PRINCIPLES
OF
REAL ESTATE
SYNDICATION

by

Samuel Freshman

BEVERLY HILLS PUBLISHING

PRINCIPLES OF REAL ESTATE SYNDICATION

Samuel K. Freshman

THIRD EDITION

"This publication is designed to provide accurate and authoritative information in regard to subject matter covered. It is sold with the understanding that the publisher is not engaged in rendering legal, accounting, or other professional services. If legal advice or other expert assistance is required, the services or a competent professional person should be sought"

(From a Declaration of Principles jointly adopted by Committee of American Bar Association and a Committee of Publishers and Associations.)

International Standard Book Number

ISBN-10: 0-9777074-2-3
ISBN-13: 978-0-9777074-2-3

Library of Congress Control Number: 2006927851

Printed in the United States of America

_____

Published by
BEVERLY HILLS PUBLISHING
BEVERLY HILLS, CA. USA.
TEL: 1-800-LA1-KNOW
WWW.BEVHILLSPUB.COM

ABOUT THE AUTHOR

Samuel K. Freshman, formerly a principal in Freshman, Marantz, Orlanski, Cooper & Klein Law Corporation, of Beverly Hills, California, now the Century City office of Kirkpatrick, Lockhart, Nicholson & Graham, has lectured and written extensively on real estate financing and syndication. A graduate of Stanford University and Stanford Law School, he is a general partner in numerous real estate syndications.

As a member of the California Real Estate Commissioner's and California Corporations Commissioner's Advisory Committees, he assisted in drafting state syndication legislation. Mr. Freshman has served as Chairman of the Legal Committee of the California Real Estate Association, Syndication Division; Secretary of the National Real Estate Securities Institute; and Chairman of the Real Property Committee, Beverly Hills Bar Association; as well as Vice-Chairman of the American Bar Association Real Property Section Sub-Committees on Trade Associations and Real Estate Options, and as a member of the Arbitration Panel of the American Arbitration Association.

He has qualified as an expert witness in both the federal and state courts in matters relating to real estate trade practices, finance, syndication, escrow, fiduciary duties, property management, due diligence, lease interpretation, and related subjects. He is a former Adjunct Professor of Real Estate Law at the University of Southern California Graduate School of Business and has more than forty-five years experience in acquiring property, forming syndications, and managing real property.

Mr. Freshman is active in creating real estate financing structuring and solutions, and heads up a property management firm that controls several hundred millions dollars worth of property. He has owned property in 15 states and 24 cities. His investors have included life insurance companies, pension funds, banks, and high net-worth individuals.

PREFACE

Having been successively President of the California Real Estate Association, Real Estate Commissioner of the State of California, a charter member and National Vice President of the Real Estate Securities Institute, and President of the successor to that institute (the Real Estate Syndicate Securities Institute, of the National Association of Realtors), I have had many occasions to work closely with Samuel K. Freshman on improving and developing standards for the syndication industry.

The first edition of Principles of Real Estate Syndication (published in 1971) was extremely helpful to me and I have recommended it whenever asked by anyone interested in real estate syndication for an authoritative work on the subject.

Sam's expertise, imagination, and depth of real estate knowledge comes through even stronger in later editions. It is being used as the basic text by several colleges for courses in syndication and real estate development and is a good, practical working tool for those active in the industry, rounding out and supplementing their own individual experiences.

BURTON A. SMITH
Orange County, California

FOREWARD

I've had the opportunity of learning the principles of real estate syndication from Sam Freshman long before he wrote the first edition of this book.

Up until 1968, my then partner and I were quite content in doing what we had been doing successfully since 1958 - selling apartment houses to individuals using customary brokerage procedures. I recall a luncheon meeting during late 1968 when Sam tried to convince us that with syndication as an additional marketing tool we would be able to expand our sales volume at a much faster rate.

Frankly, we were a bit hesitant in taking his advice; not because he hadn't convinced us that syndication was the right direction but because we were some- what apprehensive about the unknown. After all, to be successful in syndication required revamping our marketing program - not to mention learning the legal and practical aspects of putting a syndicate together.

Finally, during the early part of 1969, Sam said to us, "Look, you select a suitable property for syndication, and I'll tell you what to do from there even if I have to do it myself." Subsequently, we selected one of our best listings for our first syndication, conducted a meeting in our own office for a number of investors, and were on our way with a marketing process we had long ignored.

Although our initial offering was sold out the first evening, we made a number of mistakes in our presentation and Sam stayed with us at our office until almost two o'clock in the morning following that presentation. That meeting was an example of his in-depth understanding of the practical aspects of syndication because his coaching was directed to the organizational and psychological aspects of the presentation including matters concerning our timing, the content, and the overall selling approach.

You'll discover by reading Principles of Real Estate Syndication that the success of an offering is not necessarily limited to the manner in which the legal material is put together. It takes good business judgment as well. Mr. Freshman's understanding of how to combine legal expertise with that good business judgment is reflected in the material which follows.

NORMAN JACOBSON
Los Angeles County, California

INTRODUCTION

This work arose as a result of a need expressed by many attorneys, accountants, contractors, investment bankers, mortgage bankers, real estate brokers, and educators for a practical discussion of the basic principles behind real estate syndication to serve as a basic reference and text. It is intended as an over-view of the functions of the syndicator and the place of syndication in the development and operation of real estate. It will acquaint the reader with the economic background and operation of syndication and leaves the discussion of the historical development of real estate syndication to other publications.

The book is written from the standpoint of real estate syndication in California, but the techniques described should be operable in other jurisdictions as well. Many of the principles relate not only to real estate syndication, but have broader application to the general field of syndicating or joint venturing other types of property and businesses.

The reader who intends to acquire an in-depth background may want to review the glossary before reading the chapters, so that he will have a thorough understanding of the terms used. In this edition the text has been expanded over prior editions. The reader who wants to review sample offering circulars and promotional material can get copies of same from any investment banking firm active in the solicitation and sale of limited partnership interests.

In response to numerous requests, a teaching manual is being prepared and will be available to institutions which have adopted the book as part of their curriculum in a syndication or real estate development course upon written request from the instructor accompanying orders for the student edition.

Chapters 5 (What to Syndicate), 6 (How to Acquire the Property), 7 (Selecting a Real Estate Broker), 8 (How to Negotiate Financing), 9 (Selecting the Form of Entity), 10 (Tax Considerations), and 11 (Formation of the Entity) will be helpful to anyone interested in investing in real estate, whether through a syndicate or as a sole proprietor. Persons interested in raising venture capital for industrial enterprises may find chapters 12 (Documentation of the Syndicate), 13 (Drafting Syndicator's Provisions of Entity Documents), 14 (Drafting Impound Provisions in a Securities Offering), 16 (State and Federal Regulation of Syndicate Activities), 17 (How to Market Syndicate Shares), 18 (Guarantees and Real Estate Syndicate Securities), and 19 (Providing Liquidity for Syndicate Interests) helpful.

Every attempt has been made to see that the material contained in this text was current as of the date of preparation, but the reader should check tax matters, various quoted statutes, rules, and office policies of governmental agencies to make sure that the latest law is being applied to the particular situation.

Syndication and real estate are complex matters involving legal and tax considerations. The reader should consult an attorney and an accountant before starting a project, to assure himself that he is familiar with local law as it applies to the particular proposed transaction.

ACKNOWLEDGEMENTS

It is not possible to list the many people and organizations whose help and assistance over the past years made this book possible. The author apologizes for being unable to devote the many pages of space that would be necessary, but hopes that all who have given their help know that it is deeply appreciated.

I particularly want to thank the staff of the Securities and Exchange Commission, the U. S. Treasury Department, the California Corporation Commissioner's office, the California Real Estate Commissioner's office, the National Association of Securities Dealers, and the National Association of Realtors for material that appears in this edition. The inclusion of this material does not in any way constitute an endorsement or approval of any portion of the text by any of the organizations mentioned.

Also thanks to cover artist Allyce Balson, cover photographer Louis Beltran, typesetter Kelly Sheffer, web designer Duke Jabed, editor Heidi Clingen, and publisher David Silvers of Beverly Hills Publishing.

My sincere thanks also, to my wife, Ardyth, my children, my grand-children, my special friends and my associates at Standard Management Company for their support in the work on this revision.

Samuel K. Freshman

TABLE OF CONTENTS

CHAPTER 1
WHAT IS A SYNDICATE?

A syndicate is a joining of two or more persons for making an investment. A syndicate, for purposes of this text, will imply that one or more of the parties will take an active part in the operation and management of the investment, and one or more of the parties will be passive. The parties who supply the principal amount of the investment capital are normally the passive investors, although the active investors may also supply a portion of the capital. The active investor may receive an override and/or a management fee for its services in addition to a return on any cash it invests.

While this work will discuss real estate syndication, the principles involved apply to the syndication of other types of investments as well. Natural resources (oil, gas, timber, crops or minerals) entertainment (theatrical and motion picture products, and related products) and various kinds of business investments have the same potential for joining together multiple investors in one project.

Note that syndication is not a form of legal ownership or description of a legal form of entity, but is rather a term used to describe multiple party ownership of an investment.

It is the means whereby investors of limited resources pool their financial resources with experienced and skillful management to benefit from projects frequently only available to wealthy investors and institutions. The method is not, however, limited to such investors but may involve very wealthy investors pooling their funds to purchase large properties.

Group Investment

Because of adverse connotations to the words "syndication" and "syndicate" in the eastern part of the United States where the public associates the word "syndicate" with organized criminal activities, many syndication organizers prefer to use the words "group investment" in place of the word "syndicate" and the words "group investing" or "organization of a group investment" as opposed to the noun "syndication" and refrain from any reference to the former words.

Types of Syndicates

A syndicate can be a simple agreement between two investors to purchase a single-family residence for resale or can be as complicated as the syndication of the Empire State Building that involved hundreds of people in group ownership of a large commercial office building. Syndications are used to acquire ownership in land, to construct new tract housing, to rehabilitate older properties, to acquire and operate shopping centers, industrial parks, commercial office buildings, mobile home parks, camper parks, resorts, and all types of real estate investment. As will be seen later, the syndicate can be formed as any one of many different legal entities, including a:

(1)   tenancy in common,
(2)   joint tenancy,
(3)   joint venture,
(4)   general partnership,
(5)   limited partnership,
(6)   common law trust,
(7)   real estate investment trust,
(8)   corporation,
(9)   limited liability company, or
(10) investment association or club

The various entities differ from each other with regard to investors' rights of control and participation, rights of survivorship, personal liability, tax treatment and many other respects. The selection of the proper entity is one of the first considerations of the syndicator often before securing control of the project proposed to be syndicated.

Necessity for Sound Project

Syndication involves the same elements as any good investment plus the addition of the syndicate vehicle. The start of any syndication is a soundly conceived investment. A large sum of money is not required to make syndicate principles work and be of advantage to a syndicator and investors. Good sense, careful preparation, diligent investigation, and a little luck are the elements of syndication, the same as they are in any other field of endeavor.

CHAPTER 2

WHY REAL ESTATE SYNDICATE INTERESTS ARE PURCHASED

Real estate syndicates exist for the same reasons some people invest in property and others prefer different investments. Without an understanding of conflicting investor motivations, no one can build a successful syndicate.

There are seven main reasons why people invest in real estate: (1) to gain net spendable cash flow; (2) to take advantage of favorable treatment the tax laws give to real estate investment; (3) to acquire equity through leverage;(4) to hedge against inflation; (5) to profit from appreciation in property values; (6) to secure capital (low risk), and (7) to achieve overall higher investment yield as a combination of the foregoing.

1. Spendable Cash

Spendable cash is total cash income from operations during a given period of time, less cash disbursements (including payments on current debt and obligations as well as reasonable allowances for contingencies and future obligations) during the same period of time, but prior to any distribution to partners, general or limited, other than management fees and fixed expenses, and without consideration of depreciation. It generally is expressed as a percentage of invested capital. ("Invested capital" is the total initial and deferred amount the investor spends for a syndicate interest, and any subsequent assessments paid to the investment entity, less any return of invested capital due to re-financing or sale of partnership assets.)

There are many advantages to real estate investments from a spendable cash standpoint. The returns on real estate as of 2006 may run anywhere from 4 to 20% annual spendable cash on a successful cash flow project and are often a higher yield than is realized from other forms of investment. Real Estate Syndication distributions may provide partly tax sheltered cash flow as well. In addition, there is of course mortgage amortization. Stock dividends are often less than 6%, long-term government bonds, as of 2006, are about 4.5%, thrifts and banks pay 3% to 5% on six month time deposits, and all of these are fully taxable at ordinary or dividend income rates. Long-term tax-free municipal bonds may be partially or wholly tax free and are, as of 2006, paying 3 to 4.5%. Nevertheless, as with government or corporate bonds, they have no appreciation potential. There is not much in the investment field when other advantages of real estate are considered that can be bought with the same kind of a spendable cash return combined with appreciation.

Spendable cash is an important motivation in syndicate investment. The reason this becomes extremely important to understand is that the motivation of the individual non-syndicate purchaser of property may be (1) solely for tax reasons, (2) for some specific use for the property, (3) to own something that he can be proud of, the so-called pride of ownership, (4) for an inflation hedge, (5) for speculation. In syndicates, however, the number one motive is most often spendable cash. In such situations, it often outweighs everything else. Those projects that show high spendable yields sell better than those that rely for yield on other factors such as appreciation by adding value or from inflation. The public is not sophisticated in the area of spendable yield related to total return.

2. Tax Advantages through Depreciation

The term "depreciation" is not used here in the sense of actual economic obsolescence or physical deterioration of a specific project but in the conceptual sense as an allowable income tax deduction. Federal and State income tax law assume that a building will depreciate every year over the estimated life of the structure and allows this assumed depreciation to be written off as an expense item, although actual cash reserves for replacement may not be established or required. This results in excess tax shelter when a syndicate generates losses for tax purposes greater than the profit for tax purposes, creating excess losses that may offset and thereby shelter other income of the investor. Only syndicates that have a large ratio of depreciable assets to total investment and are appropriately debt leveraged will generally qualify as tax sheltered.

Non-depreciable property purchased with interest is not a tax shelter, although it may create "tax deferral" in that taxable income of the investor offset by the payment of interest will be deductible from his current return, while appreciation continues to increase the value of the investment. A resale of the property at a later date, in an amount sufficient to return original investment plus expenses, can result in depreciation losses being taken back at time of sale as ordinary income or capital gain (depending on holding period).

The payment of certain expenses, if they result in immediate deductions, may be a "tax deferral" but not a tax shelter technique. The paying of certain expenses, where these qualify under the Internal Revenue laws as a deduction in the year of payment, may result in shifting taxable income from a current tax year to a later tax year. This is "tax deferral" rather than tax shelter.

Although the average person who invests in real estate syndicates often gives spendable cash as the most important reason, remember that there is a class of investors in certain high income tax brackets who are very interested in the depreciation coverage of their income as well as spendable cash returns. A number of properties carry heavy mortgage debt and little or no spendable cash is left after debt is serviced, but a large depreciation loss may be created even after debt amortization credits. People in certain high income-tax brackets may prefer an investment that carries a high depreciation allowance in order to shelter other income from taxation. High depreciation usually only is found in highly leveraged properties.

Note, of course, that part of book depreciation might actually represent lost value due to obsolescence or physical wearing out. Nevertheless, appreciation caused by inflation, rising incomes and an increased population have often more than counteracted actual depreciation in recent years.

3.   Equity Through Leverage

Another important element motivating real estate purchase is the accumulation of equity through leverage financing. Leverage results where there is a purchase of property whose debt is several times the amount of the original equity. "Positive net spendable leverage" exists where the income return (cap rate) in the absence of financing will exceed the debt service constant, so that the override results in a higher net spendable rate on the invested capital than would be present if the property were purchased for all cash. When the debt service constant exceeds the net income return from the property in the absence of financing, there is "negative net spendable leverage." "Appreciation leverage" exists where the annual estimated appreciation rate exceeds the debt service interest rate. Appreciation leverage contributes to equity build-up where it exceeds the debt interest rate. A combination of spendable income, equity build-up, and appreciation build-up that exceeds the debt service constant would be "combined leverage."

Mortgage amortization leverage becomes important in syndication because investors generally do not purchase syndicate interests for immediate resale. The typical syndicate of improved property is held for more than five years and equity build-up through mortgage amortization can be very substantial.

SEE FOLLOWING PAGES FOR:
DEBT LEVERAGE; POSITIVE LEVERAGE; AND
NEGATIVE LEVERAGE ILLUSTRATIONS

LEVERAGE - PART I

ILLUSTRATION OF DEBT LEVERAGE (Equity Build-Up)

	All Cash	Leveraged
[1]Price	$500,000	$2,500,000
[2]Annual return before debt service	50,000	250,000
Down payment	500,000	500,000
[3]Loan	-0-	2,000,000
Annualdebt service constant	-0-	200,000
Annual net spendable return on down	50,000	50,000
[4]Value of property at loan maturity	500,000	2,500,000

[1]The illustration assumes a group has $500,000 to invest and alternative of buying a $500,000 property for all cash or a $2,500,000 property for 20% down.

[2]Assumed cash return of 10% on purchase price.

[3]Assumed 80% loan amortized over 20 years at an annual constant rate (principal and interest) of 10% of original loan balance.

[4]Assumes market value of each property remains constant.

    BY OBTAINING A LOAN AT A CONSTANT RATE EQUAL TO OR LESS THAN THE RATE OF NET SPENDABLE BEFORE DEBT SERVICE, THE INVESTOR MAINTAINS HIS SPENDABLE YIELD AND BUILDS UP AN EQUITY IN THE "LEVERAGED" PORTION OF THE PURCHASE THROUGH AMORTIZATION OF THE MORTGAGE. In the illustration the investors property will be worth five times what they originally paid at loan maturity from mortgage amortization. Other factors such as appreciation from inflation can further increase the value.

LEVERAGE - PART II

ILLUSTRATION OF "POSITIVE SPENDABLE LEVERAGE"
(Increasing Rate of Spendable Return)

	All Cash	Positive Leveraged
Price	$500,000	$500,000
Loan	-0-	400,000
[1]Cash Investment	500,000	100,000
[2]Annual spendable before debt service	50,000	50,000
[3]Annual loan constant	-0-	32,000
[4]Annual net spendable	50,000	18,000
Annual spendable yield on down	10%	18%

[1]Assumes an 80% loan at a term and interest rate that results in an annual constant payment of principal and interest equivalent to 8% of original amount of the loan.

[2]Assumes property returns 10% before debt service on purchase price.

[3]8% x 400,000 = 32,000.

[4]50,000% - $32,000 debt constant

    THE INCREASED ("LEVERAGED") YIELD RESULTS FROM HAVING A LOWER ANNUAL CONSTANT RATE (8%) ON THE MORTGAGE THAN THE ANNUAL NET SPENDABLE RATE ON THE PURCHASE PRICE (10%) RESULTING IN AN OVER-RIDE (2%) TIMES THE MULTIPLE OF THE LOAN IN RELATION TO THE DOWN PAYMENT ($400,000 ÷ $100,000 = 4), THE RESULTING OVERRIDE (2% X 4 = 8%) ADDED TO THE RETURN IN ABSENCE OF THE LOAN (12) GIVES A HIGHER RETURN RATE (10% + 8% = 18%) BECAUSE THE INVESTOR RECEIVES THE BENEFIT OF THE OVERRIDE ON THE DEBT.

LEVERAGE - PART III

ILLUSTRATION OF "NEGATIVE SPENDABLE LEVERAGE"
(Decreasing Rate of Spendable Return)

	All Cash	Negative Leveraged
Price	$500,000	$500,000
Loan	-0-	400,000
[1]Cash Investment	500,000	100,000
[2]AnnualSpendable before debt service	50,000	50,000
[3]Annual Loan constant	-0-	48,000
AnnualNet spendable	50,000	2,000
AnnualSpendable yield on down	10%	2% [footnotes]

[1]Illustration assumes an 80% loan at a term and interest rate that results in an annual constant payment of principal and interest equivalent to 12% of original amount of the loan.

[2]Illustration assumes property returns 10% before debt service on purchase price.

[3]12% x 400,000 = 48,000.

[4] $50,000 – $48,000 = $2,000

THE DECREASED YIELD ON EQUITY (Equity of 100,000) RESULTS FROM HAVING A HIGHER ANNUAL CONSTANT RATE (12%) ON THE MORTGAGE THAN THE ANNUAL RATE ON THE PURCHASE PRICE (10%) RESULTING IN A REDUCTION 2% TIMES THE MULTIPLE OF THE LOAN IN RELATION TO THE DOWN PAYMENT ($400,000÷ $100,000 = 4), SO THAT THE RESULTING REDUCTION (2% X 4 =8) SUBTRACTED FROM RETURN IN ABSENCE OF THE LOAN (10%) GIVES A LOWER RATE (10%-8%=2%) OF RETURN ON THE DOWN PAYMENT.

4. Speculation (Appreciation)

Everyone has heard stories about uncles or friends who could have bought a lot on Wilshire Boulevard for fifteen hundred dollars ($1,500.00) that is worth one million dollars ($1,000,000.00) now and thinks back to the day "when." There is still a great deal of this feeling and it works as a strong motivator. This, combined with the other reasons for purchasing real estate, may be the final factor in someone deciding to put money into real estate. Thus, if there is a prime location which has been bought at an advantageous price, it may be possible that investors will accept rather low returns in the hope that a particular piece of property will increase in value and that they will receive a substantial bonus return on a future sale.

5. Hedge Against Inflation

Appreciation of value is the so-called hedge against inflation. A general assumption is that as price levels rise, the price of real estate, particularly improved property with a high ratio of labor and material costs to duplicate, will rise with the price level rise. This is not entirely true because operating against this rise is the fact that good real estate is usually under lease and the owner's return is set for a period of time even though the cost of building keeps rising and therefore the cost of replacing a building keeps rising. Long term fixed rent leases without rent escalation provisions hold back the value of a particular property. The continued population growth in many areas serves to help not only the appreciation factor but the hedge against inflation factor as well. A rise in property value, which more than covers expenses, may provide an economic profit even where there is negative leverage going into the investment initially. The following is an example of the differential in return when inflation factors are considered.

INFLATION ILLUSTRATION LEVERAGED PRE TAX

	1. Unleveraged	2. Leveraged
Price	$500,000	$500,000
Inflation Rate @ 4%	4%	4%
[1]Down Payment	$500,000	$100,000
[2]Inflation Return on Down Payment	4%	20%

The return from inflation on the leveraged down payment at only 4% per anum on the total cost is 20% alone! This explains why even at very low rates of current return some investors buy real estate.

[1]Assumes 20% down payment.
[2]4% x $400,000 = $16,000 + 4% on $100,000 down of $4,000 = $20,000 or 20%

INFLATION

The construction cost indexes and graphs on pages 11 and 12, prepared by the General Appraisal Company and published in their April 1973, Clients Service Bulletin, dramatically illustrate the effect of inflation on construction costs. Costs, on the average, have increased more than four-fold for the period from November 1946, through February 1973. Note that since 1964, as indicated on the graph, there has been a very sharp rise in the rate of increase. These increases eventually showed up in increased prices for existing properties as present leases expired and were replaced by higher current rental.

Factors that could slow this process in the future are (a) a dramatic downturn in the rate of inflation, (b) an unforeseen change in construction methods and building codes that would serve to reduce or level off the construction costs, (c) rent control freezing rentals at uneconomic artificial levels, or (d) a combination of these factors taking place.

There are many indicators of the impact of inflation (I call it "silent value growth") when combined with the miracle of compound interest have a dramatic effect on value. For example, the NAREIT equity index shows that since 1971 through 2005 the average stock price of REITs (whose primary assets are real estate) has increased sixty

Cost Indexes of Average Construction and Representative Items of Material and Labor

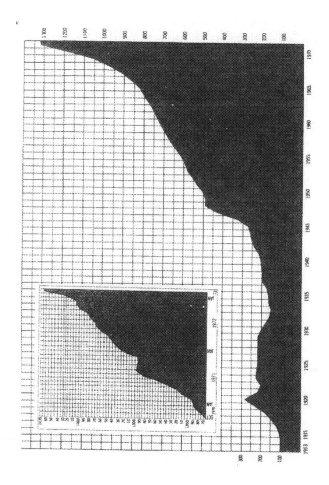

NOTE—This index applies to construction only and does not include building fixture items such as plumbing, heating, lighting, sprinkler system, etc. It is based on average costs under normal conditions with no allowance for overtime, premiums on materials, or special conditions. It is the composite of four types of industrial buildings—frame, brick, concrete, and steel — in 30 repre-sentative cities, and therefore should be used only as a trend as it is not applicable to specific buildings. Indexes are based on 100 for 1913. They reflect the cost trend in each city but do not indicate the relative costs between cities.

	Depression Avg. 1926	Low Avg. 1933	Prewar Decontrol Avg. 1939	November 1946	DEC. 1972	JAN. 1973	FEB. 1973
NATIONAL AVERAGE (30 Cities)	217	150	200	352	1407	1426	1464
Twenty-two Typical Cities							
Boston	224	163	210	351	1399	1412	1533
New York	234	167	219	356	1443	1456	1513
Buffalo		150	205	364	1600	1613	1654
Baltimore	224	158	198	364	1543	1557	1579
Philadelphia	225	156	196	343	1416	1430	1464
Pittsburgh	236	161	219	352	1377	1390	1406
Cincinnati	217	151	209	344	1450	1465	1486
Cleveland	233	151	206	359	1475	1488	1505
Chicago	219	156	205	330	1251	1261	1299
Indianapolis		150	206	358	1387	1402	1437
Detroit	224	146	208	368	1579	1592	1614
Milwaukee	218	141	209	355	1540	1550	1582
Minneapolis		146	202	333	1322	1331	1386
Kansas City	220	149	209	349	1265	1281	1299
St. Louis	230	156	208	344	1320	1335	1372
Atlanta		142	187	377	1592	1670	1696
Dallas	204	139	171	323	1174	1189	1246
New Orleans	217	141	194	346	1439	1455	1486
Denver	204	141	195	326	1127	1141	1183
Seattle	199	136	195	351	1244	1271	1335
San Francisco	188	138	183	323	1319	1349	1406
Los Angeles	195	134	167	344	1318	1338	1391

COMMENTS Scattered wage rate increases and spiraling lumber costs caused the National Average Index to rise 38 points in February. The increase since the beginning of the year (2005) amounts to 38 points, as compared with 11 points for the same period in 1972.

6. Foreign Investment

The United States has developed, over the recent past, an adverse balance of payments (the amount of money leaving the United States being greater than the amount of money coming into the United States). This means that foreign investors, particularly in Europe and Japan, have large amounts of United States dollars that they must invest. A substantial amount of this investment has been directed into prime real estate in this country. As the supply of domestic prime real estate is limited fluctuations in the demand from foreign investors for prime real estate is a factor in the market price of this type of property.

7. Combined Factors

In a given syndicate, the motivations for purchasing an interest in that syndicate can be a combination of two or more of the different items discussed (spendable cash, tax advantages through depreciation, equity through leverage, appreciation and the hedge against inflation). The total yield on investment by combining these factors can be quite high, often 10 to 25% per annum. The most important of these is spendable cash and other items will add to or detract from that motivation, depending upon whether or not, in a given project, they are favorable to the purchase. High yields with minimal risk are rare, but through the pooling of equity capital under the skilled direction of the experienced syndicator, they are possible.

Objections to Real Estate Investment

The reasons other forms of investment are preferred over real estate are also necessary to an understanding of the continuing interest in real estate syndication

1. Marketability (Liquidity)7

The most important reason people do not purchase real estate is that it has less marketability than other forms of investment. There is not as ready a market for real estate as there is for stocks, bonds, and other types of investment. No one can list a piece of property and be assured that it will sell promptly. There are occasions where some particular types of property cannot even be given away. There are some cities where property in certain sections has been so depressed that the owners could not give it away and have let it go for taxes. Even when property is a bargain there may not be a quick market, and an owner cannot put a piece of property on the market and sell it the same day unless, possibly, he happens to have extremely good connections at the title company.

The sale of real estate takes anywhere from three days to many weeks to complete, assuming there is an immediate buyer. Timing is often extremely important. If we assume that, for a particular piece of property, there are buyers ready, willing and able to buy at all times, there will still be a time lag between the time that the buyer is discovered and the sale is consummated.

2.   Obsolescence

There are two types of obsolescence: functional obsolescence and geographic obsolescence. Functional obsolescence is intrinsic to the property itself and may be caused by style of architecture, lack of air conditioning, elevators, or parking facilities, and so forth. Geographic obsolescence relates to location and occurs when there is a deterioration of the neighborhood. Almost everyone has seen such neighborhoods where the houses need repair and paint, and the gardens have been trampled on and allowed to die. This is generally the result of the gradual moving away of former owners and tenants, and their replacement by a less fortunate economic class. Why the former owners have moved may be a simple reason such as the need for a larger home, or the ability to purchase a better home. There may also be a specific economic or geographical change in the neighborhood which has come about as the result of the building of a shopping center on the corner or across the street, the erection of a dump a mile or so away, the coming of industry to the area, relocation of major highways, job losses, increase in crime rate, etc.

The possibility of obsolescence occurs because every parcel of real estate is unique, no two parcels being exactly alike. A good example of obsolescence may be found in motel investment. For example, a large motel may have been located with the idea of appealing to highway traffic patronage and the operator has built up a profitable business during four or five years. If the highway is relocated and access is cut off, or traffic diverted, the property becomes relatively worthless.

Old motion picture theatre buildings are another example. At one time, it may have been a good investment; today, unless they are extremely well located, the property on which they are located might be worth more if the building was removed. There are many other types of buildings that, because of their special purpose and the change in the market, have become obsolete. In certain areas, the competition in apartment rentals has reached the point where buildings that do not have air conditioning and elevators are considered obsolete.

3.   Management

The third reason against investing in real estate, and one that is probably emphasized the most concerning smaller properties, is the necessity of personal supervision and management. Unless the property is a high credit triple-A tenant who pays on a net-net basis, the owners' own time, energy, and skill is required successfully to operate the property. The most difficult property to run, generally, is an apartment building and, of course, the larger it is, the more problems there are involved. This means that if a tenant's toilet overflows in the middle of the night, the owner will get a call. If the screens do not fit, if the heating unit is not working, if the neighbor's children on the second floor are making too much noise, the owner hears about and must correct the situation or lose his tenant.

Net properties pay lower returns than management intensive property. The average investor is not interested in investing for the type of return these properties will show; they are looking for the properties that will show higher returns with minimal risks and these are hard to find. If they do not want to invest in properties that show a low return with minimal risks, they have to consider properties that require supervision.

4.   Specialized Acquisition Knowledge

In addition to the element of supervision, the real estate owner must, of necessity, have specialized knowledge and experience upon which to base his decisions. It is still possible to make an error and purchase property for more than it is worth, and this applies to all parts of the country. Not every piece of property is a bargain, and not every piece of property can be resold for its original purchase price or its reproduction value. In fact, this is always true at any given time with regard to some property. It takes a great deal of skill and experience to select a property that is a bargain in the market at a given time. Many people feel a great deal of inadequacy where real estate is concerned because they are not familiar with the market. These are usually the people who have money to invest in syndicates and are the most likely prospects for syndicators. They are extremely hesitant to purchase property on their own because of lack of market knowledge and prices may appear to them to be very high in comparison to what they have been used to historically.

5. Timing

Choosing the proper time to sell a property is also an important element in the success of a project. There are many property owners today who, when offered $700,000 for their property, say that just two years ago they were offered $1,000,000, and want to know why it is worth only $700,000 now. The answer is that the timing for the maximum sale of that property is past. Either the highway has relocated, the neighborhood has changed, the use of the property has changed, or the buyer who would have been the highest and best user has bought something else. Timing of a sale is extremely important for syndicate profits.

6. Changes in Governmental Policy

One of the factors given consideration by investors is the continuing change taking place in governmental policy.

7. Environmental Risks

The geographic location of a property may lend itself to certain environmental risks such as flooding, periodic fires, hurricanes, tidal surges, tornados, landslides, land subsidence, and or contraction, or man-made hazards related to the location of the property. While a number of these risks can be covered by insurance, others are excluded. The cost of insurance or its lack of availability needs to be included in the calculation of income and expenses as well as the likelihood of the occurrence of a catastrophe.

8. The presences of hazardous and toxic materials

Hazardous conditions which may exist on the property or migrate to the property from adjoining property, including asbestos radon, gas, chemicals and other toxic materials needs to be considered. The science of assessing toxic risks is constantly evolving and conditions, which may at an earlier time have been considered toxic, are now considered no longer toxic, or are containable while others that were not so considered now are. The degree of tolerance from a regulatory or health standpoint generally continues to be reduced making what might have been acceptable in the past no longer acceptable. While there are some provisions that an owner may take to protect itself from liability for certain toxic materials that were present prior to purchase if proper due diligence is conducted the law is constantly changing and evolving.

9. Marketability of Title

The title may be impaired by easements, conditions, and restrictions of record as well as conditions that may be determined from a site inspection of the property. These conditions can usually be protected against somewhat by title insurance that will provide a degree of reduction of risk.

10. Credit Worthiness of Tenants

In a commercial property that contains commercial leases, the credit of the tenant and the possibility of bankruptcy of tenants is always a risk that needs to be considered. Other issues that relate to tenants can be the enforceability of existing leases and assessment of the tenants' responsibilities versus those of the property owner.

11. Physical condition of the property

Deferred maintenance that could add to risk such as roof leaks, elevator failures, lack of appropriate fire, and other safety measures can have a profound impact on the future operation of the property and its income stream.

12. Competition

The possibility of competing properties being developed and whether there are any barriers to entry.

13. Population Trends

Is the area improving in population both in numbers and in social economic status or are the population numbers and social economic status of the residence of the area declining?.

14. Financeability

Certain types of properties may be difficult to finance although they may be economically sound. Institutions tend to shy away from properties that may have a moral risk such as a lap dance club, gambling casino etc. Special purpose properties that can only be used for a single use may also be more difficult to finance or require a higher rate of interest to secure debt.

The syndicator who can develop (1) a successful track record, and (2) a team of experienced acquisition personnel with the proper expertise to evaluate acquisition management decisions, improves its ability to provide assurance that all the risks have been properly considered.

Syndication as a Disincentive

Syndication can be a marketing disincentive to real estate investment when (1) the project area has recently experienced a decline in real estate values or (2) a number of investors have suffered losses through defalcations and unsuccessful real estate investment. Usually a rising real estate market will cover up inadequate due diligence and management mistakes. However, when a market moves sharply downward which it does periodically, these errors in judgment (particularly were the project is leveraged) can result in loss of the entire equity.

Many factors affect the rate of appreciation. Increases in rental income from year to year are somewhat under the control of the syndicator and dependent on its expertise and management skill. Real estate projects sell at a multiple of their spendable income (cap rate).

The annual return in relation to the original purchase price is referred to as the cap rate. A 5% return is a 5% cap rate. A given type of property may sell at ten times its spendable income (a 10% return) or twenty times (a 5% return). A dollar increase in cash flow at a 5% cap rate project can result in a $20.00 increase in the market value of the property on a free and clear basis (without debt service). Likewise, if a rental drops $1.00 the value of the property may drop $20.00. Leverage when present will cause the fluctuation in value or equity to be even more dramatic.

A second factor that is outside the control of the syndicator but is common to real estate is inflation. As the construction cost increases, it becomes more difficult for new projects to be built and rented at the same rate as projects that were built earlier at a lower cost basis. When I started in the real estate business in the early 1960's, you could build an apartment building in West Los Angeles including land and all improvements for $8.00 a square foot for a two-story frame and stucco building of one- and two-bedroom units. Rents on such apartments were $50. As of 2006, the same building would cost approximately $200 a square foot, approximately 25 times as much and rents on that same apartment as of 2006, would be upwards of $1,200 in the same neighborhood per unit.

Conclusion

All the aforementioned elements contribute to the success or failure of a project. Each element requires skill in its respective field, and because of this, many people stay away from real estate investment. This is the reason why there has developed an industry of syndicators who try to give investors the advantages of real estate investment and satisfy their apprehensions against investing in real estate.

CHAPTER 3

THE SYNDICATOR

The Syndicator

A syndicator is an individual or entity who endeavors to satisfy the investors' desires while mitigating their fears concerning real estate investment. Often a syndicator is a real estate broker, accountant, or real estate lawyer. Clients seek his (or her) advice in investment matters. When he hears of a worthwhile project that he would like to develop but hasn't sufficient finances, he can invite clients and friends to join in a deal, with each investing smaller amounts for a project that none of them could afford to purchase individually. In this manner, he becomes a syndicator.

A syndicator represents himself as having particular skill, knowledge, and the experience to handle all the problems involved in the investment. He satisfies the time lag required to find a good investment by presenting an already developed package.

A successful syndicator never approaches investors until (1) the property is under control by being in escrow under option or under contract to be purchased, (2) has a conceptual drawing of the building to be erected, (3) costs determined, (4) financing has been arranged, (5) title insurance on the property has been secured, and (6) it knows exactly what it is going to do with the property.

The syndicator needs to know where the returns are going to come from, who is going to build the structure, who the architect is going to be if construction is involved, and who the attorney and accountant are going to be. He then presents a proposal to prospective investors and starts to solicit interest in the syndicate.

He endeavors to create a market for syndicate shares once sold, keeping in mind, of course, the SEC and state regulations and the difference between a public and a non-public offering. Ability to re-sell syndicate interests (creating a secondary market) is an extremely important aspect of syndication to anyone who goes into the syndicate business on a long-term basis. The long-term profits are in developing a pool of investors who have reliance on the syndicator and who will keep investing continuously in one project after another.

The syndicator should not guarantee the return of an investment, for both legal and business reasons. To make such a guarantee may create a public offering out of an otherwise exempt offering, requiring a permit to solicit sale of interests in the project, and limit the syndicator's bank credit by creating contingent liabilities.

What the syndicator can do, and should be ready, willing, and able to do if he is going to be successful, is to purchase out investors interests if they become dissatisfied. He should not guarantee that he will do so, but if he does it as a practice, the investors will begin to know that this is its practice that may have the same effect, practically, as if he did guarantee a return of the investment. There is no law preventing him from paying off a dissatisfied investor or one who has agreed to liquidate his interest voluntarily.

A syndicator must have the ability to handle dissatisfactions. He should never undertake a project that is beyond his means to handle in this manner because most troubles in syndication are with people who become dissatisfied before the contemplated dissolution of the syndicate. This dissatisfaction may have nothing to do with honesty or dishonesty. The syndicator may have had the best motives; legal counsel may have very carefully advised him; he may have picked his project carefully; but in spite of all these precautions, something just went wrong. If the syndicator is not able to buy out the dissatisfied investor or investors, they will complain to the authorities and probably, more importantly, to their fellow investors. As a result, there will be a run on the syndicate by other investors who then will have also lost confidence and want their investment returned, and before he knows it, the syndicator will be out of business.

As was shown in Chapter 1, a syndicate is a type of real estate investment (in terms of this work), that endeavors to meet some of the qualifications for real estate investment, and to give the investor the advantages of real estate investment, as well as some of the aspects or attributes of other types of investment. The syndicator makes it easier for investors to buy real property since units can be purchased in small shares. Thus, an investor through a syndicate buys an interest in a project (the subject realty, just as stock is an interest generally in a business venture) and does not have to put up all of a large down payment. The syndicator selects who manages the building. There is no personal supervision or attention required on the part of the investor. The project is planned to take on as many as it can of the desirable attributes of the form of investment chosen offers. The more of these attributes a syndicator can create without violating the law, the easier it is for him to sell interests in the syndicate and the better job he performs for his investors.

Issuer vs. Dealer Functions

The activities of a real estate syndicator can be divided into two major categories:

(a) Issuer functions which involve acquiring control of the property and formation of the entity which is to own or operate the property; and

(b) Dealer functions which concern the marketing and sale of syndicate interests themselves. Some syndicators act exclusively as issuers, some only act as dealers, and some perform both functions.

The issuer function involves four basic stages:

(a) The organization of the owning entity, sometimes referred to as the formation stage;

(b) The acquisition of the subject property ((a) and (b) are often referred to as the "packaging" process);

(c) The operation of the property often referred to as the management process; and

(d) The disposition of the property including determining when to sell, how to market and managing the sale process.

Each of these stages consists of a number of activities. The acquisition process includes not only the negotiations for the property, but the arrangements for financing it as well. The operation stage includes not only operating the property but the responsibility for later resale when a decision is made that the syndicate should dispose of the property.

A syndicator may perform all of the functions involved in the process or select only certain ones, relinquishing to others the remainder of the functions. For example, many syndicators are only interested in the "packaging" process and do not become involved in the continuing management of the syndicate, leaving management of the property and the entity to another who serves as operator of the syndicate. In some cases, the syndication or operator does asset management and a property manager does property management. An individual who desires to become a syndicator should carefully examine the entire syndication process and determine, based on his inclination, experience, and resources, which of the functions he desires to undertake and which he desires to associate with other professional for.

The following charts prepared by Larry Keating (as president of the former Real Estate Securities Institute) illustrate the entire syndication process. The author is indebted to the Institute and its successor, the Real Estate Syndicate Securities Institute, an affiliate of the National Association of Real Estate Boards, for permission to reproduce them. Others have now replaced these organizations.

SEE FOLLOWING PAGES FOR
PROCESS CHARTS

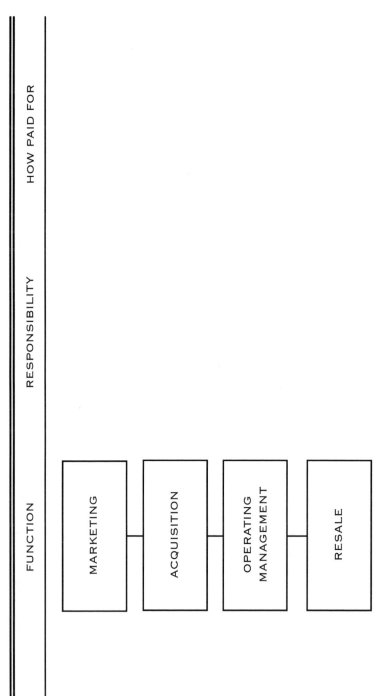

THE ANATOMY OF A REAL ESTATE SECURITY SYNDICATION

FUNCTION   RESPONSIBILITY   HOW PAID FOR

MARKETING

ACQUISITION

OPERATING
MANAGEMENT

RESALE

THE ANATOMY OF A REAL ESTATE SECURITY SYNDICATION

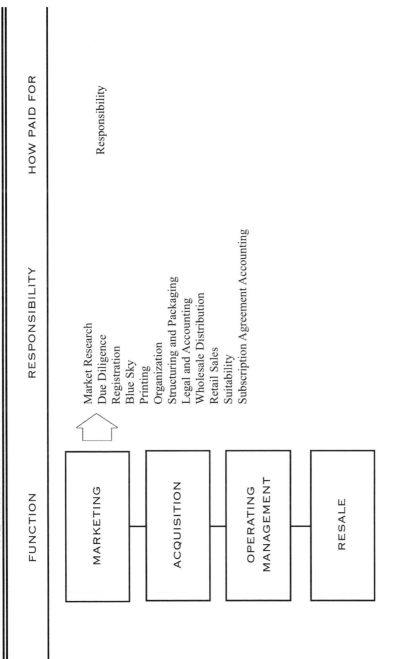

FUNCTION	RESPONSIBILITY	HOW PAID FOR
MARKETING	Market Research Due Diligence Registration Blue Sky Printing Organization Structuring and Packaging Legal and Accounting Wholesale Distribution Retail Sales Suitability Subscription Agreement Accounting	Responsibility
ACQUISITION		
OPERATING MANAGEMENT		
RESALE		

THE ANATOMY OF A REAL ESTATE SECURITY SYNDICATION

FUNCTION	RESPONSIBILITY	HOW PAID FOR
MARKETING		

ACQUISITION	Research
	Market Analysis
	Located Prospective Property
	Analyze All Properties As Follows
	  Income Analysis
	  Expense Analysis
	  Verification of Sales Information
	  Title and Zoning Analysis
	  Survey of Competition
	  Review of Seller
	    Financial
	    Track Record
	  Location and Window
	  Financial Structuring and Analysis
	  Negotiation of Terms and Conditions
	  Review Plans and Specifications
	  Review Tax Bills
	  Review Personal Property
	  Review Ground Lease
	  Deferred Maintenance Analysis
	  Tax Analysis
	  Decision On Purchase
	  Appraisal
	  Beneficiary Statement and Lender Approval of Sale
	  Income Reports and Balance Sheets
	  Operating Statement and Rent Rates
	  Copies of All Leases
	  Copies of All Permits and Licenses to Transfer
	  Corporate Resolution Authorizing Sale
	  Escrow and Purchase and Sales Agreements
	  Audit of Property — Real and Personal
		Real Estate Commission
		Or
		Acquisition Fee

OPERATING MANAGEMENT		
RESALE		

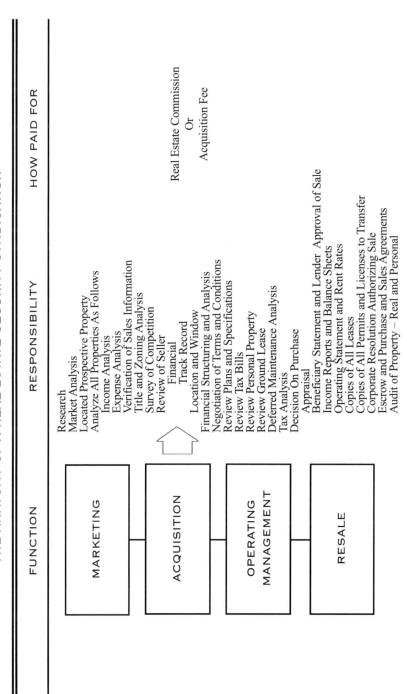

©Real Estate Securities Institute, August, 1972

THE ANATOMY OF A REAL ESTATE SECURITY SYNDICATION

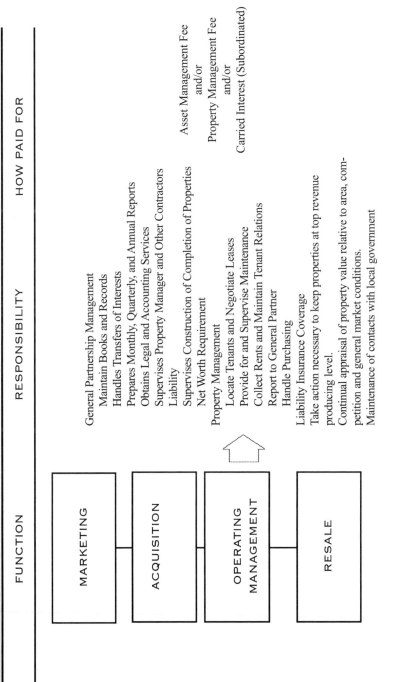

FUNCTION	RESPONSIBILITY	HOW PAID FOR
MARKETING		
ACQUISITION	General Partnership Management Maintain Books and Records Handles Transfers of Interests Prepares Monthly, Quarterly, and Annual Reports Obtains Legal and Accounting Services Supervises Property Manager and Other Contractors Liability Supervises Construction of Completion of Properties Net Worth Requirement	Asset Management Fee and/or Property Management Fee and/or Carried Interest (Subordinated)
OPERATING MANAGEMENT	Property Management Locate Tenants and Negotiate Leases Provide for and Supervise Maintenance Collect Rents and Maintain Tenant Relations Report to General Partner Handle Purchasing Liability Insurance Coverage Take action necessary to keep properties at top revenue producing level. Continual appraisal of property value relative to area, competition and general market conditions. Maintenance of contacts with local government	
RESALE		

THE ANATOMY OF A REAL ESTATE SECURITY SYNDICATION

FUNCTION	RESPONSIBILITY	HOW PAID FOR
MARKETING		
ACQUISITION		
OPERATING MANAGEMENT		
RESALE	Prepare Marketing Materials Including Income, Expense and Return Analyses Locate and Call on Prospects Show Property and Prepare Material Requested by Prospects. Select a Buyer Documentations Continual Contacts with Potential Purchasers Advise General Partner on Timing and Market Condition. Determine Value and Asking Price.	Real Estate Commission

The Syndicator's Leverage

A sophisticated real estate investor has two opportunities on how he uses his own funds. The first is to purchase properties on his own, hold them, operate them, and resell them at a profit, or secondly, to use his own funds as a portion of a down payment, controlling larger properties and making an override on the investment of passive investors (as well as other profits which will be discussed later in Chapter 4.)

For example, a syndicator has $10,000 of his own funds to invest and is faced with two alternatives:

(a) Purchase a $50,000 property for 20% down, owning the entire property himself and receiving as a return on his investment the entire spendable income and profits on sale. Assume that the spendable income shown on the project is 10%. If we further assume that the property will be held for 5 years and then resold for a $10,000 profit, the syndicator under this method will have received all of the profit and all of the spendable income for a 10% spendable yield on his investment together with a 100% profit at the end of a five-year holding period.

(b) Purchase a $500,000 property through a syndicate with $100,000 down and arrange for nine investors to put up $10,000 each with him. Assume that he is able to retain a 25% interest in spendable income and profits on sale for syndicating and managing the property, and then he would end up with instead of a 10% return on his investment, a spendable return of 32% on the project together with a profit at the end of 5 years of $32,500 rather than $10,000.

SEE THE FOLLOWING PAGE FOR
SYNDICATOR'S LEVERAGE ILLUSTRATION

ILLUSTRATION OF SYNDICATOR'S LEVERAGE

ASSUME: (a) 10% gross net spendable, (b) 10% gross profit on purchase at resale, (c) 25% of both spendable and excess proceeds of sale to syndicator, (d) 1 year hold, (e) all-cash purchase, and (f) the syndicator invests 10% of capital as investor in syndicate

	Sole Ownership	Syndication
Price of Property	$100,000	$1,000,000
Syndicate's Capital	100,000	100,000
Investor's Capital	–0–	900,000
Spendable Income	10,000	100,000
To Investors	–0–	67,500 (90% of 75%)
To Syndicator	10,000A	32,500 (25,000+7,500)C
Sale Profit	10,000B	100,000
Sale Profits to Investors	–0–	67,500 (90% of 75%)
To Syndicator	10,000B	32,500 (25,000+7,500)D
Total Profit to Investors	–0–	135,000 (2 x 67,500)
Total Profit to Syndicator	20,000 (A+B)	65,000 (C+D)

To the extent the syndicator invests, his capital is treated the same as other investors, therefore, 10% of the 75% of spendable and profits attributable to investor capital goes to the syndicator as well as his 25% share for acting as a syndicator.

Syndicator's Risks and Responsibilities

There are of course disadvantages to syndicating property as against owning it as a sole proprietor.

First, the syndicator must put up the deposit money, take the risk of loss of the deposit if it is not successful in closing, and in some cases be liable for a specific performance suit. The syndicator also has the responsibility (since it provided the funds to make the purchase deposit) in the event that the syndicate should fall short in order to protect the deposit to supply the necessary funds to purchase a sufficient number of unsold syndicate interests to make up the balance of the down payment. (As will be seen in the chapter "How to Acquire Property" the purchase contract can modify or reduce this risk using contingencies and a liquidated damage clause.)

As was explained in the preceding chapter, one of the reasons for purchasing a syndicate interest in property is marketability of shares and therefore, the syndicator must stand ready to repurchase the interests of anyone who wants to sell. Quite often, the syndicator will establish a policy that he will personally purchase any interest that cannot be resold after it has been offered for a period (often 90 days) to other investors.

An important factor is the syndicator's cash position. Does he have the cash, credit, or resources to handle the project if something should go wrong? Can he pay off his investors? As a good rule of thumb for a small project, the syndicator should be able to, if required, pay off at least 60% of the investors if they should request it. As the project gets larger and the syndicator gains a reputation for honesty and success, that percentage can go down to about 20%. However, if he intends to go into this business as a profession, and to be successful, he must have the personal resources to carry through.

The syndicator must select the profit formula before he goes to his investors. If it starts to talk to investors about a formula, each investor will have his own idea of what he desires, and confusion and argument will result. In California, the Corporation Commissioners has set out in regulations the profit participations that it feels should be fair, just and equitable under normal circumstances. Where a syndicate must be qualified with the Commissioner, reference should be had to the formulas that are discussed in the chapter, "Licensing and Regulation of Syndication Activities."

Choice of Projects

The syndicate market (which is what other syndicators are doing) and investor expectations will also influence the form of entity and profit formula chosen. The syndicator must evaluate a number of factors before deciding whether or not a particular project is worthwhile syndicating. First, he must consider alternative properties available. A syndicator is selling a personal service and, therefore, he has only so much time that he can give. Is there another project available in which more money could be made? Or less risk taken? Or that he could work on in the same time period?

Good properties are not easy to find. The usual syndicator will look at approximately ten to twenty submissions a week, and it is not possible to physically inspect all the properties. He, therefore, has to have screening procedures. He generally works through brokers who send submissions; he examines the submissions carefully and then picks one out of ten or one out of twenty actually to visit. Out of the ones he inspects he may find another one out of ten or twenty that is suitable. Successful syndicators this writer has worked with chose less than one property out of every hundred submitted. A syndicator often spends more time looking for property than in actually syndicating it.

.

The Disadvantages of Syndication

The syndicator operates under certain rules, depending upon the size and nature of the syndicate, which may restrict his activities and profits. He has developed a fiduciary relationship with his investors and, therefore, there are certain things he cannot do with the property that he might have done if it had been his own. His circumstances may have changed in a month or two, after acquisition and he may want to sell, but if he has not made adequate provisions and the investors having bought the property for a long-term investment, he may be locked in for a period.

The reverse could happen. He may want to keep the property and the investors may want to sell. He may have certain moral obligations to his investors that he must honor if he wants them to invest with him in the future, or in order to maintain his reputation and, therefore, he must sell the property even though he feels the price is not the best price and it is not the right time to sell. This is a very serious disadvantage, and while limited partners do not, theoretically, have too much say, a good lawyer can make their voices heard loudly.

Investors are at a disadvantage in that they have little control over the project. In a properly organized syndicate, the control is vested primarily in the developer or general partner in order to protect the investor from personal liability. If the investors have any more than a limited say about sale of the property and a few others restricted areas, that is, if they try to manage the property in any way or if they get involved in the rental or too involved in the financial negotiations, they will lose their protection from liability. However, a limited partner under Section 15507 of the California Corporations Code and similar state statutes in other states is not deemed to take part in the control of a business by virtue of exercising a power given him in the certificate to vote upon matters affecting the basic structure of the partnership including:

(1) Election or removal of general partners;

(2) Termination of the partnership;

(3) Amendment of the Agreement;

(4) Sale of all of the assets;

(5) Many legal writers feel that (4) includes power to vote on hypothecation of assets.

The investors must rely on the syndicator. They may also be locked into a project in that the syndicator may have set it up in such a manner that even though they want to sell, they cannot.

Since investors are relying on the experience and expertise of the syndicator, it is important to them that he has control and that investors cannot interfere with his business decisions.

CHAPTER 4
THE SYNDICATOR'S MOTIVATION AND PROFIT

In Chapter 2, the reasons for public interest in real estate syndicates and the motives for investor purchase of these interests were explained. Chapter 3 outlined the functions of the syndicator in relation to the syndicate and pointed out that the syndicator has the advantage of extended leverage. That is, not only does he have the same opportunity as the other investors to participate in real estate leverage of a prime investment property by pooling the investment funds of a number of individuals with his own, but he has the further additional advantage of being able to take an "override" by participating in a portion of the profits earned by funds invested from people other than himself.

Even without this extended leverage, there are numerous other opportunities for profit directly and indirectly to the organizer of a real estate syndicate. These will depend on the type of syndicate, the relationship with the investors, the relevant regulatory laws, the syndicator's marketing ability, and his other collateral professional activities. It is seldom that a project will have the proper set of circumstances to allow the use of extended leverage together with all of the other potential areas of profit and therefore, the syndicator will develop the particular profit areas which fit themselves to the respective project and reduce or eliminate those profit areas which are not in harmony with that project.

The Real Estate Broker

The most obvious beneficiary of the real estate syndicate industry is the real estate broker. The broker makes use of syndication in the following ways:

1. In order to sell listings which require a greater down payment or greater continuing payments than any one of his individual clients he is in a position to command, a group of clients who are pooled together so that their combined resources are sufficient to meet the cash required for the down payment and possible continuing payments, and the syndicator is able, as a real estate broker, to sell a property which he might not otherwise be able to market. Where he has an exclusive listing on the property, he may be able to avoid having to cooperate on the sale of the property (share his commission) by "creating" his own buyer in the form of a real estate syndicate.

2. The broker may have a number of clients who are interested in purchasing prime commercial real estate or acreage on a wholesale basis or management-free residential income, but each does not have individually sufficient funds to purchase the quality and type of property that they would like to own. Again, by pooling their

resources he may "create" a buyer that he would control on an exclusive basis. In California, the Real Estate and Corporation Commissioners may look with disfavor upon an exclusive listing to purchase property for a group. However, as a practical matter a real estate broker who forms his own syndicate will generally be in the most advantageous position to find the property that the syndicate will purchase. In this phase of syndication, the broker puts to work a very valuable asset: his client files of potential buyers who, but for syndication, would not be in a position to purchase a property through him.

3. While the broker cannot normally negotiate with a seller for an exclusive listing on the property for more than a short period of time, through syndication he will generally, as a syndicator, have a continuing interest in the property and be the first person to know when it will be placed on the market for resale. This places him in a unique position to make a second sale and builds up a backlog of what amounts for all practical purposes to non-exclusive listings for the life of the partnership. He may even be able to negotiate for a disposition fee for marketing efforts as the sponsor, whether or not he is the procuring cause of the sale.

4. The activity and interest, which is created through syndication, puts the syndicator-broker in contact with a large number of potential investors. Many of these investors may ultimately not purchase syndicate interests but purchase an individual property directly themselves, although their first introduction to the broker was through syndicate marketing activity of his organization. In addition, those who initially made smaller investments in the form of syndicate interests may later, if satisfied with their relationship, become purchasers of individual properties.

Others who Benefit

In addition to the real estate broker, business entrepreneurs, property managers, accountants, attorneys, insurance brokers, asset managers, business managers, financial planners, and contractors have obvious direct and indirect benefits from acting as syndicators or participating in the organization of syndicates with professional syndicators.

Areas of Profit

Among the areas of profit that may be available to the syndicator are the following:
a. A resale profit on the subject property from the syndicator to the syndicate.

Where the property to be acquired is owned by the syndicator, the full amount of the profit must be disclosed in the syndicate agreement. Where the syndicator has direct knowledge that the seller is making a profit but is not the seller himself, usually a simple statement that the syndicator believes that a profit is being made on the sale will be adequate without having to specify the amount unless the syndicator knows the amount. Where the syndicator knows the amount of profit being made, generally his fiduciary duty will require him to disclose this to the investors so that they may have the same knowledge in making their decision to invest as he has.

b. Commissions on the sale of the property. These should not exceed the arms-length commissions prevalent in the area for the sale of the particular type of property and need to be disclosed.

c. Commissions on the sale of syndicate interests. In addition to commissions for the sale of the subject property to the syndicate, reasonable securities commissions are allowed to appropriately licensed personnel (see the chapter, "Licensing and Regulation of Syndication Activities") on the sale of interests in the syndicate. In many states, total selling expenses of syndicate interests may be limited to a percentage of the price of the syndicate interest. Where the expenses of organization are being paid by a third party rather than the syndicate itself, such as the seller of the property or out of real estate commissions, the full percentages may be available as a commission on the sale of syndicate interests.

d. Building fee. Where construction is involved, the syndicator may be serving as the builder and receive the usual compensation for acting as contractor.

e. Participation in the spendable income stream. The syndicator usually takes a share of the spendable income.

This will range anywhere from 5% up to 50% of the spendable income. The rest of the income goes to the investors. Disclosure to prevent misunderstanding and lawsuits and full written disclosure of all the syndicator's benefits is required.

f. Participation in profits on sale. Almost every syndicate provides that when the property is sold, the investors receive back their investment, and then the profits on the sale are split on an agreed-upon ratio. This profit split can run anywhere from 20% to 75% to the syndicator, but most commonly, he receives between 20% to 50% of the sale profits after a return to or against a percentage return to the investor. He often receives a much smaller percentage of the income or the profits generated from the income than of the profits from the sale. The profit sharing formula is often referred to as cash-flow "waterfalls" between the investor and the sponsor.

g. Leasing fees. A commission or fee for leasing the property for the syndicate.

h. Master lease profits. The syndicator may master lease the entire property, giving the investors a set rate of return, and then re-lease or sublease the property to others at a profit.

i. Management fees. In the case of income property, they are generally expressed as a percentage of the gross income and payable as an expense of the property before any participation in profits. In some partnerships, the management fees of the syndicator (after reimbursement for actual out-of-pocket expenses) may be subordinated to a return of a stated amount to the investors. Where the property is vacant, which is the case for acreage; a "monitoring fee" is common, usually expressed in a small percentage (1/4 to 1%) of the original purchase price of the property, to be paid on an annual basis. Monitoring fees are usually "recaptured" from any real estate commissions due the syndicator-broker, if he should be entitled to a commission on the resale of the subject property by the syndicate. Management fees are sometimes broken down into asset management and property management as well as various sub-categories.

j. Options to repurchase the property from the syndicate after giving the investors a stated minimum profit. If such options are to purchase at the investor's original capital contribution, they may have the effect of giving to the syndicator the benefit of all the equity build up (both amortization and appreciation). Careful consideration of tax consequences should be made. If the option to repurchase the equity of the investor is at the then fair-market value of said equity, the purchase price can be computed either on a:

> (1) formula basis, valuing the equity at so many times the average cash credited to the investor over a certain period, or

> (2) by appraisal by an independent third party.

k. Right to borrow money from the project. Such a clause authorizes the syndicator to borrow surplus funds or reserve funds from the syndicate for specified periods at specified interest rates. This gives the syndicator the use of "tax free" cash flow, which can be applied to the control of other property and in the light of long-term inflationary factors, is a very valuable form of compensation. At a future date these funds together with the agreed interest must be returned to the project or to the investors.

l. Loans from the investors to the syndicator to purchase interests in the syndicate. This gives the syndicator additional leverage to the extent that the investors, as part of the project, may have lent to the syndicator a portion of the funds which he uses to purchase his own interest in the syndicate.

m. Ability to defer income. By taking a subordinated interest in the project, the syndicator may be able to postpone income tax and have a greater equity build-up and spendable return than where he would have taken a normal commission or fee for his services that would have been ordinary income. This may be of interest to real estate brokers, accountants, attorneys, and others, who for their services would be entitled to substantial fees. By having the fee on a contingent basis, under the circumstances, the long-term return to them can be substantially greater than receiving a non-contingent fee at the initiation of the project. This is explained in more detail in the chapter "Tax Considerations."

Profit Formulas

Participation may be qualified or contingent such as being subordinated (see subordination clause), to cumulative and/or compound returns to the investors. This is applied to both to distribution of spendable income and profits on sale. It is quite common for the syndicator's return to be expressed as a percentage of distributable cash after a priority cumulative return has been made to the investors. In California, in a public syndication, a cumulative priority of at least 5% non-compound annual return is often required by the market to be given to the investors before the syndicator can participate in spendable income or proceeds from the sale of assets. With respect to proceeds from the sale of assets, in addition to the cumulative priority return, the investors normally will have had to receive the return of their actual cash investments regardless of what their basis for tax purposes may be at the time of distribution.

The actual amount of preference depends on the syndicator's track record and the perceived risk of the project. The range is 5% to 20%.

Another formula widely used is to provide that all distributable income goes to the investors until they have received the return of their initial cash investment and then distributable funds are divided in some agreed upon ratio between the investors and the syndicator.

Both full disclosure and adequate tax planning are essential to the syndicate agreement with respect to division of spendable income and proceeds from sale as well as all other benefits accruing to the sponsors. Potential profits even under the most rigid present regulatory formulas generally offer adequate compensation to the syndicator for his services. While state regulatory authorities generally recognize certain standards, the underlying philosophy of most state regulation is that the division of profits, as well as the overall plan and operation of the syndicate, must be fair, just and equitable to the investors. Therefore, where there are unusual circumstances and an adequate objective showing can be made, state regulatory authorities may allow a greater division of spendable income or proceeds on sale, management fees, etc., than would normally be allowable if such would not violate the fair, just and equitable philosophy.

Examples of profit formulas will be found in various offering circulars readily available in the market place. In some cases, the syndicator will be taking little or no interest in a syndicate other than an arms-length management fee, making his profit at the time of the creation of the syndicate entirely in real estate commissions or profits on the sale of the subject property to the syndicate. Current tax laws appear to dictate emphasis on front-end profits to the syndicator in tenancies in common (tic)'s. In other cases, the syndicator may be receiving a very substantial interest in spendable income and proceeds from sale but making little or no front-end profits on the creation of the syndicate. There is also a middle ground where the syndicator will make a profit on the initiation of the project as well as some participation in spendable income and proceeds from sale.

No one should give services for nothing, and most investors realize this. If an investor does not want the syndicator to make a reasonable profit for his efforts, he should not invest in the project, because he is going to be unhappy from start to finish.

Private vs. Public Syndication

As will be explained further in the chapter "Licensing and Regulation," there is a considerable difference in lawful compensation between private and public syndication. Private syndication, consisting of a small group of closely associated and/or highly sophisticated investors, involves contractual compensation based on the relative bargaining power of the parties. Knowledgeable investors will grant the syndicator liberal contingent compensation, often as much as 50% or more of profits, after a minimum return to the investor. In such cases, the profit of the syndicator on the front end for acquisition is severely restricted to reimbursement for out-of-pocket costs. Such contingent compensation is expressed as a percentage of income after or against a return to the investor.

The concept of a large part of income going to the syndicator has been difficult for regulatory agencies to accept and as a result, public syndication relies more on the regulator's concept of what is fair, rather than the bargaining of the parties or the marketplace. The regulatory concept is sometimes expressed as a proportion of income remaining after a set return to the investor, or if from the first distributable dollar a relatively low participation (such as 10% to 33-1/3% of cash flow). Therefore, the distribution of income to the syndicator is usually more restricted in public syndication. For this reason, the emphasis in public syndication must be on front-end compensation to adequately reward the syndicator for his risks and efforts in obtaining qualified properties. While state securities agencies profess to deplore this development, it is a practical result of the application of present blue-sky regulations.

SEE FOLLOWING PAGE FOR ILLUSTRATION

ILLUSTRATION OF PRIVATE VS. PUBLIC EFFECT

	Private	**Public**
Net price for seller's equity	$100,000(1)	$100,000(1)
Total Cost	$100,000	$120,000
Projected net spendable on equity	$8,000 per annum	$8,000 per annum
Syndicator participation in income	25% against 6%[2] return ($2,000 per annum)	10% of cash [2] flow ($800 per annum)
Front end compensation	None	$20,000 [3]
Total investor cost	$100,000	$120,000
Cash Flow	$8,000	$8,000
Amount available for distribution	$6,000	$7,200 [4]
Investor annual return	6%	6% [4]
Syndicator annual return	$2,000	$800

[1] Amount seller to receive after acquisition fee to syndicator.

[2] The investor in the public syndication will receive 90% of any increase in distribution but suffers 90% of any reduction in projected income starting from the first dollar. This is a far more precarious position than in the private illustration where he only gets 75% of increases but none of the reductions until income drops more than 25% below original projections!

[3] 16-2/3% of cash raised.

[4] While more money is available for distribution to investors in the public program (if projections are met), the return to the individual investor is the same. The public investor has greater risk because he has had to bear acquisition and qualification costs and the property must produce $1,200 more than the private project to make the 6% return.

In the private illustration, the compensation formula gives the syndicator nothing up front and $2,000-a-year from cash flow. In the public syndication, the syndication gets $20,000 up front and $800 per annum. These numbers will vary greatly depending on state regulations and the circumstances of the transaction.

CHAPTER 5

WHAT TO SYNDICATE

Selection of Project

The selection of the project involves a careful consideration of the investment desires of the potential investors. Investors such as entertainment personalities, physicians, dentists, airline pilots, and others with high incomes are generally interested in properties that have good potential for future growth and appreciation and favorable tax aspects. Retired persons and individuals whose income is more limited are generally interested in supplementing their current income and are more concerned with stability and freedom from risk as against potential growth and tax aspects.

The dominant investor motivation is either (a) spendable income, (b) the opportunity to make substantial capital gains through high appreciation, or (c) tax benefits. Examples of the extreme between cash flow and appreciation would be a project which was a leasehold with a relatively short life but throwing off a very high spendable return (where there would be no opportunity for appreciation as the leasehold would expire before additional incremental value could be added through inflation or changes to the property), versus raw land which produced no income (and which would actually require advancing cash flow for taxes and interest payments) but because of projected population growth in the immediate area, has the potential of increasing several hundred percent in value over a given period of time.

In addition to considering potential investors' needs, current market conditions will be an important factor in the selection of the project. Just as with the stock market, there are various styles that are popular in real estate from time to time, and these styles are subject to change. Adverse publicity respecting a particular type of investment or changes in the tax laws will cause what had been a popular investment medium to go out of current favor. This does not mean that the basic economics may have changed or any of the assumptions relating to the demand at some future date for the property, but merely that the public has become "disenchanted" currently with that type of investment. In addition, there may be actual economic changes in the makeup of the population that affect the demand or attractiveness of the investment. Builders may have filled the need for the particular kind of project and developers over a period of time to the extent that where the particular type of property was once in short supply, it is now in surplus supply.

A good example of cyclical demand would be motion picture theatres. For a period, motion picture theatres were considered an excellent investment. With the advent of television, the motion picture exhibiting industry suffered greatly for a time. Now, with "high ticket" movies and resurgence of interest in theatres, many new stadium seated theatres are being constructed and are proving to be attractive investments once again.

Cash resources of the syndicator will restrict his selection of available properties. Certain types of property may require substantial down payments or option money and the syndicator will be limited to selecting those that he can secure within his own resources.

The amount of time available to syndicate may limit the type of property that can be used. Toward the end of the year, many investors are interested in properties which have favorable short term tax aspects so that they can deduct their initial cash investment or a high degree of same, or secure a great deal of write-off within the year of acquisition. To the extent that there is a limited time available to accomplish this, the type and selection of property will be seriously affected. The short time allowed for designating 1031 exchange property has created a billion dollar industry in marketing tenancy in common syndications.

The kind of marketing program that the syndicator has to use will also affect his selection of property, for if he intends to market through local real estate brokers or securities broker dealers their opinion as to what they can market will be important. To the extent that he needs to have a certain amount of mark-up, profit factor, or commission to successfully market, the gross profit margin will determine the types of property that he can select to make that profit and still offer the yield and appreciation returns which the potential investor will desire. The following is a very short summary of several different types of property and some of their investment aspects:

Types of Projects

1. Residential Income

While apartments in the past have shown good spendable returns from 4% to 12% (depending on location and tenant quality), they require considerable management and are subject to geographic and physical obsolescence to a higher degree than commercial property. Generally, there is a demand for residential income property in most areas and they can be kept rented, even in times of adverse economic circumstances by reduction in rental. However, if the project is highly leveraged, as apartment rentals fluctuate depending on general economic conditions, they will be a risky investment. Where there is a high ratio of improvements to land and considerable personal property such as carpeting, drapes, stoves, refrigerators, and furnishings that can be written off over a short life, they may offer a good tax shelter. Public acceptance of apartment syndication, as of 2006, has been good. Large syndication companies have been able to market apartment complexes at spendable yields of 6% and less by emphasizing tax shelter and appreciation factors. The potential for conversion to condominium conversion at large profits can also make them attractive.

2. *Shopping Centers*

Shopping centers generally are offered with national tenants paying a substantial portion of the rent that is often sufficient to cover taxes and mortgage payments. There is often a smaller degree of risk regardless of the leverage because leases are long and tenancy is relatively stable. However, loss of an anchor tenant can result in other tenants leaving the center and it may take a long time to secure a replacement anchor. Appreciation factor is minimal unless the leases call for overages and population projections indicate that such overages might be increased in the future. They generally do not offer favorable tax shelter because the ratio of land to building is high. They can be acquired on the current market to show 6 to 12% spendable return and generally are syndicated at 6 to 8% (2005) distributions. Because of the inability of the small investor to acquire a property with such a minimum amount of risk and high spendable return without personal management, shopping centers are an excellent investment vehicle for sale to retired persons, pension funds and others who are looking for good income with minimal risk.

3. *High-rise Office Buildings*

Because of the management specialization required for multiple-tenant high-rise, it should only be attempted by organizations that have depth of management experience to handle them. The yields are generally high and they often can be acquired on a basis to show 9% spendable or better (2005). They are usually syndicated to show the investor 8 to 10%. Because of increasing replacement costs, there is potential appreciation for well-located properties of this type. Newer properties will generally have a good improvement-to-land ratio creating favorable tax shelter. Where there is a good percentage of long-term leases to strong tenants, the risk factor will be relatively low. Nevertheless, there is a wide variance in risk factor depending on the project. Those projects that have good anchor tenants covering a substantial portion of taxes and mortgage payment obviously having less of a risk factor than those where tenants are local and leases are short. Smaller office buildings are generally not advisable because if a tenant moves out it is difficult to justify an intensive marketing campaign to secure a new tenant. The trends both in general office structures and in medical buildings are toward larger buildings where people of various specialties can be convenient to each other. Smaller single-tenant properties are usually owner-occupied and more difficult to lease in the event of vacancy.

4.   Speculative Land

Speculative land offers an extremely high degree of leverage in that it often can be controlled and purchased with as little as a 10% down payment. The carrying costs may be interest only for a number of years that may be deductible. If well selected, the returns on investment can run very high, but a great deal of skill is required in carefully selecting the property. Raw land should be attractive to those who have a "gambling instinct" and are looking for high returns or have expendable dollars where the carrying charges would be borne largely by the deduction for interest and taxes that will reduce the actual cash outlay to carry the property.

In some cases, land can be net leased to agricultural companies to reduce the carrying costs. Where there are groves of trees there may be certain depreciation advantages, although the investment in the improvements will tend to reduce the leverage available, except where a property improved with groves can be purchased for the same price as land in the area similarly situated without groves.

While income property does not generally require the investor to continue to put up money each year, vacant acreage normally does require annual assessments. Therefore, the amount of investment which an investor can make on this property is restricted, not by the funds he has currently available to invest, but by what he can lay out annually from his regular income. This means that the investor normally will be purchasing a smaller share of this type of property than he would be where he is making a one-time investment and has no further cash flow demand on his personal income to carry the investment. Except for investors in relatively high tax brackets, a typical investor should not commit more than 10% of his total income to making payments on this type of investment.

Because of the speculative nature of land investment and in particular the inability to predict holding periods, many syndicators purchase land without leverage to reduce holding costs.

5.   New Construction vs. Existing

There are certain tax advantages allowable with respect to new construction of residential income property in that a 200% declining balance depreciation schedule may be used. Generally, a syndicate that involves itself in the construction of a project should receive a larger spendable income from that project than if it bought the project completed and fully rented to compensate for higher risk. There is a loss of income on the investment during the construction period and certain risks involved in the construction for which compensation should be received in terms of a higher yield. In the case of residential income, particularly in a rising rental market, the differential in yield can be substantial and it is often possible to obtain spendable income levels of 9% or more once the project is completed and fully rented versus buying existing property at 6% or 7% cap rates.

6.   Rehabilitation of Older Properties

Some syndicates make a specialty of buying older properties and renovating them. This requires a great depth of management experience and skill. Although there is considerable risk involved in that it is not always possible to accurately determine the cost of rehabilitation and the success of the proposed plan of redevelopment of the property, the returns can be very high. Properties which have vacancy factors of 50% and greater, can normally be bought for a fraction of the replacement value, and those which appear to have little or no current use can also be bought at low prices in relation to replacement cost.

7.   Government Financed or Subsidized Projects

These often offer a very high degree of leverage as financing of 90% and more may be available. They require a skillful developer and there is a considerable time lag required from the conception of the project until the respective governmental approvals can be secured. Care must be taken to see that there will be appropriate funding available at the time the formal application for the governmental loan is approved. While the owner's flexibility as to rent that can be charged and/or who can be rented, to this may be restricted more than offset be the leverage and tax benefits offered. Note that the above observations are the author's only and that there is considerable difference of opinion as to the factors involved and the relative attractiveness of various types of government-subsidized investment.

8.   Industrial Plants

Industrial property may consist of a single tenant under long-term lease, a multi-tenant industrial building, or an industrial tract for future development. While industrial properties generally require less supervision and management than residential income or commercial property, because of their specialized nature even greater care must be given to their location and the availability of supporting facilities. An industrial building with multiple tenants may operate similarly to a large office building with multiple tenants. Industrial property, under long-term lease to a single tenant with good credit on a triple-net basis, has the same advantages as a lease to a commercial tenant under the same circumstances. The length of lease is particularly important as industrial buildings are of purpose that is more limited and in the event of vacancy, it may be more difficult to find a replacement tenant than in a well-located commercial property. This property often requires extensive environmental due diligence.

9.   *Agricultural Production*

Syndication of citrus, various nut crops (such as pistachios, walnuts, and almonds), avocados, grapes, etc., has become increasingly popular. A distinction must be made between the syndication of a mature grove or a vineyard, which is providing an annual yield in the near term, and the development of a new one, which will take as much as five to seven years or longer before meaningful cash flow can be developed. The remaining lives of the crops need to be taken into account as well. Tax considerations often play a more important part in agricultural syndication than in conventional income-oriented projects, particularly in those that are of the development type requiring the passage of time until positive cash flow is generated. Agricultural syndications have a high risk factor because of the vicissitudes of the crop market as well as the danger of loss through disease and adverse weather conditions. They can, under certain circumstances, provide unusual tax benefits and, if successful, extremely high rates of return. When near growing population centers, there is the prospect of major appreciation.

10.   *Use Programs*

These are developments such as condominium communities, campgrounds, resorts, skiing facilities, equestrian centers, golf clubs, and similar projects where the motivation for purchase of the participating unit is the purchaser's planned use of the facility rather than investment. While the form of the project may be in the nature of a condominium, a limited partnership, a non-profit membership corporation, or a tenancy in common, all of these projects are distinguishable from investment-oriented projects by the motivation for purchase by the end user. Such projects require accessibility to the property use for the proposed buyers, emphasis on amenities, and an entirely different marketing effort from that used in investment-oriented projects. The return to the purchaser is the satisfaction he will receive from the use of the project (the ability to participate in an activity and/or environment that he could not afford to do on his own.) Care should be used to disclaim investment motivation to avoid regulatory violations and litigation from purchasers claiming investment representations were made.

11. Hybrid Projects

In some cases an income-producing property has been coupled with a speculative land project producing a hybrid investment wherein the income property carries the payment required on the land. The emphasis here, obviously, is on protection from inflation and building equity as opposed to cash flow. It is often common, in a recreational-use project, to combine certain investment aspects that might result from agricultural activities. These might be conducted in connection with the project or from the ability of the participants to lease out the facilities while using them themselves, realizing some return on their investment through the availability or a rental pool.

12. Non-Specified Funds ("Blind Pools")

Because of the cost of marketing syndication and the difficulty of controlling property until the marketing effort has been completed, several major syndicate organizations have organized entities where money is raised and placed into the fund prior to purchase of any specific property. Generally, to be successful in marketing such funds, the syndicator must have a good reputation and track history so that investors will be willing to place their funds with him without any knowledge of a specific property to be purchased. Among the problems facing such funds is the necessity of promptly investing the monies raised to create a cash flow to service the investors' objectives within a reasonable period. Regulatory authorities are becoming more and more restrictive on the requirements for the establishment of such funds, and some jurisdictions prohibit such funds in their entirety.

Such funds have the advantage of (a) diversification of investment over many properties, (b) because of the size and reputation of the sponsors the possibility of a secondary market in the syndicate shares themselves, and (c) the ability on the part of the fund to make a fast investment decision to take advantage of bargain opportunities that may arise.

Some jurisdictions are requiring that a portion of the funds to be raised be committed to specific projects in order to give the investors some idea of the type of project to be purchased. There is disagreement as to whether or not the public interest is better served by a broad investment policy that enables the syndicator to move with flexibility in securing the best possible investment, or a limited and narrowly defined investment policy that will give the investor the ability to determine property to be selected and the nature of the fund.

13. Personal Property

Syndication of chattels, airplanes, ships, computer systems, office equipment, and other forms of personal property should also be considered. While technically leaseholds are personal property, they would be handled generally in the same way as real estate syndicates. The basic principles of syndication apply to personal property as well as real property, but risk factors will vary depending on the property and the use to which it is put. Syndication of cattle is subject to many of the risk factors of other types of agricultural investment such as disease, weather, variation in market price, etc. A syndicate of an airplane leased to a major airline of good credit would have many of the investment aspects of a triple net lease of real estate to the same type of lessee. Tax benefits often are a major objective in personal property syndication. Legal principles relating to security interests and title questions are handled somewhat differently than in the case of real property.

14. Oil and Mineral Exploitation

As in the case of agricultural projects, a distinction must be made between syndicating of proven reserves with established positive cash flow and speculation in exploring for minerals. Various types of mineral wealth such as oil, gas, ferrous and non-ferrous metals, etc., are subject to differing tax treatment. The cost of exploration and potential success vary depending on the individual mineral involved. Generally, mineral resources are subject to depletion (that is, the resource will diminish as it is withdrawn from the ground, the estimated amount of reserve remaining in the ground being reduced with each withdrawal). Because of inflation and other factors, depreciation in a real estate project may be more hypothetical than real. In the case of minerals, there is a real reduction in production as the particular mineral field is exploited.

Risk factors can be extremely high. Often the probability of recovery being as low as one in twenty where "wildcatting" (exploration in the area where there are no proven reserves) is taking place. While the potential returns are greatest in wildcatting the amount of risk is greatly reduced where the method of exploration is "offsetting" (exploration in an area of established presence of the mineral being sought after).

15. Commodity Speculation

The distinction between this subject of syndication and that in the preceding paragraphs 13 and 14 is that the personal property is purchased with an expectation of the rise in the value rather than for income. Fine art speculation falls into this category as well. A high degree of skill, knowledge, and experience with the particular item being speculated in is essential to success. Consideration must be given to the cost of (a) lost opportunity (what the invested funds could have earned in other investments), (b) storing, (c) insurance, and (d) maintenance of the commodity while gold and silver fluctuate in value they as well as other commodities produce no income. Holding costs and lost income can often exceed a substantial increase in the value of the commodity over a period of time.

16. Race Horses

A category separate and distinct from all the others is the syndication of race-horses. Historically the odds of success in this field are limited and the tax laws recognize that what might appear to be an investment is in many cases in reality a hobby for pleasure rather than for profit. With respect to the breeding of racehorses, the tax law requires a substantial showing that the intent is one of profit rather than pleasure. Because of the subjective nature of making an investment decision in this area and the difficulty of ascertaining the future prospects for profit as well as the high risk factors, this type of investment is only suitable for the experienced connoisseur who can afford loss of his principal and who has the resources to carry the project until it matures.

17. Motion Pictures

The odds of making money in picture production for most independent producer are not much better than gambling in Las Vegas. An experienced producer with a good track record can improve them. Pre-sale guaranteed distribution and ancillary rights can help reduce risks associates with this type of investment.

18. Syndicating Cash to Loan

Many builders and owners of property who are interested in disposing of their property in a given market may find that general market conditions call for a low down payment and seller carry back. Depending on the type of property and the amount of cash required, down payments in residential income for example may be 10 to 15% of the gross sale price, with the seller having to carry back the difference in purchase money financing for a minimum of 5 years and payable usually 3/4 to 1% per month of the original principal balance including interest of 7 to 8%. By organizing his own syndicate to purchase the property for cash to the existing loan, the seller can save the real estate commission, which would be incurred if he employed a broker to sell the property. The brokerage commission may be equal to the cost of syndicating. He then would realize net proceeds equal to a third-party sale and still have an interest in the property.

Purchase money trust deeds may have substantially less value than cash to a loan sale would have if the seller needs to dispose of them. These trust deeds are generally discounted from 25 to 50% of their face value in the event that the beneficiary of the note and deed of trust requires cash. By paying cash to a new loan, and taking advantage of a discount for cash when available, it is possible to increase the spendable yield to the investor making the spendable yield attractive enough to make a fast syndicate sale.

The following illustrates a property with a sale price of $500,000. and 15% down compared with a sale of cash to a 70% loan. On 15% down, the investor would get a spendable yield of $14.6+% on his $75,000 cash investment. However, by discounting the second trust deed 50% and making a purchase of the property on a cash to loan basis requiring $137,500 for the equity, the investor receives a spendable yield of 17.5+%.

SEE FOLLOWING PAGE FOR INCREASED SPENDABLE
BY CASH TO LOAN ILLUSTRATION

ILLUSTRATION OF INCREASED SPENDABLE
ON CASH TO LOAN

	15% Down	Cash to Loan
Sale price	$500,000	$500,000
First trust deed	350,000	350,000
Second trust deed	75,000	–0–
Discount on second trust deed	–0–	37,500
Cash required	75,000	112,500
[1]Net spendable	20,000	20,000
[2]Debt service on second trust deed	9,000	–0–
Net after debt service second	11 ,000	20,000
Cash Investment	75,000	112,500
Spendable yield	14.6%+	17.5%

[1]After debt service on the first trust deed and before debt service on second trust deed.

[2]1% per month principal and interest.

The above results from there being no necessity for making payments on secondary financing and the amount that normally would go to secondary financing is available to service the cash investment coupled with the benefit of a more favorable purchase price. There is also a substantial reduction in investment risk due to the fact that the financing on the property is a much smaller percentage of the overall purchase price and therefore the future ability to sell for a lower price to recover investment if there is a necessity of doing so at a later date. Investors do not have to face the problem of servicing a balloon payment at the maturity date of secondary financing. Normally, conventional first trust deed financing is fully amortizing and the project does not become subject to the whims of the mortgage market at the time a second trust deed would fall due.

SEE FOLLOWING PAGE FOR REDUCING PURCHASE.
PRICE BY CASH TO LOAN ILLUSTRATION

ILLUSTRATION OF CASH TO LOAN VS. PURCHASE MONEY SECONDARY FINANCING ON PURCHASE PRICE IF SELLER MUST SELL PURCHASE MONEY LOAN[1]

	15% Down	Cash to Loan
Sale price	$500,000	$462,500
Down payment	75,000	112,500
Balance purchase price	425,000	350,000
First trust deed	350,000	350,000
Second trust deed	75,000	-0-
[1]50% discount on second trust deed	37,500	-0-
Seller's net proceeds	112,500	112,500

[1]Assumes a 50% discount will be required to market a ten year maturity date second trust deed.

Syndicating For All Cash

During certain years there exists a "tight money" loan market. Interest rates (including initial loan costs) will exceed, in many cases, 10% on first trust deeds, and the "constant factor" on debt service could exceed 12%. Lenders may request participation in gross rentals and in some cases, substantial equity ownership.

Where the constant factor on debt service is higher than the cap rate it is more advantageous for the syndicator to syndicate for all cash when the public will except a spendable return of the net cap rate (net meaning return on total costs) in the absence of debt payments. Syndicating for all cash substantially reduces the risk of real estate investment in that gross income at its lowest point need only be enough to service taxes and operating expenses. Generally on an all cash basis, a property can carry operating expenses and taxes with as little as a 40% occupancy. The "no-risk" or "minimum-risk" factor has a strong appeal to elderly persons who recall the foreclosures during down turns in the real estate market..

By raising all cash in a construction deal, it is possible to secure a more favorable loan after completing and renting the building than the loan that may be available prior to construction in that all the speculative elements of rental and construction costs are no longer present. The actual gross income and actual spendable are known when the project applies for its permanent loan if it has been self-financed during the construction stage.

Where debt service constant is high and investors are principally interested in spendable income, serious consideration should be given to syndicating the project for all cash. On the other hand, if investors are primarily tax-motivated, they will want a great deal of leverage and despite the high loan costs and interest rates, may prefer maximum financing in order to leverage their tax benefits with a minimum cash investment.

Syndicating cash to existing loan may eliminate the cost of a new loan and interim construction interest and usually allows the syndicator to offer a higher return (it can lower the overall cost of the building as much as 15%). The funds not being used during the construction period can be invested in short term Treasury Bills, Certificates of Deposit, Banker's Acceptances, or other money market instruments or continue to be used by investors until called.

Money Market Conditions

The rate of interest available to the investor on Certificates of Deposit, commercial paper, Bankers' Acceptances, Treasury Bills, and other money market investments fluctuates greatly from time to time. If the rate of return available to the investor from a money-market instrument is higher than the return available from real estate on an all-cash investment basis, syndicating for all cash at that time on existing projects will not be attractive. When mortgage rates are low and the total constant required to service debt is below the net cap rate available on real estate projects (positive leveraged), it is more advantageous to take as much debt as possible. However, when rates are high and the constant required is above the yield on the property (negative leverage), syndication for all cash may be the only way to market the property. Because of fluctuations in both the cap rate of return available and the mortgage rate, reference to local money-market conditions must be had at the time of syndication to determine the relative advantage of syndicating for all cash as against maximum debt financing.

SEE FOLLOWING PAGE FOR ALL CASH VS. CONVENTIONAL
FIRST TRUST DEED FINANCING ILLUSTRATION

ILLUSTRATION OF ALL CASH VS. FIRST TRUST
DEED FINANCING CONSTRUCTION PROJECT

Total cost exclusive of financing	$500,000	$500,000
Cash invested on completion	500,000	150,000
LOAN on construction	-0-	350,000
Loan payments	-0-	30,125[1]
TOTAL COST	500,000	530,500

[1] 2 points on $350,000 = $7,000 plus 9% interest, 18 months, average loan of $175,000 = $23,125 Total $30,125

[2] Without consideration of return on surplus funds during construction.

Classes of Syndicates

Earlier in this chapter we explored various types of developments and properties which lend themselves to syndication. In the chapter "Selecting the Form of Entity" the different legal forms which syndication can take will be examined. Beside the subject of the syndicate itself and the type of form which the syndicate takes, syndications can be further divided into classes. Among the classes of syndication are the following:

1. *Specific Property.* In this class, the property is accurately described and already selected as opposed to the blind pool.

2. *Blind Pool.* As previously discussed, this is where the properties have not yet been selected and the investor relies entirely on the ability and experience of the syndicator to properly select the property.

3. *Master Registration.* A series of partnerships to purchase similar properties are formed over a period of time wherein the common elements are contained in a master registration, which is amended from time-to-time to describe the specific individual property. The investor may, under these circumstances, buy "participation interests" which would be later converted into the respective individual limited partnerships.

4. Multi-Class. A program where there are two or more classes, with each class having different rights. The differentiation may consist of:

(a) Priorities as to rights to participate in distributions, or

(b) Different tax treatment of the relative classes, with one class participating more heavily in the tax losses and the other group receiving a greater degree of spendable distribution. Accomplished by one class owning equity another owning debt.

5. Transfer or Exchange Fund. A program whereby property is contributed on a tax-free basis in exchange for shares of ownership in the fund at the time of the formation of the fund. Often called "a tax-free transfer," as distinguished from a tax-free exchange. These funds provide diversification of risk and may, when they gain size and record of accomplishment, offer opportunity for fractionalization and liquidity.

6. Open-End Fund. A program that provides for additional offerings of interests over a period of time and an expanding portfolio of properties.

7. Closed-End Fund. A limited amount of shares offered for a set period. When the specified number of participation units is sold, no additional units would be offered.

8. Repurchase Fund. A program wherein there is a provision to "redeem" or repurchase units that are offered back to the fund.

9. Assessable fund. Where a portion of the investment is not needed initially and may be called for later.

CHAPTER 6
HOW TO ACQUIRE THE PROPERTY

Once the decision has been made as to the type of project, after considering the investment needs of the potential investors, current market conditions, resources of the syndicator, the properties available, and the time available for syndication, the syndicator must gain control of an appropriate property.

Prefer Local Properties

Where the syndicator plans a small syndicate among his immediate friends and associates, local properties are most suitable. Larger syndications that are to be marketed statewide or inter-state can consider properties that may be at some distance from the syndicator's field of operation. For management purposes, however, the closer the property is to the syndicator's base of operation, the more effective will be the management of the property and the marketing of syndicate shares.

Sources of Projects

There are many good sources for locating property and among these are the following:

1. Real Estate Brokers, when using them the type of property desired, the amount of cash down payment available, whether or not the broker must cooperate (share) with the syndicator the commission, the contingencies required, and the amount of time necessary to complete investigation and eliminate contingencies, should be clearly defined. There follows a chapter on how to select and work with brokers.

2. Title and Escrow Companies are in close contact with the real estate market in which they operate and can be good sources of potential property.

3. Advertising and Classified Sections of metropolitan newspapers contain a broad offering of properties of all types.

4. Selected Publications such as The Wall Street Journal. Various trade magazines such as motel, hotel, farm and ranch, shopping center, industrial journals, etc., also are good sources of leads.

5. Builders and Construction Companies will have properties or projects available.

6. Trust Departments of Banks have property for sale and may be able to put you in touch with other owners who desire to sell.

7. Chambers of Commerce and Community Development Organizations are excellent sources of leads to local properties within the area.

8. Transportation Companies such as railroads, trucking companies, freight forwarders, etc., have an interest in keeping track of properties available for sale within their service areas. They are a particularly good source of industrial locations.

9. Public Utilities also monitor available industrial properties and may be in contact with the major builders and developers.

10. Financial Institutions such as insurance companies, pension funds, banks, savings and loan associations, mortgage companies, finance companies, real estate hedge funds, etc., through their lending functions may be cognizant of properties for sale in the area as well as a direct source for property as a result of properties in their real estate owned portfolio which they have received as a result of loans going into default.

11. Churches, schools, universities, and other similar organizations may have surplus property for sale.

12. Attorney, accounting, insurance brokers and other financially related principals may have clients who want to sell.

13. Property owners are good sources for both their own properties and those of their friends.

Controlling the Property

Before syndicating and going to the expense of having an offering circular prepared and other documentation prepared, the syndicator will want to make sure that he "controls" the property by either having an option or having the property under contract or in escrow. A sample Agreement for Purchase and Sale of Real Property appears in the Appendices. The sale contract should cover all of the areas of agreement between the buyer and seller.

It is important to remember that in most situations an "agreement to agree" is not a contract and therefore is not binding on the parties. If all the terms and conditions are not fully spelled out, one party or the other, or both, may be able to take the position that there has not yet been a full contract and they are therefore free to withdraw or to sell the property to another party.

Options, Contingencies, and Price

It is a common practice to tie up a piece of real property for the time necessary for the syndicator to get firm commitments from his investors to provide the equity capital necessary for the purchase. Depending on the size of the transaction, the syndicator's resources, and market acceptance of the particular project, this requires anywhere from thirty to one hundred twenty days, in the typical situation. Most owners of property, while willing to enter into a transaction where there are contingencies, or to give an option for a short period of time, will want a higher price for the property under such circumstances than if the buyer makes a firm offer with a sizable deposit up front. The longer the option or contingency period, the greater premium the seller of the property will require for taking his property off the market for the period requested.

Suggested Purchase Agreement

Each real estate transaction is unique, and the laws of the various state jurisdictions vary greatly, with respect to real property. For these reasons, the forms in the Appendices should be considered suggestive only, and an offer should not be made by anyone inexperienced in dealing in real property until after careful consideration has been given to the project and the buyer's attorney has reviewed the form of the offer. There are many items in both the letter of intent and the Agreement for Purchase and Sale that may require more elaboration in the escrow instructions (settlement agreement).

The forms in the Appendices are for use in California and must be adapted to the state in which the property is located. In a competitive market, many of the clauses may have to be modified to make them more "Seller Friendly."

Property in Construction

With the present emphasis on tax considerations, it is common to enter into an agreement to purchase a building to be constructed, or in the process of being constructed, with title to transfer to the buyer, before the commencement of construction or during the construction period. This is to enable the buyer to take advantage of certain tax benefits for interest and other deductible costs incurred during the construction stage. Where the buyer is to give to the seller a sum of money prior to the commencement of the cash-flow return, the investment of the purchase price, or a portion thereof during a period when no return is received, must be taken into consideration in determining the actual yield to the buyer. In some cases, the seller will commence to pay to the buyer a return from the date of receipt of buyer's funds, even though the building is not yet completed. In such situations, it is essential to provide for adequate guarantees of completion and other safeguards to assure the buyer that the building can be finished for the total cost estimate represented by the seller.

Price Provisions of A Contract of Sale

The most important provision in the purchase agreement is often the one that receives the least attention. Hours maybe spent discussing with the seller who bears the risk of loss until close, what form of warranties the seller is to give, the nature and extent of contingencies and conditions of purchase. However, little or no thought in many cases is applied to the manner and method of payment of the purchase price.

In real estate transactions there are two purchase prices: the "ostensible or stated price," which is the gross figure generally agreed upon between the parties in initial negotiations, and the "true or net price" which is the actual price received by the seller after adjustment for prorations and allowances.

Discharge of Existing Encumbrances

Where the sale is for all cash and an existing encumbrance is to be paid off, the seller's net proceeds will be affected by whether or not it is the seller's or the buyer's duty to discharge the present existing encumbrance. There are often prepayment penalties and other costs involved in payoff of the existing encumbrance. Obviously, where the discharge of that encumbrance is the seller's obligation, the net cash proceeds will be less than where the buyer has assumed this responsibility. The converse is also true, in that the buyer who has this responsibility will end up paying more for the property than the ostensible purchase price.

Purchase of Seller's Equity

Most sale contracts call for a gross purchase price that has been computed by including the balance on existing encumbrances at the time of execution of the purchase contract. The transaction is completed later (usually several months) and the cash required to purchase the seller's equity increases during the period by the amount of mortgage amortization from the date of execution to the date of the close of the transaction. The syndicator must know precisely the amount to be paid for the seller's equity at the close in order to determine the capital contributions that must be raised from the participants in the syndicate. Therefore, the syndicator should require that the purchase price be expressed as an amount to be paid for the seller's equity, plus the then-balance on the underlying encumbrances at the close of the transaction. (This gives the purchaser the benefit of any mortgage amortization that accrues in the interim.)

In some cases, there is a compromise whereby a portion of the amortization will be paid to the seller. Another common provision is to provide that, if the escrow should extend beyond a certain length of time, the price be adjusted. How this issue is finally resolved, as all other provisions of the contract, will depend on the relative bargaining strength of the parties.

Subject to vs. Assumption

If the buyer assumes the underlying encumbrance existing at the time of execution of the purchase agreement he will be personally liable to the seller for paying the encumbrance and depending on the terms of that assumption may also be personally liable to the lender. If the buyer purchases subject to the existing encumbrance he is not liable to either seller or lender. In those cases where the buyer is to retain the existing encumbrance it must be determined whether the loan is transferable and if transferable who bears the expense of transfer. Often a lender will want a substantial service fee to approve transfer of title.

Purchase Money

Where the seller is carrying back a portion of the purchase price in a note secured by a pledge of the real property, (said note usually is junior to existing encumbrances that are going with the property at the time of sale) the note and security instrument are referred to as "purchase money." It should be specified (1) whether the buyer would be personally liable on the note or whether the seller can look only to the property, (2) whether it is junior or senior to other encumbrances, and (3) such other clauses as maybe appropriate to the circumstances. In some jurisdictions, holders of purchase money notes (California is one) are barred from recovering a deficiency judgment (the amount by which the note exceeds the sale proceeds of the property on foreclosure) against the buyer, regardless of the intent of the parties or the wording of the document. Purchase money protection against deficiency judgment, where it is available, may be narrowly construed, for example, applying only to a note that is secured by the property being sold. An unsecured note, there-fore, would allow the seller to recover a deficiency and to sue the buyer personally, as would a note secured by property of the buyer other than that which he is purchasing from the seller.

Subordination

Where the buyer has given to the seller a junior purchase money note and security agreement and believes he may desire to refinance the underlying encumbrance prior to the maturity date of the purchase money note, in order to secure with respect to that underlying financing (a) a better interest rate, or (b) more funds to reduce capital investment, or (c) a lower constant rate (payment) to provide more spendable, or (d) a combination of the above, the buyer will want to include in the purchase money note and security agreement a subordination clause. Such clauses should not be drawn until there has been consultation with the proposed title insurer and legal counsel to assure that the provisions will be enforceable and accomplish the intended purpose under local law.

Personal Property Security

Where personal property is being included in the purchase price, or the installation of personal property of substantial value by the buyer is part of the consideration, a separate security instrument is generally required. Sellers are often embarrassed, on default of the purchase money note and security agreement, to find that their real property security agreement did not enable them to recover personal property received in the sale and which the buyer in turn had (1) used as security for a bona fide lender, (2) is sold to a purchaser, or (3) removed from the premises. Requirements of the personal property security agreement, including the place where it is to be filed, and the manner of documentation, are often different from the requirements of real property security agreements

Contingencies in the Contract

A number of conditions to the buyer's obligation to purchase are outlined in the letter of intent and purchase agreement in the Appendices. Those listed are not intended to be all-inclusive, and additional contingencies will suggest themselves in individual transactions.

When new financing is to be secured, the purchase should be subject to the availability of such financing. Where such a contingency is to be included, the seller may want the right to meet the contingency by adjusting the terms of the purchase money financing to provide the buyer with the same payment terms overall (combined third-party and purchase money) as the buyer would have had, if the desired third-party financing had not been available.

A right to approve may be (a) absolute, (b) subject to reasonable exercise (i.e. "approval will not be unreasonably withheld"), or (c) qualified. In some jurisdictions, if the right to approve is absolute (i.e., in buyer's sole discretion), the court may also grant the seller an absolute right to withdraw from the transaction until the condition has been satisfied. This result can sometimes be avoided by using an option agreement rather than a purchase contract.

Before drafting the agreement, it is a wise idea to make a checklist of all of the reasons and motivations for purchase of the particular property. The checklist will serve as a reminder to include appropriate warranties and conditions in the purchase contract to assure that these objectives will be met.

While sophisticated sellers often require that the buyer purchase the property "as is" without warranty, they are usually willing to give an amount of time for inspections and completion of the buyer's contingencies and conditions, although in "seller's markets" that time may be very short. Because of the cost, time, and effort involved in making a thorough examination of the property, it is advisable to make sure that the seller will sell on agreeable terms and is irrevocably committed to sell, before going to the expenses of inspection and investigation.

Escrow

The purchase contract should provide that the sale will be consummated pursuant to an escrow ("settlement") in a specific escrow company, title company, or attorney's office, and that the parties will execute appropriate escrow instructions that will incorporate their agreement by reference. It should be provided that unless the escrow instructions state to the contrary, there will be a provision in them that, as to any conflict between the escrow instructions and the agreement of sale, the agreement of sale will prevail. In some cases, the agreement of sale, if properly drafted, can serve as the escrow instructions without the necessity of additional instructions to the escrow holder, or the parties may prefer to have the escrow instructions serve as the agreement of sale. The escrow holder often has its own indemnification and instruction form that must be carefully reviewed to make sure it is acceptable and does not modify the contract between the buyer and the seller.

Where promissory notes, deeds of trust, or other documents are to be executed prior to the close of escrow, the specific form of document should be designated in the instructions or the documents themselves attached to them. Escrow instructions should be drafted to make the escrow company's functions merely ministerial and its actions predicated upon objective standards that you could rely upon, without independently ascertaining the existence or non-existence thereof. Interest on deferred payments, evidenced by notes, normally accrues from the close of escrow. However, in situations where prepaid interest may be being used or the property is to be tied up for a considerable period of time, it is not unusual for the escrow instructions to call for interest to accrue from a certain date, regardless of whether or not escrow has actually closed.

Escrow Instructions

Escrow instructions should distinguish between the performance date, which is the final date by which each party agrees to fulfill his obligations under the escrow instructions, and the closing date, which is the date when the deed and other documents affecting title are made a matter of record and title is transferred. The "performance date" usually has to be not later than the business day prior to the "closing date." Prorations of taxes, insurance, and rentals must be specifically provided for and it should be clearly stated whether the prorations are to be made in cash or by an adjustment in purchase money financing being carried back by the seller.

The escrow instructions must define whether the buyer is taking (a) "subject to," (b) "assuming," or (c) paying off existing financing. If (c), the contract states who is responsible for pay-off penalties and charges. A "time of essence" clause should be included where the closing date is not intended by the parties to be extended by a court's allowance of "reasonable time" for a party to fulfill its obligations.

The buyer should ascertain all of the following before committing himself unconditionally to purchase:

(a) The objectives, both with respect to equity build-up, cash flow return on investment, potential appreciation, and tax benefits, should be clearly defined after consultation with buyer's attorney, tax advisor, and accountant where appropriate;

(b) True plat map or survey of the property and exact state of title and legal description;

(c) The location and extent of all easements, both record and non-record, and copies of all documents and other matters of record affecting the subject property should be received and reviewed. A current survey of the property is normally required to assist in this examination;

(d) An estimate of the prorations and closing costs, in order to ascertain the exact amount of money to be required at close of escrow;

(e) All taxes and assessments and whether or not any increases are contemplated;

(f) All leases;

(g) An area inspection for comparable prices, leasing information on competing buildings;

(h) All appropriate hazardous and environmental reports, insurability risk assessments, mechanical and structural reports, etc.;

(i) Termite and pest control report where appropriate;

(j) With respect to raw land, (i) a report from the County Public Health Service concerning endemic diseases, (ii) information regarding humidity and temperature, (iii) census projection, (iv) future highway locations, (v) soil conditions, (vi) availability of water and utilities, and (vii) elevation, particularly how much is less than 15% grade, how much less than 25% grade, and how much in excess of 25% grade;

(h) Soil conditions;

(k) Physical inspection (if the buyer is not familiar with the type of construction, it is advisable to take along a contractor, architect or other person who will be familiar with the quality and type of construction), including separate (i) plumbing, (ii) roofing, (iii) structural, and (iv) electrical inspections, where appropriate;

(1) In the case of improved property, it is a good idea to check with the local Building and Safety Department as to whether or not there are any outstanding violations on the property. A fire insurance inspection may be requested to determine whether the building has proper fire protection to qualify for minimum fire rates;

(m) The effect of present zoning, probable future zoning, present environmental and ecological laws, and probable future environmental and ecological laws. This is particularly important with respect to projects to be built and raw land investments;

A partial list of sources of background information on the area is set out hereafter. These companies and agencies should be consulted whether or not the syndicator is familiar with the particular area in which the subject property is located.

INFORMATIONAL SOURCES (partial list)

1. Financial institutions such as banks, savings and loans, finance companies, credit unions, and mortgage correspondents;

2. Local and state chambers of commerce;

3. Telephone companies;

4. Post offices (for number of households, volume of mail, etc.);

5. Gas companies;

6. Electric companies;

7. Water companies or water districts;

8. State and country highway departments;

9. State, county, and local planning commissions;

10. U. S. Coast and Geodetic Survey;

11. U.S. and state departments of agriculture and local agricultural societies (Farm Bureau, Grange, etc.);

12. U. S. Department of Commerce;

13. U. S. Department of Labor and State Labor Department;

14. U. S. Department of Health, Education, Welfare, state, and local welfare agencies;

15. Newspapers and other publications;

16. Local appraisers and market survey organizations;

17. State, county and local health agencies;

18. Local professional and trade organizations such as legal, medical, engineering, etc., societies;

19. Educational institutions: public, private and parochial;

20. Local realty boards;

21. Railroads, bus lines, airlines and other transportation companies and agencies;

22. State and local historical societies;

23. Churches and fraternal organizations;

24. Auto clubs; and

25. Title and escrow companies.

From the foregoing (a) maps, (b) projections, (c) current statistics on population, ethnic and economic back-ground, (d) income, spending habits, education, etc., (e) availability of utilities, transportation, highway access, (f) information on health characteristics and climate, and (g) comparative sales data can be secured which will give the syndicator a profile or the specific area in which his project is to be located.

Leverage Techniques

One of the principal reasons for the purchase of real property is leverage. Leverage is the ability to control and receive a return on an asset greater than the cash invested, therefore giving to the investor an "override" on that portion of the asset which represents borrowed money. This override can take a number of different forms related to all of the various benefits from ownership, as follows: (1) If the cash invested is 20% of the total value of the property (the loan being 80%) and the property shows a spendable yield of 9% and the money can be borrowed at a loan constant of 8% in addition to the 9% spendable being received on the dollars invested, there is an additional 4% return (1% X 4 = 4%) of spendable by reason of the override on the cash flow, making the net spendable 13% (9% on cash plus 4% loan constant override). (2) If the appreciation of the property is 2% per year, there will be of course 3% appreciation on the 20% of the asset represented by the original down payment, plus 3% on four times that amount represented by the debt, or a total appreciation return on the equity of 15%. (3) The same may be true of other benefits such as excess depreciation, equity build-up, etc. Therefore, in order to gain maximum leverage, the syndicator and the investor are often interested in keeping the original cash investment as low as possible and diminishing the opportunity or requirement of additional cash investment.

Various techniques for improving the leverage and keeping the initial cash requirement down are as follows. These techniques generally are designed for the purchase of speculative land, although some of them will have applicability to income property as well:

1. Securing a certain portion of the property released with the down payment. This enables you then to re-borrow on that portion of the property or to retain the entire proceeds of the sale of that portion of the property without making a reduction on encumbrances. Getting a portion of the property released from the encumbrance upon the payment of additional principal. In a land situation, this would mean that with each principal payment, additional acreage would be released, which then could be sold, and the entire proceeds of the sale retained by the new owner.

2. Use of assumable multiple deeds of trust and notes (that do not include due on sale clauses). This means that the property covered by an individual deed (one of these deeds of trust) can be sold subject to that deed of trust, without there being the necessity of paying any release price.

3. Use of a release and security substitution clause. This would mean that, when it was required to release property from the blanket encumbrance, the seller would agree to take back, as a portion of the release price in lieu of cash, a new note and deed of trust on the portion of the property being released.

4.   Use of condemnation charges. The condemnation charges would apply to the release of property according to the previously agreed upon release schedule, if possible, and to the extent that the condemnation award exceeds the release price, the balance may be retained by the purchaser.

5.   Agreements that the escrow or purchase may be extended by paying additional deposits or option payments. In the case of land, this would postpone the time when the payments on the underlying encumbrance would start. The interest on the property being purchased may be much greater than the price of controlling the property, by increasing the down payment from time to time into the escrow. For example, if a property is being bought for $1,000,000, the seller might be willing to extend the escrow for a series of six-month periods by receipt of $10,000 option money out of escrow for each six-month period. Whereas the interest rate at 8% for six months would amount to $40,000. It is important to indicate when the option money applies to the purchase price, if the option is exercised, and when it does not.

6. It may also be possible to purchase a small portion of the property and to option the remaining part. Again, the option price may be much less than the interest charges on an encumbrance on the balance of the property.

7. Option vs. Purchase. From a tax standpoint in certain cases, it may be advantageous for the buyer to purchase the property rather than option it, for

interest on the purchase price and payment of taxes are fully deductible, whereas option payments need to be capitalized.

8. When the seller's proration credits are to be added to the purchase money mortgage rather than paid in cash and when the buyer's proration credits are to be paid in cash or deducted from the mortgage balance.

9. Buyer's escrow costs, etc., when to be paid out of down payment and added to purchase money mortgage.

10. Loans from brokers and other short-term bank loans.

11. Use of a trust or holding agreement allowing subdivision, sale, and development without triggering release clauses.

12. Splitting the down payment over a period of time.

ANALYSIS AND PROJECTIONS

The property analysis, due diligence, and projection preparation is a subject that could fill several volumes. While this chapter focuses on the mechanical aspects of acquisition, it is not intended to provide guidance on how to buy, and in particular, how to analyze whether a property is a good buy. One who is not thoroughly familiar and experienced in real property acquisition should associate such an individual in the effort or prepare his or herself, by taking appropriate education and studying the process in depth. It is very easy to make mistakes in what is not an easy or simple task.

CHAPTER 7

SELECTING A
REAL ESTATE BROKER*

Many syndicators are themselves licensed real estate brokers active in locating property not only for themselves but also for others. Few syndicate organizations can afford full-time acquisition staff and must rely largely on outside parties. Early in the development of a syndication practice, the syndicator must make a basic policy decision concerning his acquisition methods and use of real estate brokers. The "packager" of real estate projects has generally six alternatives:

1.   To deal only with principals on a direct basis, purchasing the property net from the seller, to the exclusion of any real estate broker.

2.   To indicate a policy of cooperation with outside brokers, wherein the real estate commission will be divided between the seller's brokerage representative and the syndicator. In this case, care must be used in the documentation to indicate to the seller that the syndicator is acting as both a broker and a principal, and will share in the commission.

3.   To deal directly with selling principals only based on a full brokerage commission being paid to the syndicator. Again, the disclosure referred to in the second method must be made.

4.   To use the services of an "exclusive broker," indicating that no property will be purchased which is not submitted through the exclusive broker. Where a syndicator does not have his own acquisition department and desires someone to be full time aggressively looking for property for his operation there are advantages to the exclusive brokerage representation, which will be discussed hereafter.

5.   To accept submissions from any broker without participation in commission by the syndicator. This generally results in the greatest number of submissions

6.   In order to increase submissions (deal flow) pay, a finder's fee to brokers and finders who present property that is not listed or where the listing broker will not share commissions.

*Taken from an article by the Author appearing in the University of West Los Angeles Bar Review, Fall 1972. Permission to reprint is gratefully acknowledged.

Importance of Proper Representation

The failure to properly select brokerage representation, or, if it has been properly selected, to adequately use such representation to full advantage, often has a material affect on the outcome of the transaction. Many sellers are motivated by consideration other than price and it is often the broker's "sixth sense" to ascertain the subjective motivations and personality of the seller, which leads to a successful close of the transaction. The ability to be imaginative with respect to tax considerations, timing of the sale, possibility for an exchange, and other factors weigh importantly, whether or not one is buyer or seller.

The Establishment of Rapport

A broker can often succeed in diluting the antagonism, which arises between buyer and seller in a given transaction. Failure promptly to communicate between the parties, particularly during early negotiations, is often the principal cause of the existence of such antagonism. The broker who is familiar with his client's objectives, tax position, economic position, and personality can suggest a course of action based on his interpretation of these factors, which will enable him effectively to perform his function of bringing the parties together to complete the transaction.

It is wise in the initial stage of the transaction to establish the respective responsibility of the syndicator's representatives including the broker, the attorney, the appraiser, the accountant, and such other advisors as he may have in connection with the acquisition of the property. It should be made clear whether a syndicator is looking to his representatives, or some of them, for guidance on the economic merits of the transaction, as well as in their specific areas of responsibility. Are the representatives merely to assist in the generation of deal-flow conclusion of the transactions and the documentation to see that it reflect the syndicator's desires, or, are they to be involved in economic decisions as well. In order to prevent conflict between the various representatives and to assure their team effort, it should be made clear between them as to their respective functions.

Selecting A Broker

When selecting a real estate broker, the syndicator should check with the appropriate state agency and trade association to determine whether the broker is currently in good standing, and inquire in the local community whether the broker has the particular skills, knowledge, and experience, which may be required for the given transaction. The following questions should be directed to the broker being considered:

1. How many years experience has the individual had as a licensed real estate professional? How many of those years in the property type being sought?

2. What proportion of the individual's time is devoted to real estate brokerage as opposed to management, insurance, syndication, non-real estate, and other activities?

3. What is the extent of the broker's staff, organization, and access to listings (note I have however made some of my best buys through small independent brokerages that had good local contacts).

4. Is the broker familiar with the particular type of transaction and can he give references of clients who have successfully engaged him in similar transactions in the past?

5. What professional and other organizations is he a member of and active in?

6. Is he able to give references concerning his general character and financial integrity?

7. What proportion of this time does he plan to devote to your project?

8. (Sale) In order to provide maximum exposure to the client's listing, (or purchasing criteria in a purchase), is he willing to advertise, and does he have a policy of cooperating with other brokers?

Preparing the Broker

The buyer should furnish his agent with information that he is a serious buyer. That is, his financial ability to complete the transaction, his experience with the particular type of property, and where appropriate, information concerning the number of similar transactions which the buyer has participated in the past. As a minimum, a list of financial references should be provided. Such background information cannot fail, at least subjectively, to improve the broker's enthusiasm to devote time and effort to the project and will serve as important negotiating points for the broker to use when he is in direct contact with the seller's representative. The broker should also be given full and adequate background as to the criteria for purchase. The following points are among the criteria that should be clearly outlined.

1. A specific geographic area in which the project must be located, where appropriate;

2. A maximum and minimum size of project and a maximum and minimum price;

3.   The type of project including the quality of tenancy desired;

4.   The kind of financing desired and the amount of down payment available;

5.   If land is to be purchased for the erection of industrial property whether or not railroad siding and/or freeway access is required, freight zone, telephone rate zone, airport access, etc., and;

6.   Utility needs.

Where the client is the seller, the broker should be given initially all of the information he would normally want to see on behalf of a prospective buyer, as this will prevent misunderstandings later. If the property is to be sold "as is," it should be clearly spelled out in the initial listing. The broker should be supplied with copies of tax bills, appraisals, lease digests, plot plans, and any other information which seller may have in his files that would be of interest to the serious buyer.

The Agency (Listing) Agreement

Whether a buyer or seller, in order to obtain maximum results, the client should be encouraged to deal exclusively with the agent selected for a period of time. A buyer by dealing with one broker exclusively can avoid inadvertently "bidding against himself." An agent can devote more time and effort to his principal's needs if he knows that all prospective properties will be channeled through him. Brokers devote more effort to exclusive listings than to open listings. This is understandable as they are normally working on a contingency and success in relation to effort has historically been greater under exclusive arrangements than open ones.

Among the type of agency arrangements that can be entered into are the following.

1.   Exclusive right to sell. For a specific period, the broker is given an exclusive right to sell a particular property and will be entitled to receive his commission if the property is sold during that time, regardless of who is the procuring cause of the sale, including the owner. The opposite, of course, of an exclusive right to sell would be an exclusive right to buy, wherein the broker would receive his commission if the purchaser purchased a particular property during the listing period, which was substantially the same as that he was authorized to procure.

2.   Exclusive Listing. The broker will be entitled to his commission if a sale takes place because of the efforts of anyone other than the owner.

3.   Open Listing. The broker will receive a commission if the sale takes place on the terms and conditions of the listing, because of the efforts of the broker during

the listing period. He will not, however, receive a commission if the sale takes place because of the efforts of others, or, because of the efforts of the owner.

4. One Party Listing. Listing authorizing a commission if the sale is to a named party only. It further indicates that there is no obligation to pay a commission on the sale to any person other than the named party or parties. It usually provides that the broker may register with the owner additional named parties under certain circumstances.

In combination with the above, the formula for determining commission may be any one of the following.

1. Percentage of Sale Price or Purchase Price;

2. Net Sale Listing, in which event the broker receives any amount paid in excess of the net listed price;

3. Net Purchase Listing, which is any amount less than the price the buyer was willing to pay;

4. Flat Fee, which is a set sum regardless of the final sale price in the event a transaction as described in the listing agreement takes place, or

5. Combination of the above contingent on a transaction taking place.

Selection of Fee

Careful consideration should be given to the manner in which the broker is to be paid. While a contingent fee based on a percentage of the purchase price may initially appear attractive in that if there is not a successful transaction nothing is owed, a fee that is based on a percentage of the sale price would motivate the broker to secure the highest price possible. Therefore, it would seem to be appropriate only where the broker is representing the seller. If a broker has been given an acquisition assignment, it would seem to be more appropriate to provide that the fee to be paid (where the fee is to be paid by the buyer) be either a set fee based on successful conclusion of the transaction, or a fee based on him being able to secure for the buyer proper property meeting certain basic criteria as to net spendable return, equity build-up, tax benefits, etc. The percentage could be based on the broker's ability to secure a property meeting certain criteria with a participation or formula price based on the extent to which the property found exceeds the minimum criteria established. Particularly in the acquisition area, consideration should be given in placing a broker on a retainer or set fee rather than a percentage.

Whether the fee, where the broker is representing the buyer, should be contingent or not is a question that must be carefully considered in light of the particular circumstances. A compensation formula that encourages the broker to secure the lowest possible price for the buyer would seem to make more sense when the broker is the buyer's representative, than the more customary one of allowing the broker, regardless of whose agent he is, to be paid by the seller, in a percentage of the sale price. Balanced against these considerations, of course, is the broker's knowledge that if he is not successful in negotiating the seller to a point where the price and terms will be acceptable to the buyer he will receive no compensation at all. Under normal circumstances, such should be a sufficient incentive for him to use his best efforts on behalf of the buyer.

Counsel for the client will generally request a provision that commission is only due and payable in the event of successful completion of the transaction. The agent will press for a provision that he be entitled to the commission if he brings together ready, willing, and able parties who agree on the transaction, regardless of whether or not the transaction is successfully concluded. Where the broker controls a particular piece of property because of a unique relationship with the seller or has outstanding reputation and ability (his services being unavailable on any other basis), the client may agree to the latter clause.

Time Limit

It is advisable to provide the listing will be for the minimum period considered necessary to evaluate the broker's efforts, with the right to extend by mutual agreement. Therefore, if the circumstances indicate that the wrong broker has been selected, the client will be free as soon as possible to discharge the present broker and select another one. Absent certain provisions, a listing agreement is generally construed to be an agency at will revocable by the principal at any time prior to the terms of the agency having been met. It is not suggested, however, that the principal rely solely on this provision, as the broker may be able to prove an agency coupled with an interest because of his efforts, etc. Brokers listing forms often contain language that gives the broker compensation if the listing is cancelled before it expires

Representations

The listing should contain a statement that the broker is not authorized to make any representations concerning the property other than those that are contained in the listing agreement. It should further state that the agreement could only be modified in writing.

Complete Listing Required

The terms of the listing should clearly spell out all of the contemplated provisions of the purchase contract, including (a) whether or not the purchase will be subject to or require an assumption of existing loans, (b) whether the prorations would be in cash or in secondary financing carried back by the seller, (c) the length of escrow, (d) the escrow agent, (e) the title company to be used, (f) the type and nature of title policy to be given, (g) the period of time which will be allowed for contingencies, etc. (This list is by no means meant to be exhaustive, as what is to be included in the listing is not within the scope of this article.) Of particular importance is a provision which will state for what period of time after the expiration of the listing the broker will receive protection if the property should later be purchased (in the case of a representation of the seller) by a party introduced to the property by the broker, or, if the buyer (in the case of the broker representing the buyer) should purchase a property introduced to him by the broker.

The broker generally can be of help in problem solving with regard to clearing up matters of title, securing information, and zoning. In order to encourage the broker to assist in these matters consideration should be given to advancing out-of-pocket costs and reasonable expenses where appropriate. In some cases, it is the practice for the principal to advance a portion of these expenses, which will thereafter be deducted from the commission if the transaction is closed.

Right to Cancel or Withdraw

Seller will often want the right to withdraw the property, cancel the listing before the term expires, and/or reject offers. When such as provision is included in the listing, it is often accompanied by a provision to reimburse the broker for its expenses and/or time.

Conclusion

If handled properly, the services of a licensed real estate broker can be of material assistance to the client and his counsel in selecting, negotiating, and completing the purchase, sale, or leasing of real property. Considering the foregoing will improve communication between the broker, the client, and counsel so that the broker's experience, knowledge, and reputation can be fully utilized.

CHAPTER 8

HOW TO NEGOTIATE FINANCING

The success of a project is determined at the time the subject property initially is acquired, as the amount of profit the developer or new owner can realize is often set during the acquisition and development stage by how the purchase and financing are structured. Acquisition factors may outweigh the importance of marketing efforts later. For this reason, consideration of the nature and type of financing to be secured is essential, and effort in this area brings the highest returns in relation to time spent. Careful projections must be made of the long-term effects of financing alternatives. Because of the diversity of legal treatment by various jurisdictions of rights to pre-pay, personal liability, rights to collateral, interest rates, priority of liens, forms of documentation required, etc. no attempt is made here to discuss the differences between the various state laws. This chapter only outlines a few of the general principles to be considered when initiating financing in a given project.

Financing Effect on Market Value

As was clearly illustrated in the earlier discussion on leverage, the constant rate (see Glossary) on loan payments can have either a positive or a negative effect on spendable income. A property equity may sell in the market place to sophisticated investors at a multiple of the net spendable on that equity. (Net spendable on the equity is the spendable remaining after debt service.) The reasons for this are as follows:

A. Many investors are cash-flow oriented. That is, they are concerned with what amount of actual cash they will receive on their net dollars invested.

B. Equity buildup resulting from mortgage amortization may be given some consideration, but the actual dollars that such equity buildup represents are to be received at some future time and must be discounted in terms of present value. The investor considering the value of future cash flow will consider the rate of inflation together with the discounted value of future money. Therefore, the value that is placed on equity buildup may be substantially less than receiving equivalent current cash income.

C. Tax benefits that can be derived from the ownership of property resulting from excess depreciation, as is seen in the chapter on tax considerations are often speculative. Congress may place continuing limits on and/or reduce such benefits, placing into question the future value of excess depreciation. The need of the government for new revenue sources from federal income tax places a transitory aura around future tax benefits, together with the current recapture provisions of the income tax laws, and indicates that tax benefits have to receive a much lower valuation in the relative scale of considerations, as against present cash flow, when making a determination to purchase or develop the real estate project.

D. Interest rates can have a positive or negative affect on the return on the down payment (see Chapter 2 concerning leverage)

Financing Considerations

The considerations that should be examined, in preparing oneself for negotiations with the prospective lender, will fall into several categories:

A. Those that relate to most types of financing, whether the project is being developed as a syndication or a sole proprietorship;

B. Those that relate specifically to construction projects wherein funds are being provided for construction on an interim basis, as opposed to permanent financing upon completion of construction;

C. Those considerations that relate primarily to the fact that the project is being syndicated rather than held as a sole proprietorship;

D. Those that relate to the form of entity chosen. For example, tenancies in common present greater financing challenges than limited liability companies do;

E. Those which are specified to the characteristics of the project, including (1) environmental and toxic issues, (2) use of the property, (3) demographics (4) traffic, and (5) growth rates; and

F. The financial statement, credit, reputation, and record of accomplishment of the borrower are important to a lender, even though a loan may be non-recourse.

General Negotiating Points Affecting Cash Flow

The following will serve to improve the owners' and developers' cash flow when negotiating financing:

A. Points and Service Charges: These should be paid only at funding of the loan, and where possible, by some means other than cash, as follows:

(1) A promissory note, usually non-interest bearing and due on funding of the loan (to be preferred by the borrower) or on the issuance of a firm commitment (to be preferred by the lender) with interest to accrue from the maturity date;

(2) A letter of credit from a commercial bank guaranteeing payment of the loan or service charge upon the funding or issuance of the commitment. (Charges for a letter of credit are often less than the interest costs of an equivalent cash loan.); and

(3) Provide, at the execution of the application, that the points or service charges will not be due until the commitment is issued or the loan funded, which will avoid the necessity of the note or letter of credit.

B. First Payment on Loan: Negotiate a delayed payment on the principal and interest of the loan. Most loans usually call for the first payment to be due 30 days after funding. Negotiate with the lender that the first payment is due some extended period after funding (usually 60, 90, or 120 days).

C. Additional Advances: The loan amount is usually based on a percentage of the value of the property at the date of funding of the loan. If the borrower intends to make improvements or materially to increase rentals during the relatively short period after the initial funding date that would materially improve the appraised value of the property, negotiate a provision in the loan that additional advances would be made, increasing the loan amount under certain conditions. If these advances are repayable over the term of the loan and the loan is a permanent long-term loan, the constant on these advances will be much lower than would be a constant required to serve short-term secondary financing from another lender.

D. Release Clauses: Where the loan covers a series of properties, as has been indicated elsewhere in the acquisition chapter, release clauses can be important.

E. Annual Financial Reports: Many formal loan commitments require the borrower to supply to the lender an audited, independent, certified financial statement within 90 days after the end of each fiscal year of the project. The cost of securing an audited statement can be substantial. Many lenders will accept, as a suitable alternative, a compilation statement prepared by an independent certified public accountant, not audited but certified by an officer of the borrower to be true and correct to the best of his knowledge.

F. Impounds: Where impounds are required, provide for the payment of interest on the impounds equivalent to those which the borrower could receive if he had deposited them in an insured savings and loan demand account, or an insured commercial bank demand savings account. An alternative would be to provide that they be placed into such an account on which only the lender can draw, with the interest to be paid to the borrower.

G. Appraisals: Commitments often call for an appraisal to be made by an appraiser selected by the lender. The borrower may already have an existing appraisal that has previously been prepared by a qualified appraiser. The lender should be requested to accept the existing appraisal or, as an alternative, an update by the appraiser of the existing appraisal (where it is acceptable to the lender). That appraiser has a full file on and is familiar with the property, which will expedite the receipt of the appraisal. Sometimes the lender will consent to a less expensive review/appraisal by the lender's appraiser where it is not familiar with the borrower's appraiser.

H. Late Charges: Include a provision that late charges are not effective until a specified period from the due date. Request that the late charge be a reasonable one, bearing some relationship to the actual amount late, rather than being based on the total amount of the loan and that a grace period, as long as possible, be provided.

Non-Cash-Flow Elements of Loan Negotiations

The following additional matters should be considered in applying for and negotiating a real property loan:

A. Subject-To, Rather Than, Assumption: If there is an existing loan, consideration should be given to providing that the purchase will be made subject to the existing loan, where this is possible. When a property is purchased subject to the existing loan, the property alone serves as security for the loan. If the existing loan is assumed, then, under most circumstances, the purchaser will be personally liable for any deficiency that might result from a foreclosure on that loan.

B. Right of First Refusal: A right of first refusal to purchase the loan if the lender at some future time should elect to sell the loan at a discount. With the changes in money market rates, lenders will, from time to time, place loans on the marketplace at discounts below their face value. It could be an important advantage to the borrower to have notice of this and a reasonable opportunity to pay off his loan at the discount when the lender should so elect.

C. Application of Insurance Proceeds: Many loans contain provisions that casualty insurance proceeds are to be used to reduce the loan balance. These provisions should be modified to provide that, at the election of the borrower, the proceeds would go into a special account for rebuilding the property, if they are adequate to do so.

D. Acceleration:

(1) On Sale: Many loans will contain an acceleration clause providing that the loan mature on the transfer of any interest in the real property. The borrower needs to negotiate the elimination or modification of these provisions. Among the kinds of modifications often available are the following:

(a) That the transfer is subject to the approval of the lender, which approval the lender agrees not to unreasonably withhold;

(b) That the borrower may transfer a certain percentage of interest in the property (usually not more than 50%) without accelerating the maturity of the loan;

(c) That the borrower can transfer to another entity in which he holds a percentage of interest, such as a corporation or a limited partnership so long as he has operating control;

(d) That there is a right to transfer provided the original borrower remains personally liable on the loan; and

(e) That family transfers, or transfers to the borrower's estate planning trusts, are approved, and transfers among original investors and syndicator are approved.

(2) On Placement of Junior Encumbrance: Acceleration on placement of junior financing can usually be eliminated. Even if not eliminated, it can often be modified to provide that, if the net proceeds of the junior financing are used for improvements on the property, such junior financing will not serve to accelerate the senior encumbrance. If junior encumbrance is to be allowed, an enter-creditor agreement form should be added to facilitate such financing.

(3) On Foreclosure of Junior Financing: A modification in this clause can often be secured, indicating that the taking of title by a junior lien holder, particularly a specifically named junior lien holder, will not serve to accelerate the senior encumbrance, provided the junior lien holder, upon taking title, agrees to assume the note and deed of trust.

(4) On Demise: A modification can often be secured in respect to the acceleration on sale or transfer, provided that if the sale or transfer is the

result of the demise of the trustor, upon the heir or legatee assuming the note and deed of trust, acceleration for transfer will be waived.

E.   Lock-In and Prepayment Penalties: Many loans will contain a lock-in clause prohibiting prepayment for a period of time. The borrower should endeavor to secure a prepayment privilege by paying a certain percentage of unearned interest. Usually these provisions are granted upon the payment of from six months to one year's unearned interest as a prepayment privilege on the then-loan balance. Another form of modification provides that the borrower can pay off 20% of the principal of the loan in any one year without penalty, or under certain penalties.

F.   Balloon Payments: (A balloon payment provides for the unpaid balance to be due at some date prior to what would normally be the maturity date of the loan if it were fully amortized.) Negotiate for a provision that, if the borrower experiences difficulty in refinancing on the balloon payment date the balloon payment will be divided over several months or that, at the election of the borrower, the balloon payment can be amortized over an extended period at a higher interest rate and/or amortization rate.

G.   Dragnet Clause: A provision that any other property that serves as security to a loan made from the same lender also serves as additional security for the respective loan contained in the note and deed of trust being executed. Most lenders will agree to eliminate this clause when it is brought to their attention. The presence of such a clause will be objectionable to sources of junior financing. This is often called "cross collateralization." A modification in the clause can often be secured so that it only applies as long as the present trustor owns that other property.

H.   Automatic Default: Provide that the borrower will be given written notice of a default and an opportunity to cure. A compromise provision is that no notice will be given as to defaults in monetary payments, such as failure to make the monthly payment or to pay taxes, etc., on the grounds that the borrower knows whether he has made the payment. Notice would be given, however, for other provisions, such as failure to commit waste, to carry insurance, etc., which may have been inadvertently overlooked by the borrower rather than by a conscious act of the borrower.

I.   Attorney's Fees and Costs: Loan applications provide that the borrower will pay for the lender's attorneys' fees and costs. They often call for the borrower to pay an appraisal fee. It is advisable to specify, in the application, the maximum amount of these fees for which the borrower agrees to be liable. The author's experience has been that by such specification the amount of the fees incurred are usually equivalent to or less than the amount specified, whereas without such a specification, the amount charged may exceed what the borrower would consider reasonable for the respective service.

J.   Borrower's Contingencies: Loan applications provide that the borrower is liable for, and the lender and/or broker have earned, their fees upon the issuance of a loan commitment. In some circumstances, this commitment may be issued and then there is a failure of the borrower's purchase. There is a method to protect the borrower from being liable for a commitment that he is unable to use. Provide, where the application is being signed prior to the borrower having completed all his contingencies of purchase, that the obligation to accept the loan and pay for the commitment is contingent upon the completion of the conditions for purchase or development. An alternative may be to provide to pay a reduced fee to the lender for its efforts.

Liability Considerations

As has been noted in the chapter, "Tax Considerations," it may be necessary to include a provision in the loan that there is no personal liability on the part of any party. This can be done either by means of an exculpatory clause providing that the borrowers are released from liability and the lender looks solely to the property, or by a provision that the sole security for the loan is the real property. In addition to the tax considerations that may dictate a non-recourse loan, the borrower may be concerned about a deficiency judgment in the event that it should be necessary to default on the loan in the future.

Personal liability also affects the borrower's credit and ability to borrow by having to report his direct or contingent liability in his financial statement. In reporting liability on a financial statement, one of several circumstances will be present:

A. There is probably no truly non-recourse institutional loan, in that an experienced and sophisticated lender will require personal liability for "the usual carve-outs" such as, (1) misuse of funds, (2) environmental issues, (3) voluntary bankruptcy and, (4) fraud of misrepresentation;(B. The individual is directly liable on the loan or has primary liability on it, in which case the full amount of the loan, under general accounting principles, should be shown on his balance sheet;

B. The borrower and/or the guarantor is directly liable on the loan or has primary liability on it, in which case the full amount of the loan, under general accounting principles, should be shown on his balance sheet;

C. It is indirectly or secondarily liable, in which case it may be shown as a contingent liability in a footnote, explaining the circumstances of the liability;

D. There is no personal liability, in which case it need not be reported either in the footnote or directly on the balance sheet, the amount of the loan merely being offset against a total value of the property in determining the net equity; or

It. He has contingent liability, wherein liability only arises under certain circumstances, such as the failure of a major tenant. It is quite common for a loan to be non-recourse "except for the usual carve-outs" (often termed the "bad boy" clause), see "personal liability" above.

Liability can be of varying degrees as follows:

A. Full liability,

B. Partial liability, such as

(1) A certain percentage of the entire principal and interest on the loan, or the top portion of the loan (often called "first loss");

(2) A specific lease (where the borrower guarantees the rental payments of one of the major tenants);

(3) All or part of the gross income of the property but not of the principal balance of the loan; or

(4) The interest, but no portion of the principal.

There are a number of substitutes for personal liability that the borrower can offer the lender in exchange for a non-recourse (often termed exculpatory) clause:

A. Mortgage insurance purchased from a conventional mortgage insurance company, guaranteeing all or a portion of the loan;

B. Lease insurance, where a conventional lease insurance company or the Small Business Administration (which also may be a source of mortgage insurance) guarantees certain of the leases;

C. A guarantee of the mortgage or lease from a private party;

D. A letter of credit guaranteeing the lease or the mortgage from a commercial bank;

E. An agreement from an individual or institution to purchase the loan on default (put agreement);

F. Supplying additional security or collateral over and above the project itself;

G. A standby loan from another lender agreeing to make a loan on the property in an amount sufficient to pay off the present lender under certain circumstances;

H. The use of a higher amortization rate, which will pay off a substantial portion of the loan at an earlier time (This is often referred to as split amortization.) wherein perhaps half of the loan may be amortized during the first five years and half of the loan over a ten or fifteen year period, so that the lender has, at a relatively early stage, a much smaller loan in relation to value than where the whole principal balance was amortized over the longer time;

I. Offering the lender a higher rate of interest than would be present where there would be personal liability; or

J. Offering an "equity kicker" giving the lender a participation in the net rental income derived from the property in addition to his interest rate. The equity kicker can either take the form of a participation in the then current income stream at the time the loan is initially funded or, as an alternative, a participation in the increase in the income stream occurring thereafter.

Construction Loans

Where a loan is being made for construction purposes, the following items should be considered:

A. Dutch Interest: (Interest accruing from the date of commitment on the amount of funds committed rather than the amount of funds actually used is often termed Dutch Interest.) Where possible, the loan should be written in such a manner that commences when funding takes place;

B. As drawn, interest does not accrue until the funds are actually disbursed, and then only on the funds so disbursed from date of disbursement;

C. Voucher System vs. Draws: It will generally be advantageous for the borrower to provide that construction expenses be paid by means of a voucher on a per item basis rather than on a stage draw system at various stages of completion. The draw system requires the borrower to advance the funds until the particular stage has been completed, entitling him to the next draw. However, where the expense of a voucher system makes such a program impractical, a larger number of stages, such as a seven or nine stage draw rather than a three or five stage draw, will serve to reduce the burden on the borrower's cash resources. The more frequent the draw, the less the burden on the borrower to come up with outside funds to carry the construction loan;

D. Holdbacks: Construction loans will generally provide for the holding back of a percentage of the progress payment until some period after completion. If possible, a guarantee of completion, or the supplying of a letter of credit guaranteeing completion, would be advisable to encourage the lender to make a 100% advance of the cost of construction at each particular stage. An alternate method is to supply outside collateral until the project has been completed, to give the lender the extra protection usually provided by the holdback;

E. Guarantees of Completion: Where lenders might, under certain circumstances, on permanent loans, be willing to provide for no personal liability provided the building is finished according to plans and specifications, the borrower will normally have to guarantee completion of the building according to plans and specifications. Again, the supplying of additional outside collateral or of a completion bond might relieve the borrower of personal liability at this stage;

F. Additional Advances: In order to provide for unexpected costs during the construction stage, the construction loan agreement should make provision for the supplying of additional amounts of funds over those estimated in the event of such difficulties. The borrower, of course, may have to provide additional collateral in such eventualities. It is advisable to negotiate such provisions at the time of the initial loan, when the terms for such additional advances might be more favorable due to the lender's desire for the loan than at the time the unexpected difficulties occurred and when the lender has no obligation to make the advance if it has not already been provided for;

G. Commencement of Work: Title insurers are reluctant to insure a lender where construction may have started prior to recordation of a construction loan. It is, therefore, essential to complete your negotiations for the construction loan prior to the actual commencement of work. Where you desire to commence work before having selected a construction lender, considerate recording with a particular construction lender forms generally in use. Secure an agreement with that lender that they will make an assignment of the construction loan documents to another lender for a nominal service charge. This works well if you are unable to reach final agreement on the terms and conditions of the construction loan with the original recorded construction lender.

Sources of Financing

The best source of financing for a particular project will depend on a consideration of the following:

A. The amount of equity which the borrower has, as some sources are willing to lend a higher percentage of value than others are;

B. The length of loan desired: Some sources will have a lower rate of interest for short-term loans and others are more interested in long-term loans and will offer their best rate for the longer term;

C. The type of property;

D. The quality of the income stream: Some sources will be extremely competitive where the income stream is AAA tenancy, while other sources are more interested in the rate available than the credit quality of the tenant;

E. Whether or not a non-recourse loan is desired;

F. Geographic location: Certain lenders are restricted in how far from their head office they may lend; others may prefer certain geographic areas; and

G. Amount of loan: Each lender has a maximum amount that it can lend. In some cases, the lender is able to arrange participation with other lenders, while in other cases the lender is restricted to those loans that it can make without the necessity of participation.

Among the sources of loans secured by real property are the following:

A. Commercial banks;

B. Savings and loan associations (thrifts);

C. Mutual savings banks;

D. Life insurance companies;

E. Pension trusts;

F. Trust companies;

G. Small Business Administration and other agencies of the federal state, or local government;

H. State and local development companies;

I. Real estate investment trusts;

J. Private individuals;

K. Mortgage correspondents;

L. Mortgage brokers;

M. Utility companies, construction companies, etc;

N. Finance companies;

O. Industrial loan companies;

P. Credit unions;

Q. Labor unions;

R. Vendors;

CHAPTER 9

SELECTING THE FORM OF ENTITY

Principal methods of holding title to syndicate ownership of real property are as follows:

TYPES OF ENTITIES

1.   Tenancy in Common

Often referred to as TICs. This is a method whereby each investor's name appears in the title of the property as to an undivided interest. Legally, absent any agreement to the contrary, each tenant is entitled to the use of the entire property. The profits and losses would be divided among the investors in relation to their percentage interest in the property. Agreement of all owners would be required in order to convey the property, borrow money, hire a property manager, grant leases or to make substantial improvements. A co-owner who advanced funds for the benefit of the property would be entitled to contribution from his other co-tenants in common. Usually where this type of agreement is in effect, there will be a management agreement between the owners and a managing agent that gives the agent a power of attorney to maintain and operate the property. Most important, the sponsor or syndicator cannot have a continuing "promotional interest or override" under current IRS regulations.

2.   Joint Tenancy

This is similar to a tenancy in common with the exception that upon the demise of any joint tenant that tenant's interest is divided prorata among the remaining joint tenants, the last surviving joint tenant succeeding to the entire ownership of the property.

3.   Trusts

There are various kinds of trusts. A trust arrangement is where the title is placed in the hands of a trustee who operates the property on behalf of the owners who are called "beneficiaries." There is usually a written trust agreement specifying the duties and obligations of the trustee and his method of compensation. These arrangements generally are referred to as *common law trusts*. There is also a *qualified real estate investment trust* (REIT) which is a trust formed pursuant to Sections 856-858 of the Internal Revenue Code. Providing the trust meets the requirements of the code, there will be flow-through accounting treatment provided to some extent. That is, the profits will be taxed in the hands of the individuals rather than at the entity level.

In order to qualify as a real estate investment trust, it must comply with various state and federal regulations. The trust activities must be passive and its assets invested in certain restricted categories. Because of the requirement of a minimum of a large number of beneficiaries at all times and the fact that the trust cannot provide excess tax shelter (it only can pass the tax shelter through to the extent that it has distributable income), the REIT is not suitable for the typical individual real estate project. Most REITs are extremely large because the market and state laws limit the fees and profits that can be made on their operation and generally, a very large capitalization is required in order to make the operation of a real estate trust profitable to a syndicator.

4. (a) Joint Venture Agreements, and (b) Co-Partnerships

These are agreements usually between partnerships or other entities for the operation of a specific piece of property. They are very similar to general partnerships and normally are not used in public syndication. A general partnership or co-partnership is one where all partners have joint and several liability. Title is placed in the partnership name rather than in the names of the individual partners, as in the tenancy in common. A general partnership can elect flow-through accounting treatment.

5.   Corporations

(a) 'C' Corporations

A 'C' corporation is an entity formed pursuant to the corporation laws of a particular governmental jurisdiction. It generally is considered a tax paying entity, the same as a trust. It is an entity therefore taxable as an association except as otherwise noted. A 'C' corporation has the advantage that it will protect the investors from personal liability, but you cannot pass through excess depreciation normally in a C corporation. A 'C' corporation will have shareholders and the ownership is represented by share certificates. In California, the jurisdiction over the selling of syndicate interests in a 'C' corporation lies with the Corporation Commissioner. Certain other forms of syndication also require compliance with corporation commissioner rules. See the chapter on "State and Federal Regulations of Syndicate Activities."

(b) 'S' Corporporations

A n 'S' corporation is a corporation taxable as a partnership and does have the benefit of flow-through accounting. This is a corporation organized pursuant to an 'S' Corporation of the Internal Revenue Code with not more than 100 shareholders. A husband and wife count as one shareholder. However, a trust or corporation cannot be a shareholder of an 'S' corporation. See the chapter "Tax Considerations" for reasons why an 'S' corporation should not be used for real estate investment.

(c) Section 1244 Corporation

This is a corporation organized pursuant to Section 1244 of the Internal Revenue Code, which provides that corporations that meet the requirements of that section qualify with regard to a loss on their capital stock investment in such corporations as an ordinary loss. This can be very important where a corporation is being used in a speculative enterprise and there is a high risk of loss.

(d) Domestic vs. Foreign Entity

Where an entity is to be involved in holding title, it is usually a domestic corporation, meaning one chartered within the state in which the syndicate is organized and the syndicate property is located. A foreign state entity is an entity that has as its state of formation a different state than that in that the syndicate is doing business or the property is located. A foreign nation entity would be one that has formed in a jurisdiction of a nation other than the one in which the property is located. Domestic entities are most often used because of a desire to qualify for the intra-state exemption from the Securities and Exchange Commission regulations and to avoid conflicts between the law of the state of the entity and the state where the property is located (see the chapter "State and Federal Regulations of Syndication Activity").

(e) Membership Corporations

This is a special type of corporation wherein the members own the assets of the corporation and are entitled to the profits and losses. The ownership of the corporation is represented by membership certificates rather than by stock certificates. A membership corporation might be organized to own and operate a golf course, beach or recreation club, etc. With increasing emphasis on planned developments, second home communities, ecology and vacation-oriented facilities, a membership corporation may in the future replace conventionally subdivided recreation communities. By having all of the facilities owned by the club (or a cooperative or condominium-type organization), further control over the environment can be had and subdivision laws concerning minimum lot sizes, set-backs, etc. may be avoided by having an entire development owned by one entity. A more efficient land use can be made leaving substantial areas for greenbelt and recreational activity.

6. Condominium or Co-Operative Corporation

A condominium is a planned development where the participants each hold in fee individual title to a separate portion of the property (usually their own residence) and share common ownership of certain facilities (park areas, laundry, rooms, recreation facilities, etc.). In a multi-story building, those who have offices or apartments on the upper floors hold title to the air space occupied by their unit. Distinguishing feature between a condominium and a cooperative corporation is that in the cooperative corporation, the corporation holds title to the entire property and each share of stock carries certain use rights to a specific area as well as certain general areas, whereas in the condominium, title to the office or residence unit is held directly by the owner in his own name with the common areas being held by the condominium for the benefit of all owners of the units.

7. Limited Partnerships

The limited partnership is a partnership formed pursuant to the Uniform Limited Partnership Act (in California Section 15501 of the Corporations Code). In this form of entity, the limited partners only have such personal liability as they specifically undertake in the partnership agreement and that agreement can provide that their interests are non-assessable. Care must be used in the preparation of the agreement to comply with the statutory provisions. A corporation may serve as general partner, but in certain cases, this can have adverse tax consequences. (See also definition of Limited Partnership Interest in the Glossary.)

8. Limited Liability Company

Similar to a limited partnership. This agreement covering the rights of members is called "the operating agreement" and the owners are called members.

9. Miscellaneous Forms of Entity

As will be seen in the Chapter "State and Federal Regulation of Syndication Activity," the definition of securities in California is extremely broad. Various other types of agreements may be considered to be securities. For purposes of our discussion and study, "syndicate securities" include agreements to share profits or profits participations, various forms of certificates of indebtedness (particularly where such certificates call for profit participations), participations in the income from leases, option agreements, franchise agreements, etc. The key here as to whether or not there is a syndicate entity is a consideration of the relationship between the investor and the active party. Where one party is a passive investor and the other is active, there may be a syndicate arrangement constituting a regulated security, unless such arrangement is exempt from syndicate and securities regulations pursuant to some statute or regulation of the respective Government regulation.

Considerations in Selecting the Entity

The following are considerations in choosing the form of entity:

1. Liability Aspects

(a) Contractual liability undertaken by the syndicate or the syndicator on its behalf, including the purchase contract, operational agreements, leases, etc. These are agreements that arise voluntarily by interaction between the syndicate and various parties doing business with it.

(b) Involuntary liabilities that arise from negligence laws, public health laws, and other acts that impose liability upon the owners of property without their consent. Most forms of involuntary liability can be insured against, but contractual liabilities are not normally the subject of insurance protection.

It is for this latter reason that most investors desire to invest in an entity where their liability will be limited. In some cases, investors may be willing to undertake certain areas of liability such as prorata obligations on encumbrances because of the economic aspects of the project that may tend to make such liability remote. In projects with a great proportion of equity, the investor would be more willing to undertake prorata liability on encumbrances than where the proportion of equity protecting him against a deficiency is small.

2. Legal Certainty

The status of the investors in relation to the syndicator and the entity itself is more certain and established in some forms of entity than others. Limited partner-ships, for example, are well defined in the Uniform Partnership Act. It is not as clear in the cases of some trusts and joint ventures as to what their status is and whether or not they will be treated for all purposes as separate entities from a liability standpoint. The ability to secure opinions from qualified legal counsel as to (a) the relationships of the investors to the entity, (b) liability, and (c) tax treatment therefore, has weight in selecting a form of entity.

3. Operational Considerations

The centralization of control in a limited partnership, limited liability company, and the corporation make them ideal vehicles for a syndicate. The tenancies in common and general partnership are usually more awkward vehicles to work with, due to the fact that absent elaborate agency agreements, etc.; the signatures of all of the participants may be required for many transactions. Third parties are more willing to deal with the entity and not as likely to require the signatures of all parties where a corporation, a limited liability company, or a limited partnership is used, as opposed to some of the other forms of entity.

4. Marketability

Corporations, limited liability companies, and limited partnerships have generally received wide acceptance in the investor market. Other forms of entity such as the tenancy in common, joint venture agreement and general partnership due to their liability aspects, may be less acceptable. The need for the ability directly to participate in 1031 exchanges or sale of the syndicate properties has led to greater activity in the formation and marketing of tenancies in common (TICs).

5. Tax Considerations

Probably the most important factors in selecting a form of entity are tax considerations. In general, the objective is flow-through accounting treatment and avoidance of a double tax. For this reason, the vehicle most often selected is the limited partnership or limited liability company. This is because they offer the advantage of freedom from liability among the various partners, allow for allocation of income and expense among owners where there is a sound business basis, and are accorded flow-through accounting treatment. They can be therefore non-taxable entities as opposed to the corporation, which is generally a taxable entity. The trust is not generally used. In rare circumstances, a trust that can prove that it is not formed for the purpose of carrying on a business and dividing profits (a so-called "passive trust") and is merely a title-holding device with no other function, may qualify for treatment as a non-taxable entity. In general, trusts are taxed as associations unless they are real estate investment trusts, in which case they are afforded special tax treatment as noted in the chapter "Tax Considerations."

CHAPTER 10
TAX CONSIDERATIONS*

Tax considerations affect all aspects of real estate syndication, from choice of entity to acquisition, operation, and eventual disposition of the property. It is necessary to give effect to these considerations when evaluating the actual expected return on an investment and the suitability for the needs of the investor.

The first edition of this book emphasized that there was a significant division between "hard dollar" and "soft dollar" investments in real estate, with the former designed to provide maximum cash flow, and the latter often marketed as tax shelters. Generally, "soft dollar" investments are highly leveraged with little cash outlay from the investors, while "hard dollar" investments are less leveraged.

There is still an economic distinction between the "hard" and "soft" dollar investments, but there have been massive changes in tax law over the last 25 years or so, which have significantly impacted the tax treatment of real estate investments, often with materially different consequences than would have been realized in the past. Perhaps most significant are the passive loss rules, promulgated in the Tax Reform Act of 1986.

Furthermore, the complexity and volume of the Internal Revenue Code (IRC) and related Regulations, Revenue Rulings, Revenue Procedures, and other related documents has mushroomed over the last 25 years. In large part, this is a result of the United States Congress fiddling with the tax code to increase revenues while giving the appearance that taxes are not being raised. The result is as would be predicted; there is confusion and inconsistency. Indeed, much of the Federal tax law is a big mess. Often answers to questions cannot be found because the laws are too new to have had rulings or regulations issued, or to have had any cases come before the tax court.

The various states may or may not conform to the Federal rules. For example, California now partially conforms to the Federal rules. The areas of non-conformity have significant impact on real estate investors. While this chapter gives some general guidelines, in any situation, especially if significant amounts of money are involved, it is crucial that competent tax counsel review the tax implications of any proposed transactions.

---

*The author of this chapter is Patricia Bates, CPA, we gratefully acknowledge her contribution and permission to use same.

Choice of Entity:

In the current tax and legal environment, the entity of choice for many real estate syndications is the Limited Liability Company, which elects to be taxed as a partnership, or a limited partnership. For tax purposes, the type of entity is decided under the Internal Revenue Code (IRC) § 7701 "check-the-box" regulations. If the entity is incorporated in a state, or meets certain other conditions (such as a publicly traded limited partnership), it will be taxed as a corporation. If the entity is organized as a limited partnership or limited liability company, it will generally be classed as a partnership if it has more than one member. It could elect to be taxed as a corporation, but this would generally not be prudent for an entity holding real estate.

Corporations:

It commonly is considered inadvisable to use any type of corporation to hold real estate investments. Since the repeal of the General Utilities doctrine, it is not possible to remove appreciated (or in some cases, any) property from a corporation without incurring tax. This is generally true even in the case of an 'S' corporation, which is a corporation whose shareholders elect to be taxed individually on the income of the corporation. In the case of a 'C' corporation, there is tax at the corporation and shareholder level on distributions, an especially unpleasant result, making 'C' corporations very unsuitable for holding real estate.

There are additional issues with holding real estate in an 'S' corporation which are not desirable. Perhaps foremost among these is the fact that losses are limited to the shareholders' at-risk amounts (tax and direct loans to the entity from the shareholder). There is no flexibility to do special allocations to different classes of owners, and there is a limit on the number of shareholders and the types of entities that are permitted shareholders. The limit is currently 100 shareholders with all members of a family consisting of 6 generations treated as one shareholder. Therefore, while the 'S' corporation is probably the entity of choice for small operating businesses, it is not desirable for real estate investments.

Limited Partnerships and Limited Liability Companies:

Most syndicated real estate investments now are organized as Limited Liability Companies (LLCs). There is little difference in tax treatment of syndicated real estate investment held by LLCs as opposed to Limited Partnerships. However, with limited partnerships there has to be a general partner, who does not have limited liability exposure.

The investors in partnerships generally are called "partners" and investors in LLCs generally are called "members." Because an LLC electing to be taxed as a partnership is treated the same as a partnership, the terms "partner" and "member" are considered interchangeable for the current discussion, as are "partnership" and "LLC."

LLCs are entities which may now be formed in any state, which have the tax attributes of partnerships (if more than one member and unless corporate status is elected) but which are purported to limit the liability of the members. There are many favorable tax aspects to being treated as a partnership. Special allocations are possible within certain constraints, there may be different classes of members, the number of members is unlimited, and there is no limitation on the type of entity that may be a member (but pension plans and other exempt organizations must use caution). Very significantly, for entities holding real estate, the members will receive "basis" for their share of certain debt, described in more detail below, which may allow them to claim losses from the property in excess of their cash investment.

One consideration for California syndications is California has imposed a gross receipts tax on LLCs (called a "fee") which can be as high as $11,790 on gross receipts of $5,000,000 or more. The writer is not aware of any other states that impose an LLC "fee," but it is certainly possible they exist.

Start-Up and Acquisition:

Year end: Generally LLCs and partnerships are required to be on a calendar year. The exception would occur with a majority of ownership by an entity (generally a 'C' corporation), which is on a fiscal year, requiring the partnership to have the same year. This is very unusual. Generally, a syndicated real estate investment will be report on a calendar year basis.

Accounting method: Generally, either the cash or accrual basis of accounting may be used by the entity. In the past, it was common to use cash-basis entities so the timing of income and deductions could be "fiddled" with. With changes in the tax laws, there are significant limitations on the ability to do very much "fiddling" now, and often accrual basis is preferred to give a more accurate picture of operations.

Organization costs: Costs incurred for organization of an LLC may, upon election, be expensed up to $5,000 with the balance amortizable over 15 years. The $5,000 "phases out" dollar-for-dollar if the expense exceeds $50,000. This is a significant change from the prior treatment of organization costs, and was a provision of the American Jobs Creation Act of 2004. Organization costs generally include the legal and related costs incurred in forming the entity.

Syndication costs: Syndication costs, related to marketing the entity to investors, are not deductible or amortizable. They generally are carried on the entity's balance sheet until dissolution and then are "distributed" to the members to be treated as an item of capital loss.

Other payments to the organizer: : Other costs paid to the organizer may include a commission on the property acquisition, which would be added to the property basis. Caution must be used to avoid having compensation to the organizer being construed as syndication cost, and if questionable, a tax opinion should be requested.

Interest granted for services: Historically, partnership profits interests granted in exchange for services to the entity have been not subject to tax at the time of the grant, and have not been taxed as compensation but rather as sale of a property interests when realized at some point in the future, as when the property is sold. However, at the present date there are proposed regulations (NPRM REG-105346-03, I.R.B. 2005-24, 1244) which would require that such profits interests be valued at the date of grant, and an IRC § 83(b) election be made by all partners and the partnership to recognize ordinary income at grant date. If the § 83(b) election was not made, any subsequent income would be compensation (ordinary) income to the profit participant. This will be effective on the date the proposed regulations become final. Even under current law, some practitioners make § 83(b) elections (at zero value) to ensure that receipt of a profit participation will not be subsequently taxable to the recipient as ordinary (as opposed to capital gain) income.

Acquisition of the real property: Generally, all costs related to the acquisition of the property are added to the basis of the property. These include, but are not limited to, the cost of the property per se, attorney fees, title insurance, survey cost, escrow fees, past due property taxes on the property, broker commission, and appraisals. These costs should be distinguished from costs incurred to obtain financing for the purchase (loan fees, attorney fee related to the financing, etc), as these are treated differently for tax purposes.

Tenancy in Common: It has become increasingly common to see investors acquiring fractional interests (tenancy in common) in real estate. In many cases, these interests have been marketed as replacement properties for entities which are executing a § 1031 exchange and are desperate for a replacement property because of the timing rules for § 1031 exchanges. The IRS has issued safe harbor guidelines (Rev. Proc. 2002-22) describing the conditions which should be met to avoid having a tenancy in common categorized as a partnership. Rev. Proc. 2002-22 and any subsequent updates should be consulted and the rules adhered to for any investment of a tenancy in common real estate interest.

Operation of the Property:

Depreciation:

Depreciation is required by the Internal Revenue Code on business real estate improvements and personal property, and is treated as a current ordinary operating expense, reducing the tax basis of the depreciated property. Current federal tax law provides statutory rates and lives over which various categories of property must be depreciated. It is provided for under IRC §168 and related regulations and rulings, and is termed "Modified Accelerated Cost Recovery System" or MACRS. The array of rules under this IRC section are rather complex, so it is best to consult a tax professional to prepare depreciation schedules. If depreciation is allowable, it is deemed to have been taken, thus reducing the tax basis of the property, so it is not an optional deduction.

The common categories, lives, and rates applicable to real estate investments are as follows at the present date. Please keep in mind that congress can change these in a heartbeat. It is always best to check with knowledgeable tax counsel before proceeding. In some cases, there may be different rules for state and federal depreciation.

Residential rental real estate	27.5-year straight line
Commercial real estate	39-year straight line
Land improvements	15-year see IRS tables for rates
– Sidewalks, parking lots, etc.	
Furnishings	5 year, see IRS tables for rates
Other equipment, etc.	7 year, see IRS tables for rates
Land	not depreciable
Intangible assets	15-year straight line

If the property purchased includes land and building, generally the buyer will want to allocate the maximum possible amount of the purchase price to the building, which is depreciable property. In some real estate purchases, there is also some personal property that should be separately stated. Be aware that if the purchase is considered that of an operating business (for example – a hotel) buyer and seller may be required to execute an IRS Form 8594, Asset Acquisition Statement, agreeing on the allocation of price to the different classes of property.

Generally, with rental real estate purchases, the agreed allocation is not required. The buyer must use the best available evidence to allocate purchase price among building, land, and other categories. This may involve use of appraisers or other experts, assessed valuations placed on the land and improvements by the local tax assessor, or other reasonable valuation methods.

At the time of purchase, or later, a Cost Segregation study may be done to determine the relative values of the different classes of property inherent in the investment. Generally, such a study will support an allocation that results in a larger amount of current depreciation. Because of relatively recent federal tax law changes, there may be a significant tax benefit from a retroactive reclassification of property, pursuant to a Cost Segregation study. Watch out for any future IRS rulings regarding recapture of the ordinary depreciation on the sale of the property.

Inherited /purchased partnership interests:

A special tax election under IRC §754 and §743 is available to partnerships to adjust the basis of partnership property to market value, when interests are transferred either by sale or by death of a partner. In the (hopefully) usual case where real estate is appreciating, this will result in more depreciation deduction for the receiving member.

Loan costs and fees:

Loan costs and fees incurred to finance investment properties are generally deductible as operating expenses over the life of the loan. They may be deducted if the loan is paid off early, as by refinancing. Prepayment penalties are generally deductible as interest when incurred. Defeasance costs may be another matter and a tax professional should be consulted if defeasances costs are to be incurred. Now, the IRS seems to have a "don't-ask-don't-tell" policy on the treatment of defeasance costs.

Operating expenses, interest, and taxes:

Generally, all expenses related to the operation of the property, property taxes, and interest on debt incurred to acquire the property, are deductible within the constraints of the chosen accounting method. Even if on the cash basis, there are limitations on deductibility of prepaid expenses.

Property taxes are generally deductible in the year paid by a cash-basis taxpayer (as long as they have actually been incurred). Accrual-basis taxpayers generally must deduct property taxes when paid, unless they elect to either deduct them as of the lien date (assuming they are paid within 8-1/2 months of the prior year end), or to deduct them ratably over the definite period they apply to.

Interest on debt incurred to acquire property is generally deductible as accrued and paid. Prepayment of interest is deductible over the term of the loan. There are numerous limitations and complications on the deductibility of interest, generally arising in the case of refinancing of the property to "pull equity" from appreciated real estate for distribution to the partners. In such a situation, tax advice should be obtained to determine the amount of interest that would be allocable to the debt-financed distribution. Such interest would not be deductible as an operating expense, but would rather be separately stated for each partner, and the deductibility would depend on what they did with the distributed money.

There are restrictions on accrual of otherwise deductible payments to related parties.

Leasing Commissions:

Leasing commissions are deductible over the life of the related lease.

Passive Loss Rules:

The passive loss rules of § 469, enacted in the 1986 Tax Act, have had a major impact on real estate investments. These rules virtually put an end to marketing real estate investments as 'tax shelters', generating losses (primarily from depreciation and a high degree of leverage) which could offset an investor's ordinary income from sources such as interest, dividends, wages, etc.

Losses from passive activities (this generally includes improved rental real estate and businesses the investor does not participate in) may only be applied against income from other passive activities. Any excess losses in a tax year carry forward to the next year. There are seemingly endless definitions of what constitutes passive investments, and the meaning of the words "participation," "significant," "material," perhaps even "is." A reasonable person reading the passive loss rules (and many of the other rules) would conclude that Lewis Caroll is alive, well, and writing U.S. tax law.

The bottom line is most syndicated real estate investment projects and their investors are subject to the passive loss rules. Unless investors have passive income, they will not get current benefit of losses. This is not to say they may have more cash flow than taxable income due to depreciation (a non-cash expense), but they cannot use passive losses to offset their non-passive income.

There are some exceptions, of course. Federal law treats passive losses of a "Qualified Real Estate Professional" as ordinary for activities in which the individual and/or spouse participates actively (again, there is detailed definition of the terms, consult a tax professional). In an example of state non-conformity, California does not recognize the different treatment of real estate professionals, often resulting in substantial differences between state and federal results. There are some other carve-outs for small amounts of loss by relatively low-income taxpayers.

Basis:

An investor may only recognize losses in a partnership equal to at-risk basis in the investment. While generally this would be the investor's cash investment plus share of recourse debt, there is an exception for non-recourse debt incurred to carry rental real estate. Such debt is termed 'Qualified non-recourse debt and investors can use their share of such debt as part of their basis. It is important to consult a competent authority to ensure that debt meets the requirements.

Special allocations:

§ 704 of the IRC generally regulates what can and cannot be done with respect to "special allocations" among the partners, and provides rules for equalizing basis when appreciated depreciable property is contributed by certain partners. These rules are generally very complicated and well beyond the scope of this chapter. A general principle is that there must be an economic effect to any special allocations. As example, they cannot be used to give all the capital gain to one partner, and all the ordinary income to another partner who might have a big net operating loss carry forward. They cannot be used to simply play with the timing of allocations. They can be used, for example, to give a preferred return to one class of partners, and differing allocations of gain to different classes of partners.

Disposition of Real Estate:

Generally, real estate is disposed of by a partnership by sale or exchange. Involuntary conversions can also occur and there are special rules for involuntary conversions in IRC §1033 and related regulations and rulings. Of course, the partner or member incurs the tax consequences of these events. The partnership (LLC) is merely a conduit.

Sale:

Gain or loss on sale of improved rental real estate is generally taxed as a §1231 gain – gain is treated as capital, with some exceptions, and loss as ordinary loss. The capital gain for federal purposes is figured, as of 2006, at a 25% rate with respect to all gain attributable to prior depreciation on real property, and 15% on the excess. Gain on any personal property is ordinary with respect to the portion attributable to prior depreciation and 15% on any excess. § 1231 losses taken by an investor in the prior five years will be "recaptured," converting a like amount of the current § 1231 gain to ordinary income. State taxes also need to be taken into consideration.

Commissions, title fees, escrow costs and other costs incident to the sale, including but not limited to professional fees, are expenses of sale and reduce the gain on sale. Unamortized leasing commissions generally are treated as capital assets when sold. They are added to selling expenses. Conversely, unamortized loan fees and prepayment penalties generally are treated as ordinary operating expenses in the year of sale. The exception might be if a portion of the debt had been allocated to debt-financed distribution; then the related expenses would be separately stated and the partner would have to decide as to their deductibility.

Investors and syndicators alike should be aware that if they have refinanced the property and distributed the excess proceeds out to the investors, and the property has been held and depreciated for several years, the taxable gain on the sale might be far in excess of the cash proceeds. It seems that the investors never remember they already got the money!

It is possible, using an installment sale, to spread the gain out over several years. Generally, if property is sold using an installment note, the partnership will continue to exist until the note is paid off. The profit recognized each year would be equal to the principal payment received times the gross profit percent (gross profit divided by contract price). There should also be interest on the note, which would pass through to the partners.

Exchange:

IRC § 1031 governs exchanges of like-kind property held for business use or investment. If the appropriate conditions are met, the investor can sell its property and acquire replacement property, without recognizing any gain as of 2006. There is a substantial body of rulings and cases describing the requirements for exchanges, including delayed (Starker) exchanges and reverse ("parking") exchanges. Any taxpayer contemplating doing a § 1031 exchange should obtain advice to ensure they are complying with the rules, many of which are extremely specific and enforceable.

In the usual delayed exchange, the partnership will use a third-party exchange accommodator to sell its property and hold the proceeds. The partnership must designate up to three replacement properties within 45 days of transfer, and must acquire the replacement property by the earlier of 180 days after transfer or the date the tax return for the year of transfer is filed. There are also detailed "safe-harbor" rules (Revenue Procedure 2000-37) for "parking" exchanges, where the replacement property is acquired and held by a third party until the partnership can sell the property it wishes to exchange for the "parked" property.

Generally, any excess cash or other "boot" (unlike property) which a taxpayer receives from an exchange will be gain to the taxpayer. Liabilities assumed or incurred in the exchange offset liabilities the exchanger is relieved of. However, excess liabilities received will not offset cash or other "boot" taken from the exchange. Generally to avoid gain, it is necessary to give cash and other boot at least equal to the amount of cash or boot received, and that debt received plus any excess boot or cash given at least equal to amount of debt relieved.

A much more complicated situation occurs when some of the partners want to exchange the property and others just want to sell and recognize any gain as of 2006. There is a specific prohibition in the tax code, IRC §1031(a) (2) (D), stating that nonrecognition treatment will not apply to exchanges of partnership interests, so the appearance of exchange of a partnership interest must be avoided.

In some situations, the partnership has dissolved and distributed tenancy in common interests to each of the partners prior to sale. This gives the former partners the option to either sell or exchange. If cash is available, it is also possible to redeem out the partner who wants to "cash out" prior to the sale. These situations are very tricky and a tax professional should be consulted for an opinion on whether a con-templated transaction conflicts with either the § 1031 rules or the partnership rules.

Computation of Effective Tax Rate

Estimation of an investor's marginal income tax rate for purposes of comput-ing the after-tax rate of return of an investment was at one time an easy task. Now, because of the various capital gains rates and the operation of the Alternative Minimum Tax (AMT), it is not so simple. If investors do not have significant amounts of capital gains and their "regular" tax is more than their AMT, they will have a current maximum federal rate of 35%. The state rate should be factored in and any federal benefit of the state tax deduction should be added back to the over-all percentage.

If the investor is subject to AMT and has no capital gain income, his maximum federal rate is now 28%, and the state rate should be added to this. There would be no benefit of the state tax deduction for taxpayers with AMT liability in excess of regular tax liability. There are also relatively small changes in the effective percentages because of the various "phase-ins" and "phase-outs" depending on the amount of Adjusted Gross Income.

Just as an example, accountants doing a projection for a high-income California taxpayer often use an effective tax rate of 41% for a taxpayer not subject to AMT, and about 37% for one with AMT in excess of regular tax. If the taxpayer has significant amounts of long-term capital gain income, the computation can become seriously complicated, and it is best at least to verify it using tax projection software.

In conclusion, the current U.S. federal and State tax environment is a minefield for the real estate syndicator and investor alike. It is not unusual for questions to arise for which no certain answer can be found. Solutions include (1) commissioning an opinion from reputable tax counsel, (2) requesting a private letter ruling from the IRS if the question involves an area they will rule on, or (3) restructuring the nature and format of the transaction to comply with existing IRS guidelines, safe harbor rules, or established case law. Caution and continued vigilance of the tax laws need to be practiced by all associated with the syndicate.

CHAPTER 11
FORMATION OF THE ENTITY

Timing

One of the details to which careful attention must be given is the timing of the formation of the entity. This can become acute at the proposed closing date for the purchase of the subject property, if the entity has not been properly formed. The title company may refuse to insure, and adverse tax consequences can result. While this discussion relates to the state of law in California, it is probably equally applicable in most jurisdictions in which the project is located.

Existence of Entity

It is probably erroneous to say that an entity can exist before its Certificate of Formation is recorded in the county where its principal place of business is located or its formation documents executed if not required to be recorded. While there may be situations in which the circumstances are such that a court would treat a purported entity as if it had come into existence before its certificate was recorded or formation documents executed, one cannot be sure that an entity has any existence at all until the required recording has been made.

Formation of a California limited partnership, for example, is authorized by and governed exclusively by Corp. C. 15502 (in the "Uniform Limited Partnership Act"). That section says, and cases have uniformly reiterated, that "a limited partnership is formed if there has been substantial compliance in good faith with the requirements" of the first paragraph of the section, which specifies the contents of the certificate, requires signing and acknowledgment by the persons forming it, and requires that they "record said certificate in the office of the recorder of the county in which the principal place of business of the partnership is situated."

It appears from certain cases that if a partnership exists at all before the certificate is recorded, it may be a general partnership, not a limited partnership. (See Tiburon National Bank v. Wagner (1968 71 Cal Rptr. 832, 265 CA2d 868; Solomon v. Polk Development (1966) 54 Cal Rptr. 22, 245 CA2d 488).

There is some authority for the proposition that some delay between execution of the certificate and its recording will not necessarily prevent substantial compliance; this being dependent upon the circumstances. (See Stowe v. Merriless (1935) 6 CA2d 217). However, there appears still to be a lack of authority indicating that the time of creation of the limited partnership can be any earlier than the recording of the certificate in the county where the principal place of business is located.

Consequently, until such recording there may be no limited partnership at all, just as there is no corporation until its articles are filed with the Secretary of State.

Similar consequences may arise if there are recording requirements for the entity such as a limited liability company.

Delivery of Deed

Before such recording of the Certificate, purported delivery of a deed to the supposed limited partnership is probably ineffective. No operative deed, for want of a grantee and for want of anyone to whom to deliver it, and the purported recording being a nullity. After formation by recording the certificate, the same deed would probably operate if (re-)delivered and again recorded. However, there may be no automatic "breathing of the breath of life" into the recorded but undelivered deed that was recorded before its grantee existed. With respect to any conveyance to a limited partnership, there should be no attempt to record until the Certificate of Limited Partnership is already recorded – preferably a day, at least, sooner, but passable if certificate recorded earlier the same day.

Conveyances Out

Assuming there is no problem of having effectively put title in the new limited partnership, how about conveyances out? A conveyance out of a limited partnership might be valid if the purported signing by the expectant general partners occurred before the limited partnership grantor came into existence by recording of its certificate. The general partners perhaps would be able, after the partnership is formed, to deliver a conveyance at that time by impliedly adopting their former signatures by their act of delivery. It is safer, however, if the deed is not even signed before the partnership certificate is recorded. Moreover, such a conveyance, to be insurable without question, should not be dated any earlier than the certificate recording, because of the presumption that a deed or other conveyance was delivered at its date.

Acknowledgements

Nevertheless, what about acknowledgments? It is the view of some authorities that a partner cannot effectively acknowledge execution of a conveyance in which a purported limited partnership is the grantor, until that partnership has come into existence. If a notary takes his acknowledgment before the certificate is recorded, the purported act of acknowledgment and the notary's certificate thereof are probably void, and would not be made valid by subsequent recordation of the certificate forming the partnership. The result probably would be a failure of the "recorded" conveyance to impart constructive notice until it had been of record for one year.

Use of Sole Limited Partner

In certain circumstances, not all the limited partners are known at the time the certificate is recorded. Some practitioners will record with only one limited partner who takes a nominal interest in the partnership, with the agreement to be amended later, adding the names of the additional partners. An alternative procedure often used is for a sole limited partner to take title as trustee, so that the designation of the limited partner is "John Jones as Trustee" for the limited partners, and an amendment is filed at a later date, substituting the names and other relevant information concerning the partners for whom the Trustee was acting. The method used should only be determined after careful consideration of its effect on the tax positions of the respective parties and the applicability of local limited partnership law.

Affect on Conveyances

The result of the foregoing is that any conveyance (deed, deed of trust, lease, etc.) out of a limited partnership, or any documents affecting title which it is to execute, should not be dated, be executed or be acknowledged before the Certificate of Limited Partnership is recorded in the county where its principal place of business is located. Recording of the certificate "concurrently" will always produce questionable results from a title insurer's standpoint, and should not be contemplated as normal routine. Rather, recordation of the certificate in advance is the only practice that will avoid the difficulties above discussed. Whatever inconvenience there might be in getting the certificate ready for recording before other documents are executed, or at any rate before they are acknowledged or recorded, is regrettable, but unfortunately necessary to make title insurance insurable without serious risk.

The foregoing discussion would relate to Limited Liability Companies and other entities as well.

Conclusion

Where a tenancy in common is the entity to be used the operating agreement among the tenants and their identity needs to be determined, so that the required information can be supplied the title company, and the management agreement executed and operative at the time of transfer of the property to the tenancy in common.

CHAPTER 12

DOCUMENTATION
OF THE SYNDICATE*

Types of Documents

The documentation of a real estate syndicate falls into the following six categories:

Acquisition documents
Marketing documents
Qualification documents
Entity documents
Management documents
Dissolution documents

The syndicator, in preparing such documents, must make the initial decision as to which of the documents he is going to take full responsibility for, and which of the documents he desires to associate legal counsel in connection with their preparation.

A highly experienced syndicator may retain counsel for the sole purpose of preparing reviewing entity and at the appropriate time, dissolution documents, preferring to maintain full control over acquisition, marketing, qualification, management and dissolution documents. An inexperienced syndicator will probably need legal assistance throughout the entire documentation process.

If the syndicator is able to prepare preliminary documentation for a private offering so that counsel can concentrate on legal and tax aspects of the transaction, legal expenses generally will be within the $5,000-$20,000 range. In a private placement project of this type, legal expenses can run anywhere from approximately $5,000 to $10,000, depending on the amount of time required of counsel to prepare documents, review the application, and his extent of involvement in negotiations. This allowance assumes that the attorney will not be responsible for any investor contacts or explanation and that while he will review the acquisition, marketing, and qualification documents, the only documents that he will be responsible for preparing will be the entity documents after receipt of a comprehensive preliminary draft from the syndicator. It is assumed that the attorney will process the application with the appropriate State Commissioner in a public offering that will entail additional legal costs. A checklist of documents required for the typical syndicate follows.

*This chapter is an update of an Article appeared originally in "How to Syndicate an Apartment House" published by the California Real Estate Association in 1971. The Author gratefully acknowledges permission to reprint herein.

1. Acquisition Documents

1. Letter of Intent
2. Contract of Purchase (often termed the Deposit Receipt, or, in some cases, an "underwriting agreement")
3. Escrow instructions
4. Loan Documents
5. Due Diligence Documents (including environmental, survey, and inspection vendor contracts)

2. Marketing Documents

1. Advertisements
2. Brochures
3. Letters to Prospects
4. Subscription Letters
5. Charts, Slides, and Maps

3. Qualification Documents

1. Application
2. Amendments to and Exhibits of Application
3. Appraisal
4. Tax Opinion

4. Entity Documents

1. Instruction Letter
2. Offering Circular or Prospectus
3. Summary of Investment
4. Certificate of Fictitious Firm Name
5. Entity Documents
6. Subscription Agreement

5. Management Documents

1. Management Contract
2. Rental Agreement
3. Service Contracts
4. Manager's Contract (where there is one with the resident manager)
5. Agreements with Suppliers
6. Leases

6. Dissolution Documents

1. Resale Documentation (such as Offer to Sell, Listing Agreement, Escrow Instructions, etc.)
2. Abandonment of Fictitious Firm Name
3. Dissolution of Entity Agreement

Combined Factors

The preparation of syndicate documents involves the careful balancing of legal, tax, and marketing considerations. Depending on the nature of the project, the relationship of the syndicator with his investors, and the appropriate regulatory rules and statutes, emphasis in documentation will vary from one syndicate to another. While the basic material required is generally available to the syndicator to put together the documentation involved in a typical project, the balancing of these factors can be said to be "an art rather than a science." A considerable savings of time and money will be had if the syndicator will study carefully the offering circulars, partnership agreements, brochures, etc., which have been prepared by his predecessors in the industry. A few hours of reading this material will be highly productive of excellent ideas that can be incorporated into the proposed syndicate, and make more complete the presentation. The more information the syndicator can present to the professionals who are assisting him in putting together documentation, the quicker it can be finalized and the more likely it is accurately to reflect the objectives of the organizer.

Offering

The offering document for intrastate offerings is generally known as the "offering circular." The "prospectus" is appropriate terminology for national interstate offerings. For private placements, the term "offering memorandum" is used.

The first material that usually comes to the attention of the investor is the offering document. Among matters that must (or if not, should) be required in the offering document are:

1. An adequate description of the property;

2. A summary of operating history, if available, and if not available a pro forma projection of estimated future operating performance (in some cases the regulatory authority may object to the pro forma where it appears to be overly optimistic

or where, in the opinion of the reviewing deputy, there is not adequate evidence presented in the application to support the pro forma);

3. An outline of the proposed offering, including the method of distribution;

4. A discussion of any risk factors that may be present, including reference to environmental and toxic hazard reports;

5. A discussion of the acquisition and financing of the subject property;

6. A discussion of the capitalization of the partnership and the use of proceeds;

7. A discussion of the operation and the management of the partnership, including background of the principals;

8. A discussion of tax factors involved in the investment, where appropriate;

9. A summary of the provision of the limited partnership and an explanation of the legal consequences of the relationship between the investors and the manager of the entity;

10. The expert's qualifications, outlining the names and professional designations of those attorneys, accountants and other experts who may have been retained to assist the organizer in preparing the offering;

11. A disclosure statement concerning any profits directly or indirectly being made or to be made in the future by the organizers and entity manager which are not clearly delineated in any of the foregoing paragraphs;

12. A reference to permit with the appropriate commissioner, where qualification is required, and that additional information is available at the commissioner's office in connection with the application;

13. Exhibits to the offering circular, including the entity agreement in full, the subscription agreement, and in some cases a copy of an appraisal of the property, where appropriate.

The style of offering circulars varies all the way from a simple typewritten one in a small private offering to an elaborate printed booklet of as many as 40 to 60 pages on good quality paper with numerous illustrations and charts. Here we are assuming that a relatively simple offering circular will be prepared by offset process on 81/2 x 11 ordinary grade paper with a total number of pages being approximately 30, not including the partnership agreement, subscription agreement, etc.

A budget of $2,500 for production of documentation of this type should be generally adequate. If a more elaborate offering circular and material should be desired, including illustrations, slick paper, special covers, etc., a budget of $10,000 to $25,000 would be more appropriate. The style and format will depend a great deal on the marketing method used. Where the organizer is relying on previously established contacts, it would not seem necessary and appropriate to incur substantial production expenses in connection with documentation. The law requires that the Offering Circular be given to each investor prior to each investment.

Limited Liability Operating Agreement

The most common entity in syndication use today is the Limited Liability Company, for the reason discussed in the chapter "Tax Considerations." The key governing document is the operating agreement that defines the rights of the various classes of members, set out the provisions for determining distributions, sets and describes the managing member's duties, obligations, and compensation. A sample is provided in the Appendices. Do not use the form without review and approval of an attorney familiar with the laws of the state in which the entity is to be formed and the circumstances of your offering.

Appraisal

An appraisal is required for a number of purposes and in some cases, several appraisals may be made. In a project the size and nature contemplated here, there will be normally, however, only one appraisal. The appraiser himself should be qualified by having a familiarity with the geographic areas and types of investment. For most purposes, an appraisal will be sufficient if made by an experienced appraiser who has no direct or indirect financial interest in the outcome of the proposed offering either by way of receiving a commission on sale of the property, commission on sale of the interests, brokerage fee, or indirectly by the fact that he may be an office associate of one of the organizers of the syndicate. If an experienced appraiser who is a member of a recognized appraisal society, such as the American Institute of Real Estate Appraisers (MAI) is available, such an individual's appraisal will, of course, carry more authority. Where qualification is required, an appraisal is necessary as part of the application. The appraisal should also support the value of the property for fire insurance purposes, and for allocation of land and building for depreciation. Even where the project is exempt from qualification and no application is going to be made, an independent appraisal will serve to assist in insulating the organizer against a charge of negligence or poor judgment if, for some unforeseen reason, the project should turn out to be unsuccessful and the appraisal contains good supportive evidence that, at the time the project was organized, fair market value was paid for the property.

Articles of Limited Partnership

The basic contract between the investors and the general partner or organizers has in the past been most often articles of the limited partnership. The reason for the use of a limited partnership was the syndicator's attempt to provide his investor with the benefits of "flow-through accounting" so that no tax will be imposed on the entity itself and profit (or tax loss) will go directly to the investor to be included in the investor's own personal tax return, projection from liability, and control by the organizer.

In use in the early 1970's it was similar to the forms most syndications today use. Other entity forms such as limited liability companies and tenancies in common, are now more popular. The limited partnership agreement that might be used today will have more elaborate and sometimes different provisions, including different classes of limited partners, more restrictions on transfer, and rights of first refusal. Do not use any form without review and approval by an attorney familiar with syndication in your state.

You will note that the operating agreement in the Appendices contains a Power of Attorney authorizing the managing member to execute further documents, so that it is not necessary to continue to solicit the individual members for technical changes in the documentation. Provisions of the California Corporation Code allow amendments to the operating agreement where the agreement so provides, to be executed only by general partner, even in the absence of a specific Power of Attorney. The signature page should be organized in such a manner that it can be executed in counterparts, so that all limited partners do not have to sign the same specific document.

Risk Factors

Liability continually is being extended by the courts to all those involved in syndication. A careful review and conduct of due diligence to disclose errors and omissions, as well as representations that are required during the formation have become more and more important. The risk factors of real estate syndication investment are brought fully to the attention of the prospective investor, either in the offering circular or in the partnership agreement. Because of the capability for emphasis in the offering circular through change of type styles, etc., the most appropriate place is often in the offering circular.

Some authorities suggest that risk factors should be contained in the subscription agreement rather than, or in addition to, in the offering circular and/or partnership agreement. Including them in two documents or in all three documents may tend to confuse the prospective purchaser or to discourage (by adding to the length of the documentation) careful reading. The better practice would be to put them in one document, but in a manner in which they stand out dramatically. Among the matters that should be considered for emphasis and appropriate disclaimer are:

1) The tax effect of the investment and whether or not the investment will receive the proposed tax treatment by the Internal Revenue Service;

2) The validity and probability of attaining income and expense projections;

3) Unusual circumstances with respect to title and/or the marketability of the property;

4) The property may not have access to a dedicated public roadway;

Certain utilities such as gas, telephone, electricity and water may not be readily available or, if available, only at more than ordinary cost and expense;

5) Other parties may have interest in surface or sub-surface rights due to retention of mineral rights, etc.;

6) Unusual easements have been allowed which might affect the subject properties' marketability;

7) Known claims exist (even though considered to be invalid) by third parties to interests in the property, which claims, if valid, would affect the marketability or value of the investment;

8) Environmental and toxic hazards;

9) Unusual insurance risks; and

10) Competitive conditions.

Partnership or Operating Agreement Check List

The following is a checklist of some fifty items that may be included in a partnership or operating agreement. It is not intended to be all-inclusive. The review of agreements of other syndicators would suggest further provisions.

1. Introductory clause

2. Partnership name

3. Principal place of business

4. Certificate of limited partnership

5. Certificate of fictitious firm name

6. Purpose

7. Term

8. Representations of the limited partners

9. Representations of the general partner

10. Acquisition of the subject property

11. Sale of the subject property

12. Exchange of the subject property

13. Apportionment of profits and losses for accounting purposes

14. Distribution of net spendable cash from operations

15. Distribution of net proceeds from refinancing

16. Distribution of net proceeds from sale or liquidation of all or a portion of the subject property

17. Special options of general partner

18. Original capital contributions of limited partners

19. Additional capital contributions of limited partners

20. Adjustment of the capital accounts and shares in profits and losses of limited partners upon failure to meet obligations

21. Provision for withdrawal of capital

22. Requirement of annual accounting and audit

23. General partner's duties and powers

24. Restrictions of general partner's powers

25. Special compensation to general partner for services

26. Special rights of limited partners

27. Restriction on limited partners' liability

28. Special power of attorney of the general partner to execute amendments

29. Partners' rights to deal in other properties and to compete with the partnership

30. Partners' rights to lend money to the partnership and collect interest

31. General partner's authority to deal with affiliates

32. Employment of attorneys and accountants

33. Death or legal incapacity of a limited partner

34. Death or legal incapacity of general partner

35. Act of bankruptcy of limited partners

36. Act of bankruptcy of general partner

37. Assignment of limited partner's interest

38. Assignment of general partner's interest

39. Rights of first refusal

40. Substituted and additional partners

41. Transfer charge

42. Arbitration of disputes

43. Notices

44. Termination of the partnership

45. Execution of articles in counterparts

46. Binding on heirs and assigns of the partners

47. Amendments to the articles

48. Execution of additional required documents

49. Articles of the full agreement of the parties, and

50. Paragraph headings, index, singular, and plural designations.

Securities and Exchange Commission Registration

All syndications must not only be qualified with the respective state authority (if not exempt from such qualification), but also registered with the Securities and Exchange Commission (SEC), unless exempt from such registration. The principal SEC exemption usually relied upon is the intrastate exemption requiring that all contact with the syndication be within one state. This requires that

> The property
> The general partner,
> The investors solicited, and
> The syndicator

all be residents of the same state. In order to provide adequate information to the syndicator to determine whether a prospective investor is a resident of a particular state, some attorneys advise the execution of a rather elaborate statement of residency by prospective investors.

As has been noted, this chapter assumes qualification with a state authority and that the cost estimates and documentation are illustrative of what can normally be expected under such circumstances. Documentation that is much more elaborate is usually required for registration with the SEC. The registration documents generally are printed, whereas documents for state qualification are often merely typed and duplicated by an inexpensive duplication process. Legal fees and printing fees for SEC registration generally run several times greater than those for state qualification do. In addition, the period for preparation of documents is often much longer than if only state qualification is involved. See Chapter 16 "State and Federal Regulation of Syndication Activities.

CHAPTER 13

DRAFTING SYNDICATOR'S PROVISIONS
OF ENTITY DOCUMENTS

Contractual Considerations

Operating Agreements or other governing documents.

Operating Agreements, Articles of Limited Partnership or other governing documents constitute a contract between three parties: (a) The syndicator/sponsor, (b) The investor(s), (c) The entity itself. For purposes of this discussion, we will assume a limited partnership is the foregoing document. The term manager and general partner are used interchangeably.

In certain cases, the articles also constitute a third-party beneficiary contract, wherein rights are created in favor of persons who are not parties to the contract, specifically or by implication. Among the third parties who may have acquired rights through the execution of the partnership agreement between the general partner(s) and the limited partners are: (a) The seller of the subject property, (b) persons who are named in the agreement and who are supplying services to the entity, such as accountants, attorneys, real estate brokers, etc., (c) certain tenants, where the possibility of leasing to them is mentioned in the agreement, etc.

For these reasons, a clause should be inserted in the partnership agreement that no third party is given any rights in the subject matter thereto, and there is no intention to create any third-party beneficiary of the agreement.

In the absence of express agreement between the parties, the Uniform Limited Partnership Act, or other statutes relating to the form of entity used in many jurisdictions (and similar acts in those states where the acts have not been adopted) sets forth the rights, privileges, and duties as between the various parties to the syndication contract. The acts do not cover all the problem areas that can become the subject of dispute not specifically covered by a written understanding. In the absence of statutory provisions, the parties are generally free to contract with each other except for agreements, which maybe against public policy. For example, an agreement to commit a violation of law would not be enforceable.

Protective Provisions

With the promulgation of the "safe harbor rule" (See chapter on "Tax Considerations") by the IRS setting forth substantial net worth requirements for a corporate general partner as a condition to the service's issuing a ruling acknowledging flow-through accounting treatment, use of a substantial individual or a well capitalized entity as sole or as co-general partner may be used. As the general partner does not have available to it the protection against personal liability which is available to the limited partners, individual general partners should require protective provisions in the partnership agreement, reducing exposure and risk of loss. Such contractual limitations of the general partner's liability need not result in a loss of flow-through accounting treatment, if there is a properly drawn agreement, nor do they diminish the limited partner's protection from personal liability under state law.

Balancing of Interests

The drafting of the articles of limited partnership involve careful balancing of the interests of the general partner in reducing its exposure while protecting the interest of the partnership and limited partners in securing its good faith services to accomplish their objectives in the respective project.

This chapter approaches the subject from the viewpoint of representation of a general partner. The comments will also be applicable to the interests of the managing partner, active co-partners of a general partnership, members of a limited liability company and sponsors of the entity. In most instances, the suggested provisions will benefit a corporate general sponsor as well as individual sponsors.

Narrow vs. Broad Definition of Rights, Privileges, and Duties

The first issue to be faced in drafting entity documents is whether to provide for a limited definition of the sponsor's rights, duties, and privileges or to provide for an extensive and very broad definition of these rights, duties, and privileges. Marketing considerations have generally compelled the use of the limited definition form because of:

(1) Natural suspicion on the part of the offerees and their legal and accounting advisors of potential conflicts of interest;

(2) Past abuses of the syndicators; and

(3) The desire of the investor to exercise maximum control over the project, to the extent it can be done, without destroying the protection against personal liability.

The success of a project is generally dependent upon the skill, experience, knowledge, and imagination of the general partner. There are many different entity forms in use as of 2006 for ventures and real estate projects. Timing and the ability to adjust to changing economic circumstances is generally essential to the success in these activities. In order to secure the most capable syndicator/manager, investors are often better served by providing for a very broad definition of his rights, duties, and privileges and the allowance of the greatest possible flexibility in the exercise of his duties and responsibilities. An experienced general partner will not want to run the risk of exceeding his authority and title insurers may require votes and approvals that could cause the partnership to lose a favorable investment opportunity if the manager is not given the broadest possible authority.

Where unusual provisions are included within the partnership agreement, it is wise to put the investors on notice that the partnership agreement contains a definition of the rights, duties, and privileges of the general partner that is more extensive than the summary of the partnership agreement set forth in the circular. It is suggested under these circumstances that the following be included in the circular:

"The articles of partnership (or appropriate entity agreements) contain provisions (a) relating to the rights, duties, and privileges of the general partner and (b) providing for indemnity of the syndicator, which provisions may be considered to be broader and more liberal than those normally found in such documents. You may desire to consult your own attorney regarding their effect on your investment in the partnership and your liability in connection with this investment."

Self-Dealing

It is quite common to include a provision authorizing self-dealing between the syndicator partnership and the entity under certain circumstances where the fees to be paid are competitive or equivalent to those which would normally be available in an arms-length bargaining situation. The standard of what are "competitive charges" or "arms-length bargaining" being subjective, such transactions could result in future litigation. Wherever possible, the charge should be specified to the fullest extent possible for the services to be rendered, in order to avoid this problem.

Right to Compete

It is wise to include a provision to allow all parties, both syndicator and investors, to compete with the entity. To exclude such a clause will not only discourage responsible individuals from serving as managers, but also discourage investors who may have other property in the area from investing. To foreclose the opportunity to purchase other property or engage in similar activities outside of the partnership itself is not generally advisable.

Accounting

An entity manager normally should have the discretion and authority, within the guidelines of the general policy of the partnership, to:

(a) Set up reasonable reserves for working capital purposes;

(b) Determine the frequency and nature of distributions. The agreement should clearly specify that the frequency and nature of distributions set forth is a general guideline and expression of intent, but that depending on circumstances, the manager, in the use of his discretion, may alter such a program where he feels circumstances require;

(c) Determine the proportion of the distribution that is to be returned as capital subject to the definitions set forth in the articles;

(d) Make an allocation between capital improvements and maintenance expense, where appropriate; and

(e) Retain, discharge, and arrange for legal, accounting services and other services.

Compensation

In order to avoid confusion, the compensation to the manager should be clearly defined by division into four areas:

1. Return on investment for actual cash invested in the project. For this purpose, the manager may also be considered a limited partner and his investment treated on a pari passu basis with all other limited partners.

2. Fees for services rendered to the entity, such as management fee, leasing fees, commissions on sale of property, commissions on sale of interests, transfer fees for handling the transfer of partnership interests, etc.;

3. Compensation for promoting the entity and the risk elements of serving as manager. This latter category is often termed the "promotional interest" or promotional compensation, and is usually subordinated to the indicated estimated rate of return for the investors (as opposed to fees for services that come out of cash flow prior to distribution to the investors). While there are good policy arguments for making the promotional interest return contingent on the success of the project and the distribution a minimum of cash flow to the investors, fees for actual services should not be contingent so the general partner can fully and properly perform it.

4. If there is to be a division between the manager and investor of tax benefits, this must also be spelled out in sufficient detail to avoid future dispute.

Loans from the Manager

Where a provision allows the manager to make a loan to the partnership (when, in his discretion, such a loan is reasonable and necessary for partnership purposes), a formula rate of interest is preferable to merely a "competitive rate" or "a generally available rate." Such a provision should make clear that the loan would have priority over the capital accounts of the investors in event of dissolution, to encourage the manager to make such funds available when required.

Manager's Right to Borrow from Partnership

In some situations, there are provisions for the manager to be able to borrow funds from the partnership. Again, a formula rate of interest should be used. This is a substantial advantage to the manager, as the cash flow that he receives from borrowing, not being currently taxable to him, may be more useful than the same receipt of cash flow as a distribution of profits. Such borrowings of surplus cash, while not income to the manager at the time borrowed, are also not deductible to the partnership or the limited partners, as are cash distributions for services or for promotional interests.

To the extent that flow-through accounting treatment is being applied, these loans represent, when they are a result of an accumulation of income to the partnership, funds on which taxes may have been paid by the investors. Where such borrowings are authorized, they must be clearly spelled out, including method of repayment, interest rate, and whether or not security will be required. If such a provision is included, clearly state under what circumstances the borrowing can be made: (a) can the manager borrow prior to the indicated distribution to the investors, (b) when must the loan be repaid; and (c) what constitutes the fund of "surplus cash" from which such loans can be made.

The manager, in addition to all other authority to borrow on behalf of the partnership or to invest the entity's funds, as is provided by general law and elsewhere herein, may be given the specific authority to lend funds of the entity to other entities in which he may be a sponsor on the following terms and conditions:

(a) Such loans to be evidenced by a written promissory note, calling for attorney's fees and costs if suit should be brought on such note for collection;

(b) Such notes are to be written on demand, and if no demand, then payable no less frequently than quarterly payments of interest;

(c) Specific or formula; and

(d) The borrower to be personally liable to the entity for the return of the principal amount, interest, and costs of collection.

Meetings and Votes

The manager should not only have the authority to call a meeting of investors to discuss and vote on questions that require their approval, but also the right to conduct a vote by writing (in the absence of the meeting).

Exculpation (Release of Personal Liability)

In some circumstances, the manager may require an exculpation clause, and such clause should be included where it is not against public policy in the particular jurisdiction involved. Such a clause is in the best interests of the investor, where they are relying heavily on the judgment of the general partner for the success of the partnership in order for him to be encouraged to exercise his judgment fully without fear of unmeritorious litigation.

Indemnity

Where the manager is personally liable on the encumbrances against the subject property, or a portion of them, it may be necessary to include a provision (sometimes called "bottom guarantee") that the investor will be liable also, in order for them to share in the portion of the basis represented by such encumbrance with respect to depreciation on the property (see the chapter "Tax Considerations"). There are a number of ways of structuring such liability. Such liability can be joint or several, and/or prorata.

The general partner may require further indemnification from the investors beyond participation in encumbrance liabilities. The extent of this indemnity, as to whether it is merely a "hold harmless" or a full indemnity, can vary from transaction to transaction. Obviously, it should include not only indemnity for direct loss, but also attorney's fees and costs in defending the manager.

In addition to the indemnity provision, the manager should be authorized to require, in his discretion, as a condition of any party contracting with the entity, a complete release of personal liability on his behalf (exculpation).

An indemnity may also run to the partnership and the general partner from each investor for any liability arising from that investor's representations being untrue.

A "hold harmless" clause should provide for indemnification in case of derivative lawsuits and that they will be defended by the entity and paid for by the entity unless the manager is found guilty. While indemnification of the manager for Securities Act violations may be against public policy in some jurisdictions, insurance can often be obtained for same, the payment for which is not against public policy. In some jurisdictions, the partnership may pay for such insurance. (However, not in California.)

Issuance and Transfer of Interests

In certain circumstances, it will be advisable to consider giving the manager the authority to admit new investors, and how broad and to what extent that authority should be.

With respect to restrictions on transferability and rights of first refusal where there are a large number of partners, such rights should normally vest only in the manager, which should be sufficient to satisfy IRS regulations regarding restriction on transferability without unduly encumbering such transferability.

It is quite common to include a provision that transfers of interest are subject to not only a right of first refusal, as indicated above, in the manager, but also that the manager has the right of approval of such substitution. If the manager's approval is subject to an agreement not to unreasonably withhold his consent or approval, some writers believe that this would amount to free transferability of interest, which could bring into question the partnership tax treatment, making the partnership taxable as a corporation under certain circumstances (see chapter on "Tax Considerations").

Common Trust Account and Investment of Surplus Funds

A manager may require authority to maintain a trust account for the particular project, in common with other projects. This often allows for greater efficiency in management operations. It should be clear; however, that such co-mingling would be only of trust finds, in a separately maintained trust account, distinct from the general partner's own funds. Provisions may be included for investment of temporary surplus cash and the inter-partnership payment of interest on overdrafts within the account, where one partnership may have a surplus balance and another may have a deficit balance. If such provisions are to be included, limitations on the amount of the surplus or deficit should set forth.

Such activities can only be provided for if all owners consent. The best way to do this is in the original governing documents. Some of these provisions may not be allowable in some jurisdictions.

Right to Rely on General Partner's Authority

The provision is often included authorizing third persons to rely on the manager's authority without further inquiry.

Power of Attorney

In order to facilitate the execution of documents, the power of attorney is often granted, allowing the manager to execute partnership documents on behalf of the respective limited partners, and in their name, pursuant to the specific power of attorney.

Marketing Representations Disclaimer

Provision can be included negating all representations other than those specifically contained in the entity documents and offering circular, and disclaiming any responsibility for representations made by agents of the entity that are contrary to such documentation. This is important in the marketing of limited partnership interests. Full disclosure should be made of all profits, and representations should be limited to full disclosure of profits. In certain cases the investors may want representations made with respect to the prior operating history of the manager, his financial condition (with regard to the "safe harbor rule") and with respect to the condition and operating figures on the property itself.

Representations of the Limited Partners

It is common for the entity to rely on the intra-state exemption from registration under the Securities and Exchange Act of 1933. Because of this reliance, a provision is often included in the subscription agreement wherein investor's represent that they:

(a) are residents of and domiciled in the state in which the entity and the property are located. (In some cases this representation goes even further, to include the representation that their automobile(s) is (are) registered, that they are registered to vote, that their children attend school, and that they spend the majority of their time all within said state);

(b) have purchased the interest for their own account and that on no other parties hold any beneficial interest therein (other than marital); and

(c) that the interest has been purchased for long-term investment and without present intent of resale.

Where such reliance is being made, a similar representation of the general partner would be advisable.

Limited Partner's Advisor

A mere disclosure of a fact is not necessarily determinative of whether or not the partner manager and the sponsors have fulfilled their duty to the investor with respect to said disclosure. Disclosure must be made in such a manner as to be understandable to the investor. This emphasizes the importance of a representation by the investor that he has independent business advice from a sophisticated advisor where there is any question as to the degree of knowledge and sophistication of the investor himself.

Duties

The partnership should spell out what responsibilities are those of the manager, the fact that he will be engaging in other activities, devoting only such portion of his time as may be required for the performance of the specific duties enumerated, and that he may delegate all duties which may be allowable to be delegated under the Act and general law of the particular jurisdiction. A statement may be desired "that with respect to any particular duty, his supervision of same shall be sufficient, rather than his actual direct performance."

Withdrawal or Removal of General Partner

The articles of partnership must define what happens to the manager's promotional interest if he should withdraw or be removed. The treatment of said interest might be different depending on whether his withdrawal is the result of his own action or is the result of being removed by vote of the limited partners. Where it is voluntary, his promotional interest could terminate with respect to any profits that have not yet been realized. Where, however, he is removed by action of the investor, a value should be placed on the interest, by either agreement appraisal or formula, and he is entitled to receive payment for same under one of the following methods:

(a) A note (or part note and part cash) executed by the entity. (It should be clarified whether or not the investors are to join in said note and the general partner may want to make those voting for removal personally liable, prorata, on the note.) The note is to be paid over time, at a reasonable rate of interest, out of the cash flow of the entity;

(b) A sum in cash at the time of termination; or

(c) Profit interest to remain (or a portion thereof), to be paid when, as, and if said profits are realized.

It should be noted that the manager retains his liability (if any) at the time he is removed or withdrawn for acts of the entity up to the date of the removal or withdrawal. It is further essential to his discharge from future liability that the entity be amended at the time of removal or withdrawal, indicating that he is no longer a manager. (This is another reason for the importance of an indemnity to the manager from the investors.) Further, if the manager's name appears in the entity name, there should be a provision that if he is removed or withdraws, his name will be removed from the entity name and the entity document amended accordingly, and properly recorded.

Repurchase Guarantee

Some writers believe that the manager is an "insider" when he purchases from other investors pursuant to a repurchase agreement, regardless of who initiates the transaction, and could be subject to liability in the same manner as if the interest were a corporate security.

In certain circumstances repurchase guarantees may be given. This is an area that requires careful consideration and is the subject of the chapter "Guarantees and Real Estate Syndicate Securities."

Derivative Suits

Stressing the importance of proper indemnity, clarification of the manager's duties, and exculpation is the fiduciary duty of the manager to the investors. In several cases, it has been held that grounds for a derivative suit may lie in some circumstances where any investor can sue the manager on behalf of all limited partners.

Rights to Deal with the Partnership

The manager may be given the right to:

(a) Lease the property beyond the term of the partnership; (specify maximum lease term);

(b) Under certain circumstances, exchange the property;

(c) Encumber or refinance the existing encumbrances on the property; and

(d) Reorganize the entity into another legal form, providing there is no adverse effect, or subject to the approval of 51% in interest of the investors.

More Than One General Partner

Where there is more than one manager, the entity document should provide that only one need sign on behalf of the entity. A decision should be made as to whether, in the event of a disagreement, the views of a particular manager are to prevail, or a majority (in interest or number) of the managers to decide.

Filing of Certificates

It is extremely important that the manager see that the entity agreement is properly filed and timely amended. If the investor's liability is not appropriately shown, an investor could end up being personally liable. He might, in turn, have an action against the manager for negligently handling the filing of the entity agreement. In some cases renewal filings may also be necessary.

Caution Re Regulatory Standards

State and federal rules may in given circumstances prohibit the use of some of the provisions recommended. (See the chapter "State and Federal Regulation of Syndication Activities.")

Partners Dealing With a Partnership and Title Insurance

Increasingly, lenders (particularly institutional lenders) are participating in loan transactions not only as a lender, but also as a member of the borrowing group or entity. In such cases, the lender is an investor. Occasionally, it is a manager in the entity. Legal problems must be considered where a loan by a lender (institutional or otherwise) is made to an entity or group in which such lender (or its parent or subsidiary) has an interest.

Concern, however, is not limited to loan transactions but also to conveyances involving parties to the entity (including joint ventures). In general, in California, the hazards are spelled out in Civil Code Section 3439.08 (Uniform Fraudulent Conveyances Act), relative to transactions entered into by an entity with a party to the entity. Corporations Code Section 15513 (Uniform Limited Partnership Act) and Section 67(d)(1), (4) and (6) of the Bankruptcy Act.

Among the transactions that could be void or subject to the claims of present or future creditors of the partnership (or other similar entity) are the following:

(a) A deed of trust on entity property from an entity in favor of a manager;

(b) A deed of trust on partnership property from an entity to an investor;

(c) A deed of trust on property from an entity in favor of a lender which wholly owns or controls the manager, or in favor of a sister entity of the manager, which sister entity and manager are owned or controlled by the same entity. (Note: this is a variation of (a) and (b) above. Several lenders, in order to exercise control over a project, require that a wholly-owned subsidiary of the lender be a manager in addition to making the lender or a different subsidiary an investor);

(d) A conveyance of property from an entity to either a manager or investor;

(e) A conveyance of, or deed of trust on, the separate property of a manager (where known to be such) from the manager to an investor in discharge of an obligation of the manager to the entity; and

(f) A conveyance of the property of an investor to the entity, and a deed of trust from such entity to the investor for more than fair market value.

Compliance with the above statutes will apparently be accommodated, at least as to transactions such as (b), (d), and (e) above. However, if, at the time, the entity is not insolvent or would be thereby rendered insolvent, such transaction, whether loan or conveyance, should be carefully reviewed with the legal counsel.

CHAPTER 14

DRAFTING IMPOUND PROVISIONS
IN A SECURITIES OFFERING[*]

Regulatory authorities often impose an impound requirement in connection with qualification or registration of a proposed syndication offering. The purpose of such impound requirements is to assure the investor that sufficient funds will be raised to meet the initial budgetary requirements outlined in the offering, circular, or prospectus as being necessary to accomplish the objectives of the offering, before any of the investor's funds will be released to the issuer. The impound provides that, in the event the offering is not successful in raising the specified amount in a given period of time, investors will receive the return of their entire investment without deduction or offset, with the issuer or sponsor paying all costs of the offering.

Even in a private offering, an impound provision indicating that the investors' funds will not be used until a sufficient amount has been raised to meet the objectives of the offering is often set forth. The degree of investor sophistication required to qualify an offering as a "private offering," exempt from securities regulations generally dictates that the issuer include impound provisions. This will give investors sufficient assurance that they will receive the full return of their funds in the event the amount required is not raised.

Types of Impounds

The following are the types of impounds commonly in use:

A. Third-Party Impound. An impound where the funds are placed with an independent third-party escrow holder, who must return the funds to the investors without deduction or offset if the impound level is not reached within a specified period of time.

B. Order Impound. An impound where the release of the funds from the impound requires an order from the regulatory body, given after certification that the required amount of funds have been paid into the depository

C. Automatic Impound. A formal impound which provides that funds be automatically released to the issuer, without further order of the regulatory body, when the funds reach a specified level.

[*]*Article by the Author published in Los Angeles Bar Journal, Vol. 48, No. 6. April 1973. Permission to reprint gratefully acknowledged.*

D. Moral Impound. An impound where the issuer or the sponsor has undertaken not to use or release the funds until the impound amount has been raised, and where funds are on deposit with and under the control of the issuer or sponsor (rather than placed in escrow with an independent depository). While some impounds are third-party impounds, in quasi-public offerings, California has allowed moral impound in limited cases. This is primarily in offerings involving issuers and sponsors of strong financial ability and proven reputation for performance.

E. Partial Impound. An impound with a provision that the impound applies to the first monies raised until a certain level has been reached. At that time, the funds then raised will be released and additional funds raised will not be subject to the impound.

F. Staggered Impound. An impound with a provision that a portion of the funds will be released for a specific purpose. Additional funds will be impounded for other purposes and released on a "staggered" basis as various levels of funds have been raised. This is quite common where the issuer plans to undertake a number of projects or purchase a series of properties. The various projects or properties generally are given a designated priority. The funds are released as they are raised in sufficient amounts to complete each stage or to purchase each respective property.

G. Investment Impound. An impound where substantial sums of money are being raised and where it is therefore advisable that the impound funds be invested by the impound holder. The investments should be relatively risk-free, such as U.S. Treasury obligations, certificates of deposit in federally insured banks or thrifts, or comparable money market instruments of unquestioned credit. The impound should clearly state whether these investments are to be made at the discretion of the impound holder or at the discretion of the issuer or sponsor. Generally, such investments should mature on or before the expiration of the impound period. Perhaps it can be clearly shown that all or a portion of the funds will not be immediately required at the conclusion of the impound. In that case, longer maturities can be permitted in order to secure higher yields, if these maturities bear a reasonable relationship to the maturing obligations that will have to be met by the issuer in connection with the plan of business.

Where there is to be an investment impound, the earnings from the investment can often be used to defray all or a portion of the expenses of the issuer in the event that the offering should be unsuccessful. The entire principal has to be returned to the investors without offset, absent agreement with investors to the contrary. If the issuer desires such an option, it must be clearly described in the offering circular or prospectus that such an application of the impound earnings will be made.

In the event that the offering is unsuccessful, the documentation should clearly state what disposition is to be made of the impound earnings. Among the possibilities are the following:

(a) They may be used to the extent necessary by the issuer or sponsor to defray expenses of the issue.

(b) They may be paid over to the issuer for distribution to the investors.

(c) They may be paid directly to the investors by the impound holder. They may be directly paid to the investors by being divided prorata among the investors or, in the case of a partnership, credited to the investor's account either (1) in proportion to the amount of the investor's initial subscription to the impound regardless of the time of investment in the impound, or (2) in proportion to the investor's subscription to the impound. But this is calculated with an additional adjustment for the relative length of time that an individual investor's funds have been in the impound, in relation to the time that the funds of the other investors have been in the impound.

The Depository Agreement

Where funds impounded are placed with a third-party depository, the depository and the issuer must enter into a depository agreement (in the nature of an escrow or agency agreement).

If securities are being offered for sale in a public offering, a copy of the depository agreement is required as part of the application for qualification or registration. In private offerings where the partnership agreement is accompanied by a "private offering memorandum," it is advisable to include a copy of the depository agreement with the other exhibits to the private offering memorandum.

The depository agreement should provide for (1) the holding of the funds; (2) the investment powers of the issuer and/or depository, if any; (3) indemnification of the depository under certain circumstances; (4) the depository's compensation; and (5) the conditions precedent to the release of the funds to the issuer or their return to the respective investors.

Providing for Flexibility

Under certain circumstances the sponsor or issuer may desire to have the funds in the impound available for use, prior to the successful completion of the offering. This is particularly true in the case of real property, where a limited escrow period may be involved, and in commercial enterprises where certain opportunities might be lost if the plan of business is not instituted promptly. In the case of real estate syndicate securities, the following are various methods that can be used to provide for a release of impound funds prior to successful completion of the offering.

(a) Each subscriber, in addition to paying a certain amount of cash into the impound, may agree to increase his subscription by a percentage of his original cash investment. The subscriber may sign a personal promissory note, which may be called at the option of the issuer. If the issuer has raised a sufficient amount in cash and notes (the subscribers meeting certain credit standards), the impound may provide that, when the total of cash and notes meets the impound limit, the impound will be released.

(b) The seller may agree that, under certain circumstances, the amount of the down payment may be reduced and the amount of any secondary financing which he is carrying back be increased, at the option of the issuer. This gives the issuer the flexibility of electing to close with a smaller amount of capital, taking the property subject to a larger amount of purchase money financing. This is a commonly used method to provide for flexibility. It is very satisfactory if there is adequate explanation in the offering circular or registration statement of the possibility of a higher ratio of financing and the concomitant higher risk to the investors.

(c) As an alternative to carrying back larger financing, the seller may agree to sell a smaller proportionate interest in the property, agreeing to hold the balance as a tenant in common with the issuer. In such event, detailed provisions must be made for the joint management of the property. Subscribers who desire to participate in the ownership of the property are usually willing to participate in an entity that owns a portion of the property as well as one that owns the whole property. While this requires careful handling in the offering material, it is preferable from the seller's standpoint, in that the seller will not be taxed on the gain allocable to the portion not sold.

(d) The seller may agree to take, at the maturity of the impound, units of the issuer up to a certain amount as a portion of the purchase price. It should be clearly indicated whether this is at the seller's option (as well as any of the foregoing methods), or whether the seller is obligated to take such a course of action and that such units taken as a portion of the seller are deemed sold for impound purposes.

(e) The sponsor can provide that he will take his commissions and other compensation in units at the closing, if required to complete the offering. It is arguable that the sponsor would have this option in any event. However it is better practice to fully disclose this possibility. That way, the investors are informed that a portion of the investment may not be paid for in cash by independent third parties, but may be purchased by the sponsor by applying his commissions and/or expenses to the purchase of an interest in the issuer. Again, it should be clearly indicated whether the sponsor has this option or whether he may, at his election, abort the deal and return the funds to the investors.

(f) The sponsor may purchase units to be held in inventory for resale. Full disclosure of such an arrangement again is required.

Promoter's Acceptance of Units

The acceptance of units in lieu of cash by the sponsor (or other persons performing certain services in connection with the offering) may have, in certain circumstances if not properly drafted, adverse tax consequences to future investors. The reason is that projections of tax deductions may be based on cash payments by all investors. It should be further noted that the entity form chosen might place certain restrictions on the ability of individuals to accept units in lieu of cash or goods for services rendered.

Under certain circumstances, the units going to the sponsor or issuer may be required by the regulatory authorities to be (a) nonvoting on certain questions, and/or (b) subordinated in various respects to the units being issued to the investors. Where the sponsor has the option of receiving cash or units prior to the closing, the imposition of any restrictions or differentiation on the units that are being issued in lieu of cash would appear to be unfair to the sponsor and contrary to the public interest. It generally is acknowledged that every incentive should be given to the sponsor to encourage him to carry units in the project and to reduce or minimize his front-end load. Restrictions, which are placed on units taken in lieu of cash, where such a decision is not within the control of and at the discretion of the sponsor, would serve to discourage him from taking the units and cause him to elect the cash alternative.

Unfortunately, for the public interest, in certain circumstances some regulators fail to distinguish between promotional interests (which are a separate and distinct means of compensation of the sponsor) and those interests that the sponsor takes in lieu of cash payment that he is otherwise entitled to. While the sponsor can reasonably expect restrictions on interests being received as promotional interests, it does not appear necessary to impose these terms on interests taken in lieu of cash.

Where the sponsor or the seller takes a substantial quantity of units and engages in resale of such units, it is clear in California that if the resale is timely and is authorized under the original permit for qualification, no amendment to the application for qualification will be required. However, under the federal securities laws, a separate and distinct registration may be required.

The Use of a Repurchase Guarantee

In order to facilitate marketing of syndication sales a repurchase guarantee on the part of the issuer, sponsor, or third party may often be useful. Such a guarantee may accelerate the rate of sales, allowing the project to reach the minimum impound level at a much earlier date than would otherwise be possible. The ability to close the impound quickly under certain circumstances can give the syndicator an opportunity for an advantageous bargain, by being able to offer to the seller a relatively short escrow period. Care should be used in determining (a) who the obligor will be, (b) the extent of the repurchase obligation, (c) the expiration date of the obligation, (d) the effect on qualification or registration under securities regulations, and (e) the tax consequences. (See chapter "Guarantees and Real Estate Syndicate Securities.")

Staging Development

It is usually impossible to predict the success that the issuer will have in raising funds. Where the business plan will lend itself to being divided into stages, all of which are independently viable, it is advisable to use a staggered impound. This way, if the full amount of funds is not raised, at least a portion of the business plan can independently proceed, and the issuer and the sponsor can have the benefit of that portion of the plan. If such a provision is not included in the original application for qualification or registration, an amendment to so provide will generally require (by the appropriate regulatory authority) the inclusion of the provision that there be a rescission offer made to all of those who have already subscribed to the impound. By including the possibility of a staged impound in the initial documentation, such rescission offer can often be avoided.

Importance of Local Law

Some jurisdictions (California is one) do not favor releasing investor funds until strict requirements are met. However, others may be more liberal and even allow a sponsor who is building a project to have access to purchaser impound before the building is completed.

Conclusion

Imagination and proper structuring in the drafting of impound provisions can contribute to the successful completion of a securities offering. Impounds serve to strengthen investor protection, increase public acceptance of an offering, and may improve the economic viability of the proposed project. In this area, counsel is well advised to set aside the form book and consider the many alternatives available for drafting provisions that fit the particular circumstances of the proposed offering.

CHAPTER 15

MANAGEMENT OF THE SYNDICATE*

Syndicate management includes comunication with investors, relations between the investors and the syndicator, and the management of the legal entity. This is distinguished from supervision and operation of the property itself, which is called property management.

Reports and Distributions

Frequent reports on the operation of the subject property to the investors generally result in good rapport between the syndicator and investors. These reports should be in sufficient detail to enable the investor to have a clear picture of present operating success of the property. However, it should not be so complicated as to generate further inquiry or confusion. Time is money in the management field and to the extent that the report can anticipate and therefore lessen investor inquiries, an additional benefit will be received from reporting functions.

Where there is close contact with the investors due to personal relationships, the reporting can be limited to the mailing of (1) an annual financial statement, (2) entity tax return or partners K1, and (3) a summary of the years' operating history. Some syndicate organizations find that it is a good policy to give the investors the complete tax return and financial statement. Some, in order to limit expense, will send the investor only the portion of the tax return that contains a schedule of the individual investor's profit and loss and capital adjustments for the year (the investor's K-1).

Similar considerations are involved in determining distributions policy and the choices usually are: (a) monthly, (b) quarterly, (c) semi-annually, and (d) annually. Smaller investors are more impressed with frequent distributions, while sophisticated substantial investors will be interested in operating costs and return on their money, rather than the frequency with which it is received.

To prepare and distribute checks and reports requires mailing costs, bank charges, and office personnel time. It probably costs a minimum of $5.00 per investor to prepare a distribution check, plus an additional sum for any enclosed report. Frequent distributions can create cash flow and operating problems. The accumulation of money for distribution helps to even out peaks and valleys in cash flow.

---

*This Article appeared originally in "How to Syndicate an Apartment House" Published by the California Real Estate Association in 1971. The Author gratefully acknowledges permission to reprint herein.

If possible, reports should be timed to coincide with distributions, to save mailing costs and office time. Generally, a quarterly distribution or semi-annual distribution will be frequent enough to maintain investor contact.

An area in which many syndicators fall down is failing to maintain contact with investors and to keep them informed. The greatest single source of future investors is the group that has already invested with the syndicator. They become important centers of influence for the marketing of new syndications. Calls and inquiries from present investors should receive priority and be treated promptly and courteously.

Annual Meetings

The question often arises as to whether or not to have annual meetings. Formal annual meetings can establish a precedent that the syndicator may come to regret later. There is the question of the expense involved in the meeting and the scheduling of it. If there is one disgruntled investor and he has the opportunity to air his views before all of the investors, dissatisfaction can spread rapidly. Probably a much better policy would be to have an annual party or social occasion at which investors have an opportunity to meet the syndicator and his staff in a relaxed, non-business atmosphere. General reports can be given on the more successful projects and investors informed that if they have particular questions or inquiries these might be handled directly with the staff of the syndicator on a one-to-one basis.

Selecting Accountant and Attorney

Probably the most important decision in selecting professional employees for the syndicate on an on-going basis is the retention of the independent accountant who will prepare the annual tax returns, depreciation schedules, etc. The accountant should be one who is thoroughly familiar with real estate investments and who will be aware of opportunities for deductions and losses for the investors. The presentation of the annual financial statement and the schedule to the entity tax return, delineating the operating results effect on each individual partner, can go a long way to filling the investors' desires for operating information. If it is in clear and in easily understood terms, this will avoid the necessity of time-consuming contact answering individual investor inquiries.

The attorney who did the work in the qualification and organization of the syndicate is usually a prestigious, experienced firm, whose background and experience may not be necessary for the day-to-day operations of leases, handling unlawful detainers, health and safety matters, etc. A young aggressive practitioner is often more appropriate for dispossessing a tenant rather than a well-established prestigious firm, which may have to charge a considerably higher rate for the same service.

Among the problem areas that may arise in connection with the management of the syndicate are the following: (a) lawsuits from investors, (b) disallowance of tax benefits, (c) cash flow deficiencies, and (d) lack of a manager.

Investor Dissatisfaction

Where a disgruntled investor sues the syndicator, the best policy is usually to offer rescission, whether or not the investor has sound grounds. If the syndicator has appropriate resources to do so, this will go a long way toward maintaining a good reputation and preventing a "run" from other investors who may have concern over the investment. As lawsuits can be costly, many entity agreements call for arbitration in the event of dispute between the investors and the manager, or between the investors and the entity itself. There are many advantages and disadvantages to an arbitration clause and such a decision can only be made after consultation with legal counsel.

Disallowance of Tax Benefits

Where alleged tax benefits have been disallowed, a decision must be made as to whether or not to challenge the position of the taxing authority. Generally speaking, such a challenge is best made by the investors as a group rather than by an individual investor. Spreading the cost of the challenge over the group as a whole, where there are no conflicts in the position of the various investors among themselves will often result in each investor obtaining counsel for a small part of the total defense costs. The decision concerning whether or not to challenge a disallowance of tax benefits is complicated and may involve consideration of a proposed compromise, wherein a portion of the benefits will be allowed, and a portion disallowed. Such decision requires the selection of experienced legal counsel thoroughly familiar with the tax law as it relates both to syndicating entities and to real property investment.

Cash Flow Deficiency

When faced with a cash flow deficiency, the best policy is to promptly lay all of the facts before the investors promptly. Where such a deficiency merely means a suspension of distribution, a wise course of action is to inform the investors of the situation as soon as possible. It is advisable to suspend spendable distribution until it may be resumed, rather than to borrow additional funds or use reserve accounts for the purpose of distributions, thereby placing the project in jeopardy and giving a false picture of financial condition. Where the deficiencies result in actual cash-flow losses, the syndicator must carefully prepare himself for the presentation of the relevant facts to the investors. An appraisal of the present market value of the property should be made so that the investors can make an informed decision as to whether they desire to continue to make payments, sell, or to allow the property to revert to lien holders.

Change of Manager

Occasionally the syndicator who is not serving as the manager (and was involved in the organization of the syndicate as a real estate agent, either with respect to the acquisition of the property by the entity or with respect to the raising of investment money), is faced with the problem of the manager resigning, or going out of business, becoming incompetent, or resigning his position. In such situations, one who has been involved in the organization of the syndicate has a responsibility to the investors to endeavor to find a qualified manager if he, himself, is unable or unwilling to serve. The responsibility of the new manager, what share, if any, he is to get in the subordinated interest of the former manager, and what responsibility he undertakes with respect to investor relations must be explored.

A new manager will insist that he be given a release and held harmless with respect to all former activities of the previous manager. Normally the investors will go along with such an indemnity and release when it is clarified to them that the original manager may have received substantial front-end compensation that is not available to the new substituted manager. Therefore, a different type of relationship may be necessary to get experienced and competent management required to preserve the value of the entity and realize its ultimate potential. The responsibility of the new manager must be clearly defined in writing.

There is also the issue of how to change managers, where the present manager should be replaced but refuses to resign.

Defaulting Partners

Where an investor ceases to make his required assessments (in the appropriate case such as purchase of raw land where continuing assessments are called for) the options open to the entity and manager may be restricted by the entity agreement. Many entity agreements provide that there is no legal liability to make continuing assessments, and while such provisions are not advisable if such continuous assessments are necessary to carry the project, marketing considerations may have outweighed the advisability of making such payments obligatory.

Obviously where possible the manager will endeavor to convince the remaining investors to take up the portion of the assessment that is deficient and attempt to secure a new investor exercising options to buy out the defaulting investor. Where neither can be accomplished, the manager must make a decision as to whether he feels his relationship with the investors and the value of the property merit his personal undertaking, by either advancing as a loan, or by purchasing the default- ing investor's share, continuing the investments required. From the standpoint of investor relations, where at all possible, the manager should do so. From a standpoint of personal credit of the syndicator this is often done as loans to the entity (with the knowledge and consent of the investors who are continuing to make their payments), rather than by taking over the equity interest. This will assure the manager of a priority to receive back his funds advanced from sale before returning capital contributions and distributions of profits.

CHAPTER 16

STATE AND FEDERAL REGULATION

OF SYNDICATE ACTIVITIES*

An interest in a real estate syndicate, whether that syndicate takes the form of a general partnership, limited partnership, tenancy in common with management agreement, joint venture, beneficial interest in a trust, lease participation, etc., constitutes a security under federal and most state laws. Any type of arrangement whereby one individual is supplying capital and relying on the efforts of another for the return on that capital may be construed to be a security. The nature of the arrangement between the investor and the seller of the interest being purchased is the determining factor, rather than the label that may be placed on the transaction.

For purposes of regulation, the syndication process can be divided into five categories:

1. The activity of the sponsor or syndicator in organizing the entity,

2. The offering for sale by the entity and the "issuance" by the entity of interests,

3. Individuals, either for themselves or on behalf of an entity or others, offering for sale and selling the interests being issued,

4. The management and operation of the project, and

5. The sale of the project.

Organization and Operations

No license may in certain circumstances be, as of 2006, required of an individual or entity that forms a real estate syndicate that takes the limited partnership or limited liability form, where such individual or entity does not receive specific compensation for the sale of interests in the program and is acting on his or its own behalf. The solicitation, sale, or formation of a real estate program for another generally may require either a real estate broker's license or a securities license from the state where the program is subject to state jurisdiction. If the program is subject to federal jurisdiction, a license to solicit and sell securities may be required from the National Association of Securities Dealers. These requirements exist whether or not the syndicate is exempt from "qualification" as a "private offering."

*Thanks to Leib Orlanski, Esq. of the Century City office of Kirkpatrick, Lockhart, Nicholson & Graham for his contributions to this chapter.

Licensing in California

The regulation of the solicitation, sale, and advising of the purchase of syndication securities falls into two categories:

1. Real Estate Syndicate Securities, for which a real estate brokers license issued by the Commissioner of Real Estate, the offering to potential offerees of interests in a limited partnership or similar entity limited to 100 or less investors and the subject of the partnership is the ownership and operation of real estate; and

2. Real Estate Syndicate Securities, to more than 100 investors require licensed as a broker-dealer by the Department of Corporation.

The California Corporations Commissioner has the following categories of licensees: broker-dealers, agents, agents of issuers, limited broker-dealers, limited agents, and investment advisors.

In general, the broker-dealer maintains a regular business and deals in securities as well as representing issuers. An agent, however, merely represents a broker-dealer or an issuer. An investment advisor is one who, for compensation, engages in the business of advising others directly or through publications or writings as to the value of securities or as to the advisability of investing in, purchasing or selling securities, or who for compensation, and as part of a regular business, publishes analyses or reports concerning securities. Banks, trust companies, savings and loan associations, attorneys, accountants, engineers or teachers whose performance of investment advisor services is solely incidental to their business and who receive no special compensation for such services, publishers of newspapers, news magazines or business or financial publications of general, regular and paid circulation and their agents and employees, are not often investment advisors.

It should be noted that the limited broker-dealer's license maybe available to broker-dealers whose activities are solely restricted to the sale of interests in real estate limited partnerships, and that such broker-dealers who hold a real estate broker's license may not need to comply with the examination requirements of the Corporations Commissioner. Examinations are required of all but the limited broker-dealer, limited agent, and agent of issuer. Generally, broker-dealers are required to meet minimum capital and ratio net capital requirements as well as post a surety bond. Broker-dealers under certain circumstances may be excused from the minimum capital and net capital ratio requirements.

The Real Estate Commissioner has a more limited category of licensees being principally the real estate broker and the real estate salesperson. Both the solicitation and sale of interests in, and the advising for compensation of the purchase of, real estate syndicate interests will require either a broker's license or a sales person's license. Sales people must be licensed under a particular real estate broker and cannot operate on their own, as may an agent under the California Corporations Commissioner. The Real Estate Commissioner also has certain rules and regulations regarding the activities of a broker and a sales person. Both commissioners emphasize fair dealing, the keeping of adequate records, the segregation of clients' funds, and the full disclosure of the licensee's interest in the transaction to all parties.

In California, a licensed broker-dealer or agent need not be licensed by the Real Estate Commissioner to sell real estate syndicate securities. Such an exemption, however, is not reciprocal in that under the Corporations Commissioner's regulations a license is required of the real estate broker or real estate sales person who engages in the sale of securities subject to the jurisdiction of the Corporations Commissioner. This license may be the "limited broker-dealer license" or the "limited agent's license."

Attorneys and accountants may perform their usual professional services in connection with the formation and operation of a syndicate. However, if they are to be compensated for the sale of syndicate interests by the syndicate or sponsor, such sales activity will generally require that they possess one of the foregoing described licenses.

Those who are business managers and invest the funds of their clients may also require a license from the Labor Commissioner to cover their management activities.

Qualification of Syndicate Shares

Most states have laws (usually referred to as "Blue Sky Laws") regulating the sale of securities. The California statute, Corporations Code Section 25019, defines a security as:

"Security" means any note; stock; treasury stock; membership in an incorporated or unincorporated association; bond; debenture; evidence of indebtedness; certificate of interest or participation in any profit-sharing agreement; collateral trust certificate; pre-organization certificate or subscription; transferable share; investment contract; viatical settlement contract or a fractionalized or pooled interest therein; life settlement contract or a fractionalized or pooled interest therein; voting trust certificate;

certificate of deposit for a security; interest in a limited liability company and any class or series of those interests (including any fractional or other interest in that interest), except a membership interest in a limited liability company in which the person claiming this exception can prove that all of the members are actively engaged in the management of the limited liability company; provided that evidence that members vote or have the right to vote, or the right to information concerning the business and affairs of the limited liability company, or the right to participate in management, shall not establish, without more, that all members are actively engaged in the management of the limited liability company; certificate of interest or participation in an oil, gas or mining title or lease or in payments out of production under that title or lease; put, call, straddle, option, or privilege on any security, certificate of deposit, or group or index of securities (including any interest therein or based on the value thereof); or any put, call, straddle, option, or privilege entered into on a national securities exchange relating to foreign currency; any beneficial interest or other security issued in connection with a funded employees' pension, profit sharing, stock bonus, or similar benefit plan; or, in general, any interest or instrument commonly known as a "security"; or any certificate of interest or participation in, temporary or interim certificate for, receipt for, guarantee of, or warrant or right to subscribe to or purchase, any of the foregoing.

All of the foregoing is securities whether or not evidenced by a written document. "Security" does not include: (1) any beneficial interest in any voluntary inter vivo trust which is not created for the purpose of carrying on any business or solely for the purpose of voting, or (2) any beneficial interest in any testamentary trust, or (3) any insurance or endowment policy or annuity contract under which an insurance company admitted in this state promises to pay a sum of money (whether or not based upon the investment performance of a segregated fund) either in a lump sum or periodically for life or some other specified period, or (4) any franchise subject to registration under the Franchise Investment Law (Division 5 (commencing with Section 31000)), or exempted from registration by Section 31100 or 31101.

"Underwriter" means a person who has agreed with an issuer or other person on whose behalf a distribution is to be made (a) to purchase securities for distribution or (b) to distribute securities for or on behalf of such issuer or other person or (c) to manage or supervise a distribution of securities for or on behalf of such issuer or other person.

Security, therefore, includes interests in any syndicate venture unless that venture or the interests therein have been specifically exempted. Certain types of securities may be exempted by specific statute and securities, when offered privately, are normally exempted. Refer to the laws of the particular state to determine whether the syndicate interests being offered are exempt from qualification under the laws of that state.

Qualification of syndicate interests usually is done by means of application for a permit from the respective state governmental authority for permission to solicit and sell interests in the syndicate. The permit is granted to the applicant, who will usually be the syndicate itself together with its organizers. A separate permit is required for each syndicate, as opposed to a license that is granted to an individual or entity to engage in certain regulated activities having to do with the sale of interests in syndicates.

Non-Public Offering

Many of the statutes provide that a non-public offering will be exempt in certain circumstances. For an offering to be "non-public," the solicitation and sale of interests must be restricted to persons other than the public. It is important to note that the test under both federal and state "private offering exemptions" is not who actually invests, but to whom the investment is offered. An offering to one person who falls under the definition of "the public" will require either registration under the Securities and Exchange Commission (SEC) and/or qualification under state Blue Sky Laws. Identifying "the public" for these purposes involves complex technical concepts and depends on the manner of solicitation, the relationship of those being solicited to each other, to the syndicator and his associates, and various other aspects of the form and nature of the transaction. These matters are discussed in various state and federal securities releases.

Interstate Offerings

Where there is contact with more than one state, often called an "inter-state offering," the interests may have to be registered with the SEC. An "intra-state offering" is exempt from SEC registration. It is one where all the contact is limited to persons resident within one state, the property is located in that state, the syndicator is a resident of that state, and all sales activity takes place within that state. Where there is any question or doubt as to whether or not the syndicate requires federal registration, the syndicator should contact the SEC itself, and secure a "no-action" letter or get a written opinion of legal counsel that the transaction is exempt from federal registration as (a) a non-public offering, or (b) an intra-state offering.

In California, the offering of real estate securities is now exclusively (except for licensing of the salesperson or brokers) under the jurisdiction of the Department of Corporations, the Real Estate Syndicate Act having repealed. As a result, the former division/jurisdiction between the Corporations and the Real Estate Commissioners' offices no longer is relevant. In the past, the Real Estate Commissioner had jurisdiction over all real estate syndicates not involving the corporate form of entity where the subject of the syndicate was solely real estate and the maximum number of investors would not exceed 100. Because of the repeal of the former law, the Corporations Commissioner retains jurisdiction over all real estate syndicates.

Finder's Fees and Brokerage Commissions

A license is required to engage in activities connected with the offering and sale of any interest in a real estate syndicate, from either the Corporations Commissioner. Depending on whether the syndicate has more or less than 100 investors, payment of a fee for the mere referral of a potential offeree may not require a license.

The Real Estate Commissioner on several occasions in the past has indicated that an unlicensed person who merely furnishes an introduction and does not personally solicit buyers or sellers or take any part, no matter how slight, in negotiations with respect to the offer or sale, may receive a referral fee from a licensed individual. It should be noted, however, that Section 1624 of the Civil Code requires a "finder" to have a written memorandum of the intention of the parties that there be payment for the introduction service where real property is involved.

The Corporations Commissioner has agreed in the past with the Real Estate Commissioner that, where the activities are those of a "finder" (providing a mere introduction), no licensing will be required.

Note that in both cases, however, that where the finder is being paid by the entity, the amount of fee paid to the finder would be included in determining allowable "selling expenses." Normally, however, the finder is being paid by the broker or agent out of his commissions that are already included in the total selling expenses and such should be disclosed in the offering circular.

A license was not required to sell interests in a limited partnership where the general partner conducts the activities. An exception was when he is receiving special compensation for the sale under the former Real Estate Syndicate Act (the act speaks in terms of "selling for another for compensation"). The Corporations Commissioner has taken a similar position and not required licensing where the sales activities are conducted solely by the general partner and incidental to his duties as general partner. However, where a commission is paid to him for sales, a license will be required.

Management Activities

In certain states, a real estate license is required to manage property for another. Unless there is a management agreement with a properly licensed property manager, it is arguable a real estate license is required of a syndicator who manages syndicate property in those states.

Leasing and Sale of Real Estate

A real estate license is generally required to sell lease and/or for compensation real property of another.

Quasi-Governmental Regulations

A number of private or quasi-governmental organizations may also have jurisdiction over a program, because the individuals engaged in the activity may, by membership in a respective organization, come under that organization's rules and standards. The National Association of Securities Dealers has its own rules and procedures for the marketing and sale of interests in real property limited partnerships. If members of this association are to be involved in the marketing of the program, it will be necessary to qualify the offering with the association.

There are many trade organizations involved in creating professional standards that apply to various aspects of the syndication process.

The former syndication Division of the California Real Estate Association had been in the forefront of developing professionalism and high ethical standards. Its membership consisted of realtors, attorneys, accountants, property managers, and others active in the syndication process. It maintained an extensive education program and had developed special forms and publications for use by the industry.

The Midwest Association of Securities Regulators has established rules that have been adopted by many states in an attempt to gain uniformity in the syndication field. The North American Securities Administrators, a national organization, also studied and worked with the Securities and Exchange Commission to improve uniformity of regulation.

State Regulation

California has adopted, with a few minor exceptions, the Real Estate Syndication Rules as recommended by the Midwest Association of Securities Regulators. Copies of these rules are available from the Department of Corporations and the rules of other states are available from the respective agency that has jurisdiction over the issuance and sale of syndicate interests.

The rules begin with a list of definitions. They set forth requirements for the sponsor (syndicator), limitations on the amount of compensation, disclosure requirements, and standards of suitability, as to whom the property may be offered. Certain conflicts of interest are prohibited and restrictions are established as to the investment of the funds raised by the syndicate.

Regulation D Rule 147

The Securities and Exchange Commission has adopted regulation D setting forth the circumstances under which it would consider an offering to be a private offering (Rule 146) and when they would consider the intra-state exemption to be effective (Rule 147). It should be noted that neither of these rules are intended to be exclusive and that there may be other circumstances under which a transaction may qualify for the intra-state or private offering exemptions.

Rules Are Guidelines

The California rules indicate they apply to qualification of real estate programs in the form of limited partnerships and will be applied, by analogy, to real estate programs in other forms. While applications not conforming to the standards are looked upon with disfavor, where good cause is shown, certain guidelines may be modified or waived by the Corporations Commissioner. The commissioner is directed by statute to make a finding that the proposed offering is fair, just, and equitable to the investing public. In reaching such a determination, the commissioner will consider, among other factors:

(a) The proposed class of offerees and their degree of business sophistication,

(b) Risk elements of the offering,

(c) The extent and nature of disclosures and precautionary legends, and

(d) The total amount of promotional interests and compensation involved in relation to the return to the investor.

Where a strong showing can be made that these purposes will be served by the application of different rules in individual respects, the commissioner's office has historically been receptive to reasonable modifications in their respective rules.

CHAPTER 17

HOW TO MARKET SYNDICATE SHARES

Each syndicator should have a marketing program fitted to his project and his own potential investor group. In structuring a marketing program, it is necessary to examine carefully the positive aspects of the project and to analyze what type of investor would be motivated to purchase shares in that project, as well as the profile of the potential investor pool. As was seen earlier, the motivations of investors differ depending on their background, economic circumstances, and personal investment inclinations.

Obviously where tax shelter is the primary advantage to the particular project, it should be marketed to persons who are in high tax brackets. A selling program directed to these high tax bracketed taxpayers would have a reasonable chance of succeeding.

Some investors will have a tolerance for risk and require larger returns than those who are risk adverse. Such investors may be good prospects for land or high leverage transactions. Conservative investors or those whose tolerance for risk is low will prefer cash flow projects such as established income properties with a known operating history but more limited upside.

Once a profile has been established as to the ideal prospective investor, a number of different marketing tools may be used. They are principally as follows:

MARKETING TECHNIQUES

1. Direct Personal Contact

Lists of potential investors are compiled from consultations with friends, business associates, and relatives. They are contacted on an individual basis by the syndicator and his staff. Syndicators using this technique prefer to contact investors on a one-to-one basis rather than having group meetings. That way, they can answer the inquiries of the individual investor without exposure to possible criticisms or heckling of other persons who may be present at a group meeting.

2. Indirect Selling on a "Third-Party Basis"

By using of "centers of influence," such as attorneys, accountants, insurance brokers, business managers, investment advisors, securities brokers, and real estate brokers who have contact with large numbers of potential investors, the syndicate shares are often marketed through "third parties" other than the syndicator. Some syndicators prefer this method on the theory that a third-party recommendation will be more easily accepted by the potential investor and that a third party is better in a position to overcome investor objections than the syndicator himself, whose arguments may be suspect or are obviously influenced by the syndicator's personal interests in the project. Several syndicate organizations have made a specialty of restricting their activity to packaging projects and marketing them through local realtors and/or investment advisors. The syndicator performs no selling function other than supplying offering circulars. Others are using securities brokers and some have even established themselves as the "syndicate department" of a securities firm.

3.   *Media Advertising*

Although it is relatively expensive, there are syndicate organizations who use advertising placed in newspapers, magazines, and professional publications as their primary investor contact. In this case, care must be given to see that the material used in solicitation meets postal regulations and in conformity with respective governmental securities regulation, yet is sufficiently attractive to motivate a response.

4.   *Lecture and Educational Programs*

One of the most successful devices used by California syndicators is to conduct a series of lectures on the general subject of real estate investment. No permit or qualification may be required to solicit the public for attendance at these lectures, providing that there are no offerings made in connection with the lectures. The lectures run one, two, or three evenings, and investors are encouraged to fill out information forms indicating their interest in various types of real estate investment. The information forms then provide the basis for further invitations to smaller meetings, at which offerings are made pursuant to permit. Such activities may require qualification and/or registration of the program under some circumstances.

5.   *Sponsorship by an Organization*

There is a group of syndicators who specialize in working with various professional organizations in offering their syndicate shares strictly to members of that profession, such as doctors, teachers, engineers, airline pilots, government employees, etc. These syndicators tailor their projects and their selling approach to the investment desires of a particular profession or group of employees. By limiting solicitation to this kind of a group, they add the aura of exclusivity to the investment.

Building a Data Bank

Once well established as a syndicator, the typical developer has a data bank of all of the individuals who have contacted him or whom he has contacted over the years for real estate investment. In some cases, these files run into the thousands of names. When he has a project suitable, he merely goes back through his file and personally invites to a meeting those on the list he feels would be interested.

A source of potential investors used by some syndicators is the limited partnership Certificates of Fictitious Firm Name. These are filed with the county recorder and which include names and addresses of all the limited partners of the partnerships on file. The county recorder has, in a metropolitan area, hundreds of partnerships on file with the names and addresses clearly delineated in the certificate. Centers of influence are listed in the yellow pages of the telephone book, with separate sections for attorneys, accountants, insurance brokers, the real estate brokers, etc. Mailings to centers of influence offering appropriate finder's fees or commissions, as the case may be, for the referral of prospective investors, is another marketing device.

Price of Entry

To the extent that initial investment can be kept to a minimum, the number of potential investors can be increased. In a particular area, there may be 100 potential investors for an investment that requires an initial investment of $100,000. There may be 1000 investors if the price of entry is $10,000 and there may be as many as 100,000 investors where the minimum initial price per unit is $1,000.

Lowering the initial capital investment to take advantage of a greater potential investor group is made possible by an arrangement with the seller of the property to take the required down payment and divide it over several payment periods. For example, if the seller wants 30% down, perhaps he would agree to take 10% down at close of escrow and the balance of 20% in four equal payments over a 24-month period. If the total down payment was $300,000, a 1% share would then be $3,000 and an investor could get in by paying $1,000 down and then four semi-annual payments of $500 each plus interest. Where the seller is not agreeable to this, it may be possible for the syndicator to arrange with a bank to do so. The bank puts up a portion of the down payment on an unsecured personal note calling for payments of the balance of the down payment over a period. Where the bank is not willing to loan based on the individual credit of the investor, the syndicator may arrange with the bank (if his credit is strong enough) to have the bank take as security for the loan the entity interest involved. The syndicator guarantees to purchase the entity interest from the bank for the balance of the loan in the event the investor should default.

The factor, which should be uppermost in the syndicator's mind, is the needs and desires of his prospective group of investors. The marketing program will be more successful if it can offer as many of these factors as possible:

(a) A low price of entry,

(b) High spendable income,

(c) Depreciation and tax shelter,

(d) Potential appreciation and inflation protection,

(e) High leverage,

(f) Minimum risk, or

(g) High potential return (speculation),

(h) Frequency of distribution

(i) Liquidity

In terms of long-term investor relationships and building a sound reputation, it is generally better to use a "soft sell" with regard to the benefits of the project. If it appears that the project will show 10% spendable, the syndicator should indicate that he estimates it will be something less than that sum. Where the investors receive more than they had expected, regardless of what the expectations were, they are generally happy and will return to purchase additional syndicate interests in new projects. Where, however, the investors receive less than they had been indicated they would receive, or the project takes a longer time to sell, they may become disillusioned with the syndicator. Regardless of his good intent, they may not reinvest with him in a later project. Good marketing is a successful balancing of the "soft sell" with proper motivational techniques to bring the investor to the point of executing the subscription agreement (and returning it with his check).

Caution Regarding Inter-state Offerings

The SEC and some state commissioners has taken the position that certain lecture activities (and by implication, other marketing activities) which pre-condition the public to the purchase of limited partnership interests through promotional seminars, without the prior filing of a registration statement, may be a violation of registration requirements. The nature and conduct of such activities must be carefully examined with a view toward the attitude of the SEC where inter-state activity may be involved, and the appropriate state agency in every state where the offering is to be made.

Offering Circulars

In addition to what may be required to conform to state and federal regulations, keep in mind that the offering circular (state) or prospectus (federal) is a sale document. It should be easy to read, contain at least one good photo of the project, and answer the typical investor's questions.

CHAPTER 18

GUARANTEES AND
REAL ESTATE SYNDICATE SECURITIES*

Guarantees as a Marketing Device

To make a proposed offering attractive to potential investors, the syndicator often considers using a guarantee as part of the marketing program. Such arrangements also have their place in the secondary market where individual owners of syndicate interests often find that the use of a guarantee helps liquidate the interest, if it should be necessary, prior to the time that the real estate project reaches its ultimate objective.

For purposes of this article, the person who agrees to guarantee is referred to as the "obligor" and the person to whom the guarantee runs is referred to as the "oblige." The offering will be more attractive if the guarantee terms are attractive and obligor has sufficient resources to perform a guarantee. The use of a guarantee not only broadens the number of potential offerees, but also often serves to shorten the marketing time required to raise the necessary capital for the down payment on the respective property.

Advantageous bargains can be secured where the contingency and/or escrow period is relatively short and the use of guarantees to shorten the time required for syndicate marketing, may give the syndicator the opportunity to negotiate on a basis of early elimination of contingencies (an escrow period of ninety days or less) and a contingency period of thirty days or less.

Definition

For purposes of this chapter, a real estate syndicate security is defined as an undivided interest in real property, subject to qualification prior to sale under either the Corporate Securities Act of 1968 in California or similar legislation in other states. It will include those interests that are exempt from qualification under the private offering exemption as defined in those acts. Except for this exemption, they would be subject to the qualification (and are nonetheless subject to all of the other provisions of the acts).

Generally, in the past, such securities were interests in limited partnerships organized pursuant to the Uniform Limited Partnership Act. In certain circumstances, however, they take the form of other entities. The discussion outlined here will be

* Taken from an article by the Author appearing in the Beverly Hills Bar Journal, November - December 1971. Permission to reprint is gratefully acknowledged.

relevant to the other forms of holding real property jointly, such as limited liability companies, tenancy in common, joint tenancy, trusts, etc., as well.

The two basic classes of guarantees are:

A. Rate of return, and

B. Return of principal.

These may both be present in a given offering, or in modified combination. Under some circumstances, only a rate of return is guaranteed and, in the alternative, in others only the return of principal. It is more common to guarantee rate of return for a period of time than to guarantee return of principal. Where the rate of return is relatively high, it is in the best interests of the offeror to guarantee only return of principal at an end of a period of time. Where the rate of return is relatively low, it is in the best interests of the offeror to guarantee only the rate of return. While return of principal is usually guaranteed by a repurchase provision, a master lease usually guarantees the rate of return to the syndicator. Such a lease may have security in terms of the syndicator or seller of the property having pledged his equity in purchase-money financing being carried back by him.

Class of Obligor

In analyzing the legal and economic effect of guarantees, it is necessary to categorize them into five classes:

(1) The obligor is the entity itself (the entity obligation is sometimes backed up by setting aside cash reserves for this purpose);

(2) The obligor is the syndicator or manager as distinguished from the entity. (Such assurance depends on obligor's ability to perform.);

(3) The obligor is an individual holder of the interest being sold (usually applicable only in the secondary market);

(4) The obligor is a third party; or

(5) A combination of the above, such as the situation where the entity itself may be the primary obligor and the syndicator or has guaranteed the performance of the entity.

Extent of Obligation

Such guarantees can be further categorized by the nature and extent of the obligation. For example, a repurchase guarantee might:

(1) require repurchase at the original purchase price, plus additional assessments or contributions and a guaranteed minimum return to the investor at any time during the period of investment;

(2) be limited to a particular period of the investment holding (A typical provision allows exercise after the first twelve months but prior to the expiration of thirty-six months of the holding period.);

(3) contain certain adjustments in the purchase price that would make the repurchase guarantee less onerous on the obligor, such as:

> (a) allow a credit for tax benefits which the holder may enjoy due to investing in and holding the particular interest during the time owned by the obligee;

> (b) allow a credit for any cash flow enjoyed by the obligee because of his investment during the holding period;

> (c) allow a credit for legal and transfer fees;

> (d) contain an arbitrary discount (such as 10% of the investment) or a discount for factors that take into consideration original marketing costs, etc.;

> (e) require an independent third-party appraisal rather than any set mathematical formula determining the price.

An appraisal might be used to create a downward or upward adjustment in the repurchase price. There might also be an option in favor of the obligor to defer the repurchase price for a period, with or without interest. If with interest, it might provide whether or not the interest is compound or non-compound and whether or not to be paid periodically or with the final installment of the purchase price.

The guarantee of return on investment could take one or more of the following forms:

A. A flat percentage of original capital investment, with no credit for amounts received in prior years in excess of that rate;

B. An average rate of return, taking credit for excess amounts received in prior years over the guaranteed rate;

C. Return computed on periodic appraised value, rather than original capital investment;

D. Rate computed on net after-tax investment (after an adjustment for an assumed tax bracket);

E. Guarantee to continue only until investor has received, due to distributions, the return of his original cash investment, without consideration of tax benefits;

F. Guarantee to continue only until investor has received, due to distributions, the return of his net after-tax investment (after adjustment for an assumed tax bracket).

The foregoing provisions would only be effective in those years where distribution available from operations does not meet original guaranteed projections.

A popular mid-way point between a guarantee of return and guarantee of original investment is for the investor to have the option to require the syndicator to repurchase the investment for a period for the net after-tax investment of the investor, taking credit for all distributions the investor has received, and all tax benefits. In this situation, an arbitrary tax bracket of the respective investor is usually what is applied in determining the amount to be paid.

Automatic Expiration

In addition to the passage of a period of time, a number of other factors should be included, which would trigger an automatic cancellation of the obligation:

A. Change in the status of one or both parties, such as death, incapacity, domicile or residence, bankruptcy, or other act of insolvency, etc.;

B. Assignment by one or both parties of their interest in the project. If this is not intended to cancel the guarantee, a provision should be included that the guarantee is binding on heirs and assigns of one or both parties as the case may be;

C. A change with respect to the investment itself, such as an increase or reduction in cash flow, net equity of the project, etc.; or

D. A certain number or dollar amount of guarantees being presented to the obligor within a limited period, creating an obligation greater (over that period)

than he might be willing to undertake. An alternative to outright cancellation in this circumstance would be the proration of the obligation to repurchase over the number and amount of guarantees being presented for repurchase and/or a spreading out of the obligation. Another would be to meet repurchase requests in order presented.

Mutuality

The consideration for the execution of the guarantee is the original purchase of the interest by the obligee either from the obligor or from some third party. In certain circumstances, however, a guarantee may be supported by independent consideration other than the original sale of the interest. The right to require repurchase need not be mutual. (Where there is consideration for any agreement in a contract, the contract as a whole does not lack mutuality. Tenant v. Wilde, 277 Pac. 137, 98 Cal. App. 437 1929.)

The obligor may be able to bargain for the right in his favor to elect to repurchase (an option on the obligee's interest in the security) at an agreed premium. Such possibility should be given consideration.

Effect on Qualification

Where a guarantee is part of the original issuance and sale, whether such guarantee is in favor of one or all of the investors, and whether it is an obligation of the entity or not, it must be disclosed to the investors and included in any application for qualification in an offering circular, because it was a material part of the original offering. When there is a provision that confers a benefit on the obligor, such as a right of first refusal, right to elect to repurchase in favor of the obligor, right to repurchase at a discount, etc., such benefits are part of the compensation earned by the obligor when they result from the initial syndication. They there-fore may affect the amount of allowable promotional interest under the rules of the commissioner.

When the guarantee is negotiated in the secondary market (not part of the original stream of distribution) between the actual holder of the interest being sold and the new purchaser (whether or not the seller was the syndicator in the original issuance), the disclosure of the guarantee to the other limited partners is probably not required. A repurchase guarantee is subject to any rights of first refusal in favor of the entity or the remaining limited partners, and a notice to those having the right of first refusal must include the full terms and conditions of the repurchase guarantee. If consent to transfer is required in connection with the sale in the secondary market, the terms of the repurchase guarantee must be included in the material submitted to the respective commissioner for approval of the transfer.

An initial offering exempt as a private offering should not lose its exemption by the mere inclusion of the repurchase guarantee. However, in some circumstances, the nature of the repurchase guarantee may be such as to convert the interest from an equity security to a debt security. In those cases, counsel may want to consider the provisions of the relevant corporate securities act with respect to exemptions for debt securities. A key factor in determining whether the particular interest is in actuality a debt security rather than an equity security is who the obligor is. Where the obligor is the entity itself, particularly if a minimum rate of return is guaranteed, the guarantee may constitute a debt security. However, if the guarantee is executed by an individual holder thereof in connection with the resale in the secondary market, it probably is not. If there is a possibility of being construed as a debt security, counsel will also want to examine the provisions of the respective usury law to make sure that the obligee has not inadvertently violated the same.

Necessity for Writing

In most real estate syndicates, the applicability of the Statute of Frauds (Cal. Code of Civil Procedure 1624 & 1971) and the Parole Evidence Rule (Cal. Code of Civil Procedure 1856) to the requirement of a writing with respect to a repurchase guarantee is academic. Either the partnership agreement itself (the better practice), or the offering circular, or both, will state that there are no agreements or representations concerning the transaction other than those contained therein. For this reason, such guarantees should always be in writing. In documenting the transfer of a real estate syndicate interest, there should be included in the assignment documents a statement that the assignment is without recourse and that there are no representations other than those that may have been specifically made in writing between the transferor and the transferee. Even absent such provision, however, the circumstances of the guarantee may generally such as to require it to be in writing. For example, where the terms indicate that it cannot be performed within one year, the obligor is guaranteeing another's obligation to repurchase, etc.

Provision should be made that notice requiring the obligor to perform be in writing. It should be sent in some manner that provides reasonable assurance that the obligor has received the written notice, such as registered mail. The securing of an affidavit of mailing executed by an independent third party is advisable.

Tax Considerations

The guarantee should be structured in such a manner as to avoid adverse tax consequences that could accrue to one or both of the parties. If the repurchase is being completed within the calendar year of original sale, the entire tax consequences of ownership for that year may be available to the obligor, if this is the expressed intent of the parties. (Applicable only where the sale is less than 50% interest in capital and profits, and the effective date of partner substitution is date of commencement of partnership year, rather than date of agreement. See IRC 706 (c). Note IRS may not acquiesce in the substitution.) In other cases, the obligor may receive a new basis for the respective share of the syndicate repurchased rather than take the obligee's basis, which may be much lower than repurchase investment. (IRC 743(b) providing election is made under IRC 754.)

Consideration also has to be given to such provisions of the tax law as the (a) recapture provisions relating to accelerated depreciation; (b) tax preference items where applicable; (c) the deductibility of investment interest: and, (d) the deductibility of investment interest and, (e) transactions structured without "business purpose" (On audit, the IRS usually will disallow alleged tax benefits if there is no business purpose – IRC 162, 183, 212.)

Whether or not the inclusion of a repurchase guarantee will be determinative of a non-business purpose is one that must be carefully examined, in the circumstances of the particular transaction. For example, the practice of having a repurchase guarantee to buy back an all-inclusive deed of trust or secondary financing at a discount from its face value is highly questionable. (For "Sham Transaction Doctrine" see Estate of Martin Melcher, et al v. Commissioner, T. C. Memo, 1970-237, CCH Dec. 30, 298 (M)).

If the repurchase guarantee should be of such a nature as to indicate, because of its attractiveness to the obligee, intent at the time of original purchase to exercise it, the Internal Revenue Service, on audit, might take the position that there was not the requisite investment intent required for capital gain treatment. (See Malat v. Riddell, 569,86S.Ct. 1030 (1966).)

Conclusion

While the guarantee is a useful marketing tool which can effectively aid the solicitation and sale of real estate syndicate securities, both in the original issuance and in the secondary market, the syndicator should give careful consideration to the alternatives open to him in structuring such guarantees and consult closely with legal and tax counsel before making a decision to use the guarantee and its type and nature.

CHAPTER 19
PROVIDING LIQUIDITY
FOR SYNDICATE INTERESTS

It is important for the long-range success of the syndicator to not only initially market the syndication, but also to provide liquidity to the investor by creating a market that the investor may want to dispose of or borrow on. This liquidity can be provided in a number of different ways:

1. By a guarantee from the syndicator or some other financially responsible entity to repurchase the interests for a set price for a certain period. These repurchase agreements are usually for a limited period starting one year after the formation of the partnership, and are for the original purchase price together with, in some cases, interest at 6 or 7%. (See chapter "Guarantees and Real Estate Syndicate Securities").

2. By raising extra funds, which serve as a repurchase fund, or withholding a certain portion of income for a repurchase fund.

3. By providing that the remaining partners will pay, on demand of the withdrawing partner, a certain formula price for the withdrawing partner's interest over a period.

4. By arranging with the investor's bank (or if they will not cooperate then the syndicator's bank) for a loan on the syndicate interest for a portion of its value (usually between 50% to 80%) backed up by an agreement from the syndicator to purchase the share pledged from the bank in the event of default for the unpaid balance of principal and interest then due on the loan.

Problem of Motivation

One of the problems of creating a resale market for syndicate shares is the lack of motivation for the resale of such shares. Reasonable compensation of from 5% to 15% of the resale price may be required to encourage individuals to market such shares and sell them. Where there is a small resale market, the amount of commission even at 10% on a $5,000 unit is only $500. This is not much money available to advertise the sale of the share or to put on a sales campaign. Psychologically, the fact that a new investor would invest in a new project as well as the old one means that the syndicator would rather have the individual invest in the new project, where in addition to the commission on the sale of the syndicate interest, he may have other advantages and over-rides (rather than sell an existing share where such advantages and overrides have already been earned).

Where an organization has many projects and therefore has a continuous supply of shares to resell, they can afford to maintain a normal resale market. A single project syndication with limited resources faces a different task in maintaining a resale market.

Sales Techniques

There are a number of sales techniques that the syndicator can use in remarketing previously sold syndicate shares:

1. Emphasize the security of the investment and the lack of risk because there is now an operating history under his management.

2. Point out the additional leverage due to the fact of faster equity build-up. In the early years on a declining balance loan, the payments have a greater proportion of interest and less amortization than they do in the later years. Therefore, one who purchases in the later years has a greater equity build-up in relation to his investment than one who purchased the partnership interest in its earlier years.

3. Take advantage of discount factor where "soft dollars" were involved in the original purchase. Take the case of a project that was purchased for prepaid interest and interest only terms. The seller, in order to realize cash, might be willing to sell for a considerable discount over what he has invested, because he had gotten a substantial tax benefit in prior years by purchasing the partnership share with "soft dollars." This means that a much smaller cash requirement may be needed. At the time of resale, the property may have matured to where the future sale of the property at a profit is much closer in point of time than it was when the partnership was organized. This would give the purchaser much greater return than if he had been an original investor.

The Entity Agreement

In designing the entity agreement, careful thought should be given to the problems involved in resale. Rights of first refusal should run generally only to the manager so that a resale can be accomplished expeditiously without having to contact large number of investors. This is particularly important in an entity where there are a large number of investors.

There should be automatic rights to transfer to certain classes of persons such as blood relatives, heirs at law, etc., without having to go through the formal transfer requirements. (However, note possible adverse tax consequences if the IRS should take the position there is "Free Transferability.")

It should be kept in mind that retirement-oriented individuals might prefer the purchase of existing entity shares, where they can buy them at a discount, or where there is more substantial equity build-up than in a newly created entity. While the tax aspects of purchasing existing interests may not be as attractive as the purchase of interests in newly formed syndicates, the already amortized debt and history of returns should make purchasing interest in successful products attractive.

From Time to Time

There are broker-dealers who maintain a secondary market in the shares of some of the larger syndicate entities. There are also private individuals who purchase shares of established syndicate entities, in the belief that they are in some cases a more advantageous purchase. They cite among their reasons for such belief the following:

(1) The seller, being motivated and having a limited market, may accept a discount off the market value of the underlying property;

(2) There is an established project operating history enabling an evaluation of how the syndicator has performed with this project;

(3) They may pick up the benefit of mortgage amortization that has already occurred; and

(4) There is an opportunity to evaluate whether value has been added, appreciation of the neighborhood has occurred, and other post acquisition factors have taken place.

CHAPTER 20
THE NEW SYNDICATION STRATEGY

The 21st century has seen a new and different approach to real estate syndication because of a number of important changes in the market for investments. These changes include:

1. Inflation Rate. A lower rate of inflation. When the rate of inflation is low, the portion of gain that can be projected from depreciation drops and a higher portion of the required investment return must come from other factors, such as cash flow and tax benefits.

2. Increase in Value. The perception of attractiveness of real estate investment has fallen and then rebounded. During the preceding decades, real estate increased in value from year-to-year at a space that often exceeded that of other investments. In the early 1990's real estate actually declined in value in many areas and the market no longer anticipated that gains would come from speculation or increased demand. Both the demand of investors for real estate, as well as the demand of users for real estate declined in many categories. Office buildings were particularly hard hit and the demand for office space declined to such a degree that many buildings no longer produced enough income to cover their operation expense in major metropolitan areas. Now rapid gains since the year 2000 have given the impression (as of 2006) that real estate is the way to quick wealth.

3. Tax Laws. Changes in the tax laws commencing in the mid 1980's reduced the attractiveness of real estate as a tax shelter. Depreciation periods were extended. More importantly, as is explained in the tax chapter, the division of income and losses in various "baskets" has the ultimate effect for many investors, preventing the use of artificial accounting losses against earned income or investment income. Syndication in the 1970s and early 1980s often emphasized the income tax benefits of owning real estate. These benefits, in many cases, more than made up for nominal or lack of cash flow.

4. Interest Rates. The decline in interest rates brought a return of opportunity of positive leverage through financing. As the market yields on real estate increased while the interest rate on debt declined, the spread between the conventional loan interest rate and the market capitalization rate on which property could be acquired increased. This created, for the first time in many years, double-digit returns on equity on a leveraged basis through the 1990s, with the financing rate of return on a free-and-clear basis (cap rate), as of 2006, often or below interests rates positive leverage is hard to come by. This now appears to be changing with interest rates increasing as of 2006.

5. Return on Investment. With interest rates down, the return on money market investments and bank deposits dropped to as low as 1%. For those on fixed incomes or who look to their investments for cash flow, real estate has become an attractive vehicle even at low cap rates. Nevertheless, rates have been on the rise.

6. Shortage of Cash Flow Investments. Conservative investors are considering real estate, since prices on some types of property are below replacement costs, providing some protection against the market competition even when cash flow yields are at historical lows.

7. Appreciation Opportunities. Investment advisors and the investing public in general has become much more knowledge and sophisticated about real estate investment. Demands for thorough due diligence and full disclosure by both regulatory authorities and the investment community are now well established. There are always opportunistic individuals who will take advantage of any investment trend by putting together unsound (and in some cases non-existent) investments. There is always the possibility of making a mistake in the selection of property today's low interest rate. Lack of new construction in certain categories makes real estate looks attractive to many. The possibility of making a real estate investment mistake post 2006, as opposed to the 1980s, may be reduced somewhat, assuming it is acquired at a proper market price. Prices are stabilizing after a sharp gain in many markets. The opportunity for further price appreciation in the near term is speculative.

8. Liquidity of Investment. One of the greatest concerns is liquidity and the fact that a syndicated real estate interest as a limited partnership share or a tenancy in common may have no resale market. In the past, one had to hold the investment until the property was eventually sold to receive the return of capital. Among the reasons for this were the following, which have not changed:

> a. Limited market of traders in limited partnership shares;

> b. The emphasis on appreciation and tax benefits in some syndications was highly speculative;

> c. The tax benefit that had been taken by the original subscribers could not be enjoyed to the same degree by later purchasers of the shares, without complication and expensive accounting and legal assistance;

9. Secondary Market Possibilities. Newly formed current real estate investments often have substantial cash flow and little appreciation and little tax benefits. There is now a greater interest in the secondary market in purchasing such shares since they not only provide higher cash flow than other investments and have the advantage of maturity and a tract record. Other factors are the existence of a larger secondary market with a number of companies handling the resale of syndicate shares.

10. Syndication Types. There are two basic forms of syndicators. Financially Oriented Syndicators have no real estate experience, background or investment motivation and receive their primary compensation from putting together the syndicate and selling the syndicate shares. Operational Syndicators make profits from operation of the property. They can be distinguished by having a long real estate record of accomplishment, a depth of management, low front-end fees, and primarily back-end compensation emphasizing performance. Just as no-load funds have grown as a percentage of the mutual fund market, syndicate investors have become more sophisticated. Therefore, Operational Syndicators should grow as a share of the total syndicate market. With the decline of opportunity for appreciation and the elimination of tax benefits, operational skills and experience is what is valued in the market place. Underwriters and institutional investors will search out the operationally oriented syndicators.

11. New Techniques. There are new techniques and software programs for analyzing syndicate offerings to predict their degree of success. They may have greater reliability than those used in the past.

12. Managed Leverage. The trend toward the securitization of real estate has resulted in a higher price for real estate in security form and reversed a long time trend. The real estate market would often place a lower capitalization rate and therefore pay a higher price for direct real estate assets than in the securities market. Real estate investment could be made by buying public vehicles such as, REITs and larger public limited partnerships in some periods at discounts off the market price of the underlying real estate.

As of 2006, the real estate syndicate market is alive and strong. Emphasis is on current cash flow rather than appreciation, although the market will give some recognition to opportunity for growth. A higher premium will be paid for current dividend and growth when there are opportunities for the use of positive leverage. However, the sophisticated market will continue to be risk averse and prefer that leverage be conservatively used. Leverage in most cases, will be confined to no more than 70% of property value in private syndications. Private syndications should be able to carry a higher debt factor, due to lower operating costs and lower front-end loads than public syndication.

14. Protecting the Public's Trust. Syndicators should watch interest rates. If they rise dramatically because of inflation expectations, there will be a shift in the type of syndicate product brought to market, with emphasis on appreciation and inflation becoming a greater part of the overall yield estimate.

Over-leveraging, high front-end fees, negligent due diligence and underwriting and withdrawal of tax benefits resulted in the demise of thrift industry, as well as lots of property sold at bargain prices by the RTC, FDIC and others, in the past. Lack of operational experience gave the real estate syndicate industry a bad reputation. Many of these factors have been addressed. Real estate syndicates are again an attractive alternate investment opportunity for the sophisticated investor who desires cash flow.

15. Inflation Protection. When the proper circumstances are present, real estate can be a low risk opportunity to protect capital against inflation. Inflation protection, while not the dominant investment motive, can be (even at the low level of 3% inflation) an advantage to holding capital in real estate over money market investment. When the interest rate payout for money market funds and certificate of deposit are 3%, and real estate investment brings 5% cash flow with 3% inflation for a real yield of 5%, real estate is extremely attractive against a money market yield of zero after inflation.

16.   Stock Market. The stock market often reaches historic highs. Overall returns from stocks at times exceed those of real estate. Nevertheless, the return is principally from appreciation rather than dividends. For those seeking portfolio balance, there is demand for well- conceived, property underwritten, and well-run real estate projects. The stock market also benefits by the desire of institutional investors, such as large pension funds, to shift from direct ownership of real estate to owning real estate in security form such as REITs.

17.   Leverage. The combination of the foregoing has generated a strong interest in acquiring real estate syndicate shares, where the overall return of the investment is based on current cash flow rather than appreciation or tax benefits. Even with real estate market prices up and capitalization rates down, it has become possible to acquire properties at 8% or better total returns (5% cash flow and 3% inflation) on an all-cash basis and put on 2/3 debt at 6%, so that the total return on equity will be 12% or better..

CHAPTER 21
HOW TO ANALYZE AN OFFERING

The following are some of the factors that apply to any syndicate offering whether it is real estate oil, gas or other resources, a motion picture, equipment leasing, recreational use project, or an operating business.

Ignore the Hype

The quality and attractiveness of the offering material and presentation is not reflective of the quality of the project itself. The greatest failures often have the most beautiful brochures and professional road show presentations. An overly elaborate brochure and/or road show is often an attempt to make up for deficiencies in the project itself. Be suspicious of any offering which appears "too good to be true" since often it is. The offering materials should be easily understood, with a clear, comprehensive summary covering the key factors that an investor should know. If projections are included, the assumptions should be spelled out and must be evaluated carefully by someone qualified to do so.

Track Record

1. Is there a record of accomplishment for the project itself, as well as a record of accomplishment for the syndicators? How detailed are they?

2. What is the reputation of the individual making the offering?

The Syndication

3. Is it blind pool or a specified project?

4. What due diligence has been performed by the syndicator? Has it been reviewed by the accountant for the syndicator, by the attorney for the syndicate, and by the underwriter?

5. Is it a single asset project or a multiple asset project?

6. Is the syndication a public or private offering?

7. What are its resources to respond to difficulties?

8. Is the syndicator an operational-experienced, hands-on real estate professional (Main Street background)? Alternatively, is he financially experienced (Wall Street background)?

9. How focused is the syndicator on this project? What is the depth of its organization; what is it track record?

10. What is the experience of professionals involved, such as, the attorneys, accountants, etc.? While not necessarily an indication of quality, large, national, or regional firms are more likely to carry errors and omissions insurance.

11. What is the total front-end load? Has it been fully disclosed, both on the total asset and on the equity portion?

12. What is the degree of debt leverage?

13. When does debt mature and is it at a fixed or a variable rate? Assess the impact of leverage on risk in relation to income stream. The stronger the equality of the income stream, the more leverage the property can accept in relation to risk. A property with AAA long-term leases and a high degree of anchors can accept more leverage than one that may have a lot of potential, but tenants of lesser credit quality.

14. What is the operational load? Property management, asset management and charge backs for items that under industry practice are normally included in management fees.

15. How is the syndicator compensated for performance?

16. Carefully examine expense projections and past history. Many syndicators in the past have failed because of inadequate provisions for operating expenses and reserves. In some product types, such as apartments, there will be industry averages available for comparison. Sources of these averages are real estate trade organizations such as the Building Owners, and Managers Association, the International Council of Shopping Centers, Institute of Real Estate Management, etc. Multi-tenant properties often have higher expense ratios than single-tenant properties.

17. What kind of property is it? Apartment expenses are dependent on the quality of the tenancy. Family oriented buildings, and buildings in disadvantage areas have substantially higher operating expenses than buildings in high-income areas. Higher rentals do not necessarily mean lower operating expenses, although in some situations that may be the case. Local factors such as taxes, utility rates, and wage rates will have an impact. There is wide variation from national averages. Try to secure expense comparison ratios that are geographically focused locally.

Search Out Conflicts of Interest

18. The nature of the investment affects what may constitute a conflict of interest. Where the operation itself is a consideration in a business investment rather than a specific real estate project, a different consideration must be given to conflicts of interest, than where the project is a single-asset project. A single property real estate project conflict assessment will focus on the fees and compensation of the syndicator. In an ongoing operating business investment, how committed the syndicator is to the business, the presence of a majority of independent directors, and internal management and staffing take on importance.

Liquidity

19. There should be an inverse relationship between liquidity and yield. Investment that is highly liquid will generally carry a lower yield than one that has little liquidity. A small private offering will not have a secondary market and should have a lower front-end operating load than a public vehicle.

20. Where there is a provision for buy-back reserves, the yield will be less, since the funds will not be fully invested.

Exit Strategy and Projections

21. These need to be carefully examined.

22. Is the going out cap rate higher (speculative) or lower than the going in cap rate (conservative)? How realistic are these in relation to the market and comparative properties?

23. How much of the motivation is tax oriented versus pre-tax economic gain?

Market Direction

24. Is the market for the type of project in an upward or a downward trend? In other words, is this a contrarian investment, or a "follow the herd" investment?

CHAPTER 22
CONCLUSION

If someone wishes to be a successful syndicator, he should start by concentrating on acquiring the skill to (a) select a proper project, (b) find qualified management for that project, and (c) the coordinate of the other elements involved. He can start on any level of investors, with one or two other people, or with a large group. If he picks his project correctly and it is successful, eventually he will be overwhelmed with investors, and future projects will be oversubscribed.

In time, he will find a rather amazing thing happening. When he is a successful syndicator, not only the investors, but institutions such as banks, insurance companies, and investment funds will start pressing money upon him. Eventually, he may be in the position where, if he sees a good property and it is an advantageous buy, he will be able to go to his bank and say, "Look, this property will cost me $1,000,000 cash down, and it is a very good buy. I only have enough investors for $500,000 and it will take me another six months to raise the rest." The bank may lend him funds based on his experience as a syndicator and the fact that they know there is a very good chance that he will sell out the project.

Syndicators generally are careful not to extend themselves beyond their immediate resources by trying to invest as little of their own cash as possible. If a syndicator buys a $100,000 property and has a $70,000 loan on it, and makes a 30% mistake, there is nothing left as equity. It is very easy to make a mistake that will destroy the cash equity. The nature of the real estate business is such that in a given market, some properties are offered at prices that are higher than their then-true value.

Therefore, the time spent in selecting a project and performing due diligence is the most important part of any syndication. The time when the project is made or broken is the first four to six months before the close of a purchase escrow, while the developer is choosing the property, drawing the documents, making plans as we have seen in previous chapters.

Generally, the safest procedure for a syndicator is to always deal with investors with whom he has established previous personal contact. He should take his time in carefully selecting the property he wants to buy, tie it up with an escrow or option agreement, select an attorney and accountant to assist in developing the syndication plan, and, finally, after the proper procedures have been followed and his plans committed to paper, solicit his investors for actual investment in the specific project.

Franchising

The franchisor often bears a similar relationship to the franchisee, in many respects, as the syndicator does to the investor. Where the franchisee is paying a substantial fee for a business plan and assistance in operation of that plan, the franchisee is relying on the representations of the franchisor as to past operations and as to the franchisor's abilities, experience, and financial standing. Therefore, the franchisor must make full disclosure of those elements that the franchisee is relying on in reaching the decision to make the franchise investment.

Obviously, the degree of disclosure that will be required will vary depending upon the nature of the franchise. If the franchise is merely a simple license agreement to sell a product, rather than a complete business plan with assistance and guidance, the nature of the disclosure will be of a different scope and degree than where the franchisee is, in a sense, buying a full business operation.

Many governmental jurisdictions have regulations governing the sale and operation of franchises. There are many special provisions that should be included in a franchise agreement to protect the respective interests of the franchisee and the franchisor, similar to provisions that would be in the investment contract between the syndicator and the investor. Among the provisions that might be considered are:

1) Buy and Sell Agreements

2) Liquidity and resale

3) Reports and their frequency

4) Disclosures

5) Minimum sales requirements

6) Exclusive territory

7) Capital requirements

8) Uniform accounting systems

9) Advertising commitments

Other Forms of Syndication

Time sharing, condominiumizing, stock co-operating, and master leasing are some of the other ways that ownership of real estate can be divided for group ownership depending on the circumstances and should be explored.

Syndication Alternatives

Franchising is the licensing of the right to use a name, process, or product, usually for a fee and percentage of income. It has been successfully used in management-intensive real estate as a way to raise capital and a substitute to syndication. The franchisor takes the position of the syndicator but in the form of a franchise or license, to operate such properties as motels, nursing homes, bars, restaurants, etc.

Conclusion

Fortunes have been made and lost in real estate syndication. Following the principles outlined in the preceding chapters combined with common sense and caution should increase the reader's chances for successful syndicating. We wish you the best.

PRINCIPLES
OF
REAL ESTATE
SYNDICATION

APPENDICES

APPENDICES
CONTENTS

APPENDIX A
LETTER OF INTENT

Date:

Re:

Dear:

Standard Management Company or assignee ("Purchaser") offers to purchase from legal owner ("Seller") the referenced property (the "Property") including all land, improvements, appurtenances, fixtures and personal property owned by Seller in connection with the Property.

1) Description: Fee simple lien free title to the Property consisting of approximately _____ acres of land (see site plan attached as Exhibit "A").

2) Purchase Price: The Purchase Price, $_____ will be paid all cash at the closing.

3) Seller's Deliveries, Review Period: Within _____ (__) days of execution of the Purchase Agreement, Seller shall, at Seller's expense, deliver the items listed on attached Exhibit "B". Purchaser shall have thirty (30) business days (the "Review Period") from receipt of the later of (a) all such items and (b) a fully executed copy of the Purchase Agreement, within which to review such items and to inspect and approve the physical structure and improvements on the Property. Failure to approve such items in writing shall constitute disapproval.

4) Deposit: Within three (3) business days of approval of all matters mentioned in paragraph 3 herein above, Purchaser shall deposit into escrow the sum of $_____ (the "Deposit") by bank letter of credit payable to Escrow Holder. Escrow Holder as security will hold such Deposit. The Deposit shall be promptly refunded to Purchaser if the closing does not occur, unless directly resulting solely from a failure by Purchaser to fulfill its obligations under the Purchase Agreement, in which case the Deposit will serve as liquidated damages and Seller's sole remedy against Purchaser.

5) Seller's Representations: Seller warrants the following:

a) There are no fire, seismic; or other civil or county code restrictions or violations exist which would affect the use of income of the Property.

b) There are no hazardous substances or material as defined by federal, state or local law on the Property; and

c) Such other ordinary and customary representations and warranties as may be mutually agreed upon between Purchaser and Seller during the documentation period set forth in paragraph 7 herein below which are not inconsistent with other provisions of this letter.

6) Tax Deferred Exchange: Each party agrees to participate in a tax deferred exchange transaction for the benefit of the other, providing such participation shall be at no cost, liability or other obligation to the accommodating party.

7) Documentation: Purchaser and Seller shall, within ten (10) business days after Purchaser's receipt of this offer signed by Seller, negotiate a consistent Purchase Agreement on Purchaser's form. During such period Seller will not offer for sale, accept any offer to purchase, advertise the Property, or employ a broker for the sale of the Property.

8) Prorations:

a) Rents, taxes and operating income and expenses will be prorated as of 12:00 midnight of the day preceding Closing. The apportionment of real estate taxes shall be pursuant to the best available evidence of real estate taxes (assessments and rates). If, after Closing, real estate taxes are for any reason to be determined to be higher than those apportioned at closing, Seller shall pay Purchaser any net increase. Seller shall pay any special assessments that are a lien at Closing.

b) Seller shall receive no credit for delinquent rent at Closing. All rental income received after the Closing shall be credited first to current rental income due. Purchaser will forward to Seller any non-prorated delinquent rentals as received.

9) Closing: The Closing of this transaction shall be at the office of Escrow Holder on a date, time and place to be specified by Purchaser within thirty (30) days after

the expiration of the Review Period. At Closing, Seller will pay the following costs and expenses:

a) Transfer and other taxes or fees on the deed;

b) To Purchaser, all tenant security and other deposits;

c) To Purchaser, all prepaid rents and other amounts;

d) All premiums for ALTA (or extended coverage) title insurance, UCC searches, endorsements and ALTA survey;

e) Real estate commissions and finders fees;

f) Recording and filing fees and escrow charges; and

g) With regard to any existing financing, mortgage transfer fees, intangible or other taxes, prepayment penalties and termination of filing fees for any UCC financing statements.

10) Counterparts: This agreement shall be effective when signed below or in counterpart, and photocopy, facsimile, electronic, or other copies shall have the same effect for all purposes as an ink-signed original.

11) Licensed Real Estate Broker: The sole shareholder of purchaser is a California licensed real estate broker and attorney. Seller agrees to pay Brokerage Company and Agents a real estate commission at close of escrow, pursuant to a separate agreement between Seller and Broker, but only if closing occurs. Purchaser and Seller represent and warrant to each other that they have had not dealings with other real estate brokers or finders regarding this transaction.

12) Risk of Loss: Risk of loss remains with Seller until Closing.

13) Purchaser's Source of Funds: Purchaser's sources of funds will be a combination of cash and bank lines of credit.

14) Purchaser's qualifications: A brief resume of Purchaser's President and a track record of property acquisitions are attached as Exhibit "C".

15) Assignment: Purchaser may sell or assign its interest in this offer or in the Purchase Agreement so long as it remains primarily liable to Seller for Purchaser's obligations.

Please indicate your acceptance of the foregoing by signing and returning a copy of this letter. THIS OFFER SHALL BE NULL AND VOID IF NOT ACCEPTED BY 5:00 P.M/PST, on _____, _____.

Respectfully,
STANDARD MANAGEMENT COMPANY

_____

APPROVED AND ACCEPTED BY THE UNDERSIGNED, WHO REPRESENTS THAT HE OR SHE IS DULY AUTHORIZED TO EXECUTE THIS OFFER ON BEHALF OF SELLER:

Signature: _____

Print Name: _____

Company: _____

Title: _____

Date: _____

Exhibit "A"
Site Plan
(To be provided)

Exhibit "B"
Seller's Deliveries

1. A current preliminary title report or commitment (the "Title Report") for the Real Property from First American Title Company, Mary Owens, 550 S. Hope Street, Suite 1950, Los Angeles, CA 90071, B:213.271.1727, F:213.271.1771, mnowens@firstam.com ("Title Company"), together with copies of all underlying documents of record referred to therein;

2. Three (3) copies of a currently dated survey ("Survey") prepared by a licensed professional surveyor reasonably acceptable to Purchaser, Purchaser's lender, and the Title Company, which shall (a) comply with the Minimum Standard Detail Requirements for ALTA/ACSM Land Title Surveys as adopted by the American Land Title Association and the American Congress on Surveying & Mapping, except that the Survey shall extend for a distance of twenty (20) feet onto adjoining properties; (b) list all title report exceptions; and (c) certify the following: (I) that, except as shown, no portion of the Real Property is located within a special flood hazard area; (II) the area and zoning of the Real Property and the dimensions, square feet and number of stories of all structures located thereon; (III) the number, location and type (standard, compact or handicap) of parking spaces; and (IV) the existing Title Policies for the Real Property in favor of Seller and its lenders as well as copies of any other Title Polices, expired or otherwise, in Seller's possession;

3. Reports regarding the presence of Hazardous Materials (including Radon) on or about the Property;

4. Copy of current rent roll including all expiration dates, prepaid rents, delinquencies, defaults, options, deposits and any special concessions (refundable of non-refundable);

5. Copies of last two (2) years' property tax assessments and bills;

6. List and copies of all management, maintenance and repair, and service and supply contracts, and other agreements, written or oral;

7. Copies of all loan documents, ground leases or any other documents evidencing obligations of Seller to be assumed by Purchaser, together with copies of all correspondence, memoranda, notes or other documents relating thereto;

8. Copies of all fire, extended risk, liability and other insurance policies in Seller's possession, and a schedule of the premiums, current claims and insurance loss claim records for the past 36 months;

9. All plans and specification in Seller's possession;

10. Evidence satisfactory to Purchaser regarding the completion of the improvements on the Real Property, including without limitation the Architect's Certificate of Substantial Completion, certificates of occupancy and all other documentation furnished to Seller's construction lender regarding such completion. If any notices are outstanding regarding any unperformed work and/or assessments for such work, Seller shall provide Purchaser with a detailed list thereof;

11. Copies of monthly and annual income and expense statements for the past three (3) years, utility and sewer bills for the last twelve (12) months and schedules of all capital improvements made over the past thirty-six (36) months;

12. Schedules of all Personal Property and fixtures with a separate list indicating personal property not being sold;

13. Schedules of current lawsuits pending or threatened and summary of the action and names of all parties and their attorneys;

14. Names, telephone numbers and addresses of architects, consultants and contractors who worked on Property, if available;

15. All feasibility studies, appraisals, demographic reports and consulting and marketing reports available to Seller.

Exhibit "C"
Brief Resume and Track Record

Samuel K. Freshman
Chairman & President, Standard Management Company

Mr. Freshman founded Standard Management Company in 1961. Since Standard's formation, Mr. Freshman's responsibilities have included implementation of Standard's investment strategy, development of business and negotiation of agreements. Mr. Freshman is a principal of all entities established by Standard and is responsible for their oversight. During his career, Mr. Freshman has been responsible for the acquisition, development and management of approximately $500 million of real property in 11 states and more than 25 cities.

Prior to his decision in 1983 to devote the majority of his time to Standard, Mr. Freshman founded and was the managing partner of the law firm of Freshman, Marantz, Orlanski, Cooper & Klein, which recently merged with Kirkpatrick and Lockhart. As a lawyer, Mr. Freshman specialized in real estate matters and real estate syndication. Prior to forming Freshman, Marantz, Orlanski, Cooper & Klein, Mr. Freshman was General Counsel of Jacob Sterns & Sons, a real estate investment company. Mr. Freshman is an acknowledged expert on real estate investment and has served as Adjunct Professor of Real Estate at the University of Southern California Graduate School of Business, and as an expert witness in over 50 cases. Mr. Freshman has also been the author of many articles on real estate syndication. Mr. Freshman received his Bachelor of Arts in pre-legal curriculum and his law degree from Stanford University.

Purchaser's Record of Multifamily Acquisitions

Property	Location	Units	Purchased
Lakeside Apartments	Burbank, CA	771	1973
Lincoln Arms Apartments	Anaheim, CA	424	1974
College Park Apartments	Santa Maria, CA	164	1974
Village Green Apartments	Lawton OK	229	1976
Timbers Apartments	Lawton, OK	149	1976
Parc Fontaine Apartments	New Orleans, LA	792	1977
Barcelona Apartments	Dallas, TX	449	1977
Front Royale Apartments	Houston, TX	195	1978
Heritage Apartments	Columbus, OH	592	1978
Tennesse Ridge Apartments	Nashville, TN	389	1978

Buena Vista Apartments	Dallas, TX	90	1978
Property	Location	Units	Purchased
Peachtree North Apartments	Atlanta, GA	236	1979
Forest Ridge Apartments	Atlanta, GA	122	1981
Highland Villa Apartments	Dallas, TX	235	1984
Colonial Square Apartments	Columbus, OH	192	1984
Lancaster Mobile Home Park	Lancaster, OH	370	1984
Oceana Apartments	Venice, CA	20	1989
Cabana Club	Las Vegas, NV	338	1996
Pacific Flamingo	Las Vegas, NV	104	1997
Sunscape Apartments	Las Vegas, NV	70	1998
Galleria Palms	Henderson, NV	216	1999
Bay Breeze Apartments	Henderson, NV	224	2000
Sunset Pointe Apartments	Las Vegas, NV	384	2002

AGREEMENT FOR SALE AND PURCHASE OF PROPERTY
AND JOINT ESCROW INSTRUCTIONS

THIS AGREEMENT OF SALE AND PURCHASE AND JOINT ESCROW
INSTRUCTIONS (**"Agreement"**) is made and entered into as of this __ day of
_____, 200_, by and between_____, a
_____("**Seller**"), and _____, a
_____ ("**Purchaser**"). In consideration of the mutual agreements
contained in this Agreement and for other good and valuable consideration, the
receipt and sufficiency of which are hereby acknowledged, Seller agrees to sell, and
Purchaser desires to purchase, the Property described below, for the Purchase Price
and upon the terms and conditions set forth below:

APPENDIX B
PURCHASE AGREEMENT (BUYER)

ARTICLE 1

CERTAIN DEFINITIONS AND FUNDAMENTAL PROVISIONS

This Article 1 sets forth certain definitions and fundamental provisions for purposes of this Agreement.

1.1. **"Purchaser's Address"** means:

_____	With a copy to:
6151 W Century Blvd. Ste. 300	_____
Los Angeles, California _____	_____
Attn:_____	Attn:_____
Facsimile: _____	Facsimile:_____
Telephone No.: _____	Telephone No.: _____
E-Mail: _____	E-Mail: _____

1.2. **"Seller's Address"** means:

	With a copy to:
_____	_____
_____	_____
_____	_____
Attn: _____	Attn: _____
Facsimile: _____	Facsimile:_____
Telephone No.: _____	Telephone No.: _____
E-Mail: _____	E-Mail: _____

1.3. **"Closing Date"** means _____, or any earlier date upon which Seller and Purchaser mutually agree upon in writing.

1.4. **"Deposit"** means: _____ Dollars ($_____). The Deposit shall be increased by all interest actually accrued on the Deposit while held by the Escrow Holder.

1.5. **"Effective Date"** means the later of Purchaser's receipt of (a) a fully-executed copy of this Agreement, or (b) all of Seller's Deliveries.

1.6. **"Seller's Deliveries"** means those items listed on Exhibit "B".

1.7. **"Escrow Holder"** means _____, whose address is:

_____

_____

_____

1.8. **"Review Period"** means the period commencing upon the Effective Date and ending at 5:00 p.m., P.S.T., on the date that is _____ (___) calendar days after the Effective Date.

1.9. **"Property"** means, collectively, the Real Property, and all of Seller's right, title and interest, if any, in the Contracts, the Intangible Property, the Leases, the Personal Property and the Security Deposits, as such terms are defined below.

   1.9.1. **"Real Property"** means the Land and the Improvements, located at _____, and commonly known as "_____".

   1.9.2. **"Land"** means that certain land more particularly described on Exhibit "A" attached hereto, together with all right, title and interest of Seller, reversionary or otherwise, in and to all easements in or upon such land and all other rights and appurtenances belonging or in anywise pertaining to such land.

   1.9.3. **"Improvements"** means all structures, improvements and fixtures located on the Land.

   1.9.4. **"Contracts"** means all assignable service, supply, maintenance and construction contracts, if any, relating to the Real Property or Personal Property.

   1.9.5. **"Intangible Property"** means all assignable intangible personal property, if any, now or through the date of Closing owned by Seller and arising out of or in connection with Seller's ownership of the Real Property and the Personal Property, including the right to use the current names, logos, trademarks and trade names of the Real Property, the goodwill of Seller in connection with the Real Property, all licenses, permits and certificates of occupancy issued by governmental authorities relating to the use, maintenance, occupancy and/or operation of the Real Property and Personal Property, all plans, specifications and drawings relating to the construction of the Improvements, and all warranties and guaranties with respect to the Real Property.

   1.9.6. **"Leases"** means any tenant leases now or hereafter affecting the Real Property.

1.9.7. **"Personal Property"** means all fixtures, furniture, carpeting, draperies, appliances, building supplies, equipment, machinery, inventory, and other tangible items of personal property owned by Seller and presently affixed, attached to, placed or situated upon the Real Property and used in connection with the ownership, operation and occupancy of the Real Property. Personal Property does not include any items of personal property leased to Seller or otherwise owned by third parties or Tenants.

1.9.8. **"Security Deposits"** means all refundable security deposits of tenants at the Property (the "Tenants"), if any, held by and in the possession of Seller.

1.10. **"Purchase Price"** means

_____ Dollars

($_____).

1.11. **"Title Company"** means _____, whose address is:

_____

_____

_____

Attn: _____

Facsimile: _____

Telephone No.: _____

E-Mail: _____

ARTICLE 2

CONSIDERATION

2.1. Purchase Price (OPTION A: ALL CASH). The Purchase Price to be paid by Purchaser to Seller for the sale and conveyance of the Property is specified in Section 1.10, and shall be payable to Seller at the closing of the transaction contemplated hereby (**"Closing"**) by wire transfer of immediately available federal funds, subject to prorations and adjustments at the Closing Date as provided in this Agreement, which funds must be delivered in a manner to permit Escrow Holder to deliver good funds to the Seller or its designee on the Closing Date. **Purchase Price (OPTION B: CASH TO EXISTING FINANCING)**.A portion of the Purchase Price specified in Section 1.10 to be paid by Purchaser to Seller for the sale and conveyance of the Property equal to the unpaid principal balance on the Closing

Date of that certain indebtedness of approxi-mately _____

Dollars ($_____) shall be deemed paid by Purchaser taking the Property subject to the lien of the deed of trust encumbering the Property dated _____(the "Existing Deed of Trust") in favor of _____, as Beneficiary, securing a promissory note (the "Existing Note") in the original principal amount of _____ Dollars ($_____), copies of which note and deed of trust are attached hereto as **Exhibits "P"** and **"Q"**, respectively; and Purchaser shall receive the benefit of reduction in the principal balance of the existing note by all payments made prior to the close.2.2The balance of the Purchase Price shall be payable to Seller at the closing of the transaction contemplated hereby ("**Closing**") by wire transfer of immediately available federal funds, subject to prorations and adjustments at the Closing Date as provided in this Agreement, which funds must be delivered in a manner to permit Escrow Holder to deliver good funds to the Seller or its designee on the Closing Date. **Purchase Price (OPTION B; CASH TO EXISTING FINANCING)**. A portion of the Purchase Price specified in Section 1.10 to be paid by Purchaser to Seller for the sale and conveyance of the Property equal to _____ Dollars ($_____) shall be payable to Seller at the closing of the transaction contemplated hereby ("**Closing**") by wire transfer of immediately available federal funds, subject to prorations and adjustments at the Closing Date as provided in this Agreement, which funds must be delivered in a manner to permit Escrow Holder to deliver good funds to the Seller or its designee on the Closing Date. 2.2 The balance of the Purchase Price shall be payable by purchase money note (the "Purchase Money Note") substantially in the form of **Exhibit "P"** attached hereto secured by a purchase money deed of trust or mortgage (the "Purchase Money Mortgage") substantially in the form of **Exhibit "Q"** attached hereto, payable as follows:

_____

_____.

2.2. **Deposit**. Within three (3) business days after Purchaser receives written confirmation from Escrow Holder that escrow has been opened ("Opening of Escrow"), Purchaser shall deposit with Escrow Holder the Deposit by a bank letter of credit payable to Escrow Holder to be held as security for performance of Purchaser's obligations under this Agreement.

2.3. **Liquidated Damages**. THE DEPOSIT SHALL BE PROMPTLY REFUNDED TO PURCHASER IF THE CLOSING DOES NOT OCCUR, UNLESS SUCH FAILURE DIRECTLY RESULTS SOLELY FROM A MATERIAL BREACH OF THIS AGREEMENT BY PURCHASER, IN WHICH CASE, THE DEPOSIT AND

ANY ACCRUED INTEREST SHALL BE PAID TO SELLER AS LIQUIDATED DAMAGES. THE PARTIES AGREE THAT (a) PAYMENT OF THE DEPOSIT TO SELLER IS INTENDED TO COMPENSATE SELLER FOR DAMAGES IT WILL SUFFER AS A RESULT OF PURCHASER'S BREACH HEREOF AND NOT AS A PENALTY OR FORFEITURE; (b) SELLER'S DAMAGES IN THE EVENT OF PURCHASER'S DEFAULT ARE IMPOSSIBLE OR EXTREMELY DIFFICULT TO ACCURATELY ASCERTAIN AND THAT PROOF OF SUCH AMOUNT WOULD BE COSTLY, TIME-CONSUMING AND INCONVENIENT; (c) THE AMOUNT OF THE DEPOSIT IS FAIR AND REASONABLE IN LIGHT OF ALL OF THE CIRCUMSTANCES EXISTING ON THE DATE OF THIS AGREEMENT AND AT THE TIME OF PAYMENT, INCLUDING THE RELATIONSHIP OF SUCH AMOUNT TO THE RANGE OF HARM TO SELLER THAT REASONABLY COULD BE ANTICIPATED; (d) THIS CLAUSE HAS BEEN THE SUBJECT OF SPECIFIC NEGOTIATION; (e) EACH PARTY HAS HAD THE OPPORTUNITY TO HAVE COUNSEL FULLY EXPLAIN THE CONSEQUENCES OF THE CLAUSE; (f) EACH PARTY FULLY UNDERSTANDS THE CONSEQUENCES OF THIS CLAUSE; AND (g) SUCH LIQUIDATED DAMAGES SHALL BE SELLER'S SOLE AND EXCLUSIVE REMEDY FOR PURCHASER'S DEFAULT AND PURCHASER SHALL HAVE NO OTHER OR FURTHER OBLIGATION OR LIABILITY UNDER THIS AGREEMENT TO SELLER ON ACCOUNT OF SUCH DEFAULT OR BREACH.

INITIALS: SELLER _____   PURCHASER: _____

ARTICLE 3

CONDITIONS PRECEDENT; REVIEW PERIOD AND TITLE

3.1. **Seller's Deliveries**. Within five (5) business days of the Opening of Escrow, Seller shall, at Seller's expense, deliver or cause to be delivered to Purchaser Seller's Deliveries as specified in Section 1.6.

3.2. **Review Period**. During the Review Period specified in Section 1.8, Purchaser shall have the right to inspect the Property, to examine and copy all of the financial books and other records of Seller for the Property, to interview persons involved in the operation of the Property, to review all of Seller's Deliveries, to have the Property inspected by its engineers, to undertake environmental surveys and assessments of the Property (including inquiries to governmental agencies), all as

Purchaser deems appropriate. Purchaser shall indemnify Seller against any physical damage to the Property arising from the negligence of Purchaser, his agents and contractors in undertaking any testing, borings, sampling or other investigations of the Property for purposes of this Agreement. Seller acknowledges that Purchaser may be obligated to disclose to the appropriate governmental authority the presence of any Hazardous Substances (as defined below) at, on or about the Property or any violation of applicable law. In such event, Purchaser shall furnish simultaneous written notice to Seller of any such disclosure to a governmental authority.

3.2.1. During the Review Period, Purchaser may, in its sole discretion for any reason, terminate this Agreement without cost or penalty; provided Seller and Escrow Holder are notified of such termination on or before 11:59 P.M., Pacific Time, on or before the last business day of the Review Period and Purchaser immediately confirms same in writing, whereupon Seller shall cause Escrow Holder to promptly return the Deposit to Purchaser, and neither party shall have any further liability to the other.

3.2.2. After expiration of the Review Period, but provided this Agreement is not terminated, Purchaser may have at least one representative on the Property during normal business hours to observe the operation thereof, which representative shall have access to all offices and records of Seller so long as he does not unreasonably interfere with the continued operation thereof in the ordinary course of business.

3.3. **Title Review and Survey**. Title to the Property (both legal and beneficial) shall be good and marketable and free and clear of all liens, restrictions, easements, encumbrances and title objections, except for the Permitted Exceptions as defined below, and shall be insurable as such at basic ordinary rate by the Title Company as specified in Section 1.11.

3.3.1. Within three (3) business days of Opening of Escrow, Seller, at Seller's expense, shall cause to be issued by the Title Company, acting in its capacity as a title insurer, and delivered to Purchaser a preliminary title report covering the Property with copies of all recorded documents or agreements giving rise to any of those title exceptions of record. The preliminary title report and the recorded documents are collectively referred to herein as the "Title Documents".

3.3.2. During the Review Period, Purchaser shall review the Title Documents and deliver to Seller in writing its approvals and objections with regard to anything contained or set forth therein. Any items not expressly objected to by Purchaser within the Review Period shall be deemed approved. All items so approved by Purchaser shall be attached as **Exhibit "C"** and referred to as "Permitted Exceptions".

3.3.3. If Seller is unable or unwilling, within fifteen (15) days after notice of Purchaser's objections, to cure such defects, then Purchaser, at his sole option, and within an additional fifteen (15) days, may (a) terminate this Agreement upon fifteen (15) days' written notice to Seller in the manner provided in Section 3.2; or (b) notify Seller that Purchaser will close subject to such uncured objections as Permitted Exceptions. Purchaser's failure to elect either alternative within the prescribed 15-day period shall be deemed an election to terminate this transaction in accordance with **Clause (a)** above.

3.3.4. On or prior to the Closing, Seller shall deliver to the Title Company, with copies to Purchaser, any and all documentation required by the Title Company to issue the Title Policies (as defined below), including without limitation any owner's affidavits, bonds, surveys, releases, evidence of ability to convey title, authorizing instruments and the like. In addition, Seller shall pay any and all costs, fees and charges which may be imposed by the Title Company or Escrow Holder in the event of the termination of this Agreement at any time.

3.3.5. If title to the Property at Closing continues to contain items to which Purchaser has objected and Seller has agreed to cure, Purchaser shall have the option of either taking such title as Seller can convey with a reduction to the Purchase Price equal to the amount of any and all monetary liens on such title and all associated costs with removing such liens, or of canceling this Agreement. In the latter event, the Deposit shall promptly be returned to Purchaser, and Seller shall reimburse Purchaser for the costs of title search and surveys with respect to the Real Property.

3.3.6. If title to the Property is not as required by this Agreement by reason of any willful act or omission by Seller after the Opening of Escrow, Purchaser shall be entitled to pursue any other remedies at law or in equity.

ARTICLE 4

SELLER'S REPRESENTATIONS, WARRANTIES AND COVENANTS.

4.1. Seller's Representations and Warranties. Seller represents and warrants the following now and as of the Closing (all of which shall survive the Closing as though made on and as of such date, except for changes occurring in the ordinary course of business, none of which changes being individually or in the aggregate materially adverse):

4.1.1. To the best of Seller's knowledge and belief, the Property is in good and physically sound condition and all vacant rentable space is currently suitable for renting (subject to tenant finish).

4.1.2. Seller has and can deliver good and marketable fee title to the Property. Title is fully insurable by the Title Company at its usual rates.

4.1.3. All documents provided to Purchaser by Seller in connection with this transaction are true, correct and complete and do not omit any information that might make such documents materially misleading.

4.1.4. If Seller is an entity, Seller is duly organized and existing in good standing under the laws of the State in which it was organized. Seller has the power to own property and to carry on its business as now being conducted, and is duly qualified to do business and is in good standing in every jurisdiction in which the nature of its business makes such qualification necessary. Seller is duly and legally authorized to enter into this Agreement and carry out and perform all covenants to be performed by it hereunder and its right to execute this Agreement is not limited by the existence of any other contracts or agreements whatsoever.

4.1.5. There are no (i) current pending or, to the best of Seller's knowledge, threatened or proposed violations of any applicable federal, state or local laws, codes, rules, ordinances or orders or of any covenant, condition, restriction, instrument or agreement affecting or relating to the use, occupation and construction of the Property, including without limitation those relating to environmental, health, safety, zoning or platting or other land use requirements, which have not been corrected to the satisfaction of the appropriate governmental authority. Seller has received no notice and has no knowledge of any violations or investigations relating to any such governmental requirements; (ii) outstanding mortgagee's requests for the performance of any work or alteration in respect to the Property which has not been complied with; (iii) defects in the Property which would render it unsuitable for Purchaser's intended use; (iv) condemnation proceedings in process or proposed affecting the Property; or (v) pending or proposed taxes or utility rate increases affecting the Property.

4.1.6. Seller has the exclusive right of possession of the Property, subject only to the leases shown on the Rent Roll attached hereto as **Exhibit "D"**, which is a true, correct and complete list, as of the Opening of Escrow, of all Leases, including commencement and expiration dates, rents, security deposits, options to extend, credits, setoffs, pre-paid rent, rental allowances, free rent and otherwise, payments due a tenant under its lease, commissions, defaults, delinquencies, remaining work to be performed by landlord, and the like. Seller agrees to indemnify and hold Purchaser harmless from and against any loss, damage or expense arising out of unsettled claims, if any, existing as of the Closing between Seller as landlord and any tenant.

4.1.7. There is not located in, on, under or about the Real Property any "Hazardous Materials", which, for purposes hereof, means any substance, material or waste which is or becomes regulated by any local governmental authority, the state in which the Property is located or the United States Government, including, but not limited to, any material or substance which is (i) petroleum; (ii) asbestos or asbestos-containing materials; (iii) aluminum wiring; (iv) polychlorinated biphenyls; (v) urea formaldehyde foam insulation; or (v) deemed to be a pollutant, contaminant, hazardous material, hazardous substance, hazardous chemical, hazardous waste, extremely hazardous waste, toxic substance or material or restricted hazardous waste pursuant to applicable laws.

4.1.8. A true, correct, and complete schedule of all Contracts as defined in Section 1.9.4 is attached as **Exhibit "M"**, identifying the contractor, his duties, the term of the contract, the rate of compensation payable, the length of notice required to cancel such contract and stating whether such contract would be binding on Purchaser and survive Closing.

4.1.9. Seller has fully performed all obligations required under any mortgages, any Leases   and any other contract, lease or agreement affecting the Property.

4.1.10. No rents, leases, concession agreements or licenses are assigned or pledged to any person other than the holder of any mortgage encumbering the Real Property.

4.1.11. All utility connections located on the Property (including without limitation gas, electricity, water, sanitary and storm sewage facilities) (i) are of sufficient size and capacity to service the Premises, (ii) have been completed, installed, activated and fully paid for and (iii) enter the Premises through adjoining public streets, or if they pass through adjoining private land, do so in accordance with valid public easements or private easements which will inure to the benefit of Purchaser. Purchaser as owner of the Premises, shall at Closing have an unqualified right to use such facilities without paying any liens, "tap-in" fees or similar charges with respect to the use thereof, except for normal water and sewer rents and nominal charges for any additional connection thereto which Purchaser's intended use may require.

4.1.12. There are presently in good standing and effect all licenses, certificates of occupancy, environmental impact reports and permits as may be required for the operation of the Property.

4.1.13. There are no legal or insurance proceedings or lawsuits threatened against or affecting the Property.

4.1.14. Seller has received no notice of any default or breach by Seller under any covenants, conditions, restrictions, rights-of-way, or easements which may affect the Property or any portion thereof, and no such default or breach now exists.

4.1.15. To Seller's knowledge, (i) all Leases set forth on the Rent Roll are in full force and effect and will be in full force and effect and unmodified at Closing, except those which expire or which have been terminated by Seller by reason of any tenant's default, (ii) there has been no default or any claim of default, and no event has occurred, which with notice or lapse of time or both would constitute a default, under any tenant lease, (iii) no tenant has asserted or has any defense, setoff, or claim with regard to his tenancy pursuant to its lease, any law or otherwise, and (iv) no rents or other obligations of any tenant exceed the maximum rent collectible under applicable law.

4.1.16. There are no notices outstanding calling for any unperformed curbing, recurbing, paving, repaving or other construction, improvements or work on or about the Real Property or any streets or roads abutting the Real Property, or the removal of any nuisance from the Real Property of any of the foregoing, and all street paving, curbing, sewer installation and other public improvements constructed or installed adjacent to the Real Property or ordered to be constructed or installed and for the cost of which the Real Property is assessable have been paid for and will not be assessed, all assessments having been paid in full.

4.1.17. There are no collective bargaining agreements or union contracts now in existence with respect to persons employed at the Property, or any part thereof, and within a three-year period prior to the Opening of Escrow, no demand has been made upon Seller for recognition of a union or collective bargaining agent for any persons employed at the Property, and Seller has no knowledge of any union organizational activity within the past three years involving persons then or now employed at the Property.

4.1.18. The heating, air conditioning, mechanical, electrical and other systems and equipment used in connection with the Property are operative and in good working condition, and any repairs required prior to settlement shall be made by Seller at its sole cost and expense.

4.1.19. No examination, investigation or operation of the Property by or on behalf of Purchaser prior to Closing shall in any way modify, affect or diminish Seller's obligations under the representations, warranties, covenants and agreements under this Agreement.

4.1.20. The Property is free from infestation by termites, other wood-destroying insects, vermin and other pests, and free from damage caused by any of the foregoing, and Seller will deliver to Purchaser at Closing a certificate issued by a reputable pest control company reasonably acceptable to Purchaser certifying the correctness of this warranty.

4.1.21. There are no underground storage tanks, sumps, grease-traps, wells and/or on-site sewage disposal systems now in use on the Real Property and potable water is and will be available in sufficient quantities for Purchaser's intended purposes.

4.1.22. The existing notes and mortgages have not been modified or amended in any respect and no defaults, monetary or non-monetary, currently exist under the existing notes or mortgages. All loan payments under the exisiting notes or mortgages shall be timely made.

4.2. In addition to all other covenants of Seller contained in this Agreement, Seller covenants and agrees that from the Opening of Escrow through the Closing:

4.2.1. The Property shall remain free and clear of all liens, superliens, encumbrances, defects in title, restrictions and easements other than the Permitted Exceptions.

4.2.2. Between the Opening of Escrow and the Closing, Seller will operate the Property and the businesses conducted thereon in substantially the same manner as conducted prior to the Opening of Escrow and will comply, at its own expense, with all environmental, hazardous waste cleanup, and similar laws and will deliver to Purchaser any certificate required thereunder.

4.2.3. If, during the Review Period, Seller (i) enters into any new leases or contracts affecting the operation of the Property; (ii) renews or amends any existing contracts for terms exceeding six (6) months, or involving a monthly expenditure in excess of that currently being paid under such existing lease or contract; (iii) commences eviction proceedings against defaulting tenants; (iv) accepts surrend-ers of leases; or (v) enters into modifications, extensions or renewals of existing leases or contracts (collectively, "New Agreements"), Seller shall given written notice thereof to Purchaser and, notwithstanding anything to the contrary contained in this Agreement, the Review Period shall be extended to the extent necessary to provide Purchaser with at least five (5) business days after receipt to review such New Agreement.

4.2.4. Following the expiration of the Review Period (provided this Agreement has not been terminated) through the Closing, Seller will not enter into any New Agreements, as defined in Section 4.2.3 above, without Purchaser's prior written consent, not to be unreasonably withheld.

4.2.5. Seller shall notify Purchaser of any written notices Seller receives regarding pending litigation affecting the Property.

4.2.6. Seller will not cause or permit any action reasonably within its control to be taken which would cause any of the representations or warranties of Seller in this Agreement to be untrue as of Closing.

4.2.7. Seller will not permit or suffer any default whatsoever under any existing mortgages and the transfer of the Property will not constitute a default thereunder, accelerate the maturity, or change any other term thereof.

4.3. If, prior to the Closing, Purchaser notifies Seller of a breach by Seller of any of its representations, warranties or covenants which occurred at any time and which can be cured solely by the payment of $250,000 or less, then Seller shall cure such breach, or, if the breach is not cured at or before Closing, give to Purchaser a credit against the purchase price equal to the amount required to cure and this transaction shall be closed as provided in this Agreement. If, prior to the Closing, Purchaser notifies Seller of a breach by Seller of any of its representations, warranties or covenants which occurred at any time and which can be cured solely by the payment of more than $250,000, then Purchaser may elect either (a) to terminate this Agreement, in which event Seller shall cause Escrow Holder to return the Deposit (plus any accrued interest thereon) to Purchaser and neither party shall have any further liability to the other, or (b) to close this transaction and receive a credit against the purchase price in the amount of $250,000 and shall be deemed to have waived the breach. Seller reserves the right to cure any breach which can be cured solely by the payment of money by payment of such curing sum to Purchaser at Closing.

ARTICLE 5

CONDITIONS

5.1. Purchaser's obligation to close this transaction under this Agreement are subject to satisfaction or waiver of the following conditions:

5.1.1. The timely and complete performance by Seller of its covenants and other obligations under this Agreement.

5.1.2. The truth and accuracy in every material respect, as of the date hereof and the date of Closing, of each and every representation and warranty of Seller, without regard to Seller's knowledge thereof.

5.1.3. Seller having marketable, indefeasible fee simple title to the Property insurable as such at standard premium rates, subject only to the Permitted Exceptions.

5.1.4. The information in the tenant estoppel certificates and the Rent Roll delivered to Purchaser at Closing is substantially the same, taking into account the ongoing operation of the Property.

5.1.5. The issuance of (i) an American Land Title Association (Form 6-1-87 or equivalent extended coverage) Standard Owner's Title Insurance Policy (the "Owner's Policy") issued by the Title Company in the face amount of the purchase price insuring Purchaser's fee title to the Property as of 10:00 A.M. on the date of Closing, subject only to the Permitted Exceptions and any updated survey exceptions permitted and the lien of the Purchaser's purchase money mortgage, and (ii) a Standard Loan Policy (the "Loan Policy") in the face amount of the purchase money loan insuring the interests of the lender designated by Purchaser in form and substance acceptable to such lender, subject only to the Permitted Exceptions. The Owner's Policy and the Loan Policy are collectively referred to in this Agreement as the "Title Policies". The Title Policies shall contain all available endorsements reasonably required by Purchaser and Purchaser's lender, including, without limitation, an inflation endorsement (if available), a usury endorsement (as to the Loan Policy only) and endorsements substantially equivalent to California Endorsement Nos. 100 (restrictions/encroachments), 100.19 (CC&Rs/no violations), 103.1 (use/maintenance of easements) and 116.1 (survey accuracy).

5.1.6. If before Closing the Real Property is prevented from being developed, expanded, rehabilitated or renovated as a result of any building moratorium or other restriction imposed by any governmental authority or public service company on the development of the Real Property or upon the availability of essential services, utilities or facilities for reasons other than condemnation or previous or threatened actions of Purchaser, then the following shall occur:

> (a). The Closing Date shall be extended one (1) day for each day that such moratorium shall remain in existence; provided, however, no such extension or extensions shall exceed, individually or collectively, more than 180 days (the "Moratorium Period"); and
> (b). If the Real Property remains subject to such moratorium at the end of the Moratorium Period, Purchaser may, upon at least ten (10) days written notice, terminate this Agreement in the manner provided in Section 3.2

5.1.7. There shall be no effective injunction or restraining order of any nature issued by a court of competent jurisdiction directing that this transaction not be consummated.

5.1.8. No consultant engaged by Purchaser to inspect the Property shall have discovered that any hazardous substance has been treated, stored, disposed of or otherwise deposited on the Property.
5.1.9. There shall not have been discovered any materially adverse defect or change in the physical, financial or other condition of the Property.

5.2. If any condition to this Agreement is not satisfied or waived, Purchaser may at its sole option terminate this Agreement. In the event of any such termination of this Agreement pursuant to the foregoing sentence the Deposit and all accrued interest thereon shall be returned to Purchaser together with a general release executed by the Seller in favor of the Purchaser in exchange for a general release executed by the Purchaser in favor of the Seller and upon such exchange of releases neither party shall have any further liability or obligation to the other under this Agreement or otherwise with respect to the subject matter of this Agreement.

5.3. Purchaser's obligations under this Agreement are contingent upon the representations and warranties contained in this Agreement being true and correct as of the Effective Date and as of the Closing Date. Nevertheless, rescission of this Agreement shall not be Purchaser's exclusive remedy for any breach of warranty by Seller.

ARTICLE 6

CLOSING

6.1. The Closing of the purchase and sale contemplated hereby shall be held at the offices of Escrow Holder on any Tuesday, Wednesday or Thursday on or before the Closing Date

6.2. At Closing (except as otherwise expressly required below), Seller shall execute and/or deliver (or cause to be delivered) to Purchaser or Purchaser's assignee:

6.2.1. A Grant Deed subject only to the Permitted Exceptions.

6.2.2. A Bill of Sale.

6.2.3. An Assignment of Intangible Rights.

6.2.4. If required by Purchaser's counsel, consent from all limited partners of Seller, if any.

6.2.5. A Tax Certification pursuant to Internal Revenue Code Section 1445.

6.2.6. Copies of notices terminating and cancelling any and all service contracts, maintenance agreements or other agreements except those agreements specified in the Assignment of Intangible Rights which will survive Closing as provided.

6.2.7. Estoppel certificates from all tenants in the form of attached **Exhibit "I"**.

6.2.8. One original and two (2) copies each of the Title Policies.

6.2.9. True, correct and complete original copies of any plans and specifications, development plans, leases and service contracts, including all modifications or amendments thereof, the keys, and copies of all default notices sent by Seller to any tenant or, if no such default notices exist, a certification to that effect.

6.2.10. A letter from Seller's liability insurance carrier dated not earlier that fifteen (15) days prior to Closing stating that (i) such company has either settled or is at present defending Seller under its existing policies of insurance against any claims arising with respect to the Property; (ii) such company will pay all claims and damages arising therefrom; and (iii) such claims and damages do not exceed the coverage therefor under the insurance policies.

6.3. At Closing, Seller shall, in addition to other amounts payable by Seller under this Agreement, pay the following costs and expenses:

6.3.1. Any transfer taxes, intangible taxes and fees on the Deed and any other conveyancing instruments.

6.3.2. The premiums for the Title Policies, all endorsements thereto, any UCC or other required record searches and all fees for the Survey.

6.3.3. Recording and filing fees and escrow charges.
6.3.4. With regard to any existing financing, mortgage transfer fees, intangible or other taxes, prepayment penalties and termination or filing fees for any UCC financing statements.

6.3.5. All special assessments or bond issues, if any, which are a lien at the time of the Closing against the Real Property.

6.3.6. The real estate commissions referred to in Section 8.1.

6.4. At Closing, Purchaser shall pay the cash portion of the purchase price and any sub-escrow charges, mortgage taxes and recording and filing fees for any purchase money financing.

6.5. Seller shall cause all utility suppliers furnishing electrical, gas and water utility services to the Property to read all utility meters on the date of Closing and to bill Seller separately for all such charges. Purchaser shall make its own arrangements regarding future utility billings and deposits. If any supplier refuses to read and bill any such utilities, such charges shall be prorated at

Closing based upon the bill for the next most similar billing period.

6.6. Escrow Holder shall return the Deposit to Purchaser at Closing.

6.7. Except as provided herein, sums due for accounts payable owing or incurred in the operation of the Property prior to the Closing shall be paid by Seller on or prior to Closing or adequate provisions reasonably satisfactory to Purchaser shall be made in respect to such payment. Seller agrees to indemnify Purchaser with respect to all such obligations. Purchaser shall furnish to the Seller for payment, promptly following receipt, any such bills to be paid by Seller.

6.8. Fees for all transferable state or local licenses required in the operation of the Property shall be paid by Seller.

6.9. Seller will hire no permanent employees for the Property nor alter the terms of any existing employment contract after the Effective Date.

6.10. Prior to Closing, no items of personal property being sold under this Agreement shall be removed from the Property, subject to replacements of like kind and quality made in the ordinary course of business.

ARTICLE 7

PRORATIONS.

7.1. Rents (including any prepaid rents), taxes, insurance premiums (if assignable and if Purchaser so elects), interest and all operating income and expenses will be prorated as of 12:00 midnight on the date preceding Closing based on the actual number of days in the month in which the Closing occurs. Purchaser shall be entitled to a credit against the purchase price for all tenant security deposits set forth in the tenant leases. The apportionment of real estate taxes shall be made pursuant to the present evidence of real estate taxes (assessments and rates) available as of the Closing. If, after the Closing, real estate taxes are (by reason of change in either assessment or rate or any other reason) determined to be higher than those apportioned at Closing, a new computation shall be made. Seller shall pay to Purchaser any net increase shown by such recomputation.

7.2. Purchaser shall give Seller no credit for rental income delinquent at Closing. All rental income received after the Closing shall be credited first to current rental income due and second to any delinquencies remaining owing to Seller. Any payments received by Seller after the Closing shall be forwarded directly to Purchaser for application in accordance with this Agreement. Upon request, Purchaser shall provide Seller with a written accounting of the application of rental payments in accordance with this paragraph.

7.3. Percentage rent (i.e., any rent payable to the landlord by the tenant under a tenant lease which is a percentage of the amount of sales or of the dollar amount of sales), if any, payable under each tenant lease shall be prorated with respect to the lease year thereunder in which the date of Closing occurs in accordance with the gross sales of tenants actually earned during the respective periods of ownership of the Property by Seller and Purchaser, and not on a straight-line basis. Purchaser shall not be required to institute any action or proceeding to collect any delinquent percentage rent.

ARTICLE 8

COMMISSION.

8.1. **Commission**. This Agreement is subject to a real estate broker's commission of _____ DOLLARS ($_____) to be divided equally between _____ and Standard Management Company, both licensed real estate brokers. Such commission shall be paid at Closing out of proceeds due Seller and shall only be due and payable if Closing occurs. Purchaser and Seller represent and warrant to each other that they have not dealt with any party that may be entitled to a finder's fee or commission for this transaction except for the above identified brokers and that no commission in excess of the aggregate commission described above will be paid to any party or parties. Seller and Purchaser each agrees to pay and protect, indemnify, defend and hold harmless the other from and against all liability, damages, attorneys' fees, court costs and expenses from causes of action, suits, claims, demands and judgments of any nature whatsoever arising out of or in any way connected with its dealings with any other real estate brokers or others pertaining to this transaction.

ARTICLE 9

RISK OF LOSS.

9.1. **Risk of Loss**. Except as provided in this Agreement, the risk of loss prior to the Closing is with Seller. Seller shall, during the term of this Agreement, maintain the fire and hazard insurance presently carried by Seller for no less than full coverage. At the Closing, Seller shall deliver the Property to Purchaser in substantially the same condition as exists as of the date hereof, reasonable wear and tear excepted.

9.1.1. If, after the expiration of the Review Period, Purchaser discovers that the Property or any portion thereof is destroyed or damaged by fire or any other casualty, and such damage or destruction is less than or equal to TWO HUNDRED FIFTY THOUSAND DOLLARS ($250,000) (including any loss of rents), then Seller shall promptly restore the damaged or destroyed portion of the Property and the Closing contemplated herein shall be postponed to a date not to exceed ten (10) business days beyond the date of such completed restoration; provided however that, if (a) the insurance carrier affirms its liability regarding such damage or destruction; (b) the available insurance proceeds are sufficient, when added to the deductible and any uninsured portion of such loss (collectively, the "Insurance Shortfall"), to pay the full cost of repairing and restoring such damaged and destroyed portions of the Property; and (c) Seller, at the time of such determination, agrees to tender to Purchaser at Closing the full amount of the Insurance Shortfall, then the parties shall promptly proceed to closing in accordance with the terms of this Agreement and, at Closing, Seller will assign all of its right, title and interest to any and all insurance proceeds to Purchaser, and the cash portion of the purchase price shall be reduced by the amount of the Insurance Shortfall.

9.1.2. If all or part of the Property is destroyed or damaged by fire or other casualty prior to the Closing, and such damage or destruction exceeds TWO HUNDRED FIFTY THOUSAND DOLLARS ($250,000) (including loss of rents), then, at Purchaser's option, Purchaser may terminate this Agreement, in which event the Seller shall cause Escrow Holder to return the Deposit to Purchaser and neither party shall have any further liability to the other. If Purchaser elects not to terminate this Agreement, this Agreement shall remain in full force and effect and Seller, at the time of Closing, shall transfer and assign to Purchaser all of Seller's right, title and interest in the insurance proceeds received or to be received by reason of such damage or destruction and shall tender at Closing the deductible plus the sum of $250,000.

9.2. **Condemnation**. If, at any time on or before the Closing, any action or proceeding is filed or threatened under which the Property or any portion thereof may be taken pursuant to any law, ordinance or regulation or by condemnation or the right of eminent domain, then at the sole option of Purchaser (a) this Agreement shall be null and void and the Deposit shall be promptly returned to Purchaser by Escrow Holder, or (b) this Agreement shall remain in full force and effect and Seller, at the time of Closing hereunder, shall transfer and assign all of Seller's rights, title and interests in and to any proceeds received or which may be received by reason of such taking, or a sale in lieu thereof, which option shall be exercisable by Purchaser by delivering to Seller written notice on or before the fifth business day following the date on which Purchaser receives notice that such suit has been filed or is threatened. If such five-business-day period extends beyond the date of Closing, as herein provided, Purchaser shall have the right to extend the date of Closing, to allow Purchaser the full five business days in which to exercise his options hereunder.

ARTICLE 10

EXCHANGE.

10.1. **Exchange**. Seller shall, at no expense to Seller, cooperate fully with Purchaser in connection with a tax-deferred exchange within the meaning of the Internal Revenue Code, Section 1031. The amount to be received by Seller and date of Closing shall not be changed.

10.2. **BENEFICIARIES**. This Agreement shall be binding upon and inure to the benefit of the parties hereto and their respective heirs, executors, legal representatives, successors and assigns.

10.3. **APPLICABLE LAWS**. This Agreement shall be governed by the laws of the state in which the Property is located.

10.4. **LICENSED REAL ESTATE BROKER**. Purchaser is a California licensed real estate broker, attorney and the principal of Standard Ma nagement Company.

10.5. **ASSIGNMENT OF AGREEMENT**. Purchaser may assign this Agreement to any person or entity, but shall not be relieved of any obligations hereunder.

10.6. **ASSIGNMENT OF RIGHTS.**   Seller hereby assigns to Purchaser all rights, claims and causes of action the Seller may have against third parties for negligence, gross negligence, willful misconduct or fraud in connection with the design or contruction of the improvements of the property. Seller also assigns any and all rights, known or unknown, which it has now or in the future, to any and all insurance policies (the "Policies") that cover the Property. Such rights include, but are not limited to, making claims for damages under the Policies and bad faith claims against the insurance companies that issued the Policies.

10.7. **EXCLUSIVE AGREEMENT**.   This Agreement is an exclusive arrangement between the parties and, after execution, neither Seller nor its agents, affiliates or employees shall negotiate or otherwise deal in the sale of the Property with anyone other than Purchaser until this Agreement is terminated in accordance with its terms.

10.8. **COUNTERPARTS**. This Agreement may be executed in counterparts each of which shall constitute an original and all of which together shall have the same full and binding effect as a single executed copy. Photocopy, facsimile, electronic, or other copies shall have the same effect for all purposes as an ink-signed original.

10.9. **NOTICES**. All notices, requests, demands and other communications under this Agreement shall be in writing and must be delivered either by personal service or by first-class mail, registered or certified, postage prepaid, return receipt requested, or by such expedited courier service where receipt by addressee can be confirmed by said courier service in writing (Federal Express, Express Mail, telecopy, etc.), and properly addressed specified in Section 1.1 and Section 1.2.

10.9.1. Notices shall be deemed received by the addressee upon the earlier to occur of (i) actual receipt; (ii) two (2) business days after mailing by registered or certified mail; (iii) one (1) business day after sending by overnight courier; or (iv) the same day if sent by telecopy, all in accordance with the terms of this paragraph. Either party may change its address for notice purposes by giving written notice of such new address to the other party.

10.10. **VALIDITY; WAIVER**.   The invalidity of any provision of this Agreement shall not affect the validity of the remainder of this Agreement. No waiver of any of the provisions of this Agreement shall be deemed or shall constitute a waiver of any other provision, whether or not similar, nor shall any waiver constitute a continuing waiver or be binding unless executed in writing by the waiving party.

10.11. **CONSTRUCTION**. Each party and its counsel have reviewed and revised this Agreement. The normal rule of construction that ambiguities are resolved against the drafting party shall not be employed in interpreting this Agreement or any amendments or exhibits thereto.

10.12. **ATTORNEYS' FEES**. In the event of a dispute between the parties hereto relating to this Agreement, the prevailing party shall be entitled to recover reasonable attorneys' fees, costs and expenses incurred in connection therewith.

10.13. **INCORPORATION OF EXHIBITS**. All exhibits attached and referred to herein are by such reference incorporated herein and made part hereof. The Exhibits attached hereto which state "Insert to Follow" or "To Be Attached" shall be completed and approved by the parties hereto prior to expiration of the Review Period and, as completed and approved, shall thereupon become a part of this Agreement.

10.14. **ENTIRE AGREEMENT**. All prior understandings and agreements between the parties respecting this transaction are merged in this Agreement and the exhibits attached hereto, which fully and completely express the agreement of the parties. No change, addition to or modification of this Agreement or any part hereof shall be valid unless in writing and signed by or on behalf of all of the parties.

10.15. **PERFORMANCE**. If the time period by which any right, option or election provided under this Agreement must be exercises, or by which any act required hereunder must be performed or by which the Close of Escrow must be held expires on a Saturday, Sunday, federal holiday or legal bank holiday in the state where the Property is located, then such time period shall be automatically extended to the close of business on the next business day.

IN WITNESS WHEREOF, the parties have executed this Agreement as of the date first set forth above.

"PURCHASER"   "SELLER"
_____ By: _____
                                Name: _____
                                Its_____

LIST OF EXHIBITS

A. Legal Description

B. Seller's Deliveries

C. Permitted Exceptions

D. Rent Roll

E. Bill of Sale

    a. Legal Description
    b. Personal Property Inventory
    c. Permitted Exceptions to Title to Personal Property

F. Indemnification Agreement

G. Assignment of Intangible Rights

    a. Legal Description
    b. Contracts and Agreements
    c. Rent Roll

H. Tax Certification

I. Tenant Estoppel Certificate

J. Joint Notice to Tenant

K. Form of Letter of Credit

L. Deposit Escrow Instructions

M. Schedule of Existing Service Contracts

N. Schedule of Litigation

O. Schedule of Full-Time Employees

P. Existing Note or Purchase Money Note

Q. Existing Mortgage or Purchase Money Mortgage

R. Lender Estoppel Certificate

EXHIBIT "A"

LEGAL DESCRIPTION

[TO BE SUPPLIED BY LEGAL COUNSEL]

EXHIBIT "B"

SELLER'S DELIVERIES

(1) (a) A current preliminary title report or commitment (the "Title Report") for the Property from _____ ("Title Company"), together with copies of all underlying documents of record referred to therein; (b) three (3) copies of a currently dated survey ("Survey") prepared by a licensed professional surveyor reasonably acceptable to Purchaser, Purchaser's lender and the Title Company, which Survey shall (i) comply with the Minimum Standard Detail Requirements for ALTA/ACSM Land Title Surveys as adopted by the American Land Title Association and the American Congress on Surveying & Mapping, except that the Survey shall extend for a distance of twenty (20) feet onto adjoining properties; (ii) list all title report exceptions; and (iii) certify the following: (A) that, except as shown, no portion of the Real Property is located within a special flood hazard area; (B) the area and zoning of the Real Property and the dimensions, square feet and number of stories of all structures located thereon; and (C) the number, location and type (standard, compact or handicap) of parking spaces; and (c) the existing Title Policies for the Property in favor of Seller and its lenders;

(2) (a) Copies of all tenant leases and any amendments, modifications and letter agreements, currently in effect; (b) the most current rent roll, including all expiration dates, prepaid rents, delinquencies, defaults, options, deposits (and whether refundable or non-refundable) and any special concessions; and (c) copies of each tenant's monthly sales reports, including sales tax filings and other pertinent information, for the past 24 months;

(3) Copies of last 2 years' property tax assessments and bills;

(4) List and copies of all management, maintenance and repair, service and supply contracts and other agreements, written or oral;

(5) Copies of all loan documents to be assumed by Purchaser;

(6) Copies of all fire, extended risk, liability and other insurance policies and schedule of the premiums, current claims and insurance loss claim records for the past 60 months;

(7) All plans and specifications in Seller's possession;

(8) Copies of monthly and annual income and expense statements for the past 36 months; utility and sewer bills for the last 12 months and schedule of all capital improvements made over the past 36 months;

(9) Schedule of all Personal Property and fixtures;

(10) Schedule of current lawsuits pending or threatened and summary of the action and names of all parties and their attorneys;

(11) Schedule of vacant spaces not suitable for renting (subject to tenant finish), and estimate of cost of work required to complete;

(12) Schedule of all outstanding commission obligations;

(13) Names, telephone numbers and addresses of architects, consultants and contractors who worked on Property, if available;

(14) All feasibility studies, appraisals, demographic reports and consulting and marketing reports available to Seller;

(15) A report issued by a reputable consultant regarding the presence of Hazardous Materials on or about the Property, to Purchaser's satisfaction; and

(16) Evidence satisfactory to Purchaser regarding the completion of the improvements on the Property, including without limitation the Architect's Certificate of Substantial Completion, certificates of occupancy and all other documentation furnished to Seller's construction lender regarding such completion.

EXHIBIT "C"

PERMITTED EXCEPTIONS

[TO BE SUPPLIED BY LEGAL COUNSEL]

EXHIBIT "D"

RENT ROLL

[TO BE SUPPLIED BY LEGAL COUNSEL]

EXHIBIT "E"

BILL OF SALE

FOR GOOD AND VALUABLE CONSIDERATION, the receipt and sufficiency of which are acknowledged, the undersigned ("Seller") bargains, sells, assigns, transfers and delivers to _____ _____ ("Purchaser"), all furniture, tangible and intangible personal property, fixtures, equipment, plans and specifications and other contract documentation, assignable insurance policies (at Purchaser's election), machinery and other items located on or used in connection with the real property and improvements described in **Exhibit "E-1"** attached here-to, and all trade names, contract rights relating to the Property, Seller's interest in and the control of the Seller over escrow accounts, insurance policies, deposits, instruments, documents of title, general intangible and business records, including without limitation the property described on **Exhibit "E-2"** attached hereto and by this reference made a part hereof (collectively, the "Property").

TO HAVE AND TO HOLD all and singular the Property unto such Purchaser, his successors, heirs, executors, administrators and assigns, to their own proper use and benefit, forever.

Seller binds itself, its successors, administrators, executors, heirs and assigns, to warrant and defend all and singular title to the Property unto the Purchaser, his heirs, executors, successors and assigns and against every person whomsoever law-fully claiming or to take claim to the same. Seller represents and warrants that it has good and marketable title to the Property and every item comprising the Property, free and clear of all liens, encumbrances and restrictions except for those liens, rights to liens and security interests existing and affecting same and the afore-said real property as of the date hereof, all of which are identified in **Exhibit "E-3"** attached hereto and by this reference made a part hereof.

IN WITNESS WHEREOF, this Bill of Sale has been executed as of _____, 20____.

"SELLER"

_____

_____

By: _____

    Name: _____

    Its: _____

EXHIBIT "F"

INDEMNIFICATION AGREEMENT

Seller agrees to indemnify and defend Purchaser against and hold Purchaser harmless from all claims, demands, debts, causes of action and suits of any nature whatsoever arising out of the ownership and/or operation of the Property prior to or on the date of Closing and any and all activities relating thereto (whether any such claims, demands, debts, causes of actions, or suits are asserted prior to or after the date of Closing).

Purchaser agrees to indemnify and defend Seller against and hold Seller harmless from any claims, demands, debts, causes of action and suits of any nature whatsoever arising out of Purchaser's ownership and/or operation of the Property subsequent to the Closing and any and all activities relating thereto.

Date: _____, 20___.

                                       "SELLER"

Signed, sealed and delivered
in the presence of:

                                       _____

                                       _____

_____   By: _____

                                       Name: _____

_____   Its: _____

                                       "PURCHASER"

                                       _____

                                       _____

_____   By: _____

                                       Name: _____

_____   Its: _____

(Add Acknowledgments Here)

EXHIBIT "G"

STATE OF _____)
) ss.
COUNTY OF _____)

ASSIGNMENT OF INTANGIBLE RIGHTS

THIS ASSIGNMENT is made and entered into as of _____, 20__ ("Effective Date") by and between _____ ("Assignor"), and _____ ("Assignee"), with reference to the following:

A.   In accordance with the terms of an Agreement For Sale and Purchase of Property (the "Purchase Agreement") dated _____ _____, 20__, Assignor conveyed to Assignee concurrently herewith the real property and improvements located thereon, more particularly described on **Exhibit "G-1"** attached hereto (the "Property").

B.   In connection with the conveyance of the Property, Assignor and Assignee intend that all of Assignor's right, title and interest in and under all contracts, guaranties, warranties, assignable insurance policies, certificates, leases, litigation and other matters relating to the Property be assigned and transferred to Assignee.

NOW, THEREFORE, for good and valuable consideration, the receipt and sufficiency of which are acknowledged, the parties agree that:

1.   **Assignment**.   Assignor assigns, conveys, transfers and sets over to Assignee any and all of Assignor's right, title and interest in and to the following set of intangible rights and Assignor shall deliver to Assignee the documents evidencing the following items:

(a)   Contracts.   All those certain contracts and agreements listed on **Exhibit "G-2"** attached hereto and previously delivered to Assignee, relating to the Property. Assignor agrees to cancel any other contracts and agreements relating to the Property

(b)   Warranties, Guaranties and Policies.   All guaranties, warranties and agreements from any contractors, subcontractors, vendors or suppliers regarding their performance, quality of workmanship and quality of materials supplied in the construction, manufacture, development, installation and operation of any and all fixtures, equipment, personal property and improvements located on or used in connection with the Property and, to the extent assignable, any and all policies of insurance regarding the Property or any part thereof..

(c) <u>Governmental Approvals and Certificates</u>. Any zoning, use, occupancy and operating permits, and all other permits, approvals and certificates obtained in connection with the Property.

(d) <u>Leases</u>. All leases with respect to the Property, including without limitation, tenant leases for those tenants specified in the Rent Roll attached as **Exhibit "G-3"** ("Leases").

2. **Construction**. Each party and its counsel have reviewed and revised this Assignment. The normal rule of construction that ambiguities are resolved against the drafting party shall not govern the interpretation of this Assignment or any amendments or exhibits.

3. **Governing Law**. This Assignment shall be governed by and construed under and in accordance with the laws of the state in which the Property is located.

4. **Additional Documents**. Each party shall, at the request of the other, execute, acknowledge and deliver whatever additional instruments, and do such other acts, as may reasonably be required in order to accomplish and carry forward the intent and purposes of this Assignment.

5. **Successors and Assigns**. This Assignment shall be binding upon and shall inure to the benefit of the parties hereto and their respective heirs, executors, representatives, successors and assigns.

IN WITNESS WHEREOF this Assignment is executed by the parties on the date first above written.

"ASSIGNOR"   "ASSIGNEE"

_____

_____

By: _____   _____

_____

Name _____

Its: _____

[ATTACH APPROPRIATE JURATS]

EXHIBIT "H"

CERTIFICATE OF NON-FOREIGN STATUS

Section 1445 of the Internal Revenue Code provides that a transferee of a U.S. real property interest must withhold tax if the transferor is a foreign person. To inform the transferee that withholding of tax is not required upon the disposition of a U.S. real property interest in _____ ("Seller"), the undersigned hereby certifies the following on behalf of the Seller:

    1. Seller is not a foreign corporation, foreign partnership, foreign trust, or foreign estate (as those terms are defined in the Internal Revenue Code and Income Tax Regulations);

    2. Seller's U.S. employer identification number is _____; and

    3. Seller's office address is _____
                                    _____

Seller understands that this certification may be disclosed to the Internal Revenue Service by the transferee and that any false statement contained herein could be punished by fine, imprisonment, or both.

Under penalties of perjury, I declare that I have examined this certification and to the best of my knowledge and belief it is true, correct and complete. I further declare that I have authority to sign this document on behalf of Seller.

Date: _____, 200____.

                                             "SELLER"

                            _____
                            _____

                            By: _____
                            Name: _____
                            Its:_____

EXHIBIT "I"

TENANT ESTOPPEL CERTIFICATE

Dated:_____

Standard Management Company
6151 West Century Blvd., Suite 300
Los Angeles, California 90045-5314
ATTN: Legal Department/Acquisitions

[Purchaser's Purchase Money Lender]_

_____

_____

Re: Lease dated _____ between _____,
       as Landlord, and the undersigned, as Tenant, for Premises located at

_____

Gentlemen:

The undersigned Tenant certifies to you as follows:

1. The Lease (a true, complete and correct copy of which is attached hereto as **Exhibit "1"**) is in full force and effect and has not been amended, modified or supplemented orally, by course of conduct or in writing, except as follows:

(If none, so state; if blank, will be conclusively presumed "none".)

2. All space and improvements covered by the Lease have been completed and furnished in accordance with the Lease, and Tenant has accepted and taken possession of the Premises;

3. Neither Tenant nor Landlord is in default under the Lease, nor is there now any fact or condition which, with notice or lapse of time or both, will become a default, and Tenant has not assigned, transferred or hypothecated any of its interest under the Lease, except as follows:

(If none, so state; if blank, will be conclusively presumed "none".)

4. There are no defenses, offsets, counterclaims or credits against rentals or other sums payable under the Lease, and neither Tenant nor any predecessor has made any payment to Landlord as a security deposit or advance or prepaid rental except (a) payments expressly provided for in the Lease or in any above-referenced amendment, modification or supplement, and (b) payments made not earlier than ten (10) days prior to the date upon which such payments are due;

5. Except as expressly provided in the Lease or above-referenced amendment, modification or supplement, Tenant has no right or option (a) to renew or extend the term of the Lease, (b) to purchase all or any part of the Premises or of the building of which the Premises are a part, (c) to receive rent concessions or other special privileges.

6. The fixed annual rent under the Lease is $_____, subject to escalation and other payments in accordance with the Lease;

7. The term of the Lease commenced on _____ and shall expire on _____, subject only to the following remaining options to renew the term of the Lease:

(If none, so state; if blank, will be conclusively presumed "none".)

8. Tenant acknowledges that (a) the address for notices to be sent to Tenant under the Lease is as set forth in the Lease, or as set forth below, and (b) Tenant has received no notice of any prior assignment, hypothecation or pledge of the rents or of the Lease

9. Tenant acknowledges that Samuel K. Freshman and/or assigns ("Purchaser") is acquiring ownership of the Property in material reliance on this statement, and agrees that, upon such acquisition, Tenant will attorn to Purchaser and recognize Purchaser as Landlord; subject to Purchaser's agreement not to disturb Tenant's possession under the Lease so long as Tenant is not in default thereunder.

"TENANT"

_____

_____

By: _____

EXHIBIT "J"
JOINT NOTICE TO TENANTS

[TO BE SUPPLIED BY LEGAL COUNSEL]

EXHIBIT "K"

FORM OF LETTER OF CREDIT

[TO BE SUPPLIED BY LEGAL COUNSEL]

EXHIBIT "L"

DEPOSIT ESCROW INSTRUCTIONS

THESE DEPOSIT ESCROW INSTRUCTIONS (the "Escrow Instructions") are made and entered into as of _____ by and between _____ ("Escrow Holder"); _____ ("Seller"); and SAMUEL K. FRESHMAN ("Purchaser"), regarding the following:

A. Purchaser and Seller have entered into an Agreement for Sale and Purchase of Property dated _____, a copy of which is attached hereto as **Exhibit "L-1"** ("Agreement"), regarding the acquisition by Purchaser of _____ located in _____ (the "Property").

B. The Agreement requires that, within three (3) business days after its execution and delivery, Purchaser shall deposit with Escrow Holder, as security for a portion of the purchase price, a bank letter of credit in the amount of _____ Dollars ($_____) (the "Deposit").

C. The Agreement grants to Purchaser a Review Period during which Purchaser is permitted to inspect the Property and perform certain due diligence with respect thereto. The Review Period shall be for a period of _____ (___) business days (excluding Saturdays, Sundays and legal holidays) after commencement thereof, which commencement shall be determined in the manner provided in **Paragraph 4** of the Agreement. Seller and Purchaser shall give Escrow Holder written notice of the commencement and expiration dates of the Review Period so as to enable Escrow Holder to comply with the instructions contained herein.

D. Purchaser and Seller desire to enter into these Escrow Instructions in order to set forth the terms and conditions governing the deposit of the Deposit in the possession of Escrow Holder as a disinterested third party escrow holder.

E. Escrow Holder is willing to hold the Deposit for the benefit of Purchaser and Seller on the terms set forth below.

NOW, THEREFORE, in consideration of the fee paid to Escrow Holder, Escrow Holder agrees to hold such security subject to the following express instructions.

1. **Deliveries**. Within three (3) business days of the date hereof, Purchaser shall deliver to Escrow Holder the Deposit in the form attached hereto as Exhibit "L-2" and made a part hereof, the disposition of which shall be governed by these Escrow Instructions, as they may be amended by the mutual written agreement of Seller and Purchaser. Escrow Holder acknowledges prior receipt of a copy of the Agreement.

2. **Instructions**.

a. If the Agreement is terminated by Purchaser for any reason on or before the end of business on the last day of the Review Period (the "Out Date"), as it may be extended by the mutual written agreement of Seller and Purchaser, Escrow Holder shall return the Deposit to Purchaser upon receipt of notice of such termination, notwithstanding any instructions to the contrary from Seller.

b. If the Agreement is not terminated by Purchaser on or before the Out Date, Escrow Holder shall retain and hold the Deposit in accordance with these Escrow Instructions. In such event, Seller and Purchaser shall give Escrow Holder written notice of the scheduled date for Closing so as to enable Escrow Holder to comply with the instructions contained below.

c. If the transaction contemplated in the Agreement fails to occur on the date scheduled for Closing, as such date may be extended or accelerated by the mutual written agreement of Purchaser and Seller, Escrow Holder shall return the Deposit to Purchaser promptly upon the expiration of five (5) business days after such scheduled Closing date (as so extended or accelerated) unless Escrow Holder receives a written statement from an authorized representative of Seller within such five-business-day period declaring that "the failure directly results solely from a breach of the Agreement by Purchaser", in which event, Escrow Holder shall hold the Deposit until the parties agree on the proper disposition thereof or until a final disposition is determined by arbitration or a court of competent jurisdiction. Notwithstanding anything to the contrary contained herein, if, by the end of business on the fifth day prior to any stated expiration date of the Deposit (as it may be extend from time to time, as provided below), Escrow Holder has not received either (i) an uncontested written instruction from either party regarding the disposition of the Deposit, or (ii) a joint instruction from both parties regarding the disposition of the Deposit, or (iii) a valid court order from a court of competent jurisdiction regarding the disposition of the Deposit, or (iv) a substitute letter of credit or an amendment to the existing letter of credit extending the expiration date of the Deposit for at least 60 days, then Escrow Holder shall automatically and immediately draw down the Deposit and hold the proceeds thereof in an interest-bearing account at the direction of Purchaser until the parties agree on the proper disposition thereof or until a final disposition is determined by a court of competent jurisdiction.

   d. Any interest accruing on the Deposit during the pendency of any dispute as to the proper disposition thereof shall be payable in the proportion in which such proceeds are ultimately distributed.

   e. Seller and Purchaser shall each pay one-half of any escrow fees charged by Escrow Holder in connection with the performance of its obligations hereunder, as amended.

3. **Counterparts**. These Escrow Instructions may be executed in counterparts, each of which shall constitute an original and all of which together shall constitute one complete instrument.

4. **Governing Law**. These Escrow Instructions shall be governed by the laws of the State of _____.

IN WITNESS WHEREOF, the undersigned have executed these Escrow Instructions as of the date first set forth above.

"SELLER"   "PURCHASER"

_____

_____

By:_____   _____
   Name:_____   Samuel K. Freshman
      Its:_____

APPROVED AND ACCEPTED AS OF _____:

"ESCROW HOLDER"

_____,

a _____

By:_____
   Name:_____
      Its Escrow Officer

EXHIBIT "M"

SCHEDULE OF SERVICE CONTRACTS

[TO BE SUPPLIED BY LEGAL COUNSEL]

EXHIBIT "N"

SCHEDULE OF LITIGATION

[TO BE SUPPLIED BY LEGAL COUNSEL]

EXHIBIT "O"

SCHEDULE OF FULL-TIME EMPLOYEES

[TO BE SUPPLIED BY LEGAL COUNSEL]

EXHIBIT "P"

EXISTING NOTE OR PURCHASE MONEY NOTE

[TO BE SUPPLIED BY LEGAL COUNSEL]

EXHIBIT "Q"

EXISTING MORTGAGE OR PURCHASE MONEY MORTGAGE

[TO BE SUPPLIED BY LEGAL COUNSEL]

EXHIBIT "R"

LENDER ESTOPPEL CERTIFICATE

To: Purchaser

Re: (Describe Loan and Property)

Gentlemen:

The undersigned is the owner and holder of the above-referenced Note and Mortgage and has been informed that Samuel K. Freshman has entered into a contract for the purchase of the Property described in the Mortgage. In connection with such purchase, the undersigned certifies to Mr. Freshman and any assignee of the contract that:

1. As of the date hereof, the principal balance outstanding under the Note is $_____.

2. The interest rate payable under the Note is _____% per annum, and the regular monthly payments of principal and interest due and payable thereunder are the sum of $_____ per month.

3. The only indebtedness secured by the Mortgage is that evidenced by the Note and the Note and Mortgage have not been modified in any respect whatsoever.

4. The amount presently held by the undersigned in escrow for payment of taxes and insurance is the sum of $_____.

5. The undersigned consents to the transfer of the Property described in the Mortgage to Samuel K. Freshman or his assignee of the above-referenced contract and acknowledges and agrees that, in connection with such transfer, Samuel K. Freshman or his assignee may further encumber the Property with one or more mortgages as described in the Agreement or in **Exhibit "R-1"**

6. The undersigned's consent will not be unreasonably withheld or conditioned upon any modification of the terms of the Note or the Mortgage to a subsequent sale of the Property described in the Mortgage by Samuel K. Freshman or the further encumbering of the Property described in the Mortgage by one or more mortgages which shall be subject and subordinate to the Mortgage.

7. The undersigned agrees that prior to any acceleration of the Note as a result of a default thereunder or under the Mortgage, the undersigned shall provide the owner of the Property described in the Mortgage with not less than ten (10) days prior written notice with respect to any monetary default and not less than thirty (30) days prior written notice with respect to non-monetary defaults.

8. Notwithstanding the provisions of the Mortgage, the undersigned hereby agrees that:

(i) Subject to approval of plans and specifications and subject to disbursement upon such invoices, lien waivers, and title insurance endorsements as the holder of the Note and Mortgage may reasonably require and subject further to such other loan proceeds disbursement procedures as the holder may reasonably require, insurance proceeds payable with respect to any damages or destruction shall be made available to the owner of the Property described in the Mortgage for the purpose of restoration.

(ii) To the extent any condemnation awards are paid for the purpose of compensating the owner of the Property, or for the purpose of restoration, repair or damage attributable to such condemnation, the undersigned consents to the application of such award for that purpose.

9. All payments of money due and payable through the date hereof under the Note and Mortgage have been received by the undersigned, and the loan evidenced by the Note and secured by the Mortgage is not presently in default.

10. The undersigned agrees that it will not transfer or assign the Note and Mortgage unless it shall give thirty (30) days' written notice to the Mortgagor prior to such assignment.

"LENDER"

By: _____
    Name: _____
    Its: _____

EXHIBIT "R-1"

OTHER MORTGAGES

[TO BE SUPPLIED BY LEGAL COUNSEL]

AGREEMENT FOR SALE OF REAL PROPERTY (SELLER)

THIS AGREEMENT FOR SALE AND PURCHASE OF REAL PROPERTY (the "Sale Agreement") is entered into as of _____, 200__ (the " Execution Date") between _____ ("Seller") and _____ ("Purchaser" or "Buyer"), with reference to the following:

A. Seller owns (i) certain parcels of land located in the City of _____, County of _____, State of _____, and more particularly described in **Exhibit "1"** attached hereto, together with all improvements situated thereon, all transferable Licenses or Permits, appurtenances, rights, privileges, servitudes and prescriptions thereunto belonging (collectively, the "Real Property") commonly known as "_____", and (ii) owns or leases certain furniture, furnishings, equipment and personal property now or hereafter attached to or used in connection with the operation or maintenance of the improvements on the Real Property (described on the schedule attached here as **Exhibit "2"** and incorporated herein by this reference) (the "Personal Property"). The Real Property and Personal Property are collectively referred to as the "Property". The foregoing are not representations by Seller but merely its under-standing of the facts. Notwithstanding the foregoing, Seller will retain all (1) mineral rights below 500 feet to the Real Property and will have the access to those rights however without right of surface entry, and (2) All rights to the names _____ (the "Excluded Property").

B. Seller agrees to sell and Purchaser agrees to buy the Property upon the terms and conditions set forth herein.

NOW, THEREFORE, for good and valuable consideration, the receipt and sufficiency of which are acknowledged, the parties agree:

1. SALE AND PURCHASE. At the Closing, and upon the terms and conditions set forth more fully below, Seller agrees to sell and convey to Purchaser, and Purchaser agrees to purchase and accept from Seller, all of Seller's right, title and interest in and to the Property with the exception of the "Excluded Property", subject to the Permitted Exceptions (as defined in **Article 6** of this Agreement"]), which Permitted Exceptions are more particularly set forth in **Exhibit "3"** attached hereto.

2. PURCHASE PRICE

APPENDIX C
AGREEMENT FOR SALE

2.1 Purchaser shall pay the purchase price for the Property equal to
_____DOLLARS ($_____), to be paid as follows:

(a)   On the Closing, Purchaser shall pay the sum of
_____ dollars ($_____) in cash.

(b)   Time is of the essence. If the transaction does not close by the scheduled Closing, Seller at its option may terminate this agreement and have no further obligation to Purchaser.

2.2 As additional consideration,

(a)   All repairs in excess of $_____ dollars ($_____) required from the Execution Date shall be the responsibility of Buyer. If Buyer does not want to make such repairs, it may cancel this Agreement prior to close as provided in Section 4.

3. CONDITION OF THE PROPERTY

3.1 Purchaser acknowledges and agrees that it is acquiring the Property "AS IS, WHERE IS" and with all faults, and that, except as expressly set forth in this Sale Agreement, neither Seller nor anyone on behalf of Seller has made any representation or warranty, either expressed or implied, with respect to the Property, or otherwise in connection with the transaction contemplated hereby or in connection with the size, value or condition of the Property or its feasibility, suitability or profitability for development, resale or condominium conversion. There is no representation as to the validity or assignability of any zoning permit, or license affecting the Property or its use.

3.2 There is no obligation on the part of the Seller, other than what it might otherwise have at law, with respect to environmental matters. Seller has no actual knowledge of Environmental Matters affecting the Property other than what has been disclosed to Buyer herein. For purposes of this Agreement the term "actual knowledge" shall mean the actual knowledge of Samuel K. Freshman or Craig Walsh only.

4. **INSPECTION**

4.1 Purchaser shall have the right, until _____ 1999, the "Expiration Date"), at its own peril and risk with no liability to be incurred by Seller, to enter upon and inspect the Property for purposes of conducting surveys, non-evasive, soil tests or other tests, engineering studies, collecting architectural data, inspecting its economic condition and viability and reviewing Lease Agreements, and all other documents in possession of Seller (at Sellers office during normal business hours) and doing any other work Purchaser deems reasonably necessary to determine the suitability of the Property; provided that (a) if Purchaser fails to purchase the Property as provided herein, Purchaser shall restore the Property to substantially the same condition as exists on the date hereof to the extent such restorations are the result of damage due to Purchaser's actions; and (b) Purchaser shall indemnify, defend and hold Seller harmless from and against any and all claims, costs, demands, fines, fees, expenses, causes of action, lawsuits and attorneys' fees resulting from or in any way related to such use of the Property by Purchaser. During the inspection period, Purchaser shall satisfy itself as to the existence or non-existence of infestation from termites, dry rot, fungi or other pests in accessible areas and, if Purchaser purchases the Property, Purchaser shall be responsible for any work called for therein. Purchaser acknowledges receipt of all the items listed as "Seller's Disclosure" attached hereto and incorporated herein as **Exhibit "A"**. Purchaser's approval shall be in its sole and absolute discretion. The indemnity provided in this Section 4.1 shall survive the closing.

4.2 This Agreement shall be automatically terminated, if Purchaser delivers written notice to Seller of its election NOT to proceed with the purchase of the above Property on or prior to the Expiration Date. If Purchaser gives written notice to Seller of its election to proceed with the purchase on or prior to the Expiration Date then the transaction will continue in accordance with this Agreement. If no notice is given by Purchaser to Seller by the Expiration Date, then Seller at its option may elect to terminate this Agreement or proceed with the transaction by giving written notice to Purchaser of Seller's applicable election within three (3) business days after the Expiration Date. If this Agreement is terminated, then Purchaser and Seller shall be relieved of all liability hereunder, except for Purchaser's obligations under this Article 4 and Article 5 below.

4.3 As further consideration for this Agreement, Purchaser shall deliver to Seller, at Purchaser's expense and as soon as available, a copy of all reports, surveys, tests, inspections proposed Subleases or Leases and other documents prepared for or obtained by Purchaser (if any) in connection with Purchaser's inspection and review of the Property

4.4 At least three (3) business days prior to the Expiration Date, Purchaser shall notify Seller in writing of all lenders with whom loan applications have been filed together with copies of any applications or other documents in connection therewith.

4.5 Purchaser shall not divulge to any third party any confidential or proprietary information obtained by Purchaser with respect to the Property and all such information shall be kept confidential until such time and to the extent such information loses its confidential or proprietary character without the fault of Purchaser. Purchaser may disclose to its agents, consultants, employees and Lenders subject to their holding such disclosures confidential.

5. DEPOSIT

5.1 Purchaser shall, on the Execution Date, pay to Chicago Title Company ("Escrow Holder"), the sum of _____ dollars by wire transfer of clear funds. If the Closing occurs, the Deposit shall be applied toward the Purchase Price. Purchaser and Seller shall instruct Escrow Holder to deposit the Deposit in an interest-bearing account or accounts; provided, however, that nothing herein shall relieve Purchaser of its obligation to cause to be delivered to Seller the Deposit when required hereunder.

6. PRELIMINARY TITLE EXAMINATION.

6.1   By executing this Agreement, Purchaser acknowledges receipt and approval of (a) Title Policy Order dated, copies of which are attached hereto as **Exhibit "3"** and (b) copies of all exceptions of record described therein. Promptly upon execution of this Agreement, Purchaser shall, at its expense, obtain a commitment (the "Commitment") from the Title Company to issue to Purchaser at the Closing a standard coverage owner's policy insuring Purchaser's interest in the Property, subject to all liens, covenants, conditions, restrictions, easements leases, rights, rights-of-way and encumbrances as may now be of record against the Property.

6.2 After the Execution Date, Purchaser may, at Purchaser's expense, obtain from a registered or licensed land surveyor or engineer an ALTA boundary survey, an original copy of which shall be delivered to Seller. Purchaser has no obligation to do so.

6.3 Purchaser shall notify Seller in writing prior to the Expiration Date (without right of extension) of Purchaser's objections (if any) to the Commitment and/or such survey (the "Title Objections"). Approval of Title is at Buyer's sole discretion. Any items not expressly objected to by Purchaser within such period shall be deemed approved. All items so approved by Purchaser shall be attached to this Agreement as **Exhibit "3"** thereto and shall thereafter be referred to as the "Permitted Exceptions". If Purchaser makes timely written objection, Seller shall have thirty (30) days from receipt within which to cure any such Title Objections, provided Seller shall not be obligated to expend any funds in connection with any curative action. If Seller fails to cure any such objections within such 30-day period, then, unless such Title Objection is waived in writing by Purchaser, this Agreement shall be automatically terminated, in which event, there shall be no further rights or obligations between the parties, except for Purchaser's obligations under **Articles 4** and **5** above.

7. **THE CLOSING**.

7.1 The Closing shall occur at the offices of Escrow Holder on or before _____ , 200_ unless an earlier date is mutually agreed to in writing. The Closing shall be on a Monday, Tuesday, Wednesday or Thursday, unless Seller agrees otherwise in writing.

7.2 At the Closing, Seller shall deliver the following:

(a) Duly executed Quitclaim Deed (or Oklahoma equivalent) substantially in the form of **Exhibit "4"**;

(b) Duly executed Bill of Sale substantially in the form of **Exhibit "5"**;

(c) Duly executed Assignment and Assumption of Leases, Contracts and Warranties in the form of **Exhibit "6"**;

(d) Schedule of all personal property being sold by Quit Claim to Purchaser, which schedule shall be attached hereto as Exhibit "2";

(g) A Tax Certification in the form of **Exhibit "7"** pursuant to Internal Revenue Code Section 1445.

7.3 The following charges shall be paid as of the Closing:

(a) All certificates, transfer fees and taxes, and recordation costs shall be paid by Purchaser.

(b) Purchaser and Seller shall pay their own attorneys' fees.

(c) Purchaser shall pay all cost, fees and charges incurred in procuring an owner's title policy for the Property in Purchaser's name Purchaser shall also pay for any title policies required by any of Purchaser's lenders.

(d) Purchaser shall pay any mortgage taxes (if any, none known) and points and any and all other charges which may be incurred in connection with any purchase money financing obtained by Purchaser.

7.4 At the Closing, Purchaser shall, at Purchaser's expense, deliver to Seller the following:

(a) Clear funds in the amount of the purchase price specified in **Article 2** and adjusted as provided for herein.

(b) A Certificate of Good Standing for Purchaser from the Secretaries of State of the state of Purchaser's incorporation and of the state in which the Property is located, if a corporation or limited liability company or partnership;

(c) Certified copies of corporate resolutions of the Board of Directors and the stockholders of Purchaser, if a corporation or resolutions of all the Members (if Purchaser is a limited liability company) or all the partners (if Purchaser is a partnership), authorizing the execution and delivery by Purchaser of this Sale Agreement and all other documents necessary or advisable to consummate the transactions contemplated hereby.

7.5 Any credits or prorations in favor of Purchaser by reason of Purchaser assuming any financing contract balances or obligations of Seller shall be prorated to the Close.

7.6 Purchaser shall pay sales tax if any on the sale of the Personal Property.

8. <u>PRORATIONS</u>.

8.1 The following items will be prorated as of 11:59 P.M. on the date of Closing: rents; real estate taxes; interest; operating income and expenses; transferred tenant deposits for which Seller is accountable; reasonable prepaid expenses and transferred escrow accounts; utilities and water charges based on readings as of the Closing; utility deposits; interest on encumbrances. The apportionment of real estate taxes shall be made pursuant to the present evidence of real estate taxes (assessments and rates) available as of the Closing. If, subsequent to the date of

Closing, real estate taxes are (by reason of change in either assessment or rate or any other reason) determined to be higher than those that are apportioned, a new computation shall be made and Purchaser shall pay to Seller any net decrease shown by such recomputation and Seller shall pay to Purchaser any increase shown by such recomputation if applicable. Special assessments, if any, which are a lien as of the Closing shall be prorated assuming the maximum time for payment permitted by the taxing authority for such items. All non refundable deposits collected by Seller prior to closing shall belong exclusively to Seller.

8.2 The following shall be prorated or adjusted in the following manner:

Seller shall receive credit for all rents billed which are delinquent thirty (30 days or less) regardless of whether or not such rents are ever collected by Purchaser.

Seller shall receive no credit for any rents which are delinquent for more than thirty (30) days regardless of whether or not such rents are collected by Purchaser.

9. BROKERAGE COMMISSION. Purchaser and Seller represent that they have employed no real estate brokers or finders in connection with the sale. Purchaser and Seller each indemnify and agree to hold the other harmless from and against any claim for a commission or finder's fee made by a claiming party through the indemnifying party.

10. DAMAGE AND DESTRUCTION; CONDEMNATION;

10.1 If, prior to the date of the Closing, a "material portion" of the Property (as defined below) is either destroyed or materially damaged by fire or other insured casualty, or taken by eminent domain, then Purchaser may, within five (5) days from receipt of written notice of such occurrence, either (a) terminate this Sale Agreement, whereupon Seller shall return the Deposit to Purchaser, or (b) proceed with the purchase, in which event Purchaser shall complete the purchase of the Property from Seller at the purchase price and upon the terms set forth in this Sale Agreement, in which latter event Purchaser shall be entitled to receive Seller's insurance proceeds or condemnation award, as the case may be, as its loss compensation. "A material portion of the property" shall be 10% or more of the aggregate gross building area.

10.2 If, prior to the date of the Closing, all or a portion of the Property is either destroyed or materially damaged by an uninsured casualty, then Seller shall give Purchaser written notice describing such damage or destruction. If the cost of repairing such damage is $10,000 or less, then Seller shall promptly undertake the repair of such damage or destruction and the purchase price shall be increased in accordance with the cost of such repair. If the cost of such repair exceeds $10,000, then Purchaser shall have five (5) business days (or 48 hours in the event of an emergency) after receipt of Seller's notice within which to terminate this Sale Agreement by written notice to Seller. If Purchaser fails to elect to terminate this Sale Agreement within such ten (10)-business day (or 48 hour) period, Purchaser shall be deemed to have elected to proceed with the sale notwithstanding the damage or destruction and Purchaser shall repair the damage at its sole cost and expense.

INITIALS: SELLER:_____   PURCHASER:_____

11. ASSUMPTION AND INDEMNITY.

11.1 Effective on the date of the Closing, Purchaser indemnifies and agrees to hold Seller, its agents, employees, partners, attorneys, legal successors and assigns, and each of them, free and harmless from and against all claims, demands, liens, obligations, indebtedness, damages, debts, liabilities, accounts, actions, causes of action costs or expenses, including attorneys' fees on account of any grounds whatsoever in law or in equity arising out of, relating to, or in connection with, from and after the date of Closing, (a) the operation, management and ownership of the Property, (b) all contracts, agreements and leases affecting the Property and (c) all claims of tenants with respect to their leases and/or security/pet deposits.

11.2 Seller indemnifies and holds Purchaser, its legal successors and assigns, free and harmless from all claims and causes of action arising out of any event occurring prior to the Closing and any liability or obligation incurred prior to the Closing with respect to the operation, management and ownership of the Property which Purchaser does not assume at the Closing; provided, however, that nothing herein shall be interpreted as expanding any covenant or warranty contained in the Deed to be delivered by Seller to Purchaser at the Closing or creating any representation, warranty or indemnification regarding the condition of the Property as of the Closing. Purchaser agrees that any liability of Seller under any claim brought pursuant to this Sale Agreement or any document or instrument delivered simultaneously or in connection with, or pursuant to this Sale Agreement, shall be limited solely to the sales proceeds received by Seller and that in no event shall Purchaser seek satisfaction for any such obligation from any of the partners of Seller.

12. REPRESENTATIONS AND WARRANTIES.

12.1   Seller represents that, through the Closing, Seller shall operate the Property in the same manner as now exists.

12.2   Purchaser represents to Seller that the representatives of Purchaser executing this Sale Agreement are authorized to enter into this Sale Agreement and to perform such acts to execute such documents as are reasonably necessary to consummate Purchaser's purchase of the Property.

12.3.   (a) Seller represents and Warrants that:

1. Seller is duly formed and in good standing

2. Samuel K. Freshman has the authority to bind Seller to this Agreement.

3. Seller has the power and authority to sell the Property.

4. This transaction will not violate any provision in the Partnership agreement or any other agreement to which the Seller is a party.

(b) To the best of Seller's actual knowledge, Seller represents and Warrants that:

1. That all the documents given to Buyer are true and accurate copies of original documents.

2. That there is no litigation presently involving the Property; that Seller has no knowledge of any facts or circumstances which would give rise to such litigation except for events which are covered by insurance

3. All information provided with respect to the income, expense, and liabilities of the property are true and correct to the best of Sellers knowledge and belief.

4. Seller has no actual knowledge of any contamination of the Property other than as disclosed in the reports described in Exhibit 7.

5. That Seller is not delinquent or otherwise in breach of any loan documents.

6. Purchaser represents and Warrant to Seller

1. Purchaser is duly formed and in good standing

2. _____ has the authority to bind Purchaser to this Agreement.

3. Purchaser has the power and authority to purchase the Property.

4. This transaction will not violate any provision in the Corporate Charter or by-laws, Partnership Agreement or Article of Organization or Operating Agreement as applicable, or any other agreement to which the Purchaser is a party.

13. **GENERAL PROVISIONS**.

13.1 Time of Essence. Time is of the essence with respect to all matters contained in this Sale Agreement.

13.2 Notices. All notices, request, demands and other communications under this Sale Agreement shall be in writing and must be delivered either by personal service or by first class mail, registered or certified, postage prepaid, return receipt requested, or by such expedited courier service where receipt by addressee can be confirmed by said courier service in writing (i.e., Federal Express, Express Mail, etc.), and properly addressed as follows:

To Seller:

    Samuel K. Freshman
    Standard Management Company
    6151 W. Century Boulevard, Suite 300
    Los Angeles, California 90045-5314

With Copy to:

    Standard Management Company
    6151 W. Century Boulevard, Suite 300
    Los Angeles, California 90045-5314
    Attn.: Legal Department/Marc Schwartz

To Purchaser:

    Attn.:

With Copy to:

    _____
    _____
    _____
    Attn:

All notices are deemed given upon actual receipt by addressee. Any party may change its address for notice by giving the other written notice of the new address in the manner specified above.

13.3 Validity-Waiver. If any provision of this Sale Agreement shall be held to be invalid, the same shall not affect in any respect whatsoever the validity of the remainder of this Sale Agreement. No waiver of any of the provisions of this Sale Agreement shall be deemed or shall constitute a waiver of any other provision, whether or not similar, nor shall any waiver constitute a continuing waiver. No waiver shall be binding unless executed in writing by the party making the waiver.

13.4 Governing Law; Heading; Gender. This Sale Agreement shall be governed by and construed in accordance with the laws of the State in which the property is located. Paragraph headings contained in this Sale Agreement are for convenience only and shall not be considered for any purpose in construing this Sale Agreement. As used in this Sale Agreement, the masculine, feminine or neuter gender and the singular or plural number shall each be deemed to include the others whenever the context so indicates.

13.5 Attorneys' Fees. In the event of a dispute between the parties hereto arising out of this Sale Agreement, the prevailing party shall be entitled to recover reasonable attorneys' fees, costs and expenses incurred in connection therewith.

13.6 Additional Documents. Each party shall, at the request of the other, execute, acknowledge and deliver whatever additional instruments, and do such other acts, as required or convenient to accomplish and carry forward the intent and purposes of this Sale Agreement.

13.7 Assignment; Successors and Assigns.

(a) Purchaser shall not sell or assign its interests under this Sale Agreement without the prior written consent of Seller, which consent May be withheld in Seller's sole discretion. If such consent is granted, such assignment shall be subject to the following conditions:(i) the assignment shall be in writing signed by both the Purchaser and the assignee, and shall contain a provision whereby the assignee assumes all rights and obligations of the Purchaser under this Sale Agreement including all exhibits referred to herein and takes subject to all conditions provided in this Sale Agreement, and (ii) Purchaser shall deliver a copy of such assignment to Seller not later than thirty (30) days prior to the then-scheduled Closing.

Notwithstanding the foregoing, any such assignment shall not in any manner whatsoever alter, reduce, modify, affect or otherwise relieve Purchaser of any of its obligations to Seller hereunder.

(b) This Sale Agreement shall be binding upon and inure to the benefit of the parties hereto and their respective heirs, representatives, successors and assigns.

13.8 Recordation. Purchaser shall not record this Sale Agreement or a memorandum thereof in any public place or register of any kind.

13.9 Tax-Deferred Exchange. Seller shall be entitled to transfer this property in accordance with Internal Revenue Service Code 1031. Purchaser will cooperate with Seller in order to effectuate the tax-deferred exchange. Seller reserves the option, however, to elect to proceed under a non-simultaneous exchange prior to the close of escrow. The sale and closing of escrow covering the Property are in no way contingent upon Seller's ability to effect an Internal Revenue Service Code 1031 Tax Deferred Exchange.

13.10 Entire Agreement. All understandings and agreements heretofore made between the parties respecting this transaction are merged in the Option Agreement, this Sale Agreement and the exhibits and schedules attached hereto, all of which together completely express the agreement of the parties. There are no representations, warranties or agreements except as specifically and expressly set forth herein and in the exhibits and schedules attached hereto.

13.11 Modification. No modification of this Sale Agreement or any part hereof shall be valid unless in writing and signed by or on behalf of all of the parties.

13.12 Construction of Language. Each party and its counsel have reviewed and revised this Sale Agreement such that the normal rule of construction that ambiguities are resolved against the drafting party shall not be employed in the interpretation of this Sale Agreement or any amendments or exhibits thereto. No delay by either party in enforcing any right, remedy, privilege or recourse under this Sale Agreement, or which either party may be or become entitled to have or exercise under this Sale Agreement, nor any number of recoveries thereon, shall affect, diminish, suspend or exhaust any such right, remedy, privilege or recourse.

13.13 Counterparts. This Agreement shall be effective when signed below or in counterparts, and photocopy, facsimile, electronic, or other copies shall have the same effect for all purposes as an ink-signed original.

13.14 <u>Government Authority</u>. This entire Sale Agreement is subject to any legislation or regulations issued by any government authority having jurisdiction over this transaction and the parties agree to cooperate with each other in complying with any such legislation or regulations.

13.15 <u>Back-up Offers</u>. Seller reserves the right during the term of this Sale Agreement to accept additional back-up offers to purchase the Property from other persons or entities.

13.16 <u>Default</u>. EXCEPT AS OTHERWISE EXPRESSLY SET FORTH IN THIS SALE AGREEMENT, IF THE CLOSING OF THE TRANSACTION CONTEMPLATED HEREIN FAILS TO OCCUR, THE DEPOSIT SHALL BE PAID TO SELLER AS LIQUIDATED DAMAGES AND AS SELLER'S EXCLUSIVE REMEDY, UNLESS SUCH FAILURE TO CLOSE RESULTS DIRECTLY AND SOLELY FROM A MATERIAL DEFAULT BY SELLER OF ITS OBLIGATIONS UNDER THIS SALE AGREEMENT, IN WHICH EVENT PURCHASER SHALL, AS ITS EXCLUSIVE REMEDY, BE ENTITLED TO THE FOLLOWING REMEDY: A REFUND OF ITS DEPOSIT, PLUS ANY INTEREST EARNED THEREON WHILE THE DEPOSIT IS HELD BY ESCROW HOLDER.

INITIALS: SELLER:_____   PURCHASER:_____

IN WITNESS WHEREOF, the parties have executed this Sale agreement as of the date first set forth above.

"SELLER"   "PURCHASER"

_____

By:_____   By: _____
    SAMUEL K. FRESHMAN
                                                  Its:_____

SCHEDULE OF EXHIBITS

(TO SALE AGREEMENT)

EXHIBIT	DESCRIPTION
1	Legal Description
2	Schedule of Personal Property Being Sold
3	Title Policies/Permitted Exceptions
4	Quitclaim Deed
5	Bill of Sale
5-1	Legal Description
6	Assignment and Assumption of Lease, Contracts and Warranties
6-1	Legal Description
6-2	Lease Agreements
6-3	Contracts and Warranties
7	Seller's Disclosures
8	Tax Certification

EXHIBIT "1"
Legal Description
(to be supplied by title company)

EXHIBIT "2"
Schedule of Personal Property
(List all personal property being transferred. (s10))

EXHIBIT "3"
Title Policy/Permitted Exceptions
(to be supplied by legal counsel)

EXHIBIT "4"
Quitclaim Deed
(Form varies depending on state in which real property is located.)

EXHIBIT 5

BILL OF SALE

THE STATE OF _____)

$\qquad$) KNOW ALL MEN BY THESE PRESENTS:

THAT _____("Seller"), for and in consideration of the sum of TEN DOLLARS ($10.00) and other good and valuable consideration, the receipt and sufficiency of which are acknowledged and confessed, bargains, sells, assigns, transfers and delivers to _____, all of Seller's right, title and interest in and to the personal property (the "Personal Property") situated upon the real property set forth and described on **EXHIBIT "5-1"** attached hereto and made a part hereof for all purposes, together with Seller's right, title and interest, if any, in and to the name _____" and any related trademarks or symbols.

THIS ASSIGNMENT IS MADE WITHOUT ANY REPRESENTATION OR WARRANTY, EXPRESS OR IMPLIED, AS TO THE OWNERSHIP, QUALITY, QUANTITY, NATURE, OR PHYSICAL OR OPERATING CONDITION OF THE PERSONAL PROPERTY.

IN WITNESS WHEREOF, Seller has executed this Bill of Sale as of _____, 200__.

"SELLER"

By:_____

EXHIBIT "5-1"
Legal Description
(repeat of Exhibit "1")

EXHIBIT 6

ASSIGNMENT AND ASSUMPTION OF LEASES, CONTRACTS AND WARRANTIES

THIS ASSIGNMENT, made and entered into as of _____, 200_, by _____ ("Assignor") and _____ _____ ("Assignee"), with reference to the following:

A. Pursuant to an Agreement for Sale and Purchase of Real Property dated _____, 200_ (the "Sale Agreement"), Assignor is selling certain real property (the "Real Property") to Assignee commonly known as "_____" and more particularly described on **Exhibit "6-1"** attached hereto and incorporated herein by this reference.

B. Assignor or Assignor's predecessors-in-title, as Landlord, and certain parties, as tenants or contracting parties, heretofore entered into the leases, contracts and warranties described on the Schedules attached hereto as **Exhibit "6-2"** (the "Leases") and **Exhibit "6-3"** (the "Contracts" and "Warranties"). All of such tenants and contracting parties are hereinafter referred to as the "Tenants" and "Vendors", respectively.

C. Assignor now desires to assign and convey, and Assignee desires to assume and accept all of Assignor's interest in the Leases, Contracts and Warranties, subject to the conditions set forth below.

NOW, THEREFORE, for good and valuable consideration, the receipt and sufficiency of which are acknowledged, the parties agree as follows;

1. **ASSIGNMENT**. Subject to the terms and conditions set forth in the Sale Agreement, Assignor assigns, transfers, sets-over and delivers unto Assignee all of the rights, benefits and privileges of Assignor under (a) the Leases, including without limitation all rents, security deposits and profits arising therefrom; (b) the Contracts and (c) the Warranties, TO HAVE AND TO HOLD all and singular subject as aforesaid, unto Assignee, its successors and assigns, forever. This conveyance is made without warranty implied or express.

2. **ASSUMPTION**. Assignee assumes and agrees to discharge and perform all duties, obligations and liabilities arising on or after the date hereof to be performed

by Assignor under the Leases, Contracts and Warranties for the duration of the respective terms thereof, and agree to indemnify, save and hold harmless Assignor from and against any and all loss, liability, claims or causes of action existing in favor of or asserted by any tenant under any Lease or any Vendor under any Contract or Warranty for the duration of the respective terms thereof based on the failure of Assignee to perform or discharge any duty, obligation or liability hereby assumed by Assignee including without limitation the failure to pay any Vendor or properly apply any advance rental, security deposit or other deposit under any Lease or Contract if such advance rental, security deposit or other deposit has been delivered by Assignor to Assignee con-currently herewith.

3. SECURITY DEPOSITS. Assignee shall hold and disburse security deposits with respect to the Leases strictly in accordance with the terms and provisions thereof and applicable law.

4. SUCCESSORS AND ASSIGNS. All of the covenants, terms and conditions set forth herein shall be binding upon and shall inure to the benefit of the parties hereto and their respective heirs, personal representatives, successors and assigns.

IN WITNESS WHEREOF, the parties have executed this instrument as of the date first set forth above.

ASSIGNEE: ASSIGNOR:

By: _____   By:_____

EXHIBIT "6-1"
Legal Description
(repeat of Exhibit "1")

EXHIBIT "6-2"
Lease Agreements
(schedule of all existing leases)

EXHIBIT "6-3"
Contracts and Warranties
(schedule of all contracts and warranties being transferred (s10))

EXHIBIT "7"
Tax Certification
(to be supplied by legal counsel)

Code of Federal Regulations][Title 17, Volume 2]
[Revised as of April 1, 2003]
From the U.S. Government Printing Office via GPO Access
[CITE: 17CFR230.501]

TITLE 17--COMMODITY AND SECURITIES EXCHANGES

CHAPTER II--SECURITIES AND EXCHANGE COMMISSION

PART 230--GENERAL RULES AND REGULATIONS, SECURITIES ACT OF 1933--Table of Contents

Sec. 230.501 Definitions and terms used in Regulation D.

As used in Regulation D (Secs. 230.501-230.508), the following terms shall have the meaning indicated:

(a) Accredited investor. Accredited investor shall mean any person who comes within any of the following categories, or who the issuer reasonably believes comes within any of the following categories, at the time of the sale of the securities to that person:

(1) Any bank as defined in section 3(a)(2) of the Act, or any savings and loan association or other institution as defined in section 3(a)(5)(A) of the Act whether acting in its individual or fiduciary capacity; any broker or dealer registered pursuant to section 15 of the Securities Exchange Act of 1934; any insurance company as defined in section 2(13) of the Act; any investment company registered under the Investment Company Act of 1940 or a business development company as defined in section 2(a)(48) of that Act; any Small Business Investment Company licensed by the U.S. Small Business Administration under section 301(c) or (d) of the Small Business Investment Act of 1958; any plan established and maintained by a state, its political subdivisions, or any agency or instrumentality of a state or its political subdivisions, for the benefit of its employees, if such plan has total assets in excess of $5,000,000; any employee benefit plan within the meaning of the Employee Retirement Income Security Act of 1974 if the investment decision is made by a plan fiduciary, as defined in section 3(21) of such act, which is either a bank, savings and loan association, insurance company, or registered investment adviser, or if the employee benefit plan has total assets in excess of $5,000,000 or, if a self-directed plan, with investment decisions made solely by persons that are accredited investors;

(2) Any private business development company as defined in section

APPENDIX D
REG D

202(a)(22) of the Investment Advisers Act of 1940;

(3) Any organization described in section 501(c)(3) of the Internal Revenue Code, corporation, Massachusetts or similar business trust, or partnership, not formed for the specific purpose of acquiring the securities offered, with total assets in excess of $5,000,000;

(4) Any director, executive officer, or general partner of the issuer of the securities being offered or sold, or any director, executive officer, or general partner of a general partner of that issuer;

(5) Any natural person whose individual net worth, or joint net worth with that person's spouse, at the time of his purchase exceeds $1,000,000;

(6) Any natural person who had an individual income in excess of $200,000 in each of the two most recent years or joint income with that person's spouse in excess of $300,000 in each of those years and has a reasonable expectation of reaching the same income level in the current year;

(7) Any trust, with total assets in excess of $5,000,000, not formed for the specific purpose of acquiring the securities offered, whose purchase is directed by a sophisticated person as described in Sec. 230.506(b)(2)(ii); and

(8) Any entity in which all of the equity owners are accredited investors.

(b) Affiliate. An affiliate of, or person affiliated with, a specified person shall mean a person that directly, or indirectly through one or more intermediaries, controls or is controlled by, or is under common control with, the person specified.

(c) Aggregate offering price. Aggregate offering price shall mean the sum of all cash, services, property, notes, cancellation of debt, or other consideration to be received by an issuer for issuance of its securities. Where securities are being offered for both cash and non-cash consideration, the aggregate offering price shall be based on the price at which the securities are offered for cash. Any portion of the aggregate offering price attributable to cash received in a foreign currency shall be translated into United States currency at the currency exchange rate in effect at a reasonable time prior to or on the date of the sale of the securities. If securities are not offered for cash, the aggregate offering price shall be based on the value of the consideration as established by bona fide sales of that consideration made within a reasonable time, or, in the absence of sales, on the fair value as determined by an accepted standard. Such valuations of non-cash consideration must be reasonable at the time made.

(d) Business combination. Business combination shall mean any transaction of the type specified in paragraph (a) of Rule 145 under the Act (17 CFR 230.145) and any transaction involving the acquisition by one issuer, in exchange for all or a part of its own or its parent's stock, of stock of another issuer if, immediately after the acquisition, the acquiring issuer has control of the other issuer (whether or not it had control before the acquisition).

(e) Calculation of number of purchasers. For purposes of calculating the number of purchasers under Secs. 230.505(b) and 230.506(b) only, the following shall apply:

(1) The following purchasers shall be excluded:

(i) Any relative, spouse or relative of the spouse of a purchaser who has the same principal residence as the purchaser;

(ii) Any trust or estate in which a purchaser and any of the persons related to him as specified in paragraph (e)(1)(i) or (e)(1)(iii) of this section collectively have more than 50 percent of the beneficial interest (excluding contingent interests);

(iii) Any corporation or other organization of which a purchaser and any of the persons related to him as specified in paragraph (e)(1)(i) or (e)(1)(ii) of this section collectively are beneficial owners of more than 50 percent of the equity securities (excluding directors' qualifying shares) or equity interests; and

(iv) Any accredited investor.

(2) A corporation, partnership or other entity shall be counted as one purchaser. If, however, that entity is organized for the specific purpose of acquiring the securities offered and is not an accredited investor under paragraph (a)(8) of this section, then each beneficial owner of equity securities or equity interests in the entity shall count as a separate purchaser for all provisions of Regulation D (Secs. 230.501-230.508), except to the extent provided in paragraph (e)(1) of this section.

(3) A non-contributory employee benefit plan within the meaning of Title I of the Employee Retirement Income Security Act of 1974 shall be counted as one purchaser where the trustee makes all investment decisions for the plan.

(f) Executive officer. Executive officer shall mean the president, any vice president in charge of a principal business unit, division or function (such as sales, administration orfinance), any other officer who performs a policy making function, or any other person who performs similar policy making functions for the issuer. Executive officers of subsidiaries may be deemed executive officers of the issuer if they perform such policy making functions for the issuer.

(g) Issuer. The definition of the term issuer in section 2(4) of the Act shall apply, except that in the case of a proceeding under the Federal Bankruptcy Code (11 U.S.C. 101 et seq.), the trustee or debtor in possession shall be considered the issuer in an offering under a plan or reorganization, if the securities are to be issued under the plan.

(h) Purchaser representative. Purchaser representative shall mean any person who satisfies all of the following conditions or who the issuer reasonably believes satisfies all of the following conditions:

(1) Is not an affiliate, director, officer or other employee of the issuer, or beneficial owner of 10 percent or more of any class of the equity securities or 10 percent or more of the equity interest in the issuer, except where the purchaser is:

(i) A relative of the purchaser representative by blood, marriage or adoption and not more remote than a first cousin;

(ii) A trust or estate in which the purchaser representative and any persons related to him as specified in paragraph (h)(1)(i) or (h)(1)(iii) of this section collectively have more than 50 percent of the beneficial interest (excluding contingent interest) or of which the purchaser representative serves as trustee, executor, or in any similar capacity; or

(iii) A corporation or other organization of which the purchaser representative and any persons related to him as specified in paragraph (h)(1)(i) or (h)(1)(ii) of this section collectively are the beneficial owners of more than 50 percent of the equity securities (excluding directors' qualifying shares) or equity interests;

(2) Has such knowledge and experience in financial and business matters that he is capable of evaluating, alone, or together with other purchaser representatives of the purchaser, or together with the purchaser, the merits and risks of the prospective investment;

(3) Is acknowledged by the purchaser in writing, during the course of the transaction, to be his purchaser representative in connection with evaluating the merits and risks of the prospective investment; and

(4) Discloses to the purchaser in writing a reasonable time prior to the sale of securities to that purchaser any material relationship between himself or his affiliates and the issuer or its affiliates that then exists, that is mutually understood to be contemplated, or that has existed at any time during the previous two years, and any compensation received or to be received as a result of such relationship.

Note 1: A person acting as a purchaser representative should consider the applicability of the registration and antifraud provisions relating to brokers and dealers under the Securities Exchange Act of 1934 (Exchange Act) (15 U.S.C. 78a et seq., as amended) and relating to investment advisers under the Investment Advisers Act of 1940.

Note 2: The acknowledgment required by paragraph (h)(3) and the disclosure required by paragraph (h)(4) of this section must be made with specific reference to each prospective investment. Advance blanket acknowledgment, such as for all securities transactions or all private placements, is not sufficient.

Note 3: Disclosure of any material relationships between the purchaser representative or his affiliates and the issuer or its affiliates does not relieve the purchaser representative of his obligation to act in the interest of the purchaser.

[47 FR 11262, Mar. 16, 1982, as amended at 53 FR 7868, Mar. 10, 1988; 54 FR 11372, Mar. 20, 1989]

SECTION 502
[Code of Federal Regulations][Title 17, Volume 2]
[Revised as of April 1, 2003]
From the U.S. Government Printing Office via GPO Access
[CITE: 17CFR230.502]

TITLE 17--COMMODITY AND SECURITIES EXCHANGES

CHAPTER II--SECURITIES AND EXCHANGE COMMISSION

PART 230--GENERAL RULES AND REGULATIONS, SECURITIES ACT OF 1933--Table of Contents

Sec. 230.502 General conditions to be met.

The following conditions shall be applicable to offers and sales made under Regulation D (Secs. 230.501-230.508):

(a) Integration. All sales that are part of the same Regulation D offering must meet all of the terms and conditions of Regulation D.Offers and sales that are made more than six months before the start of a Regulation D offering or are made more than six months after completion of a Regulation D offering will not be considered part of that Regulation D offering, so long as during those six month periods there are no offers or sales of securities by or for the issuer that are of the same or a similar class as those offered or sold under Regulation D, other than those offers or sales of securities under an employee benefit plan as defined in rule 405 under the Act (17 CFR 230.405).

Note: The term offering is not defined in the Act or in Regulation

D. If the issuer offers or sells securities for which the safe harborrule in paragraph (a) of this Sec. 230.502 is unavailable, the determination as to whether separate sales of securities are part of the same offering (i.e. are considered integrated) depends on the particular facts and circumstances. Generally, transactions otherwise meeting the requirements of an exemption will not be integrated with simultaneous offerings being made outside the United States in compliance with Regulation S. See Release No. 33-6863.

The following factors should be considered in determining whether offers and sales should be integrated for purposes of the exemptions under Regulation D:

(a) Whether the sales are part of a single plan of financing;

(b) Whether the sales involve issuance of the same class of securities;

(c) Whether the sales have been made at or about the same time;

(d) Whether the same type of consideration is being received; and

(e) Whether the sales are made for the same general purpose.

See Release 33-4552 (November 6, 1962) [27 FR 11316].

(b) Information requirements--(1) When information must be furnished. If the issuer sells securities under Sec. 230.505 or Sec. 230.506 to any purchaser that is not an accredited investor, the issuer shall furnish the information specified in paragraph (b)(2) of this section to such purchaser a reasonable time prior to sale. The issuer is not required to furnish the specified information to purchasers when it sells securities under Sec. 230.504, or to any accredited investor.

Note: When an issuer provides information to investors pursuant to paragraph (b)(1), it should consider providing such information to accredited investors as well, in view of the anti-fraud provisions of the federal securities laws.

(2) Type of information to be furnished. (i) If the issuer is not subject to the reporting requirements of section 13 or 15(d) of the Exchange Act, at a reasonable time prior to the sale of securities the issuer shall furnish to the purchaser, to the extent material to an understanding of the issuer, its business and the securities being offered:

(A) Non-financial statement information. If the issuer is eligible to use Regulation A (Sec. 230.251-263), the same kind of information as would be required in Part II of Form 1-A (Sec. 239.90 of this chapter). If the issuer is not eligible to use Regulation A, the same kind of information as required in Part I of a registration statement filed under the Securities Act on the form that the issuer would be entitled to use.

(B) Financial statement information. (1) Offerings up to $2,000,000. The information required in Item 310 of Regulation S-B (Sec. 228.310 of this chapter), except that only the issuer's balance sheet, which shall be dated within 120 days of the start of the offering, must be audited.

(2) Offerings up to $7,500,000. The financial statement information required in Form SB-2 (Sec. 239.10 of this chapter). If an issuer, other than a limited partnership, cannot obtain audited financial statements without unreasonable effort or expense, then only the issuer's balance sheet, which shall be dated within 120 days of the start of the offering, must be audited. If the issuer is a limited partnership and cannot obtain the required financial statements without unreasonable effort or expense, it may furnish financial statements that have been prepared on the basis of Federal income tax requirements and examined and reported on in accordance with generally accepted auditing standards by an independent public or certified accountant.

(3) Offerings over $7,500,000. The financial statement as would be required in a registration statement filed under the Act on the form that the issuer would be entitled to use. If an issuer, other than a limited partnership, cannot obtain audited financial statements without unreasonable effort or expense, then only the issuer's balance sheet, which shall be dated within 120 days of the start of the offering, must be audited. If the issuer is a limited partnership and cannot obtain the required financial statements without unreasonable effort or expense, it may furnish financial statements that have been prepared on the basis of Federal income tax requirements and examined and reported on in accordance with generally accepted auditing standards by an independent public or certified accountant.

(C) If the issuer is a foreign private issuer eligible to use Form 20-F (Sec. 249.220f of this chapter), the issuer shall disclose the same kind of information required to be included in a registration statement filed under the Act on the form that the issuer would be entitled to use. The financial statements need be certified only to the extent required by paragraph (b)(2)(i) (B) (1), (2) or (3) of this section, as appropriate.

(ii) If the issuer is subject to the reporting requirements of section 13 or 15(d) of the Exchange Act, at a reasonable time prior to the sale of securities the issuer shall furnish to the purchaser the information specified in paragraph (b)(2)(ii)(A) or (B) of this section, and in either event the information specified in paragraph (b)(2)(ii)(C) of this section:

(A) The issuer's annual report to shareholders for the most recent fiscal year, if such annual report meets the requirements of Sec. 240.14a-3 or 240.14c-3 under the Exchange Act, the definitive proxy statement filed in connection with that annual report, and, if requested by the purchaser in writing, a copy of the issuer's most recent Form 10-K and Form 10-KSB (17 CFR 249.310) under the Exchange Act.

(B) The information contained in an annual report on Form 10-K (Sec. 249.310 of this chapter) or 10-KSB (Sec. 249.310b of this chapter) under the Exchange Act or in a registration statement on Form S-1 (Sec. 239.11 of this chapter), SB-1 (Sec. 239.9 of this chapter), SB-2 (Sec. 239.10 of this chapter) or S-11 (Sec. 239.18 of this chapter) under the Act or on Form 10 (Sec. 249.210 of this chapter) or Form 10-SB

(Sec. 249.210b of this chapter) under the Exchange Act, whichever filing is the most recent required to be filed.

(C) The information contained in any reports or documents required to be filed by the issuer under sections 13(a), 14(a), 14(c), and 15(d) of the Exchange Act since the distribution or filing of the report or registration statement specified in paragraphs (b)(2)(ii) (A) or (B), and a brief description of the securities being offered, the use of the proceeds from the offering, and any material changes in the issuer's affairs that are not disclosed in the documents furnished.

(D) If the issuer is a foreign private issuer, the issuer may provide in lieu of the information specified in paragraph (b)(2)(ii) (A) or (B) of this section, the information contained in its most recent filing on Form 20-F or Form F-1 (Sec. 239.31 of the chapter).

(iii) Exhibits required to be filed with the Commission as part of a registration statement or report, other than an annual report to shareholders or parts of that report incorporated by reference in a Form 10-K and Form 10-KSB report, need not be furnished to each purchaser that is not an accredited investor if the contents of material exhibits are identified and such exhibits are made available to a purchaser, upon his written request, a reasonable time prior to his purchase.

(iv) At a reasonable time prior to the sale of securities to any purchaser that is not an accredited investor in a transaction under Sec. 230.505 or Sec. 230.506, the issuer shall furnish to the purchaser a brief description in writing of any material written information concerning the offering that has been provided by the issuer to any accredited investor but not previously delivered to such unaccredited purchaser. The issuer shall furnish any portion or all of this information to the purchaser, upon his written request a reasonable time prior to his purchase.

(v) The issuer shall also make available to each purchaser at a reasonable time prior to his purchase of securities in a transaction under Sec. 230.505 or Sec. 230.506 the opportunity to ask questions and receive answers concerning the terms and conditions of the offering and to obtain any additional information which the issuer possesses or can acquire without unreasonable effort or expense that is necessary to verify the accuracy of information furnished under paragraph (b)(2) (i) or (ii) of this section.

(vi) For business combinations or exchange offers, in addition to information required by Form S-4 (17 CFR 239.25), the issuer shall provide to each purchaser at the time the plan is submitted to security holders, or, with an exchange, during the course of the transaction and prior to sale, written information about any terms or arrangements of the proposed transactions that are materially different from those for all other security holders. For purposes of this subsection, an issuer which is not subject to the reporting requirements of section 13 or 15(d) of the Exchange Act may satisfy the requirements of Part I.B. or

C. of Form S-4 by compliance with paragraph (b)(2)(i) of this Sec. 230.502.

(vii) At a reasonable time prior to the sale of securities to any purchaser that is not an accredited investor in a transaction under Sec. 230.505 or Sec. 230.506, the issuer shall advise the purchaser of the limitations on resale in the manner contained in paragraph (d)(2) of this section. Such disclosure may be contained in other materials required to be provided by this paragraph. (c) Limitation on manner of offering. Except as provided in Sec. 230.504(b)(1), neither the issuer nor any person acting on its behalf shall offer or sell the securities by any form of general solicitation or general advertising, including, but not limited to, the following:

(1) Any advertisement, article, notice or other communication published in any newspaper, magazine, or similar media or broadcast over television or radio; and (2) Any seminar or meeting whose attendees have been invited by any general solicitation or general advertising;Provided, however, that publication by an issuer of a notice in accordance with Sec. 230.135c shall not be deemed to constitute general solicitation or general advertising for purposes of this section; Provided further, that, if the requirements of Sec. 230.135e are satisfied, providing any journalist with access to press conferences held outside of the United States, to meetings with issuer or selling security holder representatives conducted outside of the United States, or to written press-related materials released outside the United States, at or in which a present or proposed offering of securities is discussed, will not be deemed to constitute general solicitation or general advertising for purposes of this section.

(d) Limitations on resale. Except as provided in Sec. 230.504(b)(1), securities acquired in a transaction under Regulation D shall have the status of securities acquired in a transaction under section 4(2) of the Act and cannot be resold without registration under the Act or an exemption therefrom. The issuer shall exercise reasonable care to assure that the purchasers of the securities are not underwriters within the meaning of section 2(11) of the Act, which reasonable care may be demonstrated by the following:

(1) Reasonable inquiry to determine if the purchaser is acquiring the securities for himself or for other persons;

(2) Written disclosure to each purchaser prior to sale that the securities have not been registered under the Act and, therefore, cannot be resold unless they are registered under the Act or unless an exemption from registration is available; and

(3) Placement of a legend on the certificate or other document that evidences the securities stating that the securities have not been registered under the Act and setting forth or referring to the restrictions on transferability and sale of the securities.

While taking these actions will establish the requisite reasonable care, it is not the exclusive method to demonstrate such care. Other actions by the issuer may satisfy this provision. In addition, Sec. 230.502(b)(2)(vii) requires the delivery of written disclosure of the limitations on resale to investors in certain instances.

[47 FR 11262, Mar. 16, 1982, as amended at 47 FR 54771, Dec. 6, 1982; 53 FR 7869, Mar. 11, 1988; 54 FR 11372, Mar. 20, 1989; 55 FR 18322, May 2, 1990; 56 FR 30054, 30055, July 1, 1991; 57 FR 47409, Oct. 16, 1992; 58 FR 26514, May 4, 1993; 59 FR 21650, Apr. 26, 1994; 62 FR 53954, Oct. 17, 1997]

SECTION 504

Code of Federal Regulations][Title 17, Volume 2]
[Revised as of April 1, 2005]
From the U.S. Government Printing Office via GPO Access
[CITE: 17CFR230.503]

TITLE 17--COMMODITY AND SECURITIES EXCHANGES

CHAPTER II--SECURITIES AND EXCHANGE COMMISSION

PART 230_GENERAL RULES AND REGULATIONS, SECURITIES ACT OF
1933--Table of Contents

Sec. 230.503 Filing of notice of sales.

(a) An issuer offering or selling securities in reliance on Sec. 230.504, Sec. 230.505 or Sec. 230.506 shall file with the Commission five copies of a notice on Form D (17 CFR 239.500) no later than 15 days after the first sale of securities.

(b) One copy of every notice on Form D shall be manually signed by a person duly authorized by the issuer.

(c) If sales are made under Sec. 230.505, the notice shall contain an undertaking by the issuer to furnish to the Commission, upon the written request of its staff, the information furnished by the issuer under Sec. 230.502(b)(2) to any purchaser that is not an accredited investor.

(d) Amendments to notices filed under paragraph (a) of this section need only report the issuer's name and the information required by Part C and any material change in the facts from those set forth in Parts A and B.

(e) A notice on Form D shall be considered filed with the Commission under paragraph (a) of this section.

(1) As of the date on which it is received at the Commission's principal office in Washington, DC; or

(2) As of the date on which the notice is mailed by means of United States registered or certified mail to the Commission's principal office in Washington, DC, if the notice is delivered to such office after the date on which it is required to be filed.

[51 FR 36386, Oct. 10, 1986, as amended at 54 FR 11373, Mar. 20, 1989]

Code of Federal Regulations][Title 17, Volume 2]
[Revised as of April 1, 2005]
From the U.S. Government Printing Office via GPO Access
[CITE: 17CFR230.504]

TITLE 17--COMMODITY AND SECURITIES EXCHANGES

CHAPTER II--SECURITIES AND EXCHANGE COMMISSION

PART 230_GENERAL RULES AND REGULATIONS, SECURITIES ACT OF
1933--Table of Contents

Sec. 230.504 Exemption for limited offerings and sales of securities not exceeding
$1,000,000.

(a) Exemption. Offers and sales of securities that satisfy the conditions in
paragraph (b) of this Sec. 230.504 by an issuer that is not:

(1) Subject to the reporting requirements of section 13 or 15(d) of the
Exchange Act,;

(2) An investment company; or

(3) A development stage company that either has no specific business plan or
purpose or has indicated that its business plan is to engage in a merger or acquisition
with an unidentified company or companies, or other entity or person, shall be
exempt from the provision of section 5 of the Act under section 3(b) of the Act.

(b) Conditions to be met. (1) General conditions. To qualify for exemption
under this Sec. 230.504, offers and sales must satisfy the terms and conditions of
Sec. Sec. 230.501 and 230.502 (a), (c) and (d), except that the provisions of Sec.
230.502 (c) and (d) will not apply to offers and sales of securities under this Sec.
230.504 that are made:

(i) Exclusively in one or more states that provide for the registration of the
securities, and require the public filing and delivery to investors of a substantive disclosure document before sale, and are made in accordance with those state provisions;

(ii) In one or more states that have no provision for the registration of the
securities or the public filing or delivery of a disclosure document before sale, if the

securities have been registered in at least one state that provides for such registration, public filing and delivery before sale, offers and sales are made in that state in accordance with such provisions, and the disclosure document is delivered before sale to all purchasers (including those in the states that have no such procedure); or

(iii) Exclusively according to state law exemptions from registration that permit general solicitation and general advertising so long as sales are made only to "accredited investors" as defined in Sec. 230.501(a).

(2) The aggregate offering price for an offering of securities under this Sec. 230.504, as defined in Sec. 230.501(c), shall not exceed $1,000,000, less the aggregate offering price for all securities sold within the twelve months before the start of and during the offering of securities under this Sec. 230.504, in reliance on any exemption under section 3(b), or in violation of section 5(a) of the Securities Act.

Note 1: The calculation of the aggregate offering price is illustrated as follows:

If an issuer sold $900,000 on June 1, 1987 under this Sec. 230.504 and an additional $4,100,000 on December 1, 1987 under Sec. 230.505, the issuer could not sell any of its securities under this Sec. 230.504 until December 1, 1988. Until then the issuer must count the December 1, 1987 sale towards the $1,000,000 limit within the preceding twelve months.

Note 2: If a transaction under Sec. 230.504 fails to meet the limitation on the aggregate offering price, it does not affect the availability of this Sec. 230.504 for the other transactions considered in applying such limitation. For example, if an issuer sold $1,000,000 worth of its securities on January 1, 1988 under this Sec. 230.504 and an additional $500,000 worth on July 1, 1988, this Sec. 230.504 would not be available for the later sale, but would still be applicable to the January 1, 1988 sale.

[57 FR 36473, Aug. 13, 1992, as amended at 61 FR 30402, June 14, 1996; 64 FR 11094, Mar. 8, 1999]

[Code of Federal Regulations][Title 17, Volume 2]
[Revised as of April 1, 2005]
From the U.S. Government Printing Office via GPO Access
[CITE: 17CFR230.505]

TITLE 17--COMMODITY AND SECURITIES EXCHANGES

CHAPTER II--SECURITIES AND EXCHANGE COMMISSION

PART 230_GENERAL RULES AND REGULATIONS, SECURITIES ACT OF 1933--Table of Contents

Sec. 230.505   Exemption for limited offers and sales of securities not exceeding $5,000,000.

(a) Exemption. Offers and sales of securities that satisfy the conditions in paragraph (b) of this section by an issuer that is not an investment company shall be exempt from the provisions of section 5 of the Act under section 3(b) of the Act.

(b) Conditions to be met--(1) General conditions. To qualify for exemption under this section, offers and sales must satisfy the terms and conditions of Sec. Sec. 230.501 and 230.502.

(2) Specific conditions--(i) Limitation on aggregate offering price. The aggregate offering price for an offering of securities under this Sec. 230.505, as defined in Sec. 203.501(c), shall not exceed $5,000,000, less the aggregate offering price for all securities sold within the twelve months before the start of and during the offering of securities under this section in reliance on any exemption under section 3(b) of the Act or in violation of section 5(a) of the Act.

Note: The calculation of the aggregate offering price is illustrated as follows:

Example 1: If an issuer sold $2,000,000 of its securities on June 1, 1982 under this Sec. 230.505 and an additional $1,000,000 on September 1, 1982, the issuer would be permitted to sell only $2,000,000 more under this Sec. 230.505 until June 1, 1983. Until that date the issuer must count both prior sales towards the $5,000,000 limit. However, if the issuer made its third sale on June 1, 1983, the issuer could then sell $4,000,000 of its securities because the June 1, 1982 sale would not be within the preceding twelve months.

Example 2: If an issuer sold $500,000 of its securities on June 1, 1982 under Sec. 230.504 and an additional $4,500,000 on December 1, 1982 under this section, then the issuer could not sell any of its securities under this section until June 1, 1983. At that time it could sell an additional $500,000 of its securities.

(ii) Limitation on number of purchasers. There are no more than or the issuer reasonably believes that there are no more than 35 purchasers of securities from the issuer in any offering under this section.

(iii) Disqualifications. No exemption under this section shall be available for the securities of any issuer described in Sec. 230.262 of Regulation A, except that for purposes of this section only:

(A) The term "filing of the offering statement required by Sec. 230.252" as used in Sec. 230.262(a), (b) and (c) shall mean the first sale of securities under this section;

(B) The term "underwriter" as used in Sec. 230.262 (b) and (c) shall mean a person that has been or will be paid directly or indirectly remuneration for solicitation of purchasers in connection with sales of securities under this section; and

(C) Paragraph (b)(2)(iii) of this section shall not apply to any issuer if the Commission determines, upon a showing of good cause, that it is not necessary under the circumstances that the exemption be denied. Any such determination shall be without prejudice to any other action by the Commission in any other proceeding or matter with respect to the issuer or any other person.

[47 FR 11262, Mar. 16, 1982, as amended at 54 FR 11373, Mar. 20, 1989; 57 FR 36473, Aug. 13, 1992]

Code of Federal Regulations][Title 17, Volume 2]
[Revised as of April 1, 2005]
From the U.S. Government Printing Office via GPO Access
[CITE: 17CFR230.506]

TITLE 17--COMMODITY AND SECURITIES EXCHANGES

CHAPTER II--SECURITIES AND EXCHANGE COMMISSION

PART 230_GENERAL RULES AND REGULATIONS, SECURITIES ACT OF
1933--Table of Contents

Sec. 230.506   Exemption for limited offers and sales without regard to dollar
amount of offering.

(a) Exemption. Offers and sales of securities by an issuer that satisfy the
conditions in paragraph (b) of this section shall be deemed to be transactions not
involving any public offering within the meaning of section 4(2) of the Act.

(b) Conditions to be met--(1) General conditions. To qualify for an exemption
under this section, offers and sales must satisfy all the terms and conditions of Sec.
Sec. 230.501 and 230.502.

(2) Specific Conditions--(i) Limitation on number of purchasers. There are no
more than or the issuer reasonably believes that there are no more than 35 purchasers
of securities from the issuer in any offering under this section.

Note: See Sec. 230.501(e) for the calculation of the number of purchasers and
Sec. 230.502(a) for what may or may not constitute an offering under this section.

(ii) Nature of purchasers. Each purchaser who is not an accredited investor
either alone or with his purchaser representative(s) has such knowledge and experience
in financial and business matters that he is capable of evaluating the merits and risks
of the prospective investment, or the issuer reasonably believes immediately prior
to making any sale that such purchaser comes within this description.

[47 FR 11262, Mar. 6, 1982, as amended at 54 FR 11373, Mar. 20, 1989]

Code of Federal Regulations][Title 17, Volume 2]
[Revised as of April 1, 2005]
From the U.S. Government Printing Office via GPO Access
[CITE: 17CFR230.507]

TITLE 17--COMMODITY AND SECURITIES EXCHANGES

CHAPTER II--SECURITIES AND EXCHANGE COMMISSION

PART 230_GENERAL RULES AND REGULATIONS, SECURITIES ACT OF 1933--Table of Contents

Sec. 230.507   Disqualifying provision relating to exemptions under Sec. Sec. 230.504, 230.505 and 230.506.

(a) No exemption under Sec. 230.505, Sec. 230.505 or Sec. 230.506 shall be available for an issuer if such issuer, any of its predecessors or affiliates have been subject to any order, judgment, or decree of any court of competent jurisdiction temporarily, preliminary or permanently enjoining such person for failure to comply with Sec. 230.503.

(b) Paragraph (a) of this section shall not apply if the Commission determines, upon a showing of good cause, that it is not necessary under the circumstances that the exemption be denied.

[54 FR 11374, Mar. 20, 1989]

Code of Federal Regulations][Title 17, Volume 2]
[Revised as of April 1, 2005]
From the U.S. Government Printing Office via GPO Access
[CITE: 17CFR230.508]

TITLE 17--COMMODITY AND SECURITIES EXCHANGES

CHAPTER II--SECURITIES AND EXCHANGE COMMISSION

PART 230_GENERAL RULES AND REGULATIONS, SECURITIES ACT OF
1933--Table of Contents

Sec. 230.508   Insignificant deviations from a term, condition or requirement of
Regulation D.

(a) A failure to comply with a term, condition or requirement of Sec. 230.504,
Sec. 230.505 or Sec. 230.506 will not result in the loss of the exemption from the
requirements of section 5 of the Act for any offer or sale to a particular individual
or entity, if the person relying on the exemption shows:

(1) The failure to comply did not pertain to a term, condition or requirement
directly intended to protect that particular individual or entity; and

(2) The failure to comply was insignificant with respect to the offering as a
whole, provided that any failure to comply with paragraph (c) of Sec. 230.502,
paragraph (b)(2) of Sec. 230.504, paragraphs (b)(2)(i) and (ii) of Sec. 230.505 and
paragraph (b)(2)(i) of Sec. 230.506 shall be deemed to be significant to the offering
as a whole; And

(3) A good faith and reasonable attempt was made to comply with all applicable
terms, conditions and requirements of Sec. 230.504, Sec. 230.505 or Sec. 230.506.

(b) A transaction made in reliance on Sec. 230.504, Sec. 230.505 or Sec.
230.506 shall comply with all applicable terms, conditions and requirements of
Regulation D. Where an exemption is established only through reliance upon paragraph (a) of this section, the failure to comply shall nonetheless be actionable by the
Commission under section 20 of the Act.

[54 FR 11374, Mar. 20, 1989, as amended at 57 FR 36473, Aug. 13, 1992]

Regulation E--Exemption for Securities of Small Business Investment Companies

Authority: Sections 230.601 to 230.610a issued under sec. 19, 48 Stat. 85, as amended; 15 U.S.C. 77s.

Source: Sections 230.601 through 230.610a appear at 23 FR 10484, Dec. 30, 1958, unless otherwise noted.

Cross Reference: For regulations of Small Business Administration under the Small Business Investment Act of 1958, see 13 CFR, Chapter I.

SUBSCRIPTION AGREEMENT

Sunset Pointe, LLC
A Nevada Limited Liability Company ("The Company")

1. Subscription

(a) The undersigned ("Undersigned" or "Purchaser") hereby applies to the above Company and to purchase the initial capital interest (the "Interest") indicated below in accordance with the terms and conditions of the Subscription Agreement, the Company's operating agreement (the "Agreement") enclosed herewith as Exhibit A and the project summary previously received (the "Offering Memorandum").

By signing this Subscription Agreement, the Undersigned is (1) subscribing to purchase the Interest; (2) accepting and agreeing to be bound by the terms of the Agreement; (3) authorizing the Managing Member to act on your behalf, in matters regarding the partnership; (4) granting a Special power of attorney to Samuel K. Freshman pursuant to the provisions of paragraph 5 of this Subscription Agreement; (5) acknowledging the undersigned meets the investor suitability requirements set forth herein and that the Undersigned has been informed of all pertinent facts relating to the liquidity and marketability of the Interests; and (6) agreeing to the terms of Subscription set forth in this Subscription Agreement.

(b) Before this subscription for Interest(s) is considered, the Undersigned must complete, execute, and deliver to the Company the following:

(i) The purchaser's personal check in the amount of the Interest subscription.

(ii) This Subscription Agreement.

(c) The Undersigned understands that the cash received by the Company from each subscriber prior to the closing of the Offering will be deposited in noninterest-bearing accounts.

(d) This Subscription is irrevocable. It may be rejected in whole or in part by the Company in its sole discretion. In the event that this Subscription is rejected by the Company all funds and documents tendered by the Undersigned shall be returned without interest.

(e) This Subscription is not transferable or assigned by the Undersigned

APPENDIX E

SUBSCRIPTION AGREEMENT

(f) This Subscription, upon acceptance by the Company, shall be binding on the heirs, executors, administrators, successors, and assigns of the Undersigned.

(g) If the Undersigned is more than one person, the obligations of the Undersigned shall be joint and several and the representations and warranties shall be deemed to be made by and be binding on each such person and his heirs, executors, administrators, successors, and assigns.

2. Representations

The Undersigned represents and warrants as follows:

(a) The Undersigned has read and is familiar with the Agreement including the Project Summary.

(b) The Undersigned has carefully reviewed and understood the risks of, and other considerations relating to, a purchase of the Interests.

(c) The Undersigned has examined or has had an opportunity to examine such additional information concerning the Company and the offering of the Interests as he or she deemed necessary or appropriate to form a decision as to whether to purchase the Interests.

(d) The Undersigned has had an opportunity to ask questions of and receive answers from the Company, or a person or persons acting on its behalf, concerning the terms and conditions of this investment, and all such questions have been answered to his of her full satisfaction.

(e) No representations or warranties have been made to him or her by the Company or any agent, employee or affiliate of it, and that in entering into this transaction he or she is not relying upon any information, other than that contained in the project summary and the attachments hereto, and the results of his or her own independent investigation.

(f) The Undersigned does not intend or anticipate that his or her investment in the Company will be a source of income, is able to bear the substantial economic risks of the investment in interests being made by him or her, and that he or she could afford a complete loss of such investment.

(g) Neither the Undersigned nor his/her representatives, if any, have been furnished any offering literature other than the Project Summary and the documents attached as exhibits, and the Undersigned and his/her representatives, if any, have relied only on the information contained in the Project Summary and such exhibits and information, furnished or made available to them by the Company, its counsel, or the Managers.

(h) The Undersigned has an individual net worth in excess of $1,000,000 or had individual income in excess of $200,000 in each of the two most recent years and reasonably experts an income in excess of $200,000 in the current year or joint income together with his/her spouse of $300,000 in each of those two years and an expected joint income of $300,000 in the current year. If a limited liability company or trust, each managing member is within the above standard.

(i) The Undersigned has adequate means of providing for his/her current needs and personal contingencies, has no need for liquidity in his/her investment, could afford to lose the entire amount of his/her investment and understands that he/she may lose his/her entire investment.

(j) The Undersigned's commitment to all investments is reasonable in relation to his/her net worth.

(k) The Undersigned understands that the interests have not been registered under the Securities Act in reliance on an exemption thereunder for transactions not involving any public offering, that the interests have not been approved or disapproved by the Securities and Exchange Commission or by any other federal or state agency, and that no such agency has passed on the accuracy or adequacy of the project summary.

(l) The Undersigned is acquiring the interests of his or her own account for investment purposes only and not with a review to resale or other distribution, in whole or in part; and that: (i) the interests are speculative investment and involve a high degree of risk; (ii) the partnership has limited financial and operating history; and (iii) the transferability of the interests to be registered under the Securities Act; there will likely be no public market for the interests; and, accordingly, it may not be possible for the investor to liquidate his or her investment in the company.

(m) The Undersigned is not relying on the Managers nor any of their officers or shareholders for independent legal, accounting, financial, or tax advice in connection with the Undersigned's of such an investment.

3. Investor Eligibility

Offers and sales of interests will be made to purchasers whom the Company believes (i) are "Accredited Investors" pursuant to Regulation D of the Securities Act of 1933 and similar provisions of applicable state law or are otherwise deemed appropriate investors under applicable securities laws and, in addition (ii) meet other suitability standards, if any. Purchaser represents and warrants that (initial all applicable boxes):

_____   a. Purchaser has such knowledge and experience in business and financial matters as to be able to evaluate the merits and risks of the investment in the interests;

_____   b. Purchaser has full power and authority to enter into this Agreement and that this Agreement constitutes a valid and legally binding obligation of such Purchaser;

_____   c. Purchaser confirms that the interests to be purchased will be acquired for investment for such Purchaser's own account, not as a nominee or agent, and not with a view to the resale or distribution of any part thereof, and that Purchaser had no present intention of selling, granting any participation in, or otherwise distributing the same. Purchaser further represents that Purchaser does not have any contract, undertaking, agreement or arrangement with any person to sell, transfer or grant participation to such persons or to any third person with respect to any of the Interests; and

_____   d. Purchaser is an "Accredited Investor" as that term is defined.

4. Choice of Laws

This Agreement shall be construed in accordance with and governed by the laws of the State of Nevada except as to the manner which the Undersigned elects to take title to interests, which shall be construed in accordance with the laws of the state of his or her residence.

5. Power of Attorney

(a)   The Undersigned irrevocably constitutes and appoints, Samuel K. Freshman, acting individually; with full power of substitution as his true and lawful attorney-in-fact and agent, to execute, acknowledge, verify, swear to, deliver, record, and file, in the Undersigned's name or his/her assignees' name, place, and stead, all instruments, documents, and certificates that may from time to time be required by the laws of the United States of America, the State of Nevada, and any other state in which the partnership conducts or plans to conduct business, or any political subdivision or agent of the government to effectuate, implement, and continue the valid existence of the partnership, including, without limitation, the power and authority it execute, verify, swear to, acknowledge, deliver, record, and file the following:

(i)   The Agreement, and all other instruments (including amendments) that the Managers deem appropriate to form, qualify, or continue the Company as a limited liability company in the State of Nevada and all other jurisdictions in which the company conducts or plans to conduct business;

(ii) All instruments that the attorney-in-fact deem appropriate to reflect any amendment to the Agreement, made in accordance with the terms of the Agreement;

(iii) A fictitious business name certificate and such other certificates and instruments as may be necessary under the fictitious or assumed name statue from time to time in effect in the State of Nevada and all other jurisdictions in which the Company conducts or plans to conduct business;

(iv) All instruments relating to the admission of any additional or substituted member; and

(v)   All conveyances and other instruments that the attorney-in-fact deem appropriate to reflect the dissolution and termination of the partnership pursuant to the terms of the Agreement.

Such agent and attorney-in-fact shall not, however the right, power, or authority to amend or modify the Agreement when acting in such capacities, except to the extent authorized in this document and in the Agreement.

(b)   The power of attorney granted is a special power of attorney and shall be deemed to be coupled with an interest, shall be irrevocable, shall survive the death, dissolution, bankruptcy, incompetence, or legal disability of the Undersigned, and shall extend to the Undersigned's heirs, successors, and assigns. The Undersigned agrees to be bound by any representations made by the Managers acting in good faith under such power of attorney, and each member waives any and all defenses that may be available to contest, negate, or disaffirm any action of the Managers taken in good faith under such power of attorney.

6. Miscellaneous

(a) This Subscription Agreement is subject to all of the terms and provisions of the agreement.

(b) Purchaser may not assign any of his rights under this Subscription Agreement without the written consent of the partnership.

(c) Purchaser may not cancel, terminate or revoke this Subscription Agreement or any agreement of the Purchaser made herein.

(d) This Subscription Agreement shall be binding upon the heirs, executors, administrators, successors and assigns of the Purchaser.

(e) If the Purchaser is more than one person, the obligations of the Purchaser shall be joint and several and the representations herein contained shall be deemed to be and binding upon each such person and their heirs, executors, administrators, successors and assigns.

(f) Throughout this Subscription Agreement, as the context may require, the masculine gender includes the feminine and neuter genders.

7. Subscription for Company Interests

Class A Interest(s) totaling $_____.

Class B Interest(s) totaling $ _____.

Subscriber Information: (The information below should be consistent with the form of ownership selected below.)

Name of Company
Sunset Pointe, LLC

Name (please print):

_____

If entity named above,

By_____

Social Security or Taxpayer I.D. Number:

_____

Taxable year ends

_____

Business Address (including zip code)

_____

_____

Business Phone

(___)_____

Residence Address (including zip code)

_____

_____

 Residence Phone

(___)_____

All communications to be sent to check one:

___ Residence Address   ___ Business Address

**Type of Ownership
(select one)**

PLEASE INDICATE BY CHECKING THE APPROPRIATE BOX BELOW THE FORM IN WHICH YOU WILL HOLD TITLE TO YOUR INTEREST. PLEASE CONSIDER CAREFULLY. ONCE YOUR SUBSCRIPTION IS ACCEPTED, A CHANGE IN THE FORM OF TITLE CONSTITUTES A TRANSFER OF THE INTEREST AND WILL THEREFORE BE RESTRICTED BY THE TERMS OF THE OPERATING AGREEMENT AND RESULT IN ADDITION COSTS TO YOU. SUBSCRIBERS SHOULD SEEK THE ADVICE OF THEIR ATTORNEYS IN DECIDING IN WHICH OF THE FORMS THEY SHOULD TAKE OWNERSHIP OF THE INTERESTS, BECAUSE DIFFERENT FORMS OF OWNERSHIP CAN HAVE VARYING GIFT TAX, ESTATE TAX, INCOME TAX, AND OTHER CONSEQUENCES, DEPENDING ON THE STATE OF THE INVESTOR'S DOMICILE AND HIS OR HER PARTICULAR PERSONAL CIRCUMSTANCES. FOR EXAMPLE, IN COMMUNITY PROPERTY STATES, IF COMMUNITY PROPERTY ASSETS ARE USED TO PURCHASE INTERESTS HELD AS SEPARATE PROPERTY, ADVERSE GIFT TAX CONSEQUENCES MAY RESULT.

____   INDIVIDUAL OWNERSHIP (one signature required)

____   JOINT TENANTS WITH RIGHT OF SURVIVORSHIP AND NOT AS TENANTS IN COMMON (both or all parties must sign)

____   COMMUNITY PROPERTY (one signature required if interest held in one name, i.e., managing spouse; two signatures required if interest held in both names)

____   TENANTS IN COMMON (both or all parties must sign)

____   GENERAL PARTNERSHIP (fill out all documents in the name of the Company, by a PARTNER authorized to sign, and include a copy of the Partnership Agreement)

____   LIMITED PARTNERSHIP (fill out all documents in the name of the LIMITED PARTNERSHIP, by a GENERAL PARTNERSHIP authorized to sign, and include a copy of the corporation's Articles and certified Corporate Resolution authorizing the signature)

____   LIMITED LIABILITY COMPANY (fill out all documents in the name of the LIMITED LIABILITY COMPANY, by the MANAGING MEMBER authorized to sign, and include a copy of the corporation's Articles and certified Corporate Resolution authorizing the signature)

___   TRUST (fill out all documents in the name of the TRUST, by the trustee, and include a copy of the instrument creating the trust and any other documents necessary to show that the investment by the trustee is authorized. The date of the trust must appear on the Notarial where indicated)

Subject to acceptance by the Company, the Undersigned has completed this Subscription Agreement to evidence his/her subscription, this ____ day of _____, 2002.

Documents to be Returned:

1. A check payable to the order of THE COMPANY for the Subscription amount.
2. One copy of this Subscription Agreement completed, dated and signed with the Purchaser's (s') signature(s).

Purchaser #1   Purchaser #2 (if the Shares are to be held as tenants in common, as joint tenants, or as community property in both names)

Dated: _____   Dated: _____

By: _____   By: _____
        (Signature)   (Signature)

Name: _____   Name: _____
        (Print or type)   (Print or type)

_____   _____
Social Security or Tax I.D. No   Social Security or Tax I.D. No.
(If none, so state)   (If none, so state)

The Company has accepted this Subscription this _____ day of _____, 2002.

Sunset Pointe, LLC, a Nevada limited liability company

By: Standard Asset Managers Corp, a
         Nevada corporation
Its: Manager

         By: _____
                  Samuel K. Freshman
         Its: President

Appendix F
Operating Agreement

**OPERATING AGREEMENT
FOR
A NEVADA LIMITED LIABILITY COMPANY**

THE SECURITIES REPRESENTED BY THIS AGREEMENT HAVE NOT BEEN REGISTERED UNDER THE SECURITIES ACT OF 1933 NOR REGISTERED NOR QUALIFIED UNDER ANY STATE SECURITIES LAWS. SUCH SECURITIES MAY NOT BE OFFERED FOR SALE, SOLD, DELIVERED AFTER SALE, TRANSFERRED, PLEDGED, OR HYPOTHECATED UNLESS QUALIFIED AND REGISTERED UNDER APPLICABLE STATE AND FEDERAL SECURITIES LAWS OR UNLESS, IN THE OPINION OF COUNSEL SATISFACTORY TO THE COMPANY, SUCH QUALIFICATION AND REGISTRATION IS NOT REQUIRED. ANY TRANSFER OF THE SECURITIES REPRESENTED BY THIS AGREEMENT IS FURTHER SUBJECT TO OTHER RESTRICTIONS, TERMS AND CONDITIONS WHICH ARE SET FORTH HEREIN.

PROPERTY MANAGEMENT COMPANY:

MANAGER:

**STANDARD MANAGEMENT COMPANY PROPERTY NUMBER: 100
STANDARD MANAGEMENT COMPANY GENERAL COUNSEL:**

PRESENTED TO: _____

*PLEASE RETURN ALL DOCUMENTS IF YOU ELECT
NOT TO SUBSCRIBE*

TABLE OF CONTENTS

OPERATING AGREEMENT
FOR
SUNSET POINTE, LLC
a Nevada limited liability company

This Operating Agreement, is made as of June 18, 2002, by and between the parties listed on the signature pages hereof, with reference to the following facts:

A. On May 10, 2002, Articles of Organization for Sunset Pointe, LLC (the "Company"), a limited liability company organized under the laws of the State of Nevada, were filed with the Nevada Secretary of State.

B. The parties desire to adopt and approve an operating agreement for the Company.

NOW, THEREFORE, the parties by this Agreement set forth the operating agreement for the Company under the laws of the State of Nevada upon the terms and subject to the conditions of this Agreement.

ARTICLE I

DEFINITIONS

When used in this Agreement, the following terms shall have the meanings set forth below (all terms used in this Agreement that are not defined in this Article I shall have the meanings set forth elsewhere in this Agreement):

1.1   "Act"
shall mean the Sunset Pointe Limited Liability Company Act, codified in the Nevada Corporations Code, as the same may be amended from time to time.

1.2   "Affiliate"
of a Member or Manager shall mean any Person, directly or indirectly, through one or more intermediaries, controlling, controlled by, or under common control with a Member or Manager, as applicable. The term "control," as used in the immediately preceding sentence, shall mean with respect to a corporation or limited liability company the right to exercise, directly or indirectly, more than fifty percent (50%) of the voting rights attributable to the controlled corporation or limited liability company, and, with respect to any individual, partnership, trust, other entity or association, the possession, directly or indirectly, of the power to direct or cause the direction of the management or policies of the controlled entity.

1.3   "Agreement"
shall mean this Operating Agreement, as originally executed and as amended from time to time.

1.4   "Articles"
shall mean the Articles of Organization for the Company originally filed with the Nevada Secretary of State and as amended from time to time.

1.5   "Assignee"
shall mean the owner of an Economic Interest who has not been admitted as a substitute Member in accordance with Article VII.

1.6   "Bankruptcy"
shall mean: (a) the filing of an application by a Member for, or his or her consent to, the appointment of a trustee, receiver, or custodian of his or her other assets; (b) the entry of an order for relief with respect to a Member in proceedings under the United States Bankruptcy Code, as amended or superseded from time to time; (c)

the making by a Member of a general assignment for the benefit of creditors; (d) the entry of an order, judgment, or decree by any court of competent jurisdiction appointing a trustee, receiver, or custodian of the assets of a Member unless the proceedings and the person appointed are dismissed within ninety (90) days; or (e) the failure by a Member generally to pay his or her debts as the debts become due within the meaning of Section 303(h)(1) of the United States Bankruptcy Code, as determined by the Bankruptcy Court, or the admission in writing of his or her inability to pay his or her debts as they become due.

1.7   "Capital Account"
shall mean with respect to any Member the capital account which the Company establishes and maintains for such Member pursuant to Section 3.3.

1.8   "Capital Contribution"
shall mean the total amount of cash, fair market value of property and/or services rendered or to be rendered contributed to the Company by Members.

1.9   "Code"
shall mean the Internal Revenue Code of 1986, as amended from time to time, the provisions of succeeding law, and to the extent applicable, the Regulations.

1.10   "Company"
shall mean Sunset Pointe, LLC, a Nevada limited liability company.

1.11   "Company Minimum Gain"
shall have the meaning ascribed to the term "Partnership Minimum Gain" in the Regulations Section 1.704-2(d).

1.12   "Corporations Code"
shall mean the Nevada Corporations Code, as amended from time to time, and the provisions of succeeding law.

1.13   "Dissolution Event"
shall mean with respect to all Managers who are Members one or more of the following: the death, insanity, withdrawal, resignation, retirement, expulsion, Bankruptcy or dissolution of any such Managers who are Members.

1.14   "Distributable Cash"
shall mean the amount of cash which the Managers reasonably deem available for distribution to the Members, taking into account all debts, liabilities, and obligations of

the Company then due, and working capital and other amounts which the Managers reasonably deem necessary for the Company's business or to place into reserves for customary and usual claims with respect to such business.

1.15   "Economic Interest"
shall mean the right to receive distributions of the Company's assets and allocations of income, gain, loss, deduction, credit and similar items from the Company pursuant to this Agreement and the Act, but shall not include any other rights of a Member, including, without limitation, the right to vote or participate in the management of the Company, or except as provided in Section 17106 of the Corporations Code, any right to information concerning the business and affairs of the Company.

1.16   "Fiscal Year"
shall mean the Company's fiscal year, which shall be the calendar year.

1.17   "Former Member"
shall have the meaning ascribed to it in Section 8.1.

1.18   "Former Member's Interest"
shall have the meaning ascribed to it in Section 8.1.

1.19   "Majority Interest"
shall mean those Members who hold a majority of the Percentage Interests which all Members hold.

1.20   "Manager"
shall mean Standard Asset Managers Corp, a Nevada corporation, or any other persons or entities that succeed any of them as a Manager of the Company. The term "Managers", though plural, shall refer to that one person or entity, and that named person or entity shall have full authority to exercise all powers of "Mangers" as set forth herein

1.21   "Member"
shall mean each Person who (a) is an initial signatory to this Agreement, has been admitted to the Company as a Member in accordance with the Articles or this Agreement or is an Assignee who has become a Member in accordance with Article VII, and (b) has not become the subject of a Dissolution Event or ceased to be a Member in accordance with Article VIII or for any other reason. There shall be two classes of membership, Class A and Class B, with differing rights to profit, loss and cash distributions and with differing capital contribution requirements. .

1.22   "Member Nonrecourse Debt"

shall have the meaning ascribed to the term "Partner Nonrecourse Debt" in Regulations Section 1.704-2(b)(4).

1.23   "Member Nonrecourse Deductions"

shall mean items of Company loss, deduction, or Code Section 705(a)(2)(B) expenditures which are attributable to Member Nonrecourse Debt.

1.24   "Membership Interest"

shall mean a Member's entire interest in the Company including the Member's Economic Interest, the right to vote on or participate in the management, and the right to receive information concerning the business and affairs, of the Company.

1.25   "Net Profits" and "Net Losses"

shall mean the income, gain, loss and deductions of the Company in the aggregate or separately stated, as appropriate, determined in accordance with the method of accounting at the close of each Fiscal Year on the Company's information tax return filed for federal income tax purposes.

1.26   "Nonrecourse Liability"

shall have the meaning set forth in Regulations Section 1.752-1(a)(2).

1.27   "Percentage Interest"

shall mean the percentage of a Member set forth opposite the name of such Member under the column "Member's Percentage Interest" in Exhibit B hereto, as such percentage may be adjusted from time to time pursuant to the terms of this Agreement. Percentage Interests shall be determined annually, unless otherwise provided herein.

1.28   "Person"

shall mean an individual, partnership, limited partnership, limited liability company, corporation, trust, estate, association or any other entity.

1.29   "Regulations"

shall, unless the context clearly indicates otherwise, mean the regulations in force as final or temporary that have been issued by the U.S. Department of Treasury pursuant to its authority under the Code, and any successor regulations.

1.30 "Remaining Cash Investment".
"Remaining Cash Investment" equals the Member's capital or Equity contributions received by the Company, less any Distributable Cash provided to such Member pursuant to Section VI.5.b. of this Agreement (excluding any portion thereof related to the deficiency in a contributing Member's Priority Return, but without deduction of any depreciation or operating losses.).

1.31 "Remaining Members"
shall have the meaning ascribed to it in Section 8.1.

1.32 "Tax Matters Partner"
z as designated pursuant to Section 9.8.

ARTICLE II

ORGANIZATIONAL MATTERS

2.1 Formation.
The Members have formed a Nevada Limited Liability Company under the laws of the State of Nevada by filing the Articles with the Nevada Secretary of State and entering into this Agreement, which Agreement shall be deemed effective as of the date the Articles were so filed. The rights and liabilities of the Members shall be determined pursuant to the Act and this Agreement. To the extent that the rights or obligations of any Member are different by reason of any provision of this Agreement than they would be in the absence of such provision, this Agreement shall, to the extent permitted by the Act, control.

2.2 Name.
The name of the Company shall be Sunset Pointe, LLC. The business of the Company may be conducted under that name or, upon compliance with applicable laws, any other name that the Managers deem appropriate or advisable. The Managers shall file any fictitious name certificates and similar filings, and any amendments thereto, that the Managers consider appropriate or advisable.

2.3 Term.
The term of this Agreement commenced on the filing of the Articles and shall continue until terminated as hereinafter provided.

2.4   Office and Agent.

The Company shall continuously maintain an office and registered agent in the State of Nevada. The principal office of the Company shall be Standard Management Company, 6151 W. Century Blvd., Suite 300, Los Angeles, CA 90045 or at such location as the Managers may determine. The Company may also have such offices, anywhere within and without the State of Nevada, as the Managers determine from time to time, or the business of the Company may require. The registered agent shall be as stated in the Articles or as otherwise determined by the Managers.

2.5   Addresses of the Members and the Managers.

The respective addresses of the Members and the Managers are set forth on Exhibit B attached hereto. A Member may change his or her address upon notice thereof to the Managers.

2.6   Purpose and Business of the Company.

The purpose of the Company is to engage in any lawful activity for which a limited liability company may be organized under the Act including but not limited to the ownership of the property attached hereto as Exhibit "A" and/or any other property (herein the "Property") and incorporated herein by this reference. The Company may own the Property in its entirety, or in part, with others. The ownership structure of the Property may take the form of tenants-in-common, a limited liability company, general partnership, limited partnership, trust, or such other entity as may be approved by a majority in interest of the Members. As such, the Company may be a tenant, a general partner, a limited partner, a Member, a shareholder, a beneficiary or such other title holder as is appropriate.

ARTICLE III

CAPITAL CONTRIBUTIONS

3.1   Initial Capital Contributions.

Each Member shall contribute such amount as is set forth in Exhibit B as his or her initial Capital Contribution, which Exhibit B shall be revised to reflect any additional contributions made in accordance with Section 3.2.

3.2   Additional Capital Contributions.

No Member shall be required to make any additional Capital Contributions. To the extent unanimously approved by the Managers, from time to time, the Members may be permitted to make additional Capital Contributions if and to the extent they so desire, and if the Managers determine that such additional Capital Contributions are necessary or appropriate for the conduct of the Company's business, including without limitation, expansion or diversification. In that event, the Members shall have the opportunity, but not the obligation, to participate in such additional Capital Contributions on a pro rata basis in accordance with their Percentage Interests. Each Member shall receive a credit to his or her Capital Account in the amount of any additional capital which he or she contributes to the Company. Immediately following such Capital Contributions, the Percentage Interests shall be adjusted by the Managers to reflect the new relative proportions of the Capital Accounts of the Members.

3.3   Capital Accounts.
The Company shall establish and maintain an individual Capital Account for each Member in accordance with Regulations Section 1.704-1(b)(2)(iv). If a Member transfers all or a part of his or her Membership Interest in accordance with this Agreement, such Member's Capital Account attributable to the transferred Membership Interest shall carry over to the new owner of such Membership Interest pursuant to Regulations Section 1.704-1(b)(2)(iv)(1). Members who are Managers shall maintain in the aggregate a minimum capital account balance equal to the lesser of one percent (1%) of the total positive capital accounts. Members who are managers shall also maintain, in the aggregate, at least a one percent (1%) interest in each material item of the Company income, gain, loss, credit or deduction.

3.4   No Interest.
No Member shall be entitled to receive any interest on his or her Capital Contributions.

3.5   Return of Distributions.
The obligation of a Member to make a contribution shall be compromised only by a Majority Interest of Members. Except as is otherwise provided herein the obligation to return money or property paid or distributed shall require the consent of all Members.

ARTICLE IV

MEMBERS

4.1   Limited Liability.
Except as expressly set forth in this Agreement or required by law, no Member shall be personally liable for any debt, obligation or liability of the Company, whether that liability or obligation arises in contract, tort or otherwise.

4.2   Admission of Additional Members.
The Managers, with the approval of a Majority Interest of Members, may admit to the Company additional Members.   Any additional Members shall obtain Membership Interests and will participate in the management, Net Profits, Net Losses, and distributions of the Company on such terms as are determined by the Managers and approved by Majority Interest of Members. Any additional Members shall be required to agree to be bound by the terms of this Agreement, and the issuance of Membership Interests to such Members shall not be effective unless and until the purchaser agrees in writing to be so bound. Assignees may only be admitted as substitute Members in accordance with Article VII. Notwithstanding the foregoing there shall be no dilution of an existing Members' interest as a result of the addition of a new Member, without such existing Member's consent.

4.3   Withdrawals or Resignations.
Any Member who is under obligation to render services to the Company may withdraw or resign as a Member at any time upon one hundred twenty (120) days prior written notice to the Company, without prejudice to the rights, if any, of the Company or the other Members under any contract to which the withdrawing Member is a party. In the event of such withdrawal, such Member's Membership Interest shall terminate pursuant to Section 4.4. No other Member may withdraw, retire or resign from the Company.

4.4   Termination of Membership Interest.
Upon (a) the transfer of a Member's Membership Interest in violation of Article VII, (b) the occurrence of a Dissolution Event as to such Member which does not result in the dissolution of the Company under Article X, or (c) the withdrawal or resignation of a Member in accordance with Section 4.3, the Membership Interest of a Member shall be terminated by the Managers and thereafter that Member shall be an Assignee only unless such Membership Interest shall be purchased by the Company and/or remaining Members as provided in Article VIII. Each Member acknowledges and agrees that such termination or purchase of a Membership Interest upon the occurrence of any of the foregoing events is not unreasonable under the circumstances existing as of the date hereof.

4.5   Competing Activities.
The Members and their officers, directors, shareholders, partners, members, managers, agents, employees and Affiliates may engage or invest in, independently or with others, any business activity of any type or description, including without limitation those that might be the same as or similar to the Company's business and that might be in direct or indirect competition with the Company. Neither the Company nor

any Member shall have any right in or to such other ventures or activities or to the income or proceeds derived therefrom. The Members shall not be obligated to present any investment opportunity or prospective economic advantage to the Company, even if the opportunity is of the character that, if presented to the Company, could be taken by the Company. The Members shall have the right to hold any investment opportunity or prospective economic advantage for their own account or to recommend such opportunity to Persons other than the Company. Each Member acknowledges that the other Members and their Affiliates own and/or manage other businesses, including businesses that may compete with the Company and for the Members' time. Each Member hereby waives any and all rights and claims which they may otherwise have against the other Members and their officers, directors, shareholders, partners, members, managers, agents, employees, and Affiliates as a result of any of such activities.

4.6   Transactions With The Company.

Subject to any limitations set forth in this Agreement and with the prior approval of the Managers, a Member may lend money to and transact other business with the Company, so long as such transaction is not expressly prohibited by this Agreement and so long as the terms and conditions of such transaction, on an overall basis, are fair and reasonable to the Company and are at least as favorable to the Company as those that are generally available from Persons capable of similarly performing them and in similar transactions between parties operating at arm's length. Subject to other applicable law, such Member has the same rights and obligations with respect thereto as a Person who is not a Member.

4.7   Remuneration To Members.

Except as otherwise specifically provided in this Agreement, no Member is entitled to remuneration for acting in the Company business.

4.8   Members Are Not Agents.

Pursuant to Section 5.1 and the Articles, the management of the Company is vested in the Managers. The Members shall have no power to participate in the management of the Company except as expressly authorized by this Agreement or the Articles and except as expressly required by the Act. No Member, acting solely in the capacity of a Member, is an agent of the Company nor does any Member, unless expressly and duly authorized in writing to do so by a Manager or Managers, have any power or authority to bind or act on behalf of the Company in any way, to pledge its credit, to execute any instrument on its behalf or to render it liable for any purpose.

4.9   Voting Rights.

Except as expressly provided in this Agreement or the Articles, Members shall have no voting, approval or consent rights. Members shall have the right to approve or disapprove matters as specifically stated in this Agreement, including the following:

4.9.1   Approval by Members Holding a Majority Interest.

Except as set forth in Section 5.3.2 or in any other provision of this Agreement, in all other matters in which a vote, approval or consent of the Members is required, a vote, consent or approval of a Majority Interest (or, in instances in which there are defaulting or remaining members, non-defaulting or remaining Members who hold a majority of the Percentage Interests held by all non-defaulting or remaining Members) shall be sufficient to authorize or approve such act. Interest for this purpose is 66 2/3 percent to the Class A Members, pro-rata, and 33 1/3 percent to the Class B Members, pro-rata.

4.9.2   Other Voting Rights.

Besides the rights granted in Section 4.9.1, Members may vote, consent or approve to the extent and on the terms provided in this Agreement in the following Sections:

(i) Section 3.2 on additional Capital Contributions;

(ii) Section 3.5 on a decision to compromise the obligation of a Member to make a Capital Contribution or return money or property paid or distributed in violation of the Act;

(iii) Section 4.2 on admission of new Members;

(iv) Section 5.2 on election and removal of a Manager;

(v) Section 5.3.2 on a change in the purpose or business of the Company;

(vi) Section 5.3.2 on reorganization of the Company;

(vii) Section 5.3.2 on other limitations on the Managers' authority;

(viii) Section 5.8.1 on management fees payable to Managers;

(ix) Section 7.1 on the transfer of a Membership Interest;

(x) Section 10.1 on dissolving the Company.

(xi) Section 14.12 on any amendment of the Articles or this Agreement;

4.9.3   Member Approval.

No annual or regular meetings of the Members are required to be held. However, if such meetings are held, such meetings shall be noticed, held and conducted pursuant to the Act. In any instance in which the approval of the Members is required under this Agreement, such approval may be obtained in any matter permitted by the Act.

4.10   Certificate of Membership Interest.

4.10.1   Certificate.

A Membership Interest may be represented by a certificate of membership. The exact contents of a certificate of membership may be determined by action of the Managers but shall be issued substantially in conformity with the following requirements. The certificates of membership shall be respectively numbered serially, as they are issued, shall be impressed with the Company seal or a facsimile thereof, if any, and shall be signed by the Mangers or officers, if any, of the Company. Each certificate of membership shall state the name of the Company, the fact that the Company is organized under the laws of the State of Nevada as a limited liability company, the name of the person to whom the certificate is issued, the date of issue, and the Percentage Interest represented thereby. A statement of the designations, preferences, qualifications, limitations, restrictions, and special or relative rights of the Membership Interest, if any, shall be set forth in full or summarized on the face or back of the certificates which the Company shall issue, or in lieu thereof, the certificate may set forth that such a statement or summary will be furnished to any holder of a Membership Interest upon request without charge. Each certificate of membership shall be otherwise in such form as may be determined by the Managers.

4.10.2   Cancellation of Certificate.

Except as herein provided with respect to lost, stolen, or destroyed certificates, no new certificates of membership shall be issued in lieu of previously issued certificates or membership until former certificates for a like number of Membership Interests shall have been surrendered and cancelled. All certificates of membership surrendered to the Company for transfer shall be cancelled.

4.10.3   Replacement of Lost, Stolen, or Destroyed Certificate.

Any Member claiming that his or her certificate or membership is lost, stolen, or destroyed may make an affidavit or affirmation of that fact and request a new certificate. Upon the giving of a satisfactory indemnity to the Company as reasonably required by the Managers, a new certificate may be issued of the same tenor and representing the same Percentage Interest of membership as was represented by the certificate alleged to be lost, stolen, or destroyed.

ARTICLE V
MANAGEMENT AND CONTROL OF THE COMPANY

5.1   Management of the Company by Managers.

5.1.1   Exclusive Management by Managers.

The business, property and affairs of the Company shall be managed exclusively by the Managers. Except for situations in which the approval of the Members is expressly required by this Agreement, the Managers shall have full, complete and exclusive authority, power, and discretion to manage and control the business, property and affairs of the Company, to make all decisions regarding those matters and to perform any and all other acts or activities customary or incident to the management of the Company's business, property and affairs.

5.1.2   Agency Authority of Managers.

Subject to Section 5.3.2:

Any Manager, acting alone, is authorized to endorse checks, drafts, and other evidences of indebtedness made payable to the order of the Company, but only for the purpose of deposit into the Company's accounts. All checks, drafts, and other instruments obligating the Company to pay money in an amount of less than $50,000 may be signed by any one Managing Member , acting alone. All checks, drafts, and other instruments obligating the Company to pay money in amount of $50,000 or more must be signed on behalf of the Company by any two Managers acting together or one Manager where there is only one. Any one Manager shall be authorized to sign contracts and obligations on behalf of the Company.

5.1.3   Meetings of Managers.

Meetings of the Managers may be called by any Manager. All meetings shall be held upon four (4) days notice by mail or forty-eight (48) hours notice (or upon such shorter notice period if necessary under the circumstances) delivered personally or by telephone, telegraph or facsimile. A notice need not specify the purpose of any meeting. Notice of a meeting need not be given to any Manager who signs a waiver of notice or a consent to holding the meeting (which waiver or consent need not specify the purpose of the meeting) or an approval of the minutes thereof, whether before or after the meeting, or who attends the meeting without protesting, prior to its commencement, the lack of notice to such Manager. All such waivers, consents and approvals shall be filed with the Company records or made a part of the minutes of the meeting. A majority of the Managers present, whether or not a quorum is present, may adjourn any meeting to another time and place. If the meeting is adjourned for more than twenty-four (24) hours, notice of any adjournment shall be given prior to the time of the adjourned meeting to the Managers who are not present at the time of the adjournment. Meetings of the Managers may be held at any place within or without the State of Nevada which has been designated in the notice of the meeting or at such place as may be approved by the Managers. Managers may participate in a meeting through use of conference telephone or similar communications equipment, so long as all Managers participating in such meeting can hear one another. Participation in a meeting in such manner constitutes a presence in person at such meeting. A majority of the authorized number of Managers constitutes a quorum of the Managers for the transaction of business. Except to the extent that this Agreement expressly requires the approval of all Managers, every act or decision done or made by a majority of the Managers present at a meeting duly held at which a quorum is present is the act of the Managers. A meeting at which a quorum is initially present may continue to transact business notwithstanding the withdrawal of Managers, if any action taken is approved by at least a majority of the required quorum for such meeting.

Any action required or permitted to be taken by the Managers may be taken by the Managers without a meeting, if a majority of the Managers individually or collectively consent in writing to such action, unless the action requires the unanimous vote of the Managers, in which case all Managers must consent in writing. Such action by written consent shall have the same force and effect as a majority vote or unanimous vote, as applicable, of such Managers.

The provisions of this Section 5.1.3 govern meetings of the Managers if the Managers elect, in their discretion, to hold meetings. However, nothing in this Section 5.1.3 or in this Agreement is intended to require that meetings of Managers be held, it being the intent of the Members that meetings of Managers are not required.

5.2   Election of Managers.

5.2.1   Number, Term, and Qualifications.
The Company shall initially have one (1) Manager. During the term of this Agreement, the authorized number of Managers shall consist of not less than one (1) nor more than three (3). The number of Managers of the Company shall be fixed from time to time by the affirmative vote or written consent of a Majority Interest of Members. In no instance shall there be less than one Manager and provided further that if the number of Managers is reduced from more than one to one, the Articles shall be amended to so state, and if the number of Managers is increased to more than one, the Articles shall be amended to delete the statement that the Company has only one Manager. Unless he or she resigns or is removed, each Manager shall

hold office for a term of 10 year(s). A Manager need not be a Member, an individual, a resident of the State of California, or a citizen of the United States.

5.2.2   Resignation.

Any Manager may resign at any time by giving written notice to the Members and remaining Managers without prejudice to the rights, if any, of the Company under any contract to which the Manager is a party. The resignation of any Manager shall take effect upon receipt of that notice or at such later time as shall be specified in the notice. Unless otherwise specified in the notice, the acceptance of the resignation shall not be necessary to make it effective. The resignation of a Manager who is also a Member shall not affect the Manager's rights as a Member and shall not constitute a withdrawal of a Member.

5.2.3   Removal.

Any Manager may be removed at any time, with cause, by the affirmative vote of a Majority Interest at a meeting called expressly for that purpose, or by the written consent of a Majority Interest. Any removal shall be without prejudice to the rights, if any, of the Manager under any employment contract and, if the Manager is also a Member, shall not affect the Manager's rights as a Member or constitute a withdrawal of a Member. For purpose of this Section, "cause" shall mean fraud, embezzlement by the Manager concerning the Company or a breach of such Manager's obligations, willful misconduct or gross negligence, which breach, willful misconduct or gross negligence relates to the Manager's activities concerning the Company and have not been cured within 30 days after written notice given by a majority of the Managers specifying such breach, willful misconduct or gross negligence.

5.2.4   Vacancies.

Any vacancy occurring for any reason in the number of Managers may be filled by the affirmative vote or written consent of a majority of the remaining Managers.

5.3   Powers of Managers.

5.3.1   Powers of Managers.

Without limiting the generality of Section 5.1, but subject to Section 5.3.2 and to the express limitations set forth elsewhere in this Agreement, the Managers shall have all necessary powers to manage and carry out the purposes, business, property, and affairs of the Company, including, without limitation, the power to exercise on behalf and in the name of the Company all of the powers described in Corporations Code Section 17003 including, without limitation, the power to:

(i) Acquire, purchase, renovate, improve, alter, rebuild, demolish, replace, and own real property and any other property or assets that the Managers determine is necessary or appropriate or in the interest of the business of the Company, and to acquire options for the purchase of any such property;

(ii) Sell, exchange, lease, or otherwise dispose of the real property and other property and assets owned by the Company, or any part thereof, or any interest therein;

(iii) Borrow money from any party including the Managers and their Affiliates, issue evidences of indebtedness in connection therewith, refinance, increase the amount of, modify, amend, or change the terms of, or extend the time for the payment of any indebtedness or obligation of the Company, and secure such indebtedness by mortgage, deed of trust, pledge, security interest, or other lien or Company assets;

(iv) Guaranty the payment of money or the performance of any contract or obligation of any Person;

(v) Sue on, defend, or compromise any and all claims or liabilities in favor of or against the Company; submit any or all such claims or liabilities to arbitration and confess a judgement against the Company in connection with any litigation in which the Company is involved; and

(vi) Retain legal counsel, auditors, and other professionals in connection with the Company business and to pay therefor such remuneration as the Managers may determine.

5.3.2   Limitations on Power of Managers.
Notwithstanding any other provisions of this Agreement, no single debt or liability of more than $500,000 may be contracted on behalf of the Company except by the written consent of a Majority Interest of the Members. Additionally, the Managers shall not have authority hereunder to cause the Company to engage in the following transactions without first obtaining the affirmative vote or written consent of Majority Interest of the Members:

(i) The sale, exchange or other disposition of all, or substantially all, of the

Company's assets occurring as part of a single transaction or plan, or in multiple transactions over a twelve (12) month period, except in the orderly liquidation and winding up of the business of the Company upon its duly authorized dissolution;

(ii) The merger of the Company with another limited liability company or limited partnership;

(iii) The merger of the Company with a corporation or a general partnership or other Person shall require the affirmative vote or written consent of all Members;

(iv) The establishment of further different classes of Members;

(v) The lending of money by the Company to any Manager, Member, Affiliate;

(vi) Any act which would make it impossible to carry on the ordinary business of the Company;

(vii) The confession of a judgment against the Company;

(viii) To file a bankruptcy petition on behalf of the Company; and

(ix) Any other transaction described in this Agreement as requiring the vote, consent, or approval of the Members in which case the vote required will be as specified in the provision of this Agreement requiring such vote, approval or consent.

5.4   Performance of Duties; Liability of Managers.
A Manager shall not be liable to the Company or to any Member for any loss or damage sustained by the Company or any Member, unless the loss or damage shall have been the result of fraud, deceit, gross negligence, breach of fiduciary duty to the other members, reckless or intentional misconduct, or a knowing violation of law by the Manager.

5.5   Devotion of Time.
The Managers are not obligated to devote all of their time or business efforts to the affairs of the Company. The Managers shall devote whatever time, effort, and skill as they deem appropriate for the operation of the Company.

5.6   Transactions between the Company and the Managers.

Notwithstanding that it may constitute a conflict of interest, the Managers may, and may cause their Affiliates to, engage in any transaction (including, without limitation, the purchase, sale, lease, or exchange of any property or the rendering of any service, or the establishment of any salary, other compensation, or other terms of employment) with the Company so long as such transaction is not expressly prohibited by this Agreement and so long as the terms and conditions of such transaction, on an overall basis, are fair and reasonable to the Company and are at least as favorable to the Company as those that are generally available from Persons capable of similarly performing them and in similar transactions between parties operating at arm's length.

5.7   Liability of Manager Limited to Manager's Assets.

Under no circumstances will any director, officer, shareholder, member, manager, partner, employee, agent or Affiliate of any Manager have any personal responsibility for any liability or obligation of the Manager (whether on a theory of alter ego, piercing the corporate veil, or otherwise), and any recourse permitted under this Agreement or otherwise of the Members, any former Member or the Company against a Manager will be limited to the assets of the Manager as they may exist from time to time.

5.8   Payments to Managers.

Except as specified in this Agreement, no Manager or Affiliate of a Manager is entitled to remuneration for services rendered or goods provided to the Company. The Managers and their Affiliates shall receive only the following payments:

5.8.1   Managers' Fee. See Exhibit B

5.8.2   Services Performed by Managers or Affiliates.

Manage the activities of the Company including, but not limited to, hiring property management companies, attorneys, accountants and contractors.

5.8.2(a) Property Management Fee.

As of the date of this Agreement, Managers shall retain the property management services of Standard Management Company ("SMC"), an affiliate of Managers, to manage the assets of the Company. For its services, SMC shall receive four percent (4%) of the gross receipts from operations of the assets of the Company, as well reimbursements of their party charges fro services normally performed by third party professional management companies. Reasonable arms-length charges may be made for legal and construction supervision where such services are needed in the reasonable judgment of the Managers. For purposes of this section, "gross receipts" means receipts from all sources generated by the assets of the Company, including but not limited to, all rentals, percentage rentals, interest on delinquent rental, late charges, earned security, cleaning and other deposits, parking fees, sale of surplus personal property, cleaning and service charges, interest on funds invested, real estate taxes, insurance expenses, maintenance and utility expenses and all other common area maintenance expense payments and reimbursements but excluding condemnation proceedings, property tax refunds and casualty loss settlements. Managers reserve the right the change property management companies from time to time.

5.8.3   Expenses.

The Company shall reimburse the Managers and their Affiliates for the actual cost of materials used for or by the Company. The Company shall also pay or reimburse the Managers or their Affiliates for organizational expenses (including, without limitation, legal and accounting fees and costs) incurred to form the Company and prepare and file the Articles and this Agreement. Except where reasonably required to operate the company or as otherwise provided herein. The Managers and their Affiliates shall not be reimbursed by the Company for the following expenses: (i) salaries, compensation or fringe benefits of directors, officers or employees of the Managers or their Affiliates; (ii) overhead expenses of the Managers or their Affiliates, including, without limitation, rent and general office expenses except as provided in Exhibit B.

5.9   Limited Liability.

No person who is a Manager or officer or both a Manager and officer of the Company shall be personally liable under any judgment of a court, or in any other manner, for any debt, obligation, or liability of the Company, whether that liability or obligation arises in contract, tort, or otherwise, solely by reason of being a Manager or officer or both a Manager and officer of the Company.

5.10   Membership Interests of Managers.

Except as otherwise provided in this Agreement, Membership Interests held by the Managers as Members shall entitle each Manager to all the rights of a Member, including without limitation the economic, voting, information and inspection rights of a Member.

ARTICLE VI
ALLOCATIONS OF NET PROFITS AND NET LOSSES
AND DISTRIBUTIONS

6.1 Allocations of Net Profit and Net Loss.

6.1.1 Net Loss (a).

Net Loss shall be allocated 95% to the Class A Members and 5% to Class B in proportion to their Percentage Interests of their respective class.

6.1.1 (b) Special Provisions.

For allocation of taxable net profit and net loss all depreciation shall be allocated to the Contributing Members, provided that the Contributing Members maintain a positive Remaining Cash Investment in the Company, without regard to the interest of the Non-Contributing Members of the Company. The Contributing Members are to receive the depreciation deductions for the real and personal property owned by the Company as if the property was owned solely by them. The allocation among the Contributing Members shall be a percentage equal to the Remaining Cash Investment of a Contributing Member divided by the Remaining Cash Investment of all the Contributing Members. Taxable losses from operations shall be allocated to the Members who advance the funds required to cover such losses in proportion to their advances. Taxable gains shall be allocated among the parties in relation to their distributions from the Company including, the distribution by reason of the Priority Return. The Members are to have no taxable gain or loss beyond the distributions made to them from the Company. Any gain by reason of recapture of depreciation previously allocated to Contributing Members will be allocated to the Contributing Members. The appropriate adjustments will be made in the capital accounts of the Company to reflect these special allocations but such adjustments made to reflect the special tax allocations will not affect the distribution of distributable cash as set forth in this Operating Agreement. The purpose of these special adjustments is to allocate on the tax return of the Company the economic consequences of the Company's operation.

Notwithstanding the previous sentence, loss allocations to a Member shall be made only to the extent that such loss allocations will not create a deficit Capital Account balance for that Member in excess of an amount, if any, equal to such Member's share of Company Minimum Gain. Any loss not allocated to a Member because of the foregoing provision shall be allocated to the other Members (to the extent the other Members are not limited in respect of the allocation of losses under this Section 6.1.1). Any loss reallocated under this Section 6.1.1 shall be taken into account in computing subsequent allocations of income and losses pursuant to this Article VI, so that the net amount of any item so allocated and the income and losses allocated to each Member pursuant to this Article VI, to the extent possible, shall be equal to the net amount that would have been allocated to each such Member pursuant to this Article VI if no reallocation of losses had occurred under this Section 6.1.1.

6.1.2   Net Profit. (i).

Net Profit from operations shall be allocated to the Members in the same priority with respect to the Allocation of Distributable Cash from operations set forth in VI.5(a); (ii) Net Profits incurred in connection with any refinancing, insurance award, condemnation or sale of all or any part of the company's assets or any interest therein other than in the ordinary course of business, or any similar item which, in accordance with generally accepted accounting principals is attributable to capital, shall be allocated among the Members in the same priority with respect to the allocation of Distributable Cash from Sale or Refinance as set forth in section VI.5(b) of this Agreement, except that no allocation pursuant to this Section VI, 1.2 shall be made with respect to any distributions pursuant to Section VI.5(b) which represent a reutrn of a Member's Remaining Cash Investment in the Company.

6.2   Special Allocations. Deleted

6.2.1   Minimum Gain Chargeback.

If there is a net decrease in Company Minimum Gain during any Fiscal Year, each Member shall be specially allocated items of Company income and gain for such Fiscal Year (and, if necessary, in subsequent fiscal years) in an amount equal to the portion of such Member's share of the net decrease in Company Minimum Gain that is allocable to the disposition of Company property subject to a Nonrecourse Liability, which share of such net decrease shall be determined in accordance with Regulations Section 1.704-2(g)(2). Allocations pursuant to this Section 6.2.1 shall be made in proportion to the amounts required to be allocated to each Member under this Section 6.2.1. The items to be so allocated shall be determined in accordance with Regulations Section 1.704-2(f). This Section 6.2.1 is intended to comply with the minimum gain chargeback requirement contained in Regulations Section 1.704-2(f) and shall be interpreted consistently therewith.

6.2.2   Chargeback of Minimum Gain Attributable to Member Nonrecourse Debt.

If there is a net decrease in Company Minimum Gain attributable to a Member Nonrecourse Debt, during any Fiscal Year, each member who has a share of the

Company Minimum Gain attributable to such Member Nonrecourse Debt (which share shall be determined in accordance with Regulations Section 1.704-2(i)(5)) shall be specially allocated items of Company income and gain for such Fiscal Year (and, if necessary, in subsequent Fiscal Years) in an amount equal to that portion of such Member's share of the net decrease in Company Minimum Gain attributable to such Member Nonrecourse Debt that is allocable to the disposition of Company property subject to such Member Nonrecourse Debt (which share of such net decrease shall be determined in accordance with Regulations Section 1.704-2(i)(5)). Allocations pursuant to this Section 6.2.2 shall be made in proportion to the amounts required to be allocated to each Member under this Section 6.2.2. The items to be so allocated shall be determined in accordance with Regulations Section 1.704-2(i)(4). This Section 6.2.2 is intended to comply with the minimum gain chargeback requirement contained in Regulations Section 1.704-2(i)(4) and shall be interpreted consistently therewith.

6.2.3   Nonrecourse Deductions.
Any nonrecourse deductions (as defined in Regulations Section 1.704-2(b)(1)) for any Fiscal Year or other period shall be specially allocated to the Members in proportion to their Percentage Interests.

6.2.4   Member Nonrecourse Deductions.
Those items of Company loss, deduction, or Code Section 705(a)(2)(B) expenditures which are attributable to Member Nonrecourse Debt for any Fiscal Year or other period shall be specially allocated to the Member who bears the economic risk of loss with respect to the Member Nonrecourse Debt to which such items are attributable in accordance with Regulations Section 1.704-2(i).

6.2.5   Qualified Income Offset.
If a Member unexpectedly receives any adjustments, allocations, or distributions described in Regulations Section 1.704-1(b)(2)(ii)(d)(4), (5) or (6), or any other event creates a deficit balance in such Member's Capital Account in excess of such Member's share of Company Minimum Gain, items of Company income and gain shall be specially allocated to such Member in an amount and manner sufficient to eliminate such excess deficit balance as quickly as possible. Any special allocations of items of income and gain pursuant to this Section 6.2.5 shall be taken into account in computing subsequent allocations of income and gain pursuant to this Article VI so that the net amount of any item so allocated and the income, gain, and losses allocated to each Member pursuant to this Article VI to the extent possible, shall be equal to the net amount that would have been allocated to each such Member pursuant to the provisions of this Section 6.2.5 if such unexpected adjustments, allocations, or distributions had not occurred.

6.3   **Code Section 704(c) Allocations.**

Notwithstanding any other provision in this Article VI, in accordance with Code Section 704(c) and the Regulations promulgated thereunder, income, gain, loss, and deduction with respect to any property contributed to the capital of the Company shall, solely for tax purposes, be allocated among the Members so as to take account of any variation between the adjusted basis of such property to the Company for federal income tax purposes and its fair market value on the date of contribution. Allocations pursuant to this Section 6.3 are solely for purposes of federal, state and local taxes. As such, they shall not affect or in any way be taken into account in computing a Member's Capital Account or share of profits, losses, or other items of distributions pursuant to any provision of this Agreement.

6.4   **Allocation of Net Profits and Losses and Distributions in Respect of a Transferred Interest.**

If any Economic Interest is transferred, or is increased or decreased by reason of the admission of a new Member or otherwise, during any Fiscal Year of the Company, Net Profit or Net Loss for such Fiscal Year shall be assigned pro rata to each day in the particular period of such Fiscal Year to which such item is attributable (i.e., the day on or during which it is accrued or otherwise incurred) and the amount of each such item so assigned to any such day shall be allocated to the Member or Assignee based upon his or her respective Economic Interest at the close of such day.

However, for the purpose of accounting convenience and simplicity, the Company shall treat a transfer of, or an increase or decrease in, an Economic Interest which occurs at any time during a semi-monthly period (commencing with the semi-monthly period including the date hereof as having been consummated on the last day of such semi-monthly period, regardless of when during such semi-monthly period such transfer, increase, of decrease actually occurs (i.e., sales and disposi-tions made during the first fifteen (15) days of any month will be deemed to have been made on the 15th day of the month).

Notwithstanding any provision above to the contrary, gain or loss of the Company realized in connection with a sale or other disposition of any of the assets of the Company shall be allocated solely to the parties owning Economic Interests as of the date such sale or other disposition occurs.

6.5   **Distributions of Distributable Cash by the Company.**

Subject to applicable law and any limitations contained elsewhere in this Agreement, the Managers shall from time to time distribute Distributable Cash to the Members, which distributions shall be in the following order of priority:

VI.5(a)   All Distributable Cash from operations shall be distributed to the Members as follows:

(i). First to the Class A Members (the "Contributing Members") who have contributed cash or property to the Company (to the extent of their equity in such property after deduction for the outstanding balance of loans secured by such property as of the date of contribution of the Property to the Company) until the Contributing Members have received for each full fiscal year cumulatively non-compounded (as of the date of contribution of such cash or property to the Company) a percentage of the Contributing Members Remaining Cash Investment in the Company equal to eight (8%) percent per annum. Should the respective period involved be less than one full year or should a change result in the Remaining Cash Investment of one or more of the Contributing Members during any calendar year, then the distributions shall be prorated accordingly. After the Class A Members have received their return, then Class B Members shall receive $1.00 for every $2.00 distributed to Class A until such time that Class B Members have received an amount equivalent to 1/3 of the cash flow which participation is subordinated to the 8% return outlined above.

(ii) Second any amount equal to 1% of the cash flow to the Managers subordinated to the priority set for above.

(iii) Third any remaining Distributable Cash remaining after the distributions set forth in (i) above shall be distributed to Class A Members and Class B Members in proportion to their Percentage Interests as set forth on Exhibit B.

6.5(b)   Cash Distributions from Sale or Refinance.
If, as a result of the sale, financing or refinancing of all or any part of the Property, recasting of any mortgage or deed of trust relating to all or any part of the Property or condemnation sale or sale under threat of condemnation of all or any part of the Property, the Company has cash or other assets, and if in the reasonable opinion of the Manager such cash or other assets are in excess of the working capital needs of the Company to timely meet its obligations, then the same shall be distributed first to the remaining cash investment of Class A, second to any deficiency in any priority returns under Section VI.5(a) (i), third, any remaining cash investment of Class B, fourth, any deficiency in Class B priority, and fifth, any such excess cash or assets remaining shall be distributed to the Members in proportion to their Percentage Interests on Exhibit B, 66 2/3 to Class A and 33 1/3 to Class B

It is the intent that distributions from operations shall relate to cash flow from oper-ations in accordance with generally accepted accounting principals and

Distributions from Sale or Refinance shall relate to Non-Operating Cash Flow (including but not limited to Sale or Refinance of Company' Property). All such distributions shall be made only to the Persons who, according to the books and records of the Company, are the holders of record of the Economic Interests in respect of which such distributions are made on the actual date of distribution. Subject to Section 6.7, neither the Company nor any Manager shall incur any liability for making distributions in accordance with this Section 6.5.

6.6   Form of Distribution.

A Member, regardless of the nature of the Member's Capital Contribution, has no right to demand and receive any distribution from the Company in any form other than money. Except as provided in Section 10.4, no Member may be compelled to accept from the Company a distribution of any asset in kind in lieu of a proportionate distribution of money being made to other Members and no Member may be compelled to accept a distribution of any asset in kind.

6.7   Restriction on Distributions.

No distribution shall be made if, after giving effect to the distribution: (i) Such distribution would be in violation of any applicable law; (ii) the Company would not be able to pay its debts as they become due in the usual course of business; or (iii) the Company's total assets would be less than the sum of its total liabilities plus, unless this Agreement provides otherwise, the amount that would be needed, if the Company were to be dissolved at the time of the distribution, to satisfy the preferential rights of other Members, if any, upon dissolution that are superior to the rights of the Member receiving the distribution.

6.7.1   Managers Determination.

The Managers may base a determination that a distribution is not prohibited on any of the following: (i) financial statements prepared on the basis of accounting practices and principles that are reasonable in the circumstances; (ii) a fair valuation; or (iii) any other method that is reasonable in the circumstances. Except as provided in Corporations Code Section 17254(e), the effect of a distribution is measured as of the date the distribution is authorized if the payment occurs within 120 days after the date of authorization, or the date payment is made if it occurs more than 120 days of the date of authorization.

6.7.2   Member or Manager who votes for a distribution.

A Member or Manager who votes for a distribution in violation of this Agreement or the Act is personally liable to the Company for the amount of the distribution that exceeds what could have been distributed without violating this Agreement or the

Act if it is established that the Member or Manager did not act in compliance with Section 6.7 or Section 10.4. Any Member or Manager who is so liable shall be entitled to compel contribution from (i) each other Member or Manager who also is so liable and (ii) each Member for the amount the Member received with knowledge of facts indicating that the distribution was made in violation of this Agreement or the Act.

6.8   Return of Distributions.

Members and Assignees who receive distributions made in violation of the Act or this Agreement shall return such distributions to the Company. Except for those distributions made in violation of the Act or this Agreement, no Member or Assignee shall be obligated to return any distribution to the Company or pay the amount of any distribution for the account of the Company or to any creditor of the Company. The amount of any distribution returned to the Company by a Member or Assignee or paid by a Member or Assignee for the account of the Company or to a creditor of the Company shall be added to the account or accounts from which it was subtracted when it was distributed to the Member or Assignee.

6.9   Obligations of Members to Report Allocations.

The Members are aware of the income tax consequences of the allocations made by this Article VI and hereby agree to be bound by the provisions of this Article VI in reporting their shares of Company income and loss for income tax purposes.

ARTICLE VII
TRANSFER AND ASSIGNMENT OF INTERESTS

7.1   Transfer and Assignment of Interests.

Except as otherwise expressly set forth in this Agreement, no Member shall be entitled to transfer, assign, convey, sell, encumber or in any way alienate all or any part of his/her/its Membership Interest (collectively, "transfer") except with the prior written consent of the Managers, which consent may be given or withheld, conditioned or delayed (as allowed by this Agreement or the Act), as the Managers may determine in their sole discretion. Transfers in violation of this Article VII shall only be effective to the extent set forth in Section 7.6. After the consummation of any transfer of any part of a Membership Interest, the Membership Interest so transferred shall continue to be subject to the terms and provisions of this Agreement and any further transfers shall be required to comply with all the terms and provisions of this Agreement. This provision shall not prohibit a sale or transfer of the entire company which has been approved by a Majority Interest of the Members, as long as the Members not voting for the sale or transfer are treated the same as the Members who did vote for the sale or transfer.

7.2   Further Restrictions on Transfer of Interests.

In addition to other restrictions found in this Agreement, no Member shall transfer, assign, convey, sell, encumber or in any way alienate all or any part of his or her Membership Interest: (i) without compliance with all federal and state securities law, and (ii) if the Membership Interest to be transferred, when added to the total of all other Membership Interests transferred in the preceding twelve (12) consecutive months prior thereto, would cause the tax termination of the Company under Code Section 708(b)(1)(B).

7.3   Substitution of Members.

An Assignee of a Membership Interest shall have the right to become a substitute Member only if (i) the requirements of Sections 7.1 and 7.2 relating to the consent of Managers who are Members, securities and tax requirements hereof are met, (ii) the Assignee executes an instrument satisfactory to the Managers accepting and adopting the terms and provisions of this Agreement, and (iii) the Assignee pays any reasonable expenses in connection with his or her admission as a new Member. The admission of an Assignee as a substitute Member shall not result in the release of the Member who assigned the Membership Interest from any liability that such Member may have to the Company.

7.4   Effective Date of Permitted Transfers.

Any permitted transfer of all or any portion of a Membership Interest or an Economic Interest shall be effective as of the date provided in Section 6.4 following the date upon which the requirements of Sections 7.1, 7.2 and 7.3 have been met. The Managers shall provide the Members with written notice of such transfer as promptly as possible after the requirements of Sections 7.1, 7.2 and 7.3 have been met. Any transferee of a Membership Interest shall take subject to the restrictions on transfer imposed by this Agreement.

7.5   Rights of Legal Representatives.

If a Member who is an individual dies or is adjudged by a court of competent jurisdiction to be incompetent to manage the Member's person or property, the Member's executor, administrator, guardian, conservator, or other legal representative may exercise all of the Member's rights for the purpose of settling the Member's estate or administering the Member's property, including any power the Member has under the Articles or this Agreement to give an assignee the right to become a Member. If a Member is a corporation, trust, or other entity and is dissolved or terminated, the powers of that Member may be exercised by his or her legal representative or successor.

7.6   No Effect to Transfers in Violation of Agreement.

Upon any transfer of a Membership Interest in violation of this Article VII, the transferee shall have no right to vote or participate in the management of the business, property and affairs of the Company or to exercise any rights of a Member. Such transferee shall only be entitled to become an Assignee and thereafter shall only receive the share of one or more of the Company's Net Profits, Net Losses and distributions of the Company's assets to which the transferor of such Economic Interest would otherwise be entitled. Notwithstanding the immediately preceding sentences, if, in the determination of the Managers, a transfer in violation of this Article VII would cause the tax termination of the Company under Code Section 708(b)(1)(B), the transfer shall be null and void and the purported transferee shall not become either a Member or an Assignee.

Upon and contemporaneously with any transfer (whether arising out of an attempted charge upon that Member's Economic Interest by judicial process, a foreclosure by a creditor of the Member or otherwise) of a Member's Economic Interest which does not at the same time transfer the balance of the rights associated with the Membership Interest transferred by the Member (including, without limitation, the rights of the Member to vote or participate in the management of the business, property and affairs of the Company), the Company shall purchase from the Member, and the Member shall sell to Company for a purchase price of $100, all remaining rights and interests retained by the Member that immediately before the transfer were associated with the transferred Economic Interest. Such purchase and sale shall not, however, result in the release of the Member from any liability to the Company as a Member.

Each Member acknowledges and agrees that the right of the Company to purchase such remaining rights and interests from a Member who transfers a Membership Interest in violation of this Article VII is not unreasonable under the circumstances existing as of the date hereof.

7.7   Other Permitted Transfers.

The Interest of any Member may be transferred subject to compliance with Section 7.2, and without the prior written consent of the Members as required by Section 7.1, by the Member (i) by inter vivos gift or by testamentary transfer to any spouse, parent, sibling, niece, nephew, child or grandchild of the Member, or to a trust for the benefit of the Member or such spouse, parent, sibling, niece, nephew, child or grandchild of the Member, or (ii) to any Affiliate of the Member wholly owned by the Member. Such transfer shall continue to be subject to the provisions of this Agreement. It being agreed that, in executing this Agreement, each Member has consented to such transfers.

7.8   Rights of First Refusal.

If at any time during the term of this Agreement, the Company chooses to sell the Property, or a Member chooses to sell its interest in the Property, the Company and the Member shall offer, in writing, the opportunity to the Manager to purchase the Property or the interest on the same bona fide, arm's length economic terms and conditions agreed to by a third party prospective purchaser which Company and Member desires to accept. Manager shall have ten (10) calendar days from the receipt of the notice to accept or reject said offer. If Manger fails to accept the offer within said time period, Manager's opportunity shall expire and be of no further effect as to the perspective purchaser. Manager's opportunity shall apply to each and every offer received by Company and Member for any and all Properties or interests.

ARTICLE VIII
CONSEQUENCES OF DISSOLUTION EVENTS AND
TERMINATION OF MEMBERSHIP INTEREST

8.1   Dissolution Event.

Upon the occurrence of a Dissolution Event, the Company shall dissolve unless the remaining Members ("Remaining Members") holding a majority of the Percentage Interests which all Remaining Members hold, consent within ninety (90) days of the Dissolution Event to the continuation of the business of the Company. If the Remaining Members consent to the continuation of the business of the Company, the Company and/or the Remaining Members shall have the right to purchase, and if such right is exercised the Member whose actions or conduct resulted in the Dissolution Event ("Former Member") or such Former Member's legal representative shall sell, the Former Member's Membership Interest ("Former Member's Interest") as provided in this Article VIII.

8.2   Withdrawal.

Notwithstanding Section 8.1, upon the withdrawal by a Member in accordance with Section 4.3, such Member shall be treated as a Former Member, and, unless the Company is to dissolve, the Company and/or the Remaining Members shall have the right to purchase, and if such right is exercised, the Former Member shall sell, the Former Member's Interest as provided in this Article VIII.

8.3   Purchase Price.

The purchase price for the Former Member's interest shall be the Capital Account balance of the Former Member; provided, however, that if the Former Member, such Former Member's legal representative or the Company, deems the Capital

Account balance to vary from the fair market value of the Former Member's Interest by more than ten percent (10%), such party shall be entitled to require an appraisal by providing notice of the request for appraisal within thirty (30) days after the determination of the Remaining Members to continue the business of the Company. In such event, the value of the Former Member's Interest shall be determined by three (3) independent appraisers, one (1) selected by the Former Member or such Former Member's legal representative, one (1) selected by the Company, and one (1) selected by the two (2) appraisers so named. The fair market value of the Former Member's Interest shall be the average of the two (2) appraisals closest in amount to each other. In the event the fair market value is determined to vary from the Capital Account balance by less than ten percent (10%), the party requesting such appraisal shall pay all expenses of all the appraisals incurred by the party offering to enter into the transaction at the Capital Account valuation. In all other events, the party requesting the appraisal shall pay one-half of such expense and the other party shall pay one-half of such expense. Notwithstanding the foregoing, if the Dissolution Event results from a breach of this Agreement by the Former Member, the purchase price shall be reduced by an amount equal to the damages suffered by the Company or the Remaining Members as a result of such breach.

9.4   Notice of Intent to Purchase.
Within thirty (30) days after the Managers have notified the Remaining Members as to the purchase price of the Former Member's Interest determined in accordance with Section 8.3, each Remaining Member shall notify the Managers in writing of his/her/its desire to purchase a portion of the Former Member's Interest. The failure of any Remaining Member to submit a notice within the applicable period shall constitute an election on the part of the Member not to purchase any of the Former Member's Interest. Each Remaining Member so electing to purchase shall be entitled to purchase a portion of the Former Member's Interest in the same proportion that the Percentage Interest of the Remaining Member bears to the aggregate of the Percentage Interests of all of the Remaining Members electing to purchase the Former Member's Interest.

8.5   Election to Purchase Less Than All of the Former Member's Interest.
If any Remaining Member elects to purchase none or less than all of his or her pro rata share of the Former Member's Interest, then the Remaining Members may elect to purchase more than their pro rata share. If the Remaining Members fail to purchase the entire Interest of the Former Member, the Company may purchase any remaining share of the Former Member's Interest.

8.6   Payment of Purchase Price.

The purchase price shall be paid by the Company or the Remaining Members, as the case may be, by either of the following methods, each of which may be selected separately by the Company or the Remaining Members for the Former Member's Interest.

8.6.1   Former Member's Interest

The Company or the Remaining Members shall at the closing pay in cash the total purchase price for the Former Member's Interest; or

8.6.2   Former Member's Interest

The Company or the Remaining Members shall pay at the closing one-fifth (1/5) of the purchase price and the balance of the purchase price shall be paid in four equal annual principal installments plus accrued interest, and be payable each year on the anniversary date of the closing. The unpaid principal balance shall accrue interest at the current applicable federal rate as provided in the Code for the month in which the initial payment is made, but the Company and the Remaining Members shall have the right to prepay in full or in part at any time without penalty. The obligation of each purchasing Remaining Member, and the Company, as applicable, to pay its portion of the balance due shall be evidenced by a separate promissory note executed by the respective purchasing Remaining Member or the Company, as applicable. Each such promissory note shall be in an original principal amount equal to the portion owed by the respective purchasing Remaining Member or the Company, as applicable. The promissory note executed by each purchasing Remaining Member shall be secured by a pledge of that portion of the Former Member's Interest purchased by such Remaining Member.

8.7   Closing of Purchase of Former Member's Interest.

The closing for the sale of a Former Member's Interest pursuant to this Article VIII shall be held at a time mutually agreed upon by the parties at the principal office of Company, or at a place mutually agreed upon by the parties, no later than sixty (60) days after the determination of the purchase price, except that if the closing date falls on a Saturday, Sunday, or legal holiday, then the closing shall be held on the next succeeding business day. At the closing, the Former Member or such Former Member's legal representative shall deliver to the Company or the Remaining Members an instrument of transfer (containing warranties of title and no encumbrances) conveying the Former Member's Interest. The Former Member or such Former Member's legal representative, the Company and the Remaining Members shall do all things and execute and deliver all papers as may be necessary fully to consummate such sale and purchase in accordance with the terms and provisions of this Agreement.

8.8   Purchase Terms Varied by Agreement.

Nothing contained herein is intended to prohibit Members from agreeing upon other terms and conditions for the purchase by the Company or any Member of the Membership Interest of any Member in the Company desiring to retire, withdraw or resign, in whole or in part, as a Member.

ARTICLE IX
ACCOUNTING, RECORDS, REPORTING BY MEMBERS

9.1   Books and Records.

The books and records of the Company shall be kept, and the financial position and the results of its operations recorded, in accordance with the accounting methods followed for federal income tax purposes. The books and records of the Company shall reflect all the Company transactions and shall be appropriate and adequate for the Company's business. Any Member shall have the right, upon reasonable request, for purposes reasonably related to the interest of that person as a Member, Manager or holder of an economic interest, to inspect the Company's books and records. The Company shall maintain at its principal office in California all of the following:

9.1.1   Current List of Names

A current list of the full name and last known business or residence address of each Member and Assignee set forth in alphabetical order, together with the Capital Contributions, Capital Account and Percentage Interest of each Member and Assignee;

9.1.2   Current List of Full Name and Business Address.

A current list of the full name and business or residence address of each Manager;

9.1.3   Copy of Articles.

A copy of the Articles and any and all amendments thereto together with executed copies of any powers of attorney pursuant to which the Articles or any amendments thereto have been executed;

9.1.4   Copies of the Company's federal, state, and local income tax.

Copies of the Company's federal, state, and local income tax or information returns and reports, if any, for the six (6) most recent taxable years;

9.1.5   Copy of this Agreement.

A copy of this Agreement and any and all amendments thereto together with executed copies of any powers of attorney pursuant to which this Agreement or any amendments thereto have been executed;

9.1.6   Financial Statements.

Copies of the financial statements of the Company, if any, for the six (6) most recent Fiscal Years; and

9.1.7   Company Books and Records.

The Company's books and records as they relate to the internal affairs of the Company for at least the current and past four (4) Fiscal Years.

9.2   Delivery to Members and Inspection.

9.2.1   Request of any Member or Assignee.

Upon the request of any Member or Assignee for purposes reasonably related to the interest of that Person as a Member or Assignee, the Managers shall promptly deliver to the requesting Member or Assignee, at the expense of the Company, a copy of the information required to be maintained under Sections 9.1.1, 9.1.2 and 9.1.4, and a copy of this Agreement.

9.2.2   Members Right to Inspect and Copy Record

Each Member, Manager and Assignee has the right, upon reasonable request for purposes reasonably related to the interest of the Person as Member, Manager or Assignee, to:

(i)   inspect and copy during normal business hours any of the Company records described in Sections 9.1.1 through 9.1.7; and

(ii) obtain from the Managers, promptly after their becoming available, a copy of the Company's federal, state, and local income tax or information returns for each Fiscal Year.

9.2.3   Members representing at least five percent (5%) of the Percentage Interests

Members representing at least five percent (5%) of the Percentage Interests, or three or more Members, may make a written request to the Managers for an income statement of the Company for the initial three-month, six-month, or nine-month period of the current Fiscal Year ended more than thirty (30) days prior to the date of the request, and a balance sheet of the Company as of the end of that period. Such statement shall be accompanied by the report thereon, if any, of the independent accountants engaged by the Company or, if there is no report, the certificate of a Manager that the statement was prepared without audit from the books and records of the Company. If so requested, the statement shall be delivered or mailed to the Members within 30 days thereafter.

9.2.4   Any request, inspection or copying
Any request, inspection or copying by a Member or Assignee under this Section 9.2 may be made by that Person or that Person's agent or attorney.

9.2.5   Furnish Copies of any Amendment to the Articles or the Agreement.
The Managers shall promptly furnish to a Member a copy of any amendment to the Articles or this Agreement executed by a Manager pursuant to a power of attorney from the Member.

9.3   Annual Statements.

9.3.1   If the Company has more than thirty-five Members.
If the Company has more than thirty-five (35) Members, the Managers shall cause an annual report to be sent to each of the Members not later than one hundred twenty (120) days after the close of the Fiscal Year. The report shall contain a balance sheet as of the end of the Fiscal Year and an income statement and statement of changes in financial position for the Fiscal Year. Such financial statements shall be accompanied by the report thereon, if any, of the independent accountants engaged by the Company or, if there is no report, the certificate of a Manager that the financial statements were prepared without audit from the books and records of the Company.

9.3.2   Federal and State Income Tax Returns.
The Managers shall cause to be prepared at least annually, at Company expense, information necessary for the preparation of the Members' and Assignees' federal and state income tax returns. The Managers shall send or cause to be sent to each Member or Assignee within ninety (90) days after the end of each taxable year such information as is necessary to complete federal and state income tax or information returns, and, if the Company has thirty-five (35) or fewer Members, a copy of the Company's federal, state, and local income tax or information returns for that year.

9.3.3   Nevada requirement under Nevada Corporation Code.
The Managers shall cause to be filed at least annually with the Nevada Secretary of State the statement required under Nevada Corporations Code §.

9.4   Financial and Other Information.

The Managers shall provide such financial and other information relating to the Company or any other Person in which the Company owns, directly or indirectly, an equity interest, as a Member may reasonably request. The Managers shall distribute to the Members, promptly after the preparation or receipt thereof by the Managers, any financial or other information relating to any Person in which the Company owns, directly or indirectly, an equity interest, including any filings by such Person under the Securities Exchange Act of 1934, as amended, that is received by the Company with respect to any equity interest of the Company in such Person.

9.5   Filings.

The Managers, at Company expense, shall cause the income tax returns for the Company to be prepared and timely filed with the appropriate authorities. The Managers, at Company expense, shall also cause to be prepared and timely filed, with appropriate federal and state regulatory and administrative bodies, amendments to, or restatements of, the Articles and all reports required to be filed by the Company with those entities under the Act or other then current applicable laws, rules, and regulations. If a Manager required by the Act to execute or file any document fails, after demand, to do so within a reasonable period of time or refuses to do so, any other Manager or Member may prepare, execute and file that document with the Nevada Secretary of State.

9.6   Bank Accounts.

The Managers shall maintain the funds of the Company in one or more separate bank accounts in the name of the Company, and shall not permit the funds of the Company to be commingled in any fashion with the funds of any other Person.

9.7   Accounting Decisions and Reliance on Others.

All decisions as to accounting matters, except as otherwise specifically set forth herein, shall be made by the Managers. The Managers may rely upon the advice of their accountants as to whether such decisions are in accordance with accounting methods followed for federal income tax purposes.

9.8   Tax Matters for the Company Handled by Managers and Tax Matters Partner.

The Managers shall from time to time cause the Company to make such tax elections as they deem to be in the best interests of the Company and the Members. The Tax Matters Partner shall represent the Company (at the Company's expense) in connection with all examinations of the Company's affairs by tax authorities, including resulting judicial and administrative proceedings, and shall expend the Company funds for professional services and costs associated therewith. The Tax Matters Partner shall oversee the Company tax affairs in the overall best interests of the Company. If for any reason the Tax Matters Partner can no longer serve in that capacity or ceases to be a Member or Manager, as the case may be, a majority of the Managers may designate another to be Tax Matters Partner.

ARTICLE X
DISSOLUTION AND WINDING UP

10.1   Dissolution.
The Company shall be dissolved, its assets shall be disposed of, and its affairs wound up on the first to occur of the following:

10.1.1   The happening of any event of dissolution specified in the Articles;

10.1.2   The entry of a decree of judicial dissolution pursuant to Corporations Code Section 17351;

10.1.3   The vote of a Majority Interest of the Members

10.1.4   The Occurrence of a Dissolution Event.
The occurrence of a Dissolution Event and the failure of the Remaining Members to consent in accordance with Section 8.1 to continue the business of the Company within ninety (90) days after the occurrence of such event or the failure of the Company or the Remaining Members to purchase the Former Member's Interest as provided in Section 8.2; or

10.1.5   The sale of all or substantially all of the assets of Company.

10.2   Certificate of Dissolution.
As soon as possible following the occurrence of any of the events specified in Section 10.1, the Managers who have not wrongfully dissolved the Company or, if none, the Members, shall execute a Certificate of Dissolution in such form as shall be prescribed by the Nevada Secretary of State and file the Certificate as required by the Act.

10.3   Winding Up.
Upon the occurrence of any event specified in Section 10.1, the Company shall continue solely for the purpose of winding up its affairs in an orderly manner,

liquidating its assets, and satisfying the claims of its creditors. The Managers who have not wrongfully dissolved the Company or, if none, the Members, shall be responsible for overseeing the winding up and liquidation of Company, shall take all account of the liabilities of Company and assets, shall either cause its assets to be sold or distributed, and if sold as promptly as is consistent with obtaining the fair market value thereof, shall cause the proceeds therefrom, to the extent sufficient therefor, to be applied and distributed as provided in Section 10.5. The Persons winding up the affairs of the Company shall give written notice of the commencement of winding up by mail to all known creditors and claimants whose addresses appear on the records of the Company. The Managers or Members winding up the affairs of the Company shall be entitled to reasonable compensation for such services.

10.4   Distributions in Kind.
Any non-cash asset distributed to one or more Members shall first be valued at its fair market value to determine the Net Profit or Net Loss that would have resulted if such asset were sold for such value, such Net Profit or Net Loss shall then be allocated pursuant to Article VI, and the Members' Capital Accounts shall be adjusted to reflect such allocations. The amount distributed and charged to the Capital Account of each Member receiving an interest in such distributed asset shall be the fair market value of such interest (net of any liability secured by such asset that such Member assumes or takes subject to). The fair market value of such asset shall be determined by the Managers or by the Members or if any Member objects by an independent appraiser (any such appraiser must be recognized as an expert in valuing the type of asset involved) selected by the Manager or liquidating trustee and approved by the Members.

10.5   Order of Payment Upon Dissolution.
After determining that all the known debts and liabilities of the Company, including, without limitation, debts and liabilities to Members who are creditors of the Company, have been paid or adequately provided for, the remaining assets shall be distributed to the Members in the following order of priority as set forth in section V.1.5(b).

10.5.1   The payment of a debt or liability.
The payment of a debt or liability, whether the whereabouts of the creditor is known or unknown, has been adequately provided for if the payment has been provided for by either of the following means:

(i) Payment thereof has been assumed or guaranteed in good faith by one or more financially responsible persons or by the United States government or any agency thereof, and the provision, including the financial responsibility of the

Person, was determined in good faith and with reasonable care by the Members or Managers to be adequate at the time of any distribution of the assets pursuant to this Section.

(ii) The amount of the debt or liability has been deposited as provided in Section 2008 of the Corporations Code.

This Section 10.5.2 shall not prescribe the exclusive means of making adequate provision for debts and liabilities.

10.6 Limitations on Payments Made in Dissolution.
Except as otherwise specifically provided in this Agreement, each Member shall only be entitled to look solely at the assets of the Company for the return of his or her positive Capital Account balance and shall have no recourse for his or her Capital Contribution and/or share of Net Profits (upon dissolution or otherwise) against the Managers or any other Member.

10.7   Certificate of Cancellation.
The Managers or Members who filed the Certificate of Dissolution shall cause to be filed in the office of, and on a form prescribed by, the Nevada Secretary of State, a Certificate of Cancellation of the Articles upon the completion of the winding up of the affairs of the Company.

10.8   No Action for Dissolution.
Except as expressly Permitted in this Agreement, a Member shall not take any voluntary action that directly causes a Dissolution Event. The Members acknowledge that irreparable damage would be done to the goodwill and reputation of the Company if any Member should bring an action in court to dissolve the Company under circumstances where dissolution is not required by Section 10.1. This Agreement has been drawn carefully to provide fair treatment of all parties and equitable payment in liquidation of the Economic Interests. Accordingly, except where the Managers have failed to distribute funds as required by this Agreement, or failed to liquidate the Company as required by this Article X, or have breached their fiduciary duties to the other Members, each Member hereby waives and renounces his or her right to initiate legal action to seek the appointment of a receiver or trustee to liquidate the Company or to seek a decree of judicial dissolution of the Company on the ground that (a) it is not reasonably practicable to carry on the business of the Company in conformity with the Articles or this Agreement, or (b) dissolution is reasonably necessary for the protection of the rights or interests of the complaining Member. Damages for breach of this Section 10.8 shall be monetary damages only (and not specific performance), and the damages may be offset

against distributions by the Company to which such Member would otherwise be entitled.

ARTICLE XI
CONVERSION TO C CORPORATION

11.1   Company shall automatically convert to a "C" Corporation.
Notwithstanding anything to the foregoing set forth herein, parties listed on the signature pages hereof hereby agree that the Company shall automatically convert to a "C" Corporation on the effective date of the Company's initial public offering of shares of its capital stock pursuant to a Registration Statement filed pursuant to the Securities Act of 1933, as amended, and that no further consent of the Members or Managers shall be required for such conversion. The Members' Membership Interests shall automatically convert into shares of Common Stock at the same pro rata proportion that the Percentage Interest of each member bears to the aggregate of the Percentage Interests of all of the Members. Each of the Members and Managers agree to take all actions necessary to effectuate such conversion.

ARTICLE XII
INDEMNIFICATION

12.1   Indemnification of Agents.
The Company shall defend and indemnify any Member or Manager and may indemnify any other Person who was or is a party or is threatened to be made a party to any threatened, pending or completed action, suit or proceeding by reason of the fact that he or she is or was a Member, Manager, officer, employee or other agent of the Company or that, being or having been such a Member, Manager, officer, employee or agent, he or she is or was serving at the request of the Company as a manager, director, officer, employee or other agent of another limited liability company, corporation, partnership, joint venture, trust or other enterprise, to the fullest extent permitted by applicable law in effect on the date hereof and to such greater extent as applicable law may hereafter from time to time permit. The Managers shall be authorized, on behalf of the Company, to enter into indemnity agreements from time to time with any Person entitled to be indemnified by the Company hereunder, upon such terms and conditions as the Managers deem appropriate in their business judgment.

12.2   Insurance.
The Company shall have the power to purchase and maintain insurance on behalf of any Person who is or was an agent of the Company against any liability asserted

against such Person and incurred by such Person in any such capacity, or arising out of such Person's status as an agent, whether or not the Company would have the power to indemnify such Person against such liability under the provisions of Section 12.1 or under applicable.

ARTICLE XIII
INVESTMENT REPRESENTATIONS

13.1   Legends.

He or she understands that the certificates evidencing the Membership Interest may bear one or all of the following legends:

(i)   "THE SECURITIES REPRESENTED BY THIS CERTIFICATE HAVE NOT BEEN REGISTERED UNDER THE SECURITIES ACT OF 1933 NOR REGISTERED NOR QUALIFIED UNDER ANY STATE SECURITIES LAWS. SUCH SECURITIES MAY NOT BE OFFERED FOR SALE, SOLD, DELIVERED AFTER SALE, TRANSFERRED, PLEDGED, OR HYPOTHECATED UNLESS QUALIFIED AND REGISTERED UNDER APPLICABLE STATE AND FEDERAL SECURITIES LAWS OR UNLESS, IN THE OPINION OF COUNSEL SATISFACTORY TO THE COMPANY, SUCH QUALIFICATION AND REGISTRATION IS NOT REQUIRED. ANY TRANSFER OF THE SECURITIES REPRESENTED BY THIS CERTIFICATE IS FURTHER SUBJECT TO OTHER RESTRICTIONS, TERMS, AND CONDITIONS WHICH ARE SET FORTH HEREIN IN THE COMPANY'S OPERATING AGREEMENT, A COPY OF WHICH IS ON FILE AT THE PRINCIPAL OFFICE OF THE COMPANY"

(ii) Any legend required by applicable state securities laws.

13.2   Subscription Agreement and Purchaser Questionnaire.

All representations, warranties, and statements made by the Member in the Subscription Agreement and Purchaser Questionnaire were true, correct, and complete when made, and are true, correct, and complete as of the date of this Agreement. Each Member agrees that the representations, warranties, statements, covenants, and agreements made by the Member in the Subscription Agreement and Purchaser Questionnaire are hereby incorporated into this Agreement by reference, and remain fully binding on the Member.

ARTICLE XIV
MISCELLANEOUS

14.1   Counsel to the Company.

Counsel to the Company may also be counsel to any Manager. The Managers may execute on behalf of the Company and the Members any consent to the representation of the Company that counsel may request pursuant to the California Rules of Professional Conduct or similar rules in any other jurisdiction ("Rules"). Each Member acknowledges that Company Counsel does not represent any Member in the absence of a clear and explicit written agreement to such effect between the Member and Company Counsel, and that in the absence of any such agreement Company Counsel shall owe no duties directly to a Member. Notwithstanding any adversity that may develop, in the event any dispute or controversy arises between any Members and the Company, or between any Members or the Company, on the one hand, and a Manager that Company Counsel represents, on the other hand, then each Member agrees that Company Counsel may represent either the Company or such Manager, or both, in any such dispute or controversy to the extent permitted by the Rules, and each Member hereby consents to such representation.

14.2   Complete Agreement.

This Agreement, along with the Subscription Agreement and Purchaser Questionnaire, if applicable, and the Articles constitute the complete and exclusive statement of agreement among the Members and Managers with respect to the subject matter herein and therein and replace and supersede all prior written and oral agreements or statements by and among the Members and Managers or any of them. No representation, statement, condition or warranty not contained in this Agreement or the Articles will be binding on the Members or Managers or have any force or effect whatsoever. To the extent that any provision of the Articles conflict with any provision of this Agreement, the Articles shall control.

14.3   Binding Effect.

Subject to the provisions of this Agreement relating to transferability, this Agreement will be binding upon and inure to the benefit of the Members, and their respective successors and assigns.

14.4   Headings.

All headings herein are inserted only for convenience and ease of reference and are not to be considered in the construction or interpretation of any provision of the Agreement.

14.5 Interpretation.

In the event any claim is made by any Member relating to any conflict, omission or ambiguity in this Agreement, no presumption or burden of proof or persuasion shall be implied by virtue of the fact that this Agreement was prepared by or at the request of a particular Member or his or her counsel.

14.6 Jurisdiction.

Each Member hereby consents to the exclusive jurisdiction of the state and federal courts sitting in California in any action on a claim arising out of, under or in connection with this Agreement or the transactions contemplated by this Agreement, provided such claim is not required to be arbitrated pursuant to Section 14.11. Each Member further agrees that personal jurisdiction over him or her may be effected by service of process by registered or certified mail addressed as provided in Section 14.10 of this Agreement, and that when so made shall be as if served upon him or her personally within the State of Nevada.

14.7 Arbitration.

Except as otherwise provided in this Agreement, any controversy between the parties arising out of this Agreement shall be submitted to the American Arbitration Association for arbitration in Los Angeles, California. The costs of the arbitration, including any American Arbitration Association administration fee, the arbitrator's fee, and costs for the use of facilities during the hearings, shall be borne equally by the parties to the arbitration. Attorneys' fees may be awarded to the prevailing party at the discretion of the arbitrator. The provisions of the California Code of Civil Procedure apply to the arbitration. The arbitrator shall not have any power to alter, amend, modify or change any of the terms of this Agreement nor to grant any remedy which is either prohibited by the terms of this Agreement, or not available in a court of law.

14.8 Exhibits.

All Exhibits, attached to this Agreement are incorporated and shall be treated as if set forth herein.

14.9 Severability.

If any provision of this Agreement or the application of such provision to any person or circumstance shall be held invalid, the remainder of this Agreement or the application of such provision to persons or circumstances other than those to which it is held invalid shall not be affected thereby.

14.10   Additional Documents and Acts.

Each Member agrees to execute and deliver such additional documents and instruments and to perform such additional acts as may be necessary or appropriate to effectuate, carry out and perform all of the terms, provisions, and conditions of this Agreement and the transactions contemplated hereby.

14.11   Notices.

Any notice to be given or to be served upon the Company or any party hereto in connection with this Agreement must be in writing (which may include facsimile) and will be deemed to have been given and received when delivered to the address specified by the party to receive the notice. Such notices will be given to a Member or Manager at the address specified in Exhibit B hereto. Any party may, at any time by giving five (5) days' prior written notice to the other parties, designate any other address in substitution of the foregoing address to which such notice will be given.

14.12   Amendments.

All amendments to this Agreement will be in writing and signed by a Majority Interest of Members.

14.13   Multiple Counterparts.

This Agreement may be executed in two or more counterparts, each of which shall be deemed an original, but all of which shall constitute one and the same instrument.

14.14   Attorney Fees.

In the event that any dispute between the Company and the Members or among the Members should result in litigation or arbitration, the prevailing party in such dispute shall be entitled to recover from the other party all reasonable fees, costs and expenses of enforcing any right of the prevailing party, including without limitation, reasonable attorneys' fees and expenses, all of which shall be deemed to have accrued upon the commencement of such action and shall be paid whether or not such action is prosecuted to judgment. Any judgment or order entered in such action shall contain a specific provision providing for the recovery of attorney fees and costs incurred in enforcing such judgment and an award of prejudgment interest from the date of the breach at the maximum rate of interest allowed by law. For the purposes of this Section: (a) attorney fees shall include, without limitation, fees incurred in the following: (1) post-judgment motions; (2) contempt proceedings; (3) garnishment, levy, and debtor and third party examinations; (4) discovery; and (5) bankruptcy litigation and (b) prevailing party shall mean the party who is determined in the proceeding to have prevailed or who prevails by, dismissal, default or otherwise.

14.15   Captions.

The Section and Article captions contained in this Agreement are inserted only as a matter of convenience and reference and in no way define, limit or describe the scope of this Agreement or the intent of any provisions hereof.

14.16 Counterparts.

This Agreement may be signed in counterparts, and all counterparts, when combined, shall constitute a single Agreement. The signature pages of each counterpart of Agreement may be detached and attached to one Agreement.

All of the Members of Sunset Pointe, a Nevada limited liability company have executed this Agreement, effective as of the date written above.

MEMBERS:

_____

_____

CONSENT OF SPOUSE

The undersigned spouse(s), of the party (parties) to the foregoing Agreement acknowledge(s) on his or her own behalf that: I have read the foregoing Agreement and I know its contents. I am aware that by its provision my spouse grants the Company and/or the other Members an option to purchase all of his or her Membership Interest, including my community interest (if any) in it. I hereby consent to the sale, approve of the provisions of the Agreement, and agree that such Membership Interest and my interest in it are subject to the provisions of the Agreement and that I will take no action at any time to hinder operation of the Agreement on such Membership Interest or my interest in it.

_____

_____

EXHIBIT A

PROPERTY DESCRIPTION

A 384-unit apartment building commonly known as Sunset Pointe Apartments located at 2255 East Sunset Road, Las Vegas, V 89119.

EXHIBIT B

INTERESTS AND ADDRESSES OF MEMBERS
AND MANAGERS AS OF

_____

Sunset Pointe, LLC, a Nevada limited liability company

Managers: 1% of the cash flow subordinated to Class A and Class B priorities.
Class A Members total 66 2/3% after priorities and Managers.
Class B Members total 33 1/3% after priorities and Managers.

Member's Name Address % ClassA   Contribution

Member's Name Address % Class B   Contribution

For determining "majority in interest" for voting purposes, the Class A members hold 66 2/3% and the Class B members hold 33 1/3%.

_____

Initials

PRINCIPLES
OF
REAL ESTATE
SYNDICATION

GLOSSARIES

GLOSSARIES

CONTENTS

Note:
Many of the terms in the real estate sections will apply as well to the other sections.

REAL ESTATE TERMS

A

ABANDON   Voluntary termination of interest in property.

A & B PARTNERSHIP   Indicates a partnership with at least two CLASSES of partners. See LIMITED PARTNERSHIP INTEREST. "A&B Entity "an entity with two or more classes of equity.

ABSORPTION   A swallowing up or engulfment. Note: Land may absorb the building values, e.g., in cases where encroaching higher land uses increase the degree of obsolescence in the building, thus engulfing the building value leaving no value or a negative value to the building.

ABSTRACT   A summary or review of a detailed document or record.

ABSTRACT OF JUDGMENT   Summary of a court's order regarding a money judgment. When recorded, it creates a general lien upon all real estate and personal property of a judgment debtor in the county where recorded.

ABSTRACT OF TITLE   A history of the title, summarizing the various links in the chain of title, together with a statement of all liens, charges, or encumbrances affecting a particular property, as maintained in public records.

ABUTTING   Land touching another parcel, such as a highway or adjoining parcel. Also referred to as "adjacent."

ACCELERATION   Unless otherwise specified, the maturing of a loan upon the happening of an event. The "accelerating" of the maturity date of the loan. An event that causes an obligation to be due. Some causes of acceleration: (a) TRANSFER, caused by the transfer of an interest in the property (property transfer) or in the title holding entity (equity transfer) including a sale by contract. This can be BROAD TRANSFER, covering a transfer of any type of interest in the property, such as a lease, or a NARROW TRANSFER, which would apply only to a sale or transfer of a specific interest, such as the entire property or a defined portion thereof; (b) DEFAULT, by reason of any default in payment; (c) INSOLVENCY, by reason of an act of insolvency affecting borrower; (d) JUNIOR FINANCING, by reason of the placement of a junior lien; and (d) BREACH OF CONTRACT OR COVENANT, by reason of some contractual breach other than by the above.

ACCELERATION CLAUSE   A provision in a trust deed or mortgage that makes the balance owed immediately due and payable upon the happening of a certain event. See ALIENATION CLAUSE, DUE ON SALE CLAUSE. In Wellenkamp v.

Bank of America, 22 C3d (1978) the Court declared that an acceleration clause upon an outright sale of property is unenforceable by an institutional lender unless there is an impairment of lender's security interest or an increased likelihood of default. This holding does not presently apply to private lenders (according to the court) nor to federally chartered institutional lenders (according to The Federal Home Loan Bank Board).

ACCEPTANCE   Words or an act indicating a proposed offer is accepted, thereby creating a binding contract.

ACCESS RIGHT   Landowner's right of ingress to and egress from his property to a public highway over another's land.

ACCESSIBILITY   The manner in which a site can be reached.

ACCESSION   Additions to property by natural increase or growth, or improvements to real property.

ACCOMMODATION LENDER   See LENDER.

ACCREATION   Gradual deposit of soil by wind or water onto adjoining property.

ACCRUED DEPRECIATION   Total depreciation that has accumulated over a period of time.

ACKNOWLEDGMENT   Admitting in writing before an authorized official (usually a notary public) by a person who has executed a document, that he or she in fact did execute (sign) the document.

ACQUISITION   The process of acquiring property.

ACQUISITION EXPENSES   Relate to the cost of acquiring the property such as surveys, travel expenses, escrow charges, and legal expenses related to acquisitions.

ACRE   43,560 square feet of land area (approximately 209' x 209'); or 160 square rods (4,840 square yards).

ACRE-FOOT   A volume of water equivalent to one acre in area with a depth of one foot (43,560 cubic feet of water).

ACTION   Court proceeding.

ACTION IN PERSONAM   Court action seeking a judgment against the person rather than against property, e.g., for money against the maker of an unsecured note.

ACTION IN REM   Court action seeking judgment against property, e.g., for quiet title to property.

ACTUAL NOTICE   A notice that a party has in fact received as compared with CONSTRUCTIVE NOTICE that is implied or inferred.

ADDITIONAL ADVANCE   A provision that under certain circumstances the lender will advance additional funds for stated purposes. These funds are to be secured by the security pledged for the original loan. Such advances may be obligatory (required by the loan documents) or optional (authorized if the lender elects to make).

ADDITIONAL COMMITMENT   The amount that each investor is obligated to pay in addition to his initial SUBSCRIPTION. Generally, this phrase will be applicable only in the case of transactions where, in addition to the down payment, continuing payments will be required because income from the property will not be sufficient to service encumbrances and expenses or further payments are required to the seller. In the event of failure to make such payments an investor's interest may include one or more of the following: be

(a) proportionately reduced and the interest of those who make their payments increased;
(b) sold at public or private sale with the defaulting investor responsible for the deficiency;
(c) sold at public or private sale with the defaulting investor not responsible for deficiency;
(d) subordinated to the interest of those who are non-defaulting investors; or
(e) a combination of the above and/or subject to further restrictions and disabilities as may be provided in the entity agreement.

ADJUDICATION   Judicial determination of a matter.

ADJUSTED BASIS   Cost basis of property for tax purposes with certain additions such as improvement costs and certain subtractions such as depreciation.

ADJUSTED CASH FLOW   All cash receipts from project during the ordinary course of business for the fiscal period, without allowing deductions for depreciation, after payment of operating cash expenses, capital expenditures and any sums set aside for restoration or creation of reserves.

ADJUSTED CAPITAL CONTRIBUTIONS Each investor's capital contribution for the fiscal period, less distributions of sale or refinancing proceeds. Also called Remaining Cash Investment.

ADMINISTRATOR A person appointed by the court to administer the estate of a deceased person who left no will, i.e., who died intestate.

ADMINISTRATOR c.t.a. (CUM TESTAMENTO ANNEXO) With the will annexed; where no executor is named in the will or the named executor does not wish to act.

ADR SYSTEM– ASSET DEPRECIATION RANGE SYSTEM Internal Revenue Code Section. Method of property depreciation allowance, "useful life" determined by guideline life ranges published by the IRS.

AD VALOREM According to the value.

AD VALOREM TAX A tax varying with the value of goods or commodity.

ADVANCES – OBLIGATORY Money advanced by beneficiary under deed of trust to protect his interests, e.g., real property taxes, hazard insurance premiums.

ADVANCES – OPTIONAL Advances made which are not required to protect the security but which the lender has the right to make under the loan agreement.

ADVANCE BILLINGS See PROGRESS BILLINGS, RETENTIONS.

ADVERSE LAND USE Incompatible land use with detrimental effect on adjacent properties.

ADVERSE POSSESSION The right of an occupant of land to acquire title against the real owner, where all of the following circumstances are present for the statutory period: possession has been
    (1) actual,
    (2) open and notorious,
    (3) exclusive,
    (4) hostile (without consent),
    (5) continuous, and
    (6) in some jurisdictions, the taxes may have to be paid by the claimant for the period required. The foregoing applies to securing title by adverse possession. A non-exclusive easement by adverse possession would not require payment of

taxes or excusive use, but might result from all of the other elements being present for the required period.

AFFIANT One who affirms the statement in an affidavit.

AFFIDAVIT A statement of declaration reduced to writing, and sworn or affirmed to before some officer who has authority to administer an oath or affirmation.

AFFIRMATIVE COVERAGE Insurance policy provisions whereby the insurer affirmatively insures against specific risks not ordinarily covered by the policy.

AFTER ACQUIRED TITLE ESTOPPEL BY DEED Title acquired by grantee from grantor who conveyed land before he owned it, and then acquired it. Grantee automatically retains title to such land without having to obtain another deed from his grantor.

AFTER-COMPLETION COSTS Costs incurred for the development of real property after the regular construction has been completed.

AFTER-TAX INVESTMENT The out-of-pocket cost to make an investment after all tax considerations. Also referred to as "HARD DOLLAR INVESTMENT."

AFTER-TAX NET CASH PROCEEDS OF RESALE Resale price of property, less commissions, outstanding debts, and taxes on the ownership interest.

AGE, ACTUAL The number of years elapsed since the original structure was built.

AGE, EFFECTIVE The number of years that is indicated by the condition of the building.

AGE-LIFE METHOD Method of estimating accrued depreciation as percentage of current reproduction costs of new improvements.

AGENCY A relationship of trust. The agent represents the principal who appoints him. See FIDUCIARY.

AGREEMENT OF SALE A written agreement whereby the purchaser agrees to buy certain real estate and the seller agrees to sell upon terms and conditions set forth therein (also called LAND CONTRACT, CONTRACT OF SALE, CONDITIONAL SALES CONTRACT).

A.I.C.P.A. American Institute of Certificate Public Accountants. (See also A.P.B.).

AIR RIGHTS Right to ownership of everything above physical surface of the land.

A.I.T.D. See ALL-INCLUSIVE LOAN.

ALIENATION In real estate, to convey the ownership to another.

ALIENATION CLAUSE A special kind of acceleration clause that demands payment of a balance due upon the alienation of title.

ALL-INCLUSIVE LOAN Also called in some cases an "overriding" or "over-lapping" or "AITD" or "hold harmless" or "wrap around.". A junior loan where the beneficiary (lender or seller) covenants to pay one or more senior encumbrances and the trustor (borrower or buyer) is responsible for making only one payment on the ALL-INCLUSIVE LOAN to the beneficiary, rather than the junior and senior encumbrances separately. Normally the senior encumbrances are referred to as "underlying." The face amount of the ALL-INCLUSIVE LOAN includes the EQUITY of the beneficiary as well as the balance of the senior encumbrances at the time of its creation.

ALLOWABLE ASSETS See NET CAPITAL.

ALLOWANCE FOR VACANCY AND INCOME LOSS Deduction from Potential Annual Gross Income to reflect possible vacancy, turnover, and non-payment of rent by tenants.

ALLUVION (ALLUVIUM) Accretion by gradual action of water on a shore or bank.

A.L.T.A. American Land Title Association. Extended coverage form of title insurance usually requiring physical inspection of property and survey, as compared to Standard Coverage Policy, which only covers matters of record.

AMENITIES State of being pleasant or agreeable, as in respect to a situation, location, or climate. In residential appraising it means those peculiar and intangible benefits arising from ownership. Often refers to special features such as pool, tennis courts, clubhouse, water frontage, etc.

AMENITY PACKAGE Special features such as swimming pool, tennis courts, etc.

AMENITY VALUE The value of the pleasures of the property such as good neighborhood, schools, parks, playgrounds, etc.

AMORTIZATION The liquidation of a financial obligation on an installment basis.

AMORTIZED LOAN Principal and interest of loan reduced by a series of regular payments that are often equal or almost equal. As equal payments are made principal reduction increases and interest portion of the loan reduces.

ANCHOR TENANT One who draws enough customers to encourage smaller tenants to lease in a shopping center.

ANNEXATION
    (a) Addition of a county's unincorporated territory to a city or town.
    (b) Increasing property by adding, attaching other property to it, e.g., fixtures, improvements.

ANNUITY Series of assured payments made over a period of time.

ANTICIPATION Economic principle that value is created by anticipated benefits to be gained in the future. When property value appreciates because of an improved neighborhood.

ANTIDEFICIENCY LEGISLATION Where the buyer is unwilling or unable to pay the balance of a loan, the holder only has recourse against the property and may not obtain a money judgment against the borrower.

APARTMENT HOUSE A building with separate residential units, generally at least three units. Two units would be referred to as a duplex. Three units is a triplex. Four units is a fourplex.

A.P.B. Accounting Principles Board. An affiliate of the American Institute of Certified Public Accounts, which sets forth standards to be used in the preparation of audits and financial reports.

APPLICATION FOR QUALIFICATION A written form filed with the respective securities commissioner requesting a permit to offer and sell interests in a limited partnership.

APPRAISAL A written opinion of value prepared by an individual whose background and experience would qualify him to give such an opinion. Compensation for the preparation and rendering of such an opinion shall not be in any way contingent upon the determination of any particular value. It shall constitute the opinion of the appraiser only, and the appraiser shall not in any way be interested in the offering.

APPRAISAL BY CAPITALIZATION An estimate of value based upon the capitalization (i.e., obtaining the "present worth") of income, usually future or anticipated net income.

APPRAISAL BY COMPARISON An estimate of value based upon an analysis of current market sales, listings, and rentals adjusted to reflect major points of difference.

APPRAISAL BY SUMMATION The process of adding together parts of a property separately appraised to form an opinion as to the worth of the whole.

APPRECIATION BUILD-UP An assumed increase in value due to inflation and supply and demand factors. Should be clearly designated as speculative estimate.

APPURTENANCE Belonging to something else; something that passes as an incident to land, such as a right of way.

ARCHITECT'S PUNCH LIST Discrepancies in building plans or other construction flaws noted by architect during final inspection.

ASSESSABILITY Indicates that interests in a syndicate are assessable by action of the GENERAL PARTNER under certain limited conditions and that such assessments will generally result in personal liability for the assessment on the part of the INVESTOR. Where the assessment does not result in personal liability, but merely a penalty affecting the investor's ownership interest, the assessment may be referred to as "Non-Personal Assessability."

ASSESSED VALUATION Value of real estate as set by a unit of government for taxation purposes. Not necessarily corresponding to market valuation.

ASSESSMENT There are basically two types of assessments: (a) PROP-ERTY ASSESSMENTS are impositions by government agencies or districts as charges for improvements; (b) ENTITY ASSESSMENTS are impositions by the Entity Manager on the interests of the investors for entity purposes. Such assessments may be PERSONAL indicating that the assessed investor has personal liability therefore, or NON-PERSONAL, indicating that only the entity interest itself may be made to pay the assessment if the respective investor does not. Most interests are non-assessable unless so stated in the Offering Circular. Assessments may be OPTIONAL or MANDATORY.

ASSET BASE Value of assets can be (a) book value, (b) market value or (c) cost.

ASSESSOR Public Official who determines assessed value of property for tax purposes.

ASSIGNEE Person who receives property or a right in an assignment.

ASSIGNMENT The method or manner by which a right, a specialty, or contract is transferred from one person to another.

ASSIGNOR Person who transfers property or a right to another in an assignment.

ASSISTED HOUSING Construction, finance or purchase of housing with governmental assistance, e.g., FHA, VA, HUD etc.

ASSUMPTION AGREEMENT Agreement to take over a debt or obligation of another. Original debtor may remain secondarily liable.

ASSUMPTION FEE Lender's fee for changing and processing new records for a buyer who assumes an existing loan.

ASSUMPTION OF MORTGAGE (or trust deed) Taking over the primary liability to pay an existing mortgage or trust deed debt.

ATTACHMENT Seizure of property by court order to keep it available for payment of a debt to be collected in a pending lawsuit.

ATTORN A tenant accepting and acknowledging a new property owner.

ATTORNEY-IN-FACT A person appointed under a "Power of Attorney to act on another's behalf as an agent.

AUDITED FINANCIAL STATEMENTS Financial statements including the profit and loss statement, cash flow and source of application statement, and balance sheet, which have been attested to by a certified public accountant because of an independent audit.

AVAILABLE CASH FLOW–RETURN TO THE INVESTOR See NET SPENDABLE. Proceeds from operation of project not required to meet its obligations or operations and available for distribution to investors and sponsor.

B

BALANCE SHEET A financial statement showing assets, liabilities, and net worth.

BALLOON PAYMENT A payment on maturity of a debt that is greater than the normal payment and is the balance due on maturity date.

BANKRUPT A person relieved by a court proceeding from payment of certain debts, after surrender of certain assets to a court appointed trustee.

BASE LINE Survey line running east and west that is used in establishing township boundaries.

BASIS Dollar cost assigned to property at acquisition (less losses and depreciation for tax purposes. I.R.C. Sections 167(g), 1011.) in order to compute gains.

BASIS–ALLOCATION OF Allocation of basis among land, improvements, personal property.

BASIS – NEW ADJUSTED New owner's basis in property acquired in an exchange.

BASIS – OLD ADJUSTED Old owner's adjusted basis in property being disposed of.

BASIS POINT Used to describe the amount of change in yield in debt instruments such as mortgages – one one-hundredths of one percent.

BEARER INSTRUMENT Note or other document payable to "bearer" rather than a named party.

BEFORE – TAX CASH FLOW Cash available before payment of income taxes, after payment of operating expenses and contractual debt service. Synonym – cash throw-off.

BENCH MARK Location indicated by a land surveyor on a durable marker.

BENEFICIARY
    (1) The lender in a trust deed, or
    (2) one who receives the income (benefit) from a trust.

BENEFICIARY'S STATEMENT Statement of a creditor giving the remaining principal balance and other information concerning the debt. Usually obtained when owner wishes to sell or refinance. See OFFSET STATEMENT.

BEST – EFFORTS BASIS Security broker's undertaking to use his best efforts to sell the issue. Opposite of FIRM UNDERWRITING.

BETTERMENT Improvement to property that increases its value, as opposed to maintenance, or replacement.

BILATERAL CONTRACT Contract in which a promise is given for a promise. See UNILATERAL.

BILL OF SALE Document used to transfer title (ownership) of personal property

BLANKET ENCUMBRANCE A lien covering more than one item of security of the same class. If the security were real estate, it would be one or more parcels of real estate. (If the security were personal property, it would be more than one item of personal property of the same class.) As individual lots are sold, a partial reconveyance from the blanket encumbrance is ordinarily.

BLIGHTED AREA A declining area that is seriously affected by destructive economic forces, such as encroaching inharmonious property usages, infiltration of disadvantaged social and economic classes of inhabitants, and/or rapidly depreciating buildings.

BLIND POOL   See NON-SPECIFIED FUND.

BLUE SKY The process of qualifying a securities issue under a state securities act.

BLUE SKY LAW A state law regulating solicitation and sale of securities.

BONA FIDE In good faith, without fraud.

BONA FIDE PURCHASER Good faith property purchaser, for fair value, without notice of any adverse claims, or rights of third parties.

BOND
(a) Insurance agreement whereby one party becomes surety to pay, within stated limits, financial losses caused by specified acts, or defaults of a third party;
(b) Interest-bearing security evidencing a long-term debt may be secured by lien on property, issued by government or a corporation.

BOOK COST Cost shown in general ledger of individual or entity, usually including direct and indirect financing and all development costs.

BOOK VALUE "Value" as reflected on the "books" after subtracting depreciation from original cost of property. For income tax purposes only.

BOOT Non-qualified property received as part of an exchange of realty and/or relief of liability in an exchange.

BORROWER(S) The primary obligor(s) in a debt to a lender.

BREACH Failure to perform a duty or promise.

BREAK-EVEN POINT Amount required to cover all operating expenses and debt service, if any, on the property. Normally expressed in two formulas:
(1) break-even on operations absent debt service, and
(2) break-even operations after debt service. Break- even point can be stated as a dollar amount or as a percentage of occupancy.

BROKER One who negotiates a transaction on behalf of others.

BROKER-DEALER One who is licensed to sell securities and may employ licensed AGENTS for that purpose.

B.S.P.R.A.–BUILDER/SPONSOR PROFIT AND RISK ALLOWANCE.
Developer's return for assuming risks involved when building low-income housing. Amount subject to governmental regulations.

BUILT-INS Cupboards, appliances, etc attached as part of structure.

BUILDING LINE A line established by ordinance, or statute, between which line and street, or adjoining lot, a structure is not permitted. Also called a setback.

BUILDING RESIDUAL TECHNIQUE Method of appraising a building and one of three methods of determining accrued depreciation.

BUILDING TO LAND RATIO Ratio of value of building to value of land.

BULK SALE Large transfer out of ordinary course of transferor's business of a substantial part of the personal property of the business.

BUNDLE OF RIGHTS Beneficial interests.

BURN OFF Amortization of front-end prepayments of interest by adjusting payments in a tax-structured transaction.

BUSINESS PURPOSE When an ENTITY is primarily involved in non-trade or non-business activities, such as a hobby, sport, or recreational activity and there is no bona fide intent to operate at a profit, the IRS will disallow all expenses other than those that are deductible without regard to profit motivation. Expenses deductible without regard to profit include interest, state and local taxes, capital losses, bad debts, and casualty and theft losses.

BUYER'S CLOSING COSTS Escrow costs to the buyer, including his share of prorated expenses.

BUYER'S COMMITMENT Valuable consideration or promise given by buyer as initial investment or continuing commitment.

BUYER'S MARKET Supply exceeding demand so that market prices are relatively low, giving buyers an advantage.

BUY-OUT ESTIMATE Projected cost of construction based on price of jobs for which contracts have been completely let.

BUY-SELL AGREEMENT (Distinguished from right of first refusal. See RIGHT OF FIRST REFUSAL.) Under a buy-sell agreement, if one party desires to sell, he must sell to the other and the other must buy.

C

C.A.E. Certified Assessment Evaluator.

CALENDAR YEAR January 1st through December 31st.

CALL Option to purchase at a set price for a given period. See PUT.

CAPACITY Legal right to do something (enter a contract, etc.).

CAPITAL ACCOUNT Account established for each participant, initially equal to original investment, increased by taxable income allocated to that person and reduced by allocated tax losses, cash, and sale or refinancing proceeds distributed to that person.

CAPITAL CONTRIBUTION See CAPITAL INVESTMENT.

CAPITAL GAIN See LONG-TERM CAPITAL GAIN.

CAPITAL INVESTMENT The amount invested by a particular INVESTOR that may be his (a) INITIAL OR ORIGINAL CAPITAL INVESTMENT at the time of the organization of the partnership; (b) his CONTINUING INVESTMENT consisting of his additional assessments after initial or original capital investment; or (c) his TOTAL INVESTMENT including his initial and continuing payments. May also be called CAPITAL CONTRIBUTION.

CAPITAL INVESTMENT RETURN Ratio of capital investment to net spendable income the investor earns. Capital Investment. Remaining the amount invested less returns from sale, refinance, or otherwise designated in the entity agreement for purposes of determining share of distributable cash.

CAPITALIZED COSTS Costs, for tax purposes, recovered by depreciation over a term of years, rather than being recovered by an immediate tax deduction.

CAPITALIZATION RATE A formula applied to the net income generated from property to determine its value. If the net income were to be capitalized at 10%, the value of the property would be ten times its net income.

C.A.R. California Association of Realtors. (Formerly C.R.E.A.)

CARRYING CHARGES Non-capital costs incurred by developers in carrying the project prior to occupancy, e.g., interest on loans for land and construction, property taxes, etc.

CASH FLOW (NET) See RETURN TO INVESTORS.

CASH-ON-CASH RETURN Rate of return on investment without regard to tax savings.

CASH INCOME OR GROSS INCOME Total income of the property prior to expenses and debt service. GROSS INCOME is the preferable term.

CASH LIQUIDATING VALUE The sum that a participant in an investment program is entitled to receive upon request where a program offers liquidity.

CAVEAT EMPTOR "Let the buyer beware". Places obligation on buyer to examine property before purchasing. Less applicable than in the past.

C.C&R.'s Covenants, conditions and restrictions.

CEILING In a floating or variable rate loan, the maximum rate of interest to be charged. The opposite is referred to as a "floor" the minimum rate to be charged.

CERTIFICATE OF LIMITED PARTNERSHIP A summary of the major provisions of a LIMITED PARTNERSHIP AGREEMENT which is required to be filed in the office of the county recorder in which the particular partnership is doing business.

CERTIFICATE OF OCCUPANCY Written authorization by local authority allowing newly completed building to be occupied.

CERTIFICATE OF REASONABLE VALUE Documentation required by federally insured or guaranteed loans evidencing physical inspection of property by federal employee to determine loan to value ratio.

CERTIFICATE OF SALE Certificate issued to purchaser at an execution sale. Evidences ownership. Given in exchange for deed if there is no redemption from the sale.

CERTIFICATE OF TITLE A title company's opinion of the condition of the title to a parcel of real estate without guarantee.

CERTIFICATION A written statement under penalty of perjury, executed by an officer or principal of borrower that the material contained in a document to which it is affixed is true and correct to the best knowledge of the person subscribing thereto. This is to be distinguished from a FULL DISCLOSURE NOTICE, which is a statement executed under penalty of perjury that all material facts have, to the best of the knowledge of the person executing said notice, been disclosed in the document to which it is attached.

CESTU QUE TRUST One for whose benefit property is held in trust.

CHAIN Measurement of land equal to 66 feet in length.

CHAIN OF TITLE All of the documents transferring title to a parcel of real estate, beginning with the document originally transferring title from public to private ownership and ending with the latest document transferring title.

CHANGE ORDER Change to original plan of construction by owner or contractor.

CHATTEL REAL   Interest in land that is less than freehold, e.g., leasehold.

CHECK-O-MATIC (AUTOMATIC CHECK OFF) A contract between the borrower and the lender which provides that the borrower sign an agreement allowing lender to arrange with the borrower's bank for the bank automatically to, each period, debit the borrower's account and send to the lender the PERIODIC PAYMENT called for in the loan.

CHOSE IN ACTION Personal right recoverable by an action at law.

CLASS
>   (a) of SECURITIES indicates the securities being offered have different rights and privileges. All those having the same rights and privileges being of the same class when one class could have
>>   (1) a PRIORITY over another or
>>   (2) have greater participation or TAX BENEFITS
>   (b) of INVESTOR, referring to the holder of a particular class of securities.

CLASS ACTION Plaintiff brings suit on his own behalf and as representative for all others similarly harmed.

CLEAR TITLE Free from encumbrances or defects.

CLOSE Date on which a transaction is closed and the net proceeds generally are available to the borrower. See also FUNDING.

CLOSED END Indicating an offering or fund that after the sale of a maximum number of units is "closed," with no additional units to be offered to issue without further amendment of the agreement of partnership. An OPEN END offering would indicate that further securities could be issued without amending or changing the partnership agreement.

CLOUD ON THE TITLE Claim or encumbrance that, if valid, would affect or impair the owner's title. Removed by quitclaim deed or court action.

COINSURANCE More than one insurer sharing a single risk, each undertaking part of the whole risk often the insured retains a portion of the risk itself. The coinsurer may be the insured.

COLLATERAL Security for a loan.

COLLATERAL ASSIGNMENT Assignment of property interest for security purposes, not an absolute assignment.

COLLATERAL SECURITY Transfer to a creditor of an interest in property providing additional security for the creditor.

COLOR OF TITLE Giving the appearance of title, but not in fact title.

COMBINED FUND See EQUITY FUND.

COMFORT LETTER A letter prepared by the independent Certified Public Accountant indicating that immediately prior to the public issuance of program interests a preliminary review of the company's books and records indicates no material change from the last certified audit. A comfort letter is not an audit. It refers to a cursory review.

COMMERCIAL ACRE The remainder of an acre of subdivided land after the deduction of areas for streets, sidewalks, curbs, etc.

COMMERCIAL PROPERTY Real property, excluding residential property, acquired for investment or commercial use.

COMMISSION Sum due for services in selling an item of property; an administrative and enforcement tribunal of laws.

COMMITMENT An agreement to make or buy a loan in the future, not intended for immediate funding, often called a FORWARD COMMITMENT.

COMMITMENT TO INSURE Title insurance company report, showing condition of title and obligating insurance company to issue form of policy de-scribed upon compliance with and satisfaction of requirements stated.

COMMON AREAS Land or improvements existing for benefit of more than one tenant, or property owner.

COMMON LAW Body of law that grew up from custom and decided cases (often English Law) rather than from codified law (Roman law, Spanish law, French law, etc.).

COMMUNITY APARTMENT PROJECT Subdivision where operation, maintenance and control are exercised by governing board selected by owners of the fractional interests. Undivided interest in the property is conveyed complete with the right to occupy a certain unit or apartment. See CONDOMINIUM.

COMMUNITY PROPERTY Form of ownership of property in certain states. Real property within the state and personal property wherever located, acquired during marriage, is presumed to be community property when not acquired as the separate property of either spouse. It is owned in common by both spouses.

COMPARABLES Recently sold properties with similar characteristics to a particular property, which are indicative of fair market value of particular property being compared.

COMPARISON FIGURES In projections, comparing a particular period, normally the latest current period, with some prior period of historical operation.

COMPLETED CONTRACT METHOD Method of recording income from construction contracts where income is recorded at completion rather than during progress of the work.

COMPONENT FINANCING Borrowing from separate lenders on separate loans (referred to as "sandwich financing") on various parts of the property such as (a) the fee, normally by means of a ground lease; (b) the improvements; and (c) the personal property.

CONCLUSIVE PRESUMPTION Unequivocal inference made by the law.

CONDEMNATION Taking of private property for public use, with compensation to the owner, under the right of eminent domain.

CONDITION Provision in agreement, contract providing that a right or interest in property depends on a future event that may or may not happen.

CONDITION PRECEDENT Condition must be fulfilled before estate can vest.

CONDITION SUBSEQUENT Failure or non-performance of condition may defeat an estate that has already vested.

CONDITIONAL SALE CONTRACT Title remains in seller until condition of contract met. Sometimes referred to as a "land contract."

CONDOMINIUM Individual fee ownership of units combined with joint ownership of common areas of the building and the land.

CONFIRMATION OF SALE   Sale of property by executor, administrator, guardian, or conservator, approved by the Court.

CONFLICT OF INTEREST   Anything in the nature of a program that would cause a conflict with the motivation of the GENERAL PARTNER, PROMOTER, SPONSER, or SYNDICATOR to use his best efforts exclusively in the field of real estate investment for the benefit of the respective program. Conflicts of interest are not necessarily prohibited but must be fully disclosed.

CONSERVATOR   One appointed by Probate Court to take care of person and/or property of one unable to do so himself.

CONSIDERATION   Anything of value used to induce another to enter into a contract. Either a benefit to promisor or detriment to promisee.

CONSTANT   The amount of ANNUAL DEBT SERVICE (expressed as a percentage of the original loan balance required to fully amortize the loan in equal payments of principal and interest, monthly, quarterly or annually) over a given period of time.

CONSTRUCTION COSTS   Direct costs to improve raw land or buildings.

CONSTRUCTION LOAN   See LOAN.

CONTIGUITY INSURANCE   The endorsement on title insurance policy indicating that the perimeter survey of the property is insured.

CONTIGUOUS   (a) Actual contact. (b) Adjoining.

CONTINGENT   Dependent on uncertain future events.

CONTINUING COMMITMENT   Consideration to be given by buyer after his initial investment.

CONTOUR   A line connecting the points on a land surface that have the same elevation.

CONTRACT OF SALE   (Also referred to as a "LAND CONTRACT" or "CONDITIONAL SALE CONTRACT" in some states). An agreement whereby one party has bound himself to purchase and receives possession from the other, but no legal title, as opposed to a CONTRACT TO PURCHASE whereby one party has agreed to buy and the other has agreed to sell, but both title and possession remain with the seller until further conditions take place prior to transfer of possession.

CONTRACT RENT   Rent due pursuant to rental or lease agreement.

CONTRACTOR'S FEE A payment to a licensed contractor for overhead and profit for supervising construction.

CONSTRUCTIVE NOTICE Notice given by the public records.

CONSTRUCTIVE TRUST Trust imposed by law to prevent unjust enrichment.

CONVENTIONAL MORTGAGE One not guaranteed or insured by a federal agency

CONVERTIBLE DEBT Debt that can be converted into equity shares usually a stated amount of issuer's equity.

CONVEYANCE The means or medium by which title to real estate is transferred.

CO-OPERATIVE APARTMENT HOUSES See COMMUNITY APARTMENT PROJECT.

CO-OP SALE OR LOAN Indicates that more than one BROKER is involved in the sale and that there is a sharing of COMMISSION.

CORPORATION An artificial "person" created by law.

CORRESPONDENT See MORTGAGE CORRESPONDENT.

COST BASIS Value of property determined at time of purchase by amount of purchase.

COST CERTIFICATION Independent audit statement of FHA insured housing projects as required by Section 227 National Housing Act and FHA Regulations.

COST OF LIVING See PRICE INDEX.

COST, HISTORICAL The total cost of a project based on prices at the time of construction.

COST PLUS CONTRACT Construction contract wherein contract price is equal to cost of construction plus profit allowance to builder.

COST, REPLACEMENT The cost that would be incurred in acquiring a substitute property of equivalent desirability and utility.

COST, REPRODUCTION The cost of reproducing a new replica property on the basis of current prices with the same or closely similar material, labor, plus contractor's overhead, profits and fees.

COST OF REPRODUCTION (OR REPLACEMENT) NEW LESS DEPRECIATION The possible combinations are too numerous to list; the appraiser must study each engagement's requirements to decide which category, or categories of depreciation are applicable.

COST, TRENDED Original cost new adjusted by application of an index to develop normal cost at another date, under similar conditions of acquisition, construction and installation. Care must be exercised to insure that proper indexes are applied to historical cost involving units or structures acquired used, or to purchased assets for a lump sum wherein an allocation of the price paid may have been distributed among the various assets.

COSTS Costs are often broken down into DIRECT COSTS that are the physical items that go into the project itself, and INDIRECT costs that might be financing, carrying charges, architect's fees, engineering fees, developer's profit and over-head, etc. Cost can also be ACTUAL COST (often termed "historical cost" or "replacement cost") based on present market prices of the components of the property.

COVENANT An agreement in a deed or other instrument governing activities or uses permitted or prohibited upon real estate.

COVERAGE Percentage by which the net spendable income prior to debt service equals the constant required to service the loan. If the constant is $10,000 per year, and the net spendable income is $15,000, the coverage is 150%.

CPI Consumer Price Index of the Bureau of Labor Statistics.

C.R.E.A. Refers to California Real Estate Association, which is now called California Association of Realtors (C.A.R.).

CREDIT REPORT Report obtained by potential lender regarding credit standing of potential borrower.

G.R.V. Certificate of Reasonable Value issued by the Federal Housing Administration.

CO-TENANCY Ownership of property by two or more persons.

CUL DE SAC End of a street.

CURTAIL SCHEDULE Listing of amounts by which principal sums of a debt are to be reduced by partial payments and the due date for such payments. Synonym–mortgage amortization schedule.

CURTESY Interest in wife's property allowed to a husband.

CUSTODIAL ACCOUNTS Bank accounts used for funds belonging to others.

D

DEALER OF PROPERTY One whose occupation is the sale of real property from inventory and whose profits on such sales because of his dealer status are ordinary income rather than capital gain. One can be a dealer with respect to some property and an INVESTOR with respect to other property.

DEBT In reference to a given loan, all the elements of the loan including the instruments, the security, and the obligation of the borrower. When talking about a financial statement, the total amount owed by a borrower to all creditors.

DEBT CAPITAL See EQUITY CAPITAL.

DEBT SERVICE The amount of money (both principal and interest) required to meet encumbrances on a parcel of property. Expressed in terms of TOTAL (meaning the entire amount required to service the loan during the period it is outstanding); ANNUAL (being the amount required to service encumbrances during a calendar year); or MONTHLY (bearing the amount required to service encumbrances monthly). Specify whether the discussion concerns TOTAL, ANNUAL or MONTHLY by using the proper adjective.

DECLARATION OF ABANDONMENT Document recorded to terminate a homestead.

DECLARATION OF CC&R's (COVENANTS, CONDITIONS AND RESTRICTIONS) Restrictions placed on owner's use of property in subdivisions and condominium developments. Binding on all owners of interest in the subdivision and enforceable as equitable servitudes.

DECLARATION OF HOMESTEAD Document recorded to create a homestead.

DECREE A type of court order.

DEDICATION A grant of land or easement by an owner to some public use together with acceptance for such use by or on behalf of the public.

DEDUCTIONS Specified allowable items subtracted from income before calculating taxes to be paid, e.g., medical expenses, home mortgage interest, etc. A method of tax shelter deductions are subject to "INVESTMENT AT-RISK RULE" and "LIMIT ON INVESTMENT INTEREST RULE" of the IRS.

DEED A written instrument which, when properly executed and delivered, transfers title to real estate.

DEED IN LIEU OF FORECLOSURE Deed given by investor/owner/debtor to the trustee of a Deed of Trust for the benefit of the beneficiary/lender/mortgagee to prevent foreclosure of the property.

DEED OF RECONVEYANCE The transfer of legal title from the trustee to the trustor (borrower) after a trust deed debt has been paid.

DEED OF TRUST Written instrument transferring title to land to a trustee as security for a debt or other obligation. Also called TRUST DEED.

DEEP SHELTER Indicates a project wherein there are losses available to shelter other income of the investor. See TAX SHELTER.

DEFAULT The non-performance of a duty, whether arising under a contract, or otherwise; failure to meet an obligation when due.

DEFAULT JUDGMENT A court order after the defendant has failed to answer the complaint in a lawsuit.

DEFEASABLE Ownership with conditional restrictions that, if broken, can cause forfeiture of title to grantor or his heirs.

DEFEASANCE CLAUSE A clause in a deed that contains conditional restrictions, which if broken, can cause forfeiture of title back to grantor or his heirs.

DEFEASANCE (Loan) Relates to ability or non-ability and costs associated with prepaying a loan prior to maturity.

DEFERRAL Tax incentive structure setting up investments with deductions occurring during years of high earnings, and income and capital gains occurring during reduced earning periods or on retirement. Postponement techniques resulting in taxes being paid in the future.

DEFERRED MAINTENANCE Negligent or "putting off" care of a property. An excessive form of deterioration.

DEFERRED PURCHASE (DEFERRED PAYMENT SALE) A condition of payment of property whereby the property may be paid for in certain designated periods spaced over a specified length of time. See INITIAL INVESTMENT.

DEFICIENCY The difference between the indebtedness sued upon and the sale price, or market value of the real estate at the foreclosure sale.

DEFICIENCY JUDGMENT A court order to pay the balance (deficiency) owed on a loan after the proceeds from sale of the security are not sufficient to pay off the loan.

DELIVERY Unequivocal transfer of a deed from donor/seller to donee/buyer in such a manner that it cannot be revoked.

DEMISE Transfer of an estate for years, for life or at will.
DEPLETION Tax allowance on a wasting asset, e.g., such as mineral deposits. Percentage depletion deduction allowance throughout the production period. Effectively enables investor to recover more than his investment tax free.

DEPOSIT RECEIPT Form acknowledging deposit. May also form contract for sale and purchase of land when executed by both buyer and seller.

DEPRECIATION That sum which a qualified individual (generally a certified public accountant or public account) has determined to be the reasonable allowance (for tax purposes) charge against profit and loss for tax purposes for the depreciating value of the building due to its increasing age. There are five principle methods of computing tax depreciation:
  (a) Straight line;
  (b) 200% declining balance;
  (c) 150% declining balance;
  (d) 125% declining balance;
  (e) Sum of the years digits.

Of the above, (b) through (e) are termed accelerated methods of depreciation. Depreciation taken on a UNIT BASIS is where one estimated life is applied to all the parts of a building.

COMPONENT BASIS Where the assets are broken up and different lives are applied to the respective parts of the building. Reference should be made to the regulations of the Internal Revenue Service as to the applicability and definition of the various methods. It is also deemed a loss in value from any cause. An effect caused by deterioration or obsolescence or both is
  (a) PHYSICAL, while for tax purposes is
  (b) tax.

DEPRECIATION, NORMAL The amount anticipated under average use and ordinary conditions.

DEPTH TABLE A chart used by appraisers.

DERAIGN To prove.

DETERIORATION An impairment of physical condition, due to wear and tear, decay.

DETERIORATION (a) Physical value loss resulting from disintegration, wear, tear and action of the elements, (b) FUNCTIONAL OBSOLESCENCE, value loss resulting from decreased utility, due to deficiencies inherent in the structure, or (c) ECONOMIC OBSOLESCENCE, value loss resulting from decreased utility, due to adverse external economic influences.

DEVELOPMENT FEE Fee paid to the developer for his efforts. May or may not include general overhead and supervision expenses in connection with the development of a project.

DEVELOPMENT FUND See EQUITY FUND.

DEVISE A gift of real estate by will or last testament.

DEVISEE One who receives (inherits) real estate by will.

DIRECT CONTRACTOR A single trade contractor such as an electrician or plumber who contracts with the owner rather than a general contractor.

DIRECT COST Specific costs of labor and material for a project.

DIRECTIONAL GROWTH Direction in which a community is growing.

DISCOUNT The amount by which a loan may be purchased or made below the principal obligation of the borrower. If the balance owed by the borrower is $100 and the loan may be purchased for $95, the discount is 5%. When a loan is purchased for the principal balance owing, it is said to be bought at PAR. If interest has accrued and the purchase price is to include the interest, then it is purchased at PAR PLUS accrued interest.

DISCOUNTED CASH FLOW (Internal Rate of Return) A method of analysis that indicates the rate of return which equates the present value of future benefits to the present value of the investment outlay. An analytical measure of profitability of an investment that considers not only the amount of profit, but also that point or those points in time when the profit is received. It should be distinguished from AVERAGE ANNUAL RETURN, which computes the benefit or return being measured by totaling same for the entire time of investment and dividing by the number of years that the investment is assumed to be held. This results in an average annual profit that is then divided by the initial investment. The percentage figure computed is then called the AVERAGE ANNUAL RETURN. When projections are included, they should indicate clearly and precisely whether the projection is on an AVERAGE ANNUAL RETURN basis or a DISCOUNTED CASH FLOW basis. A DIS-COUNTED CASH FLOW basis is considered to be the superior analysis.

DISCOUNTING INTEREST Taking interest in advance, when the lender giving money on a note deducts interest in advance.

DISCOUNT POINTS Money paid by the borrower to get a mortgage at a lower rate of interest than the market. A point equals one percent of the loan.

DISCRETIONARY ACCOUNT Indicates that a broker may invest on behalf of his client without consulting him. A DISCRETIONARY REINVESTMENT clause indicates that an ENTITY MANAGER can reinvest the funds without consulting the INVESTORS.

DISPOSSES To deprive one of the use of property.

DISTRIBUTED CASH The amount of cash actually distributed. As distinguished from DISTRIBUTABLE CASH or NET CASH FLOW. The participation interest of the lender is in some cases based on a percentage of distributed cash and in other cases based on a percentage of cash available for distribution whether or not distributed (DISTRIBUTABLE CASH). The PARTNERSHIP AGREEMENT should clearly specify which method is to be used. Distributed cash is the preferable method from the borrower's standpoint.

DISTRIBUTED CASH FLOW The net income from any source distributed to the investor or distributable to the investor at his option.

DOCTRINE OF RELATION BACK The title received at trustee's sale "relates back" to same condition title was in at time the deed of trust was signed.

DOCUMENTARY TRANSFER TAX Tax on transfer of real property. Amount computed on basis of consideration paid.

DOMINANT TENEMENT The tenement benefiting by an easement appurtenant (part of) another's land. See SERVIENT TENEMENT.

DRAGNET CLAUSE A provision in a loan or security agreement indicating that any security pledged by the borrower to the same lender in connection with other loans, serves also as security for the respective loan.

DUAL IMPOUND See IMPOUND CONDITIONS.

DUE DILIGENCE EXAMINATION Due Diligence – Investigation of a property by the purchaser to determine all the circumstances required for a decision to

Purchase. Examination by the broker/dealer of the circumstances surrounding securities offered by sponsor/issuer to verify representations made.

DUE ON SALE CLAUSE Special kind of acceleration clause that demands payment of a balance due upon the alienation of title. Synonym Alienation Clause.

DUPLEX A single structure designed for two-family occupancy.

DURESS Unlawful force used to compel a person to do something against his will

DOWER Estate for life to which a married woman is by statute entitled to on the death of her husband, generally one-third of the value of all land acquired by the husband during marriage.

E

EARNEST MONEY Down payment made by a purchaser as evidence of good faith.

EASEMENT The right or privilege which one person or property has in lands of another (a right of way). May be APPURTENANT- attached to the benefited land, or IN GROSS- for personal benefit not attached to ownership of land.

ECONOMIC BENEFITS Total benefits exclusive of TAX BENEFITS. Economic benefits would include EQUITY BUILD-UP, APPRECIATION BUILD-UP and NET SPENDABLE.

ECONOMIC LIFE The period during which an improvement earns enough profit to justify maintaining it.

ECONOMIC OBSOLENCE Loss of use, value of property as a result of external factors.

ECONOMIC RENT (GROUND RENT) Profit (net income) credited to the use of land after allowing a proper credit to the improvements.

EFFECTIVE AGE An "age" usually less than the chronological age, assigned to the improvements by an appraiser to reflect less depreciation.
EJECTMENT A form of action to regain possession of real property, with damages for the unlawful retention.

EGRESS The right to leave a tract of land.

EMINENT DOMAIN The power of the government to take (condemn) private property for a public use upon payment of a fair compensation.
ENCROACHMENT A structure partly or wholly upon the land of another.

ENCUMBRANCE Anything that burdens real estate or limits the title such as a lien, easement or restriction of any kind.

ENDORSEMENT Transfer of a check or promissory note to a third person by signing one's name on the back. "In Blank" guarantees payment to subsequent holders. "Without Recourse" without guaranteeing to subsequent holders. Also can mean a rider to an insurance policy.

ENTITY The legal form chosen for the particular investment.

ENTITY THEORY Refers to the fact that under certain conditions a partnership is treated for tax purposes as a separate ENTITY. If the partnership qualifies under the ENTITY THEORY, a substituted partner may receive depreciation for an entire year even though his investment and substitution into the partnership may occur at some point after organization but prior to the close of the respective fiscal year.

EQUITY In relation to borrower, the difference between the fair market value of the property and the debt owing. An Equity Fund is a trust which purchases "equities" rather than makes loans. An institution maybe an "equity purchaser" who buys for all cash rather than lending on property. In some loan or joint venture agreements, the developer or borrower is said to have a PHANTOM EQUITY, in that it represents his share of the appraised value of the completed project rather than actual cash invested. He may be entitled to a priority return on that equity before profits are computed from the venture.

EQUITY BUILD-UP The increase in equity resulting from both APPRECIATION BUILD-UP and MORTGAGE REDUCTION.

EQUITY CAPITAL Difference between total capitalization in money and property and debt capital. DEBT CAPITAL is the amount supplied by third parties as a loan to the project.

EQUITY FUND Referring to an ENTITY. which has been formed for the purchase of purchasing equities in real estate as opposed to a MORTGAGE FUND that has been formed for the purpose of purchasing mortgages and lending money on real estate. A COMBINED FUND would be one that is formed for the dual purpose, often termed a DUAL FUND, of both purchasing equities and mortgages. A DEVELOPMENT FUND is one that is formed for the sole purpose of developing real estate projects whereas the usual EQUITY FUND is formed for the purpose of both developing projects and purchasing equity in existing projects.

EQUITY KICKER Equity participation given to a lender, broker, syndicator, as part of consideration of his services.

EQUITY OF REDEMPTION Right to redeem property after a lien foreclosure sale.

EQUITY VALUE That portion of an investment that represents the amount of difference remaining after subtracting the debt owing from the value of the property.

ESCALATION CLAUSE A clause indicating that in the event of increases in taxes or other operating costs in the case of a lease, the rental will be adjusted accordingly. It may also be tied to gross sales or net income of a tenant, or to some index such as the Bureau of Labor Standards Consumer Price Indexes. Changes in the appraised value are another basis for "escalating rentals".

ESCHEET Reverting of property to the State upon death of an owner without heirs and without a will.

ESCROW The deposit of documents, funds and instruments to an independent third party who handles the documents and funds and arranges for the close of the transaction, when all of the conditions have been met pursuant to the instructions from the respective parties. Sometimes called the "settlement."

ESCROW COSTS Costs to the buyer/seller relating to purchase, sale or financing of real property, e.g., prorated expenses, fees for title insurance policies, credit reports, recording fees, escrow fees. Synonyms are CLOSING COSTS, SETTLEMENT COSTS.

ESCROW FEES Fees charged by escrow holder.

ESCROW HOLDER Independent third party with fiduciary obligation to all parties to ensure that all the terms of the transaction are carried out.

ESCROW IMPOUND CLAUSE A provision in a lease or loan that payments for taxes, insurance or other items will be ESCROWED or IMPOUNDED so that the lessor or lender will have on hand on the due date sufficient funds to pay same.

ESCROW INSTRUCTIONS Instructions given to escrow holder by buyer, seller, lender. May constitute a valid contract of sale.

ESCROW STATEMENT Statement of the escrow transaction, given to the buyer, seller, lender at the escrow closing itemizing the terms and costs of the sale.

ESTATE The ownership interest of a person in real estate; the property left by a deceased person.

ESTATE AT SUFFERANCE A type of lease automatically resulting where there is retention of possession after expiration of the term of another type of lease.

ESTATE AT WILL A type of lease terminated immediately upon notice by either party, in some states requiring advance notice.

ESTATE FOR LIFE Estate held by a person for his life or the life of another (estate per autre vie).

ESTATE FOR YEARS A lease for a definite period of time.

ESTATE IN REVERSION The residue of an estate left in the grantor, to commence in possession after termination of some particular estate granted by him. In a lease, the lessor has the estate in reversion after the lease is terminated.

ESTATE OF INHERITANCE An estate inherited, i.e., left by will or to heirs at law.

ESTOPPEL CERTIFICATE See OFFSET STATEMENT.

ETHICS, CODE OF The code of action established by a profession to insure that its members are worthy of confidence.

EVASION OF TAXES Willfully attempting illegally to evade taxes as opposed to avoiding taxes through legal means.

EVICTION Process instituted to oust a person from possession of real estate.

EXAMINATION OF TITLE Investigation of record title to real property based upon the title search or abstract.

EXCEPTION
    (a) Reservation to the grantor, that portion which is excluded from the conveyance.
    (b) Objection to title or encumbrance on title.

EXCESS DEPRECIATION See DEPRECIATION and TAX SHELTER
EXCESS INVESTMENT INTEREST   A tax preference item for taxable years beginning prior to 1972 (see TAX PREFERENCES). Thereafter, excess investment interest will no longer be a tax preference item but will have limited deductibility. Excess investment interest is defined as that amount of interest on borrowings to carry investment property that exceeds net investment income from such property. For purposes of determining excess investment interest, property subject to a net lease is specifically treated as held for investment and not as property used in trade or business.

EXCHANGE Generally refers to a transaction whereby property of like kind is being exchanged.

EXCHANGE FUND OR TRANSFER FUND An entity organized to receive property on a basis whereby the interest in the entity issued for the property will constitute a TAX- FREE TRANSFER.

EXCLUSIVE AGENCY LISTING An agreement giving a broker the right to a commission if the listed property is sold during the listing period by anyone except the owner.

EXCLUSIVE RIGHT TO SELL LISTING An agreement giving broker the right to a commission if the listed property is sold during the listing period, regardless of who obtains the buyer.

EXCULPATORY CLAUSE A provision in a mortgage or lease indicating that the lender or lessor will look solely to the property and that the borrower or lessee has no personal liability. In a Limited Partnership Agreement a provision indicating that the General Partner has no personal liability to the Limited Partners and may provide in dealing with third parties for "exculpation" from liability.

EXECUTION PAGE A page of an agreement signed by the parties to it. Generally, the agreements provide that an execution page can be in counterparts.

EXECUTED A contract that has been fully performed. Can also mean "signed."

EXECUTION Act of completing, performance, signed by grantor.

EXECUTOR (EXECUTRIX—female) A person named in a will to carry out its provisions.

EXECUTORY A contract to be performed.

EXEMPTION Immunity from a burden or obligation

EXPANSION CLAUSE The provision in the loan that if additional funds are not available from the same lender at the same ratio of loan to value and at the then market rates, when certain specified expansion of the project is to take place, borrower may pay off the existing loan without penalty.

EXPENSE OF ACQUISITION Total costs of acquiring the property.

EXPENSE RATIO The relationship between total expenses exclusive of DEBT SERVICE to total GROSS INCOME. To the extent scheduled expense ratios

exceed or are less than those generally prevalent for the type of property involved, further inquiry should be made into their validity.

EXPENSES   Generally, project expenses fall into four categories which will receive differing tax treatment: (a) organization expenses relating to the cost of organizing the entity; (b) acquisition expenses relating to the cost of acquiring property; (c) operating expenses relating to the cost of maintaining and operating the property; and (d) costs relating to disposition of the property.

EXPENSES OF LENDER   Generally considered to be the "out-of-pocket" expenses of the lender for travel, appraisal, attorneys' fees and document costs.

EXTENSION AGREEMENT   Grant of further time within which to meet an obligation.

EXIT PENALTY   To deter breach, penalty imposed for defaulting at various points in life of project, or paying off early. Synonym – walk away risk.

F

FAIR JUST AND EQUITABLE STANDARD   Regulatory authority requirement that sponsor's/issuer's compensation be fair, just, and equitable. In some jurisdictions called the MERIT STANDARD. A substitution of the judgment of the regulatory authority for that of the parties on this question.

FANNIE MAE (FNMA)   Federal National Mortgage Association. Federally sponsored private corporation providing secondary market for housing mortgages. Another organization also federally sponsored is called Freddy Mac. The two often compete.

FEASIBILITY STUDY   A report that takes into consideration various factors relating to the investment, and concludes with an opinion as to the probability of success of the proposed project. A feasibility study is NOT an appraisal.

FEE FOR SERVICE   A fee for services as distinguished from PROMOTIONAL COMPENSATION and would include such things as REAL ESTATE COMMISSIONS or ACQUISITION FEES OF DEVELOPMENT FEES, MANGEMENT FEES, LEGAL FEES, ACCOUNTING FEES, COMMISSIONS ON THE SALE OF INTERESTS, and APPRAISAL FEES that are paid to the SYNDICATOR or to an unrelated entity. PROMOTIONAL CONSIDERATION would be a fee paid to the GENERAL PARTNER OR SYNDICATOR for the formation of the program generally expressed in a subordinated interest of (a) distributed cash and (b) net proceeds from refinance or disposal of assets.

FEE SIMPLE ABSOLUTE ESTATE   Ownership without time limitation (in perpetuity). The best and most inclusive type of real estate ownership.

FEE SIMPLE DEFEASIBLE Fee simple that can be divested upon the happening of some event after the initial grant, e.g., breach of condition contained in restriction in the deed.

FHA Federal Housing Administration. Agency of federal government insuring private loans for financing new and existing housing and housing repairs and improvements on one to four family houses and large rental projects under government approved programs.

FICTITIOUS DEED OF TRUST Deed of trust recorded by trustee disclosing all general terms and provisions in the deed of trust, but not relating to a specific transaction, used for reference.

FICTITIOUS NAME A name used for business purposes which is not the true name of the owner.

FIDUCIARY Indicates a relationship with another where there is a higher degree of responsibility then generally would be expected between strangers. The fiduciary has the duty to make full disclosure and to treat those with whom he has this responsibility in a fair, just, and equitable manner. He may be responsible for any profits arising from the relationship that he makes without the specific approval of those to whom he has the duty.

FINANCE COSTS Costs, mainly interest and loan fees incurred while financing construction of a project.

FINANCING STATEMENT Replaces chattel mortgage in California. Proof of personal property security agreement generally filed with the Secretary of State. Comm. Code Section 9401. Affects real property if relates to crops, timbers, or personal property used on the real property.

FINDER One who refrains from soliciting or selling and does not participate in any way in a transaction restricting his activities solely to the introduction of potential buyers and sellers. The finder performs a referral service and refrains from taking any part in negotiations.

FINDER'S FEE The fee paid to an individual for finding or referring a buyer to a seller or vice versa as the case may be.

FIRM UNDERWRITING Guarantee by security broker that the issue will be sold or the underwriter will purchase unsold shares.

FIRST POSITION Indicates that the lender has the SENIOR LIEN on the property.

FIRST USER Indicates that the person is entitled to use a favorable method of depreciation (see DEPRECIATION) due to being the first user. The owner of the property prior to initial occupancy.

FIXED DISBURSEMENT SCHEDULE Disbursement agreement on a construction loan between lender and borrower as to the number of payments and the stages at which such payments will be made.

FIXED PRICE CONTRACT Construction contract where specific price is set before construction begins.

FIXTURE A personal chattel that does not pass with the land but may be removed by the owner, such as awnings, carpets.

FLOATING CAPITAL Investment in current assets such as inventory and receivables.

FLOATING RATE A rate of interest which varies from time to time, also referred to as a variable rate. The rate may be tied to (a) the cost of living, (b) the prime rate charged by a named institution (see PRIME RATE), or (c) a percentage of the gross or net income from the property. A floating rate may contain both a floor and a ceiling.

FLOOR In the case of a floating rate, the minimum rate of interest that will be charged.

FLOOR LOAD The live-weight-supporting capabilities of a floor, measured in pounds per square foot.

FLOW THROUGH ACCOUNTING The use of a NON-TAX PAYING ENTITY, as defined by the Internal Revenue Code and Regulations, so that there is no imposition of federal or state income tax at the entity level, each investor reporting his share of PRE-TAX income on his own personal return.

F.M.V. Fair market value.

FORECLOSURE Procedure whereby property pledged (by a mortgage for example) as security for a debt is sold to pay the debt in the event of default.

FORCE MAJEURE CLAUSE Provision in a contract that excuses one or both parties in the event of an act of God or some other circumstance materially affecting the project and not subject to the control of the parties.

FORFEITURE Loss of anything of value due for failure to perform (default).

FORMAL CLOSING Legal transfer of title. Synonym, CLOSING, ESCROW CLOSING.

FORM OF ENTITY The method by which legal title to the syndicate is held. Among the forms of holding legal title are:

(1) Tenancy in common;
(2) Joint tenancy;
(3) Community property;
(4) Trust;
(a) Real Estate investment trust;
(b) Common law trust;
(5) Joint ventures;
(6) General partnership (co-partnership);
(7) Limited partnership;
(8) Limited Liability Company;
(9) Corporations; and
(10) Unincorporated associations.

FRACTIONALIZATION LOAN A provision in the loan allowing the lender to divide the loan among a number of lenders with the borrower to make payment directly to the respective individual lenders. Common law in many jurisdictions indicates a lender does not have this privilege unless it is included in the loan documents. A borrower may want to include a provision to prohibit any fractionalization.

FRACTIONALIZATION PARTNERSHIP Indicates that the investor may further divide his interest when re-selling same. May indicate that the issuer can sell less than a single unit. For administrative purposes many partnerships contain a clause prohibiting fractionalization.

FRANCHISE
(a) Right conferred by law;
(b) Right to engage in specified business using a trade name or designation owned by another person.

FRAUD Intentional deception causing a person to enter into a contract or in some way causing a loss of property or legal rights.

FREE AND CLEAR "Free" means a freehold estate, i.e., one of indefinite duration; and "clear" indicates no money encumbrances against the title.

FREEHOLD ESTATE An ownership of an indefinite duration.

FREE STANDING Indicates that the property is leased to a single tenant who occupies the entire premises.

FRONTAGE Front boundary line of a lot facing the street.

FRONT-END LOAD Total cash compensation received by the syndicator (on the sale of the property to the syndicate) including COMMISSION ON SALE OF INTERESTS, advance management fees, loan fees to the syndicator, and any override or mark-up on the sale of the property to the syndicate (in the event that the property was owned by the syndicator). Exclusive of PROMOTIONAL INTERESTS.

FRONT FOOT A foot of property running along the frontage (usually the portion fronting on a street)

FRONT MONEY That sum of money which is used to initiate a project prior to the raising of CAPITAL INVESTMENT. Front money is often reimbursable and would include advances to the escrow for tying up the property, advances to attorneys and accountants for preparation of documentation, advances for appraisals, and travel and investigation expense. With new construction it would also involve advances for architectural plans and renderings.

FULL DISCLOSURE Indicates that all of the material relevant facts have been disclosed.

FUNCTIONAL OBSOLESCENCE Reduction in value due to an out-of-date or poor design of equipment or building.

FUNDING A process of advancing the funds from the lender to the borrower. While this is normally on the closing date of the loan, in the case of construction loans, funding will be over a period of time. In certain other circumstances funding may occur prior to the closing of the loan, in which case it would be termed "advance funding", or after the closing of the loan, in which case the proper term would be "delayed funding."

FUNGIBILITY In securities regulation, the treatment of securities of the same class being substitutable one for another in determining the holding period of the earliest purchased of the class. In general the holding period required for the latest purchased will be applied as well to the earliest purchased.

FUTURE ADVANCE CLAUSE Provision in deed of trust allowing lender to make additional advances in the future that will also be received by a deed of trust. Synonym, OPEN END LOAN.

G

GAP LOAN　See LOAN.

GARNISHMENT　Statutory proceedings for seizure of debtor's property or wages to satisfy debt.

GENERAL CONTRACTOR　One who performs or supervises the construction or development of the property pursuant to terms of primary contract between himself and the owner/developer.

GENERAL PARTNER OR PARTNERS　Indicates that the partnership is a General (where all partners are General Partners) or a LIMITED PARTNERSHIP in which one or more persons or entities will act as the GENERAL PARTNER. The General Partner has all personal liability in connection with the partnership (other than any liability that may be specifically assumed in the partnership agreement by the individual partners). When referring to partners of a LIMITED PARTNERSHIP, it will be specifically indicated whether the reference is to
  (a) ALL PARTNERS;
  (b) the GENERAL PARTNER; or
  (c) the LIMITED PARTNERS.

In the event that the partnership is a GENERAL PARTNERSHIP, reference would be to
  (a) ALL PARTNERS;
  (b) the MANAGING PARTNER; or
  (C) the NON-MANAGING PARTNERS, as the case may be.

A partner of a GENERAL PARTNERSHIP should be referred to as a CO-PARTNER.

GENERAL PARTNERSHIP　An entity organized pursuant of the Uniform Partnership Act. All partners are jointly and severally liable for the obligations of the partnership, whereas in the LIMITED PARTNERSHIP only the GENERAL PARTNERS are normally personally liable.

GENERAL PLAN RESTRICTIONS　Restrictions on owner's use of property for benefit of all lots in the subdivision.

GENERAL WARRANTY　A covenant in the deed whereby the grantor agrees to protect the grantee against the world.

GIFT DEED　A deed used to make a gift of real estate.

GI LOANS Loans available to veterans under a Federal Government program administered by the Veterans Administration.

G.N.M.A. (GINNIE MAE) Government National Mortgage Association. Government corporation providing secondary market for housing mortgages and special assistance to mortgagee financing housing under special FHA mortgage insurance programs.

GOAL CONGRUENCY Indicate that the project is structured in such a manner that the goal of the GENERAL PARTNER and the LIMITED PARTNERS are identical. The GENERAL PARTNER profiting to the extent that the LIMITED PARTNERS profit. Where there is no goal congruency, there can be CONFLICTS OF INTEREST.

GOVERNMENT LOANS Loans made directly by government agency.

GRADUATED LEASE A lease that provides for a varying rental rate, often based upon some future determination, such as a periodic appraisal of the property.

GRANT DEED Customary document used in California to transfer title in the sale of real estate containing only two implied warranties.

GRANTEE A person to whom real estate is conveyed; the buyer.

GRANTING CLAUSE Any action words in a deed to convey the title

GRANTOR The owner of the title being granted.

GROSS INCOME Total income before deduction of expenses.

GROSS MULTIPLER A factor used in making an estimate of value based on a multiple of annual CASH INCOME before debt service. If, in the opinion of the appraiser, a property of the particular type being appraised generally sells at six times its annual cash income, the gross multiplier would be 6, etc. Whenever an estimate of value is given based on a gross multiplier factor, the assumption used in reaching the total opinion of value and the gross multiplier factor used should be clearly stated.

GROUND LEASE A lease of the ground only that may be either subordinated or unsubordinated to encumbrances for improvements.

GROUND RENT See ECONOMIC RENT.

GROUP INVESTMENT Because of adverse connotations to the words "syndication" and "syndicate" in the Eastern part of the United States where the public associates the word "syndicate" with organized criminal activities, many syndication organizers prefer to use the words "group investment" in place of the noun "syndicate", and the words "group investment" or "organization of a group investment" in place of the verb "syndicating". A joining together of persons to invest wherein one or more persons are passive investors and one or more persons are active in the control and management of the investment. The key to the definition of group investment as distinguished from JOINT INVESTMENT is the differentiation of functions between active and passive investors with respect to the particular project. Where all are to be active, the proper term would be JOINT INVESTMENT.

GUARDIAN Person appointed by the court to administer the affairs of one not able to do so himself.

GUARANTOR A surety. One who guarantees the obligation of another.

H

HABENDUM The "To Have and To Hold" clause which defines or limits the quantity of the estate granted in the premises of the deed.

HARD DOLLARS See AFTER-TAX INVESTMENT and SOFT DOLLARS.

HB&M Humboldt base and meridian lines.

HEIR One who succeeds to an estate on intestacy.

HEIRS AND ASSIGNS Phraseology indicating fee simple estate.

HEREDITAMENTS The largest classification of property; includes lands, tenements, and incorporeal property, such as rights of way. Capable of being inherited

HIATUS A gap or space unintentionally left when attempting to describe adjacent parcels of land.

HIGHEST AND BEST USE The most profitable likely use to which a property can be put. That use of land that may reasonably be expected to produce the greatest net return to the land over a given time.

HOBBY TREATMENT In connection with federal income tax, a conclusion on the part of the Internal Revenue Service that the particular transaction was not entered into for profit. In general, where a project has not been entered into for profit, maintenance expenses, utilities, salaries, etc., will not be deductible. See BUSINESS PURPOSE.

HOLDBACK That portion of a construction loan or other type of loan that is withheld until certain conditions are met.

HOLDER IN DUE COURSE Person who in good faith and for value obtains promissory note or check without knowledge or defects.

HOLD HARMLESS TRUST DEED See ALL INCLUSIVE LOAN.

HOLDING PERIOD The period for which an asset has been held by a taxpayer. In tax-free exchange dates back to when original property obtained.

HOLDOVER TENANT A tenant who remains in possession of leased property after the expiration of the lease term.

HOMESTEAD A limited exemption against certain money judgments allowed a homeowner when recorded. Varies from state to state.

HOSKOLD COEFFICIENT A present worth factor. It is the value today of a series of annual payments of one dollar, after discounting for loss of interest on each dollar to the time of its collection. It is premised upon the assumption and each dollar of payment is composed of (1) interest and (2) a partial return of capital, which is invested in a compound interest sinking fund from which the original investment is returned in a lump sum. There are two rates involved: (1) the speculative rate of return on the investment (interest) and (2) the safe rate or rate paid on amounts accumulated in the sinking fund.

HUIS A group of investors formed together to make investment. It is a term used often in Hawaii.

HUNDRED PERCENT LOCATION The best location in a community for commercial property, often because of traffic.

H.U.D. Housing and Urban Development Agency – a federal government agency.

HYPOTHECATE To make property security for a debt without giving up possession of it such as by mortgaging it.

I

IMPLIED Presumed rather than expressed.

IMPOUNDS Payments made to fiduciary (usually a lender or property owner) in addition to principal and interest portion of loan or rent for purpose of paying property taxes, assessments, insurance, etc. Gives lender or property owner protection that these items will be paid.

IMPOUND ACCOUNT Set up to receive impounds for special purposes such as taxes, insurance, replacements, etc. Use regulated such as by California Civil Code Section 2954.

IMPOUND CONDITIONS Conditions set forth in the impound which must be met prior to the release of funds from the impound. A DUAL IMPOUND is one where different sets of conditions apply to separate amounts making up a total impound.

IMPROVED LAND Land on which on-site or off-site improvements have been made.

IMPROVED TO LAND RATIO Amount showing value of building as opposed to value of land.

IMPUTATION OF INTEREST Use of present value measurements to reevaluate a note, when face amount stated interest rate does not reasonably represent present value of the consideration given or received in the exchange. Occurs where note is non-interest bearing or has stated interest rate that is different from interest rate appropriate for that debt at time of the transaction.

INCOHATE Imperfect, partial, unfinished.

INCOME (OF THE PROPERTY) See RETURN OF THE INVESTOR. Should not be used except with appropriate descriptive adjective.

INCOMPETENT One unable to manage his own affairs because of a disability. Probate Code Section 1460.

INCORPOREAL Without physical existence; intangible.

INCREMENT An increase over a figure for a previous period, such as an increment in expenses or an increment in return. That amount which would be over the preceding amount. An increment in return might be involved in a projection where the first year showed a return of 5% on initial investment, the second year 6%, the third year 7%, etc. In this case, the increment return would be 1% per year.

INDENTURE A written instrument made between two or more persons of different interests in which they enter into reciprocal and corresponding grants or obligations towards each other. The name comes from the practice of indenting or cutting the deed on the top or side in a waving line.

INDIRECT COST Development costs not included in land acquisition or construction contract, e.g., professional fees, financing costs, insurance, and taxes during construction, overhead, etc. Sometimes referred to as SOFT COSTS.

INFLATION HEDGE A subjective opinion that the particular investment will have an APPRECIATION RETURN at least equivalent to the decline in the real value of money.

INGRESS Right to enter a tract of land.

INITIAL INVESTMENT The amount of the first payment or down payment required on a purchase security as opposed to the CONTINUING INVESTMENT that is the amount due after the down payment. See DEFERRED PURCHASE.

INJUNCTION A court order to do or not to do some act.

IN PERSONAM Against the person.

IN PROPRIA PERSONA (PRO PER) Acting for oneself in a lawsuit.

IN RE In the matter of.

IN REM Against the property and not against a person.

INSTALLMENT LOAN See AMORTIZED LOAN.

INSTALLMENT SALE (for tax purposes), A sale where only a portion of the purchase price is received in year of sale. A sale where the seller receives not more than thirty percent (30%) of the purchase price in the year of sale.

INSTITUTION Generally refers to a bank, trust company, title company, insurance company, savings and loan or mutual savings bank. It may also under certain circumstances refer to a pension or profit sharing plan. An institutional lender or investor would be one that falls within the above category.

INSTRUMENT A written legal document.

INSURABLE INTEREST An interest in property of such a type that financial loss would be incurred on the occurrence of the event insured against.

INSURED LOANS Loans insured by governmental agency.

INTANGIBLE Incorporeal, without physical existence; e.g., goodwill.

INTEREST Rate of return paid for the use of money (loan) or a unit in a syndicate program. In the event that the term refers to rate of return, it should be defined whether it is:
(a) SIMPLE INTEREST, indicating that it is computed on the outstanding balance from time to time;
(b) discount or "Dutch" interest computed on the full amount of the loan commitment regardless of the fact that only a portion of the loan may be outstanding from time to time;
(c) advance interest, indicating that it is paid in advance which would make the

effective rate slightly higher than the stated rate;

(d) bond interest computed on a 30-day month;

(e) banker's rule computed on a 360-day year; and

(f) it should be further clarified whether the interest is stated or effective. Effective interest is the actual interest being charged on a simple interest basis (often referenced to as "APR1" meaning true " percentage interest on an annual basis.)

INTERIM LOAN Short-term loan. Usually made during construction stage of development. Upon completion of the building, the borrower generally arranges a permanent or take-out loan.

INTERMEDIATE FINANCING See LOAN, CONSTRUCTION LOAN.

INTERLOCUTORY DECREE Interim court decree, not finally disposing of the matter, requiring further steps to be taken in the action.

INTERMEDIARY A party other than the borrower and lender and who assists in bringing them together. Certain financial institutions, such as banks and savings and loan associations, are often called Financial Intermediaries in that they congregate together the funds of depositors and in turn make such funds available to borrowers.

INTER-STATE See REGISTRATION. More than one state contact involved in a securities offering.

INTESTATE Death without leaving a valid will.

INTRASTATE OFFERING Security offering where all contacts are restricted within one state the property, the issuer, and the investors.

INVESTMENT Any form of property that produces a return to the person investing. An investment can be a security, a loan, purchase of real estate, or the purchase of a leasehold. An investor is one who supplies the funds for the purchase of the investment.

INVESTMENT EXPENSES All expenses directly incurred in producing investment income, example taxes real and personal, bad debts, operative costs, etc.

INVESTMENT INCOME General income from investments rather than personal effort. Includes for federal tax purposes:

(1) Income derived from trade or business;

(2) Net short-term capital gain attributable to the disposition of investment property;

(3) Gross income from interest, dividends, rents and royalties; and

(4) recaptured depreciation under Section 1245 and Section 1250 of the I.R. Code.

INVESTMENT INTEREST Interest on a loan taken out for investment. Interest that can be claimed as a deduction by the borrower for income tax purposes is limited by the I.R. Code Section 163(d)(3)(D).

INVESTMENT AT RISK RULE Except when a deduction is created in a real estate project, investor may not claim a greater deduction than the sum of money invested. See DEDUCTIONS.

INVESTMENT POLICY The stated investment goals of a lender. The investment policy may place certain restrictions on the type of investment that can be made.

INVESTMENT TAX CREDIT A reduction from Federal Income Tax generally equivalent to a portion of the cost of "qualified personal property." Includes most depreciable property with useful life in excess of three years, does not include real estate.

INVOLUNTARY LIEN A lien imposed against property by operation of law without consent of the owners, such as tax lien, judgment lien or mechanic's lien.

INWOOD COEFFICIENT A present worth factor. It is the value today of a series of annual payments of one dollar. Similar to the Hoskold Coefficient, it is premised on the assumption that each dollar of annual payment is composed of
(1) interest and
(2) a partial return of capital. However, it differs in that the partial return of capital is credited against the original investment and thus decreases the outstanding investment in like amount.

There is not contemplated any reinvestment of the annual capital return. There is involved only one rate, the speculative rate.

IPSO FACTO By the very fact itself.

IRREVOCABLE That which cannot be revoked or changed.

I.R.R. The INTERNAL RATE OF RETURN taking into consideration discount factors. See DISCOUNTED CASH FLOW.

IRS INTERNAL REVENUE SERVICE of the federal government.

ISSUER The entity in which interests (units) are being offered.

J

JOINDER ACTION   The "joining" of all parties connected with injury (i.e., principal and agent, etc.) asking the court to fix responsibility.

JOINT AND SEVERAL   Indicating the obligation of each party signing thereto is for his share plus that of all other parties signing thereto. A JOINT OBLIGATION indicates that each signator is responsible for the liability of all signators. A SEVERAL OBLIGATION means that each signator is only responsible for his own liabilities with respect thereto. An obligation may also be a QUALIFICATION OBLIGATION. A typical qualification would be that the signator thereto is only liable for the amount and up to the benefits that he has received from or under the contract of investment and that the party to whom he is obliged cannot receive any judgment from him in excess of this amount.

JOINT INVESTMENT   See GROUP INVESTMENT.

JOINT TENANCY   A type of ownership of property by two or more people with the right of survivorship.

JOINT VENTURE   Two or more parties joining together to accomplish an investment objective. Where one or more parties are supplying the equity capital, and remain passive, and the other party supplies the entrepreneurial expertise, the venture is referred to as a FINANCING JOINT VENTURE. A PROJECT JOINT VENTURE is where both parties are supplying expertise and skill as well as funds for the project.

JUDGMENT   Order of a court at the termination of a lawsuit.

JUDGMENT LIEN   Statutory lien created by recording an abstract, or certified copy of a money judgment against debtor's property.

JUNIOR ENCUMBRANCE   A lien on property that is subordinate to the priority of one or more liens. Synonym, JUNIOR FINANCING and JUNIOR MORTGAGE.

JUNIOR MORTGAGE   A mortgage second in lien to a previous mortgage.

JURAT   Certificate evidencing that an affidavit was properly made before an authorized officer.

K

KICKER See CONTINGENT INTEREST. A bonus participation on a loan in addition to interest.

KEY LOT A lot so located that one side adjoins the rear of another lot.

L

LABOR AND MATERIAL RELEASE Signed document given upon completion of work by laborers and material men, waiving rights under any mechanic's lien law.

LACHES Delay in asserting one's rights, causing detrimental reliance by other party.

LAND BANKING Financing arrangement whereby landowner deeds his property to a lending institution in exchange for cash with an option to repurchase the property in the future.

LAND CONTRACT A contract for the purchase of real estate upon an installment basis; upon payment of last installment, deed is delivered to purchaser. Possession is usually delivered to buy with first payment.

LAND COST All costs connected with purchase of land, e.g., purchase price plus recording fees, escrow costs, interest on loans, pre-construction property taxes.

LAND ECONOMICS Branch of the science of economics that deals with the classification, ownership, and utilization of land and buildings erected thereon.

LAND LOAN Financing used to purchase raw land. Usually subordinated to or paid out when a construction loan is obtained.

LANDLORD See LESSOR.

LAND, MARGINAL Land from which the gross income is barely sufficient to pay the cost of production.

LAND OWNERS ROYALTY Interests in production of oil, gas, or minerals created by the owner of land, either by express reservation or by direct grant, when lease of the mineral rights land entered into.

LAND PLANNER Site planner. One who determines the appropriate land use of the site, so that it will be integrated into the local community.

LAND RESIDUAL PROCESS Method of appraising vacant land.

LAND, SUBMARGINAL Land from which receipts are inadequate to pay the cost of production, even if the land were free and clean of liens.

LATE CHARGE Amount charged by lender for late payment of amount due.

LATENT Concealed, hidden from view.

LATERAL SUPPORT Right to lateral and subjacent support is the right to have land supported by the adjoining land or soil beneath.

LAWFUL RATE See USURY.

LEASE An agreement concerning the hiring of property. It may be either written or oral although in many jurisdictions a lease for more than one year must be in writing. The lease can be GROSS or NET, depending on whether the LESSOR (OWNER) or the LESSEE (TENANT) pays all or a portion of the expenses. If NET, the degree should be spelled out. Leases are also MASTER LEASES, which indicate that the lessee will in turn SUBLEASE, or STRAIGHT LEASES, wherein the lessee has no right to SUBLEASE. Where the LESSOR has the right to SUBLEASE, the initial lease is called the MASTER LEASE.

LEASEHOLDS An estate in realty held under a lease.

LEASEHOLD FINANCING Loan to lessee using leasehold estate as security.

LEASE BACK An arrangement whereby the seller of a property has the obligation to lease the same property from the buyer pursuant to terms and conditions negotiated at time of sale.

LEGAL CLOSING Formal closing.

LEGAL DESCRIPTION A description of a parcel of real estate, as per official records.

LEGAL RATE   Amount court may award on unpaid judgments.

LEGATEE Receiver of personal property (legacy).

LEGEND CONDITION A restriction placed on the sale or transfer of the security by a governmental agency.

LENDER An entity which advances money, the primary consideration being a security position in the real property, a rate of interest, and a return in the future on the original principal amount. A lender may also get a "kicker" which would be a right to participate in profits or gross income which kicker is permanent (independent of repayment of the loan) or temporary (only during the time that the loan is outstanding). A lender may be an:

(a) INSTITUTIONAL LENDER indicating that the lending of money is one of its primary functions, or;

(b) ACCOMMODATION LENDER indicating that the lender is in some other business and that the making of the loan is incidental to some other transaction between the borrower and lender. A supplier of building materials, for example, might be an accommodation lender. The lender can further be a PRIMARY LENDER who lends some stipulated percentage of the value and normally requires a senior position, or a SECONDARY LENDER who may lend close to the full value and who often takes a junior position.

LESSEE (TENANT) A person who has the right to occupy property provided by a lease.

LESSEE'S INTEREST Is the market value of the property less the value of the lessor's interest.

LESSOR (LANDLORD) Owner of property who transfers the right to occupy property to another by a lease.

LESSOR'S INTEREST Is the present (discounted) value of the contract (lease) rents in addition to the present (discounted) value of the reversion.

LETTERED STOCK Stock purchased with a restriction that it cannot be resold for a period to the public, or only after complying with certain conditions.

LETTER OF INTENT A non-obligatory expression of intent, conditioned on receipt and approval of further documentation and/or the issuance of a qualification permit. The letter of intent may be issued by an investor, indicating an intention to purchase a security; by an underwriter, indicating an intent to underwrite an issue; a lender, indicating an intent to make a loan; or a purchaser or seller, indicating a desire to purchase or sell a piece of property. The letter of intent is merely an expression of intent and is not binding upon the parties and is used solely as a memorandum for future discussion. A GENERAL LETTER OF INTENT would be an expression of interest in a general way (merely to the subject of a kind of real estate investment such as land, apartment buildings, commercial, industrial, etc.) without reference to any particular project. A LENDER'S LETTER OF INTENT indicates an intention to lend, as opposed to BORROWER'S LETTER OF INTENT, which indicates an intention to borrow.

LEVERAGE A purchase of property whose value is more than the amount of the original cash investment using encumbrances. POSITIVE NET SPENDABLE LEVERAGE exists where the assumed income in the absence of financing will exceed debt service constant so that the override results in a higher net spendable rate on the invested capital than would be present if the property were purchased for all cash. When the debt service rate exceeds the net income from the property in the absence of financing, there is NEGATIVE NET SPENDABLE LEVERAGE. APPRECIATION LEVERAGE exists where the estimated appreciation build-up exceeds the debt service rate. A combination of spendable income, equity build-up and appreciation build-up that exceeds the debt service rate would be COMBINED LEVERAGE.

LEVERAGED BUY-OUT Purchase of property, or other asset with money obtained through issue of debt.

LEVY An assessment, obtaining money by judicially sanctioned seizure and sale of property.

LIEN A hold or claim which one person has upon the property of another as security for a debt or charge, judgments, mortgages, or taxes.

LIFE, ECONOMIC The estimated period over which it is anticipated that a property may profitably be utilized.

LIFE ESTATE An estate or interest held during the term of some certain person's life.

LIFE, PHYSICAL The period over which it would function if limited only by actual deterioration of the materials of which it is composed.

LIMITED OFFER An offering to a particular class of individuals or lenders is a LIMITED OFFERING, an offering without restriction is an OPEN OFFERING.

LIMITED PARTNER The passive investor in a LIMITED PARTNERSHIP.

LIMITED PARTNERSHIP INTEREST (OR "L.P.I.")
    (a) SPLIT CLASSES: A limited partnership, wherein one class of limited partners receives a different form of profit participation, such as a greater prorata share of equity build-up, than another; the other receiving a greater percentage of spendable income, as opposed to equity build-up;
    (b) MULTIPLE CLASSES: Where the return of one class is in the same benefits as the other but is subordinated to the other.

LIMITED PARTNERSHIP An entity organized pursuant to the Uniform Limited Partnership Act.

LINK Term of land measurement. 1 /100th of a chain.

LIQUIDITY See CASH LIQUIDATING VALUE.

LIQUIDATED DAMAGES A definite sum of money to be paid under a contract in the event of its breach.

LIS PENDENS A recorded notice that litigation (a lawsuit) is pending which may affect the title of the real estate involved.

LISTING A contract authorizing a broker to sell, buy, or lease, etc. property on behalf of another. A sales listing is also known as an AUTHORIZATION TO SELL.

LITTORAL Pertaining to the shore.

LOAN The lending of funds from a lender to a borrower that may take one or more of the following forms:

> (a) Take-Out or Permanent Loan—normally a self-amortizing loan made after construction for the purpose of providing long term financing;
>
> (b) Construction Loan, made for the purpose of providing funds for construction of a project;
>
> (c) Gap Loan – or an interim period provides the difference between the construction loan and the take-out loan;
>
> (d) Mezzanine or junior loan is subordinate to a senior loan;
>
> (e) Equity loan is on interests in the entity rather than the property.
>
> (f) Bridge loan. Short term for estimated time required an anticipated event to take place.

> Loans can be made for any purpose on all types of property. The type of property may be a security and often determines how a loan is characterized such as commercial, industrial, multi-family, single family, and/or development loan. The loan may be public financing, supplied from a governmental agency, or private investor, in that it comes from a non-governmental source.

LOAN FEE Fee charged by lender for making a loan.

LOAN TO FACILITATE Loan taken back by lender to facilitate sale of real property owned by lender.

LOAN VALUE Value set to aid in determining the amount of mortgage or trust deed loan to be made.

LOAN TO VALUE RATIO Ratio of mortgage to value of security.

LOCAL HOUSING AUTHORITY Local government entity responsible for low and middle-income housing.

LOCKED IN Indicates that the investor has a substantial profit and may not be able to sell due to the fact that taxes would equal or exceed the cash generated from the sale. In a loan, a provision that loan cannot be paid off for a period of time (lock in clause).

LONG-TERM BOND Bond that matures in 10 years or longer.

LONG TERM CAPITAL GAIN Gain on the sale of certain property held for the appropriate holding period pursuant to relevant Revenue statute.

LOCUS SIGILLI (L.S.) The place of a seal, letters L.S. may be placed on an instrument as a substitute for a seal where a seal is required.

LOT Measured parcel of land with fixed boundaries.

LOT BOOK Title company's record of all transactions, recorded by county recorder affecting a particular lot.

LOT SPLIT Division of a preexisting parcel of land. Regulated by local authorities. Creating a small number of parcels (usually two) rather than a sub-division. Local law provides maximum number that constitutes a lot split.

M

M.A.I. Title of an appraiser who is a member of American Institute of Appraisers of the National Association of Real Estate Boards.

MAJORITY The age at which a person is entitled to handle his or her own affairs.

MANAGEMENT COMPANY A company that provides property management services.

MANAGEMENT FEE A fee for services, generally performed by either the sponsor or an individual third party. Among the types of management fees are the following:
   (a) Program Management Fee – a fee for managing the relationship with the investors, including retention of entity records, investor communications, and legal and tax matters relating to the entity.
   (b) Property Management Fee—a fee for services generally performed by an individual third party property management company for off-site property management services, including leasing, rent collection, coordination of repairs, payment of bills, recordkeeping, etc.

(c) Construction Management Fee—a fee for supervision or management of construction.

(d) Asset management fee for providing oversight of the property manager.

MAP ACT Statute regulating formation of subdivisions.

MARGIN The percentage of equity in relation to the total value of the security or property.

MARGIN OF SECURITY Difference between the appraised value of the property and the mortgage on it.

MARGINAL LAND Land that barely pays its cost of operation.

MARKETABILITY State of being saleable.

MARKETABLE TITLE Title to the property free from substantial encumbrances and defects.

MARKET MAKER The firm or entity who stands ready to purchase or sell at any given time a security or loan. The MARKET MAKER is said to "MAINTAIN A MARKET" in the security or loan.

MARKET OUT CLAUSE A provision in the loan agreement or contract that states that the lender need not purchase the loan or market the loan if market conditions should be unfavorable at the time of closing.

MARKET PRICE Opinion of the price actually paid for property. Obtainable based on current prices of comparable properties.

MARKET RENT Rent obtainable based on current prices rents for comparable premises.

MARKET VALUE The price for which property can be sold on the open market if there is a willing seller, a willing buyer, and a reasonable time to make the sale. See also VALUE, MARKET.

MASTER LEASE See LEASE.

MASTER REGISTRATION Refers to REGISTRATION or QUALIFICATION of a series of entities, each entity to be for specific property but to have certain common characteristics such as one issuer, or general partner, and one general format. Often used with respect to motels or other forms of real property in different locations with the same lessee.

MASTER PLAN Comprehensive, long-term general plan for physical development of real estate in the jurisdiction.

MATERIALS BOND Assurance that the one posting the bond will supply the materials necessary to complete the work.

MATURITY Indicating a date when an obligation matures or becomes due. The maturity of an investment would be the projected re-sale date.

MAXIMUM TAX Maximum amount of tax than can be levied on personal services income.

MDB&M Mount   Diablo base and meridian lines, used to determine survey and legal descriptions of property.

MECHANIC'S LIEN A special lien on a specific property for labor, material or art if bills are unpaid.

MEDIAN STRIPS Common areas between parcels.

MEETING OF MINDS A mutual intention of two persons to enter into a contract affecting their legal status based on agreed-upon terms.

MERCHANT BUILDER One who builds for sale.

MERGER OF TITLE Joining different interests in a parcel of property into one ownership.

MESNE The middle between two extremes; intermediate; intervening.

MERIDIAN LINE Survey line running north and south, used in establishing township boundaries.

METERS AND BOUNDS A description in a deed of the land location, in which the boundaries are defined by directions and distances.

MGIC Mortgage Guarantee Insurance Corporation. Principal under writer of F.H.A. mortgage insurance programs.

MINI-MAX Indicating that there is a certain minimum amount that will be loaned and there is a maximum amount that will be loaned.

MINIMUM INVESTMENT The minimum amount of investment required of an investor in order to be qualified to purchase a particular investment. (See STANDARDS OF SUITABILITY).

MINIMUM PROPERTY STANDARDS Overall minimum technical standards acceptable to F.H.A.

MINIMUM TAX Tax preference items that ensure some taxes are paid by everyone. Some items that apply to tax sheltered investments are accelerated depreciation above straight line on real property, and untaxed portion of net long-term capital gain.

MINIMUM UNIT Refers to the minimum number of interests or shares that an investor must purchase in order to qualify as an investor for a particular offer under the STANDARDS OF SUITABILITY.

MINOR In California, a person under 21 years of age, except that any married person 18 years or over is considered an adult for the purpose of contracting. See your state's laws.

MIXED FUND A fund containing specified properties and funding for unspecified properties.

MODEL FURNISHINGS Furniture in model homes in a real estate development or in an apartment (model an apartment for show to prospective renters).

MODERNIZATION Alteration of internal plan and facilities or of external detail of property or equipment to conform to present usage, style, form, method or taste.

MONTH-TO-MONTH TENANCY See PERIODIC TENANCY.

MONUMENT Surveyor's term used to mark or fix boundaries or land location.

MONUMENT SIGN A ground-level sign designating a tenant

MORAL IMPOUND See IMPOUND CONDITION.

MORATORIUM A temporary suspension in payment of a debt as opposed to forgiveness where repayment is forgiven. The amount forgiven is discharged.

MORTGAGE A document used to make property security for payment of a loan (also to borrow money).

MORTGAGE AMORTIZATION SCHEDULE Schedule of payment s of principal.

MORTGAGE-BACKED SECURITIES Bond-type investment securities representing an undivided interest in a pool of mortgages or trust deeds. Income from underlying mortgage is used to pay off securities.

MORTGAGE BANKER One who commits his own money to funding a loan, and generally services the loan after selling it.

MORTGAGE BROKER One who arranges loans.

MORTGAGE CORRESPONDENT An agent of one or more lenders.

MORTGAGEE The lender of money under a mortgage.

MORTGAGE FUND Fund of mortgages.

MORTGAGE GUARANTY INSURANCE Insurance against financial loss available to mortgage lenders.

MORTGAGE RELEASE PRICE Prearranged amount paid to mortgagee to relinquish mortgage on property. Usually occurs when house within a subdivision is completed and sold, partial release of blanket mortgage.

MORTGAGOR The borrower of money under a mortgage.

MULTI-CLASS ENTITY Consisting of different classes of partners.

MULTIPLE LISTING (CO-OPERATIVE LISTING) A listing taken by a member of a group of brokers organized so that each member of the group shares his listings with fellow members.

MUNIMENTS OF TITLE Deeds and other original documents demonstrating a chain of title to a parcel of real property.

MUTUAL WATER COMPANY Water company organized by or for users in a given district. Stock is issued to users. Goal is to ensure sufficient water supply at a reasonable rate.

N

NAR National Association of Realtors that maintains many services of value to realtors

NASD The National Association of Security Dealers. A regulatory quasi-official body.

NEGATIVE CASH FLOW Cash expenditures in operating income-producing property exceeding cash receipts from that property.

NEGOTIABLE INSTRUMENT A promissory note or check that meets certain legal requirements, allowing it to circulate freely in commerce.

NEIGHBORHOOD An urban or suburban residential (or commercial) area exhibiting a fairly high degree of homogeneity as to housing, tenancy, income, and population characteristics.

NET CAPITAL Allowable assets versus liabilities in connection with broker-dealer licensing under BLUE SKY laws and/or under NASD regulations in connection with an underwriting. Respective regulations define the allowable asset for determining net capital. May also apply to certain regulated lenders.

NET CASH RETURN See RETURN TO THE INVESTOR.

NET LEASE Lease with provision that lessee pays some of the direct expenses associated with the leased property. Triple net lease tenant pays all but capital expenses. Bond lease tenant pays all expenses including capital expenses.

NET LISTING A price below which the owner will not sell the property and at which price the broker will not receive a commission. The broker receives the excess over and above the net listing as his commission.

NET REALIZABLE VALUE (N.R.V.) Fair market value less costs to dispose of property.

NET SPENDABLE See RETURN TO INVESTOR.

NET WORTH The difference between assets and liabilities.

NO LOAD An offering wherein there is no commission being paid on the sale of interests, no promotional interests, and the property is being purchased from an independent third party or being purchased from the syndicator without any mark-up or profit to the syndicator. There may be a commission paid by the seller of the property to the syndicator and other fees for services.

NOMINEE Party appointed to act in place of original party to the transaction.

NON-CASH CHARGES Reductions in taxable income that do not reduce spendable cash for tax purposes. This includes depreciation and depletion allowances.

NONCUPATIVE WILL Dying declaration or one made in contemplation of death.

NON-DISTURBANCE AGREEMENT Clause in a mortgage or master lease indicating that the lender or master lessee will not dispossess the tenant so long as the tenant honors his lease, if it should become necessary for the lender or master lessee to take possession of the property.

NON-JUDICIAL FORECLOSURE SALE Sale of property by trustee or mortgagee under the power of sale in a deed of trust or mortgage. No right of redemption after sale.

NON-REFUNDING PROVISION Clause in loan agreement prohibiting borrower for specified period from refunding debt with borrowed funds that have a lower interest rate.

NON-SPECIFIED FUND A limited partnership organized without commitment to purchase any specified property. Also referred to as an UNSPECIFIED FUND or BLIND POOL. The preferable term is NON-SPECIFIED FUND. A SPECIFIED FUND is one in which the property to be purchased by the partnership has already been selected. A MIXED FUND would be one consisting partly of property not yet selected at the time of SUBSCRIPTION of capital.

NOTE Written acknowledgment of debt and promise to pay.

NOTARY PUBLIC Legally authorized official to attest and certify certain documents by his hand and seal.

NOTICE OF CESSATION Recorded notice under California Mechanic's Lien Law, which shortens the time to file a mechanic's lien. CC Section 3092.

NOTICE OF COMPLETION Notice recorded within specified period days after completion of construction, under State Mechanic's Lien Law. Mechanic's liens must be filed within a specified time thereafter, generally 30 to 60 days.

NOTICE OF DEFAULT A document filed with the proper county indicating that in the event that lien or liens that have been placed on the property as described in the notice should be in default, notice of such default is to be sent to persons named therein.

NOTICE OF NON-RESPONSIBILITY A notice which, when properly recorded and posted on the property, relieves the owner from the effect of mechanic's liens under certain circumstances.

NOTICE TO PAY RENT OR QUIT A three-day notice required by law before a tenant delinquent in rental payments may be evicted by suit.

NUNC PRO TUNC Now for then; allowing acts to be done after the time they should have been done, with retroactive effect.

O

OBSOLESCENCE Impairment of desirability and usefulness brought about by physical, economic, or other changes.

OFFEREE An individual to whom an OFFER TO SELL, LEASE, OR LEND, is made to receive an offer.

OFFERING CIRCULAR OR PROSPECTUS (Correct word for State qualifications is "OFFERING CIRCULAR." For Federal Registration is "PROSPECTUS.") A written description of the proposed offering which has been submitted to the respective agency and approved (in the case of an offering which must be qualified or registered), or, in the case of an exempt offering, a brochure describing in detail the terms and conditions of the purchase. In the case of an exempt offering, the document to be described as an offering circular should contain substantially the same information as would have been required if the offering had been QUALIFIED or REGISTERED.

OFFER TO SELL Any written or oral communication offering for sale an interest in a syndicate security or property must be distinguished from educational lectures, discussions, or communications relating to the general subject of real estate investment, without discussing a proposed offering. ALL OFFERS TO SELL which come within the requirements of the respective act must be QUALIFIED or registered unless exempt from it.

OFFSET In the case of percentage rents, the right of the tenant, or in the case of the loan, the right of the borrower to offset certain increased costs against the percentage rental or payment loan.

OFFSET STATEMENT A statement supplied by a tenant or borrower indicating the status of the lease or loan also referred to as an ESTOPPEL CERTIFICATE.

OFF-SITE COSTS Costs incurred improving raw land excluding buildings, fences, landscaping costs, e.g., grading, sewers, drains, gutters, curbs, side-walks, public utilities, See California Fin. Code Section 5072.

OF RECORD See RECORDED.

OMNIBUS CLAUSE Probate court decree of distribution by which decedent's property passes to the distributees.

OPEN END See CLOSED END.

OPEN-END LOAN One with provision of additional advances.

OPEN LISTING A listing providing that the broker is to receive a commission if he is the person to obtain a buyer ready, willing and able to purchase the property on the terms of the listing, or on other terms acceptable to the owner.

OPERATING CASH EXPENSES Money spent during fiscal period in ordinary course of business.

OPERATING HISTORY Past history of a project for a given period, when available, often required by lenders for a loan, or state or federal laws to QUALIFY or REGISTER.

OPINION LETTER A written opinion of an attorney at law, admitted to practice, relating to tax and/or legal consequences.

OPM Shorthand for "use of other people's money" referring to the fact that there is an equity leverage in the investment. That amount of equity being invested by persons other than the sponsor.

OPTIMUM USE Same as highest and best use.

OPTION A written agreement by the OPTIONOR (owner of the property) giving to OPTIONEE (holder of the option) the right to purchase or lease certain property under terms and conditions as spelled out in the option. The option must be complete as to terms of purchase satisfying the legal requirements of a binding contract.

OPTIONEE The person who receives an option.

OPTIONOR The owner of the property that is being optioned.

ORAL CONTRACT A verbal or spoken contract. See PAROL CONTRACT.

ORDINANCE City, county, or district regulations.

ORIENTATION Advantageous placement of a house on the lot taking into account sun, wind, noise, etc.

ORGANIZATION FEE A one-time fee received by the promoter, sponsor or general partner for services in organizing the syndicate, often described as an ORGANIZATION MANAGEMENT FEE IN A SET AMOUNT as opposed to a PROPERTY MANAGEMENT FEE that is expressed by a percentage of gross income. The organization fee is often expressed as a percentage of the original acquisition price of the subject property, or as a percentage of the original paid-in capital of the syndicate.

ORIGINAL CAPITAL FUNDS Total initial funds contributed by investors to project.

ORIGINAL CONTRACTOR The first general contractor to perform work on a project.

ORIGINAL ISSUE Indicates that the issue is direct from the issuer and has not previously been purchased by an investor.

OUTLAWED CLAIM A claim that can no longer be prosecuted, due to the expiration of the period permitted by the statute of limitations.

OVERHEAD EXPENSES General and administrative expenses of project such as administrative salaries and wages, office equipment, rent, preparation of taxes, account and record keeping, etc.

OVERRIDING MORTGAGE (OR DEED OF TRUST) A mortgage or deed of trust securing a note whose face amount includes the amount of another note or notes that are in senior positions. See ALL-INCLUSIVE LOAN.

OVERCALL Assessment.

OWNERSHIP Right to use and enjoy property to exclusion of others can be of a fee estate, a lease, or a license.

P

PACKAGE In the case of the loan, all of the documentation relating to the loan in a sale or lease; all the offering documents.

PARCEL Any area of land contained within one description. Often the property will consist of multiple parcels.

PARENT The individual(s) responsible for initiating the organization and/or offering for a real estate program sale.

PAROL CONTRACT A verbal or spoken contract.

PARTIAL RECONVEYANCE DEED A deed used to reconvey a portion of land encumbered by a blanket mortgage or trust deed.

PARTIAL RELEASE CLAUSE A clause in a mortgage or trust deed which provides for release of part of the property from the mortgage or trust deed upon part payment of the debt.

PARTICIPANT Investor, one who subscribes to a syndicate or tax incentive program.

PARTITION Legal proceeding dividing land between former co-owners.

PARTNERSHIP AGREEMENT The agreement between partners setting forth their rights and duties. Usually a written agreement.

PARTNERSHIP CONSEQUENCES A form of entity used by persons joining for operation of a business for a profit. Tax benefits flow through partnership to the partners. There are many different legal forms available besides partnerships.

PARTY WALL A wall erected on the line between two adjoining properties, belonging to different persons, for the use of both properties.

PATENT IN REAL ESTATE An original conveyance of real estate from the federal government to a private owner.

PAYBACK PERIOD The period necessary for an investor to recapture his original investment without interest out of net cash flow. If tax benefits are considered, then the proper term is PAYBACK PERIOD INCLUDING TAX AFFECT. If interest is considered, then PAYBACK PERIOD INCLUDING INTEREST should be defined.

PEDESTRIAL COUNT A count of persons walking past a location made for use
   (1) in appraising property for business purposes,
   (2) determining possible rental value, and
   (3) selecting appropriate tenants.

PER AUTRE VIE During the life of another.

PERCENTAGE LEASE A lease under which all or a portion of the rent is computed as a percentage of the gross business of the tenant.

PERCENTAGE OF COMPLETION METHOD Method of recording income from construction contracts computed on costs incurred to date to total estimated construction costs.

PERFORMANCE BOND Insurance that the work in the contract will be performed for the contract price. A PAYMENT BOND guarantees payment will be made. A COMPLETION BOND guarantees that the job will be completed at the price quoted.

PERIODIC PAYMENT Indicates that investors are to make continuing payments for a period, in addition to the initial capital investment. The amount of each additional payment required for a unit of investment in the syndicate.

PERIODIC TENANCY Tenancy for an indefinite period that can be terminated by proper notice of either party.

PERMANENT LOAN Loan obtained for purchase or operation of completed structure for an extended term equally beyond three years. Synonym, TAKE-OUT LOAN.

PERMIT IN SYNDICATION A written order of the respective agency authorizing the solicitation and sale or the negotiation of interest in a syndicate. IN CONSTRUCTION authorization by government agency to proceed with work.

PERPETUITY The state of being continuing forever.

PERSON Any individual, partnership, corporation, trust or any other legal entity.

PERSONAL LIABILITY Indicates that the investor has personal liability with respect either to a particular obligation under a loan, lease or in general. Where there is personal liability, the investor's entire assets would be subject to liability for the claim. If the liability related only to a specific item or amount, then it may be referred to as LIMITED PERSONAL LIABILITY. Such liability may be JOINT AND SEVERAL, JOINT ONLY, SEVERAL ONLY, or PRORATA and should be properly described where it exists.

PER UNIT ALLOCATION Manner of allocating certain costs over total number of units affected.

PERSONAL PROPERTY Any property which is not real estate. Moveable. May be tangible or intangible.

PLAINTIFF The party who commences a lawsuit.

PLANNED DEVELOPMENT PROJECT Subdivision where owner also receives interest in common or reserved areas. Synonyms, PUC, RESIDENTIAL PLANNED COMMUNITY.

PLANNING COMMISSION A local government agency that plans proper physical growth of a community and recommends zoning ordinances and other laws for that purpose.

PLAT OR PLOT Map showing land subdivided into lots, showing streets.

PLEDGE Making property security for payment of a debt, may include conditional transfer of possession to the lender.

PLOTTAGE VALUE See VALUE, PLOTTAGE.

POINTS A point is one percent of the amount of a loan usually paid to the lender at the time the loan is made in order to obtain the loan. Basis points are one one hundredth of one percent.

POLICE POWER The inherent rights of a government to pass such legislation as may be necessary to protect the public health and safety and/or to promote the general welfare.

POLICY OF TITLE See TITLE INSURANCE.

POSITION In investments indicates that an investor holds a portion of a particular investment.

POWER OF ATTORNEY Instrument used to make a person an attorney-in-fact. Giving one person the right to act in the place of another.

POWER OF SALE CLAUSE A clause in a trust deed giving the trustee the right to sell borrower's property publicly, without court procedure, if the borrower defaults. This clause, when in compliance with state law as to form, may be put into a mortgage by agreement, whereby the lender may foreclose without court procedure.

PREEMPTIVE RIGHT If an owner chooses to sell, the holder has the right to purchase on the same terms as offered by a third party. See also right of first refusal.

PRELIMINARY PUBLIC REPORT Preliminary Subdivision Report issued by state authority, when a requirement has not yet been fulfilled, but can be expected to be completed. Expires in one year, when the final report is issued, or if material change occurs. Developer must give purchaser a copy. Can only accept reservation for sale or lease under such a report.

PREPAYMENT CLAUSE/PENALTY Penalty for payment of a loan before it is due.

PREPAID INTEREST Interest being paid to the seller or lender that has not yet occurred. Under certain circumstances, a portion of the interest prepaid may not be deductible in the year paid but deductible in later years when it accrues. If so, the offering circular should clearly indicate which portion is deductible in the year paid and which portion will be deductible (if at all) in later years.

PRE-PERMIT OFFERING Applicable only to a PRIVATE OFFERING pursuant to exemptions under law, wherein the offering is conditioned upon the receipt of a permit from the respective agency and no funds are received until the period is issued.

PRESCRIPTION A method of obtaining an easement by adverse use for a period and under conditions set out in state law, hostile to owner's wishes. (Easement by Prescription).

PRESENT VALUE See DISCOUNTED CASH FLOW.

PRESUMPTION A fact that will stand and assumed to be true until overcome by some evidence to the contrary.

PRETERMIT Omitted, e.g. child, spouse, or other heir omitted from will is a pretermitted heir.

PRICE INDEX Reference to a particular index such as the Wholesale Price Index, or Cost of Living Index, which can either be national, regional, or confined to a metropolitan area.

PRICE, MARKET The price paid for property regardless of pressures, motives or intelligence.

PRIMARY FINANCING Loan secured by first mortgage or trust deed on real property.

PRIMARY LENDER Entity that provides primary financing. See LENDER.

PRIME MOVER Prime mover is the individual or firm who initiated the real estate project. A number of persons may be involved as syndicators or promoters due to their participating in either the general partners' interest, the sale, development or promotion of the project in one manner or another.

PRIME RATE Minimum rate in a given period of time that an institution charges its most credit-worthy borrower. Also called base rate or reference rate.

PRINCIPAL (1) Indicates that the individual is acting on his own behalf rather than for others. Some sellers will deal only with principals and not with their representatives or brokers; (2) the original sum in the event of a loan as opposed to the interest, or (3) that portion of the amortization payment that is applied to reducing the loan, as opposed to the interest portion.

PRINCIPAL TENANT Any person, corporation, or group of related persons that is the largest single occupant of a particular piece of real property, usually occupying 25% or more of the aggregate footage.

PRINCIPLE Rule of conduct, standard.

PRIORITY Preferred rank or position. Indicating that a class of investor has a prior or senior claim in distributions ahead of another class. The class that holds a priority is the SENIOR CLASS of investors, and the class that is subordinate to the priority is the JUNIOR CLASS.

PRIVATE OFFERING Private offering can be based either on a specific exemption as contained within the respective code or on the special relation-ship between the investors and the syndicator. A decision to rely on a private offering exemption rather than qualify should be based upon an opinion letter. An offering may be private under state securities laws and not be private under federal securities laws or vice versa. When relying on the private offering exemption under the federal securities laws, it might be advisable to secure a NO-ACTION LETTER from the SEC, if time and size of the project permits.

PRIVATE PLACEMENT A placement of securities with a sophisticated investor, generally an institutional investor, under circumstances that would constitute a private offering. In some cases the terms are used inter-changeably.

PRIVITY OF CONTRACT Relationship between two or more contracting parties.

PROBATE A minimum period during which the court has jurisdiction over the administration of the estate of a deceased person.

PROBATE COURT Court that has authority over property of deceased persons, minors, and insane persons.

PROFIT A PENDRE Right to enter and take from the land or its produce.

PROFIT AND LOSS The operating results of the project. Profit and loss is an accounting figure to be distinguished from RETURN TO INVESTORS (See RETURN TO INVESTORS). Return to investors should not be referred to as PROFIT AND LOSS and this term must clearly be distinguished from the accounting concept of profit and loss for tax purposes.

PROGRAM A single legal entity, organized as a limited partnership, limited liability company, general partnership, tenancy in common, joint venture, or other entity involving a SPONSOR and group of PARTICIPANTS, designed to spend a determinable sum of money to acquire real property and to produce cash receipts for distribution to the participants. Sometimes referred to as the SYNDICATE.

PROGRESS BILLINGS Those that are made as the work progresses and at the conclusion of a particular stage of work, as opposed to ADVANCE BILLINGS that are those made prior to the work having been performed or billing on completion. See RETENTIONS.

PROJECT   The proposed property and its plan of development that is to be the subject of the investment. SINGLE PROJECT indicates that the subject property is of one type and in one location. DIVERSIFIED PROJECT indicates that the property is located in several different kinds of investment, such as an income property together with speculative raw land, the former being referred to as DIVERSIFIED AS TO LOCATION, and the latter being referred to as DIVERSIFIED AS TO KIND.

PROMISSORY NOTE   A written contract containing a promise to pay a definite amount of money at a definite future time. May be negotiable (transferable) or non-negotiable. vvPROMOTIONAL INTEREST Any interest in the project being given (or sold at a lower price than that being charged other investors) for initiating the project The promotional interest is part of the prime mover's compensation which may also include options to purchase. Commissions on the sale of interests are usually considered separate for sales services.

PROMOTIONAL NOTES   Notes on unimproved real property, or a note executed after construction but prior to first sale, or a note executed as means of financing when the note is subordinated to another.

PROMOTER   The promoter is generally the prime mover who puts the project together.

PROPERTY   See REAL PROPERTY and PERSONAL PROPERTY.

PROPERTY MANAGEMENT FEE   See MANAGEMENT FEE.

PROPERTY REPORT   Report by agency having jurisdiction concerning compliance with building codes.

PRORATA   (1) When referring to DISTRIBUTED CASH OR ASSESSMENT, that portion relating to a class of investors divided among the members of the class in relation to their respective interests in that class. (2) When referring to liability, the liability is divided among the members of the class in ratio to their interest in the class and each is liable only for an amount of total liability equal to his interest. This is as opposed to JOINT AND SEVERAL LIABILITY, wherein all members of the class are liable for the total obligation. The creditor can look to anyone for satisfaction, the individual having discharged the obligation being able to look for contribution among the other members of the class.

PRORATION   Indicating that prepaid and/or accrued but unpaid expenses and income relating to real property being purchased will be debited and credited between buyer and seller. The buyer reimburses the seller for expenses paid relating to the period after the close of escrow, as well as the expenses incurred for the period prior to the close of escrow, which the buyer assumes. Prorations may be NEGATIVE, indicating that the buyer must come up with additional cash and that the total prorations indicate that the buyer has a debit balance due to seller. POSITIVE prorations indicate that there is a credit balance due buyer from seller. Prorations are made either in cash by adjusting the cash through escrow or by adjusting the purchase money obligation in favor of the seller. If the proration is positive, it is to the buyer's benefit to have the proration in cash. If the proration is negative, it is to the buyer's benefit to have an adjustment made in the encumbrance given the seller.

PROSPECTUS See OFFERING CIRCULAR.

PROTANTO For so much.

PROVISION FOR WARRANTY Reserve to cover possible costs of repair-ing or replacing defective items on new products. Usually from a reserve in calculating part of cost of sale in year of sale.

PUBLIC DOMAIN Land with title vested in a governmental entity, local, state, or federal.

PUBLIC OFFERING A public offering is an offer to the public without any restrictions. The respective code and regulations may provide a LIMITED OFFERING under certain circumstances to a particular class of investors.

PUBLIC RECORD Government records that give constructive notice of matters contained therein.

PUBLIC REPORT Report of the agency having jurisdiction containing information about subdivided property.

PUBLISH To publicly issue or circulate by email, newspaper, mail, radio, or television, or otherwise to disseminate to the public any material, either written or oral

P.U.D. Planned Unit Development.

PURCHASE AGREEMENT See AGREEMENT OF SALE.

PURCHASE MONEY ENCUMBRANCE (MORTGAGE) A note given to the seller by the buyer secured by a lien on the property being sold.

PUT Option to sell to another at a set price for a given period of time. See CALL.

PYRAMIDING Borrowing on equity to enter into further investments. Pyramid scheme to pay to investors a return out of funds being invested rather than cash flow. Sometimes called a "ponzi scheme".

Q

QUALIFIED Indicates a PERMIT has been issued by the respective state commissioner for the syndicate. See BLUE SKY.

QUALIFYING See APPLICATION FOR QUALIFICATION.

QUIET ENJOYMENT The right of an owner or lessee to the use of the property without interference of possession.

QUIET TITLE ACTION A suit brought for establishing clear title to the real estate.

QUASI CONTRACT Contract implied by law to prevent unjust enrichment.

QUITCLAIM DEED A deed used to transfer any interest in real estate that the grantor may have. It contains no warranties of any kind.

R

RANGE LINE A line used in the location and description of townships.

RATIO Indicating a relationship between two mathematical figures. Ratio of expenses would be the amount that the expenses bear to the total income, such as total expenses being 37% of total income.

RAW LAND Unimproved land.

REAL ESTATE Real property.

REAL ESTATE INVESTMENT TRUSTS A trust organized pursuant to and qualifying under Section 857 of the Internal Revenue Code. Must contain at least 100 investors and distribute 90% of its distributable income annually.

REAL ESTATE SECURITY An interest in a limited partnership or common law trust, tenancy in common or other entity (with the exception of a corporation or real estate investment trust) where the purpose of the entity is investment in real property. By definition all or a substantial portion of the investors will be passive investors taking no direct part in the operation of the investment.

REAL ESTATE SYNDICATION Joining together of two or more persons for the purpose of making and operating an investment in real estate where at least one is passive.

REALTOR   Indicates a member of the National Association of Realtors. Membership is gained by joining a local real estate board affiliated with the National Association. Only individuals who meet the standards as established by the NAR may use the term "REALTOR."

REAL PROPERTY   Land and things attached to it. (Immovable).

RECAPTURE (INCOME TAX)   Refers to income tax aspects of "recapturing" all or a portion of depreciation on sale or abandonment of property. The recapture will be either ordinary income or capital gain depending on the type depreciation used and the nature of the sale or abandonment, the holding period, etc.

RECAPTURE CLAUSE   A lease provision that authorizes tenant to deduct certain expenses paid by tenant (such as real property taxes) from rentals usually in excess of a base rent.

RESCISSION   A procedure by which the parties to a contract agree to release each other or when there is the contract or by law a period during which one side or either may unilaterally cancel.

RECONVEYANCE   See DEED OF RECONVEYANCE.

RECORDED   Indicating a document has been filed in the records of the respective governmental agency to give constructive notice pursuant to the laws of a particular state to third parties of its existence. Also referred to as OF RECORD. Gives constructive notice of interest in real property.

RECORDING   Act of filing. See RECORDED.

RECORDING FEE   Fee charged by county to record transfer of title from buyer to seller. See ESCROW COSTS.

RECOURSE NOTE   Note giving creditor recourse against debtor personally.

RECOVERY FUND   A fund held by the State Division of Real Estate, sustained by a portion of license fees to underwrite uncollectible court judgments against licensees based on fraud, etc. In some states there are similar funds covering insurance claims.

REDEMPTION RIGHT   Indicates the right of the purchaser to have the issuer repurchase his interest at either a set or formula market price.

RED HERRING   The "preliminary prospectus or offering memorandum" of a new issue.

REFINANCE The process of borrowing on the property to pay off an existing loan.

REFORMATION Action in equity to correct a mistake in a deed or other document.

REFUNDABLE UTILITY CONTRACT Contract between developer and local utility company. Utility company undertaking to reimburse the developer, out of its revenues, for all or part of the cost of installing utilities.

REGISTERED REPRESENTATIVE An individual who has passed the NASD examination and is qualified under state law to act as a sales representative of a broker/dealer.

REGISTRATION Refers to an application with the Securities and Ex-change Commission for an interstate sale. Sales which are intrastate, that is, where all the activities take place within one state where the general partner and limited partners are residents of that state and the entire property is located in that state, need only be QUALIFIED with the respective state agency. An interstate offering, however, where the offerees are residents of more than one state, or the property is located in one state and one or more of the offerees are in another state, or where the general partner is a resident of one state and the offerees are residents of another state, must also be registered with the Federal Securities Exchange Commission.

REGISTRATION RIGHTS A right included when purchasing a restricted security, to register same, the right may be (a) "piggy back" indicating that when the issuer should have a new registration the owner of the security can join in the registration at no additional cost, (b) limited as a set time or number of times at the holders own cost, or (c) unlimited at any time. If the right to register is at any time on request of the holder of the security, it is said to be a DEMAND REGISTRATION RIGHT. Registration rights are either (a) assignable or non-assignable; (b) contingent or non-contingent. They may be triggered by the happening of a certain event. Registration rights may further be prorated among the selling security holders or absolute. A registration is a SHELF REGISTRATION wherein the issuer has registered securities without an immediate plan of distribution to have them available. SHELF REGISTRATION is looked on with disfavor and approved only when the purpose of it is to have an issue available for merger and acquisitions purposes, where the issuer is in the business of acquiring assets with securities, and cannot wait the normal period to qualify a new issue. Registration is normally good for only a limited period, and under certain circumstances may be kept EVERGREEN by updating the financial information and putting in other material to keep it active. This may be done where the distribution of securities has not been as successful as originally contemplated and additional time is required.

REGRESSION Value is decreased by anticipated disadvantages to be derived in the future. In real estate, the term is used to describe the theory that the value of the best property is decreased by adjacent properties of poorer quality. Antonym, anticipation.

REHABILITATION Re establishment of the earning capacity of the property to a former state of solvency and productivity.

REINSTATEMENT Borrower's payment of arrears, restoring loan to current status.

R.E.I.T. Real Estate Investment Trust.

REINSURANCE Occurs when an insurer transfers a portion of the risk to other issuers.

REINVESTMENT PERIOD Usually the beginning of a calendar quarter or month when depositors are putting in and taking out money from financial intermediaries.

REISSUE RATE Reduced rate of title insurance where landowner had previous owner's insurance from the same issuer within a specified time.

RELEASE
(1) From IMPOUND CONDITION indicating that the funds no longer are subject to the impound, that the impound condition has been met, and the funds are released to the seller of the security;
(2) from PERSONAL LIABILITY, indicating that the individual or entity liable has been released from an obligation.

RELEASE CLAUSE See PARTIAL RELEASE CLAUSE.

RELEASE OF LIEN The discharge of certain property from the lien of a judgment, mortgage, or claim.

REMAINDER A right to future possession after termination of a life estate.

REMAINDER ESTATE An estate in property created at the same time and by the same instrument as another estate and limited to arise immediately upon the termination of the other estate.

RENT Consideration paid for the use and possession of a property.

RENTAL CONCESSIONS Agreements between property owner and tenant forgiving portion of the rent.

RENT-UP PERIOD Time after construction for rental property to reach projected stabilized occupancy. Synonyms, START-UP PERIOD, FILL-UP PERIOD, INCUBATION PERIOD.

R.E.O. Real Estate Owned. Term used by lending institutions describing repossessed properties they currently hold.

REPLACEMENT COST A method of appraising property based on producing a reasonable facsimile.

REPLACEMENT RESERVE Cash reserved for future replacement of assets.

REPORTING REQUIREMENT The requirement of the respective government agency having jurisdiction over the program as to the frequency and content of reports to investors.

REPRODUCTION COST The cost of reproducing, brick-for-brick, a specified structure. To be distinguished from replacement cost, which would be the cost of building a structure of similar utility in square footage but not necessarily cubic footage. Important to distinguish in a case of older properties with high ceilings, large portions of public area, etc. Sometimes used interchangeably, but more correct procedure would be to define what is meant.

REPURCHASE An arrangement between the investor and the syndicate and/or syndicator indicating that under certain conditions, at the option of the investor, the syndicate, and/or the syndicator will repurchase the interest from the investor. Unless otherwise indicated, repurchase means investor's repurchase option (put). If the option for repurchase lies with the syndicator, it would be referred to as the syndicator's repurchase option (call). The repurchase may be CONDITIONAL in that it is subject to certain terms and conditions (normally if it is to be put to the syndicate, that the syndicate has sufficient funds on hand to make the repurchase). It may be LIMITED, indicating that the ability to sell the interest back is only for a certain period and, or it may be GUARANTEED, indicating that the obligation of the syndicate to repurchase is guaranteed by the syndicator on a third party. Unless otherwise described by an appropriate adjective, it will be assumed to be UNCONDITIONAL AND UNLIMITED.

REPURCHASE AGREEMENT An agreement between lenders whereon one lender has sold a loan to another and agrees under certain conditions to repurchase it.

REQUEST FOR NOTICE OF DEFAULT A recorded request made by the beneficiary of a junior loan requesting that he be notified in the event that there is a default of the senior loan.

REQUEST FOR TRANSFER A formal application to the respective agency for permission to transfer a syndicate interest from the original partner to a subsequent partner.

RESERVATION AGREEMENT See PRELIMINARY PUBLIC REPORT.

RESIDUAL VALUE In the case of a loan, the estimate of the fair market value of the property on the maturity date of the term of the loan.

RESERVE FOR REPLACEMENTS A charge made to income to set up a reserve to replace items that wear out or become inoperative. It should be distinguished from "maintenance" which is a charge related to normal operating expenses for maintaining the property and its operating parts.

RESERVES The setting aside of a specific amount of money to be used for a particular anticipated expense.

RESIDENT (ON PREMISES) MANAGEMENT To be distinguished from off-premises management expense. Resident management is usually an additional expense of the project over and above the off-premises management expense.

RESIDENTIAL PLANNED COMMUNITY See PLANNED DEVELOPMENT PROJECT.

RESIDUAL PROCESS A term applied to a method of estimating the value of the land or the building as indicated by the capitalization of the residual net income attributed to it.

R.E.S.S.I. The Real Estate Syndicate Securities Institute (an affiliate of the National Association of Realtors), an organization composed of major syndicators, marketers of syndicate interests, and professional persons such as accountants and attorneys active in the real estate syndication industry. No longer active. Replaced by committees with the National Association of Realtors.

RESTRICTION An encumbrance that limits the use of real estate in some way.

RESTRICTIVE COVENANT A clause in a deed limiting the use of the property conveyed offer for a certain period.

RETAIL DEVELOPER A developer of retail properties.

RETAIL LAND DEVELOPER A developer of a retail lot or lots.

RETAIL LOT SALES Sale of individual subdivision lots to the public rather than for resale (wholesale lot sales).

RETENTIONS Percentage withheld out of progress billings to some final and satisfactory completion of project.

RETURN TO INVESTOR Categories: The phrase should be qualified by one of the following adjectives:

(1) GROSS Or TOTAL return, which will include a calculation of the total of all of the following and should be indicated as an estimate. NET SPENDABLE (often called NET CASH FLOW, NEW CASH RETURN, NET INCOME, or CASH AVAILABLE FOR DISTRIBUTION). It means the total cash income from operations during a given period of time, less cash disbursements (including payments on debts and obligations as well as reasonable allowances for contingencies and anticipated obligations) during the same period of time, but prior to any distribution to partners, general or limited, other than management fees and fixed expenses, and without consideration of depreciation. It generally is expressed as a percentage of invested capital. (Invested capital is the total initial payment for a syndicate interest, and any subsequent assessments paid to the investment entity, less any return of invested capital due to refinancing or sale of partnership assets.)

(2) EQUITY BUILD-UP. See EQUITY BUILD-UP.

(3) TAX SHELTER. See TAX SHELTER.

(4) APPRECIATION BUILD-UP. See APPRECIATION BUILD-UP.

(5) CUMULATIVE indicates that if a specified return is not received by an investor in a given year prorata on a calendar basis, the deficiency is added to the senior investors' priority before junior classes participate in distributions.

(6) COMPOUND OR NON-COMPOUND indicates whether a distribution deficiency is entitled to a priority return as well as the original capital investment being entitled to it.

(7) SUBORDINATE indicates that return is subordinate (junior) to a priority claim of another class of investor.

(8) PRE-TAX indicates that the return is calculated before any federal or state income tax. In the case of a non-tax paying entity, before the imposition of tax at the investor's individual tax rate.

REVENUE RULING Official interpretation on taxation matters published by the IRS, in the Internal Revenue Bulletin.

REVERSION A right to future possession retained by an owner at the time of transfer of part of his interest in real estate, such as the right of a grantor to regain possession after termination of a life estate he has granted, or on certain conditions.

RIDER   An addition or endorsement to a document.

RIGHT OF FIRST REFUSAL A right in one or more of the parties to purchase under certain conditions the interest of one or more of the other parties prior to such interest being sold to a third party (A) who has made an offer or/on, (B) terms to be offered (if limited the offer to be called "right of first refusal"). A lender may have a right of first refusal to buy the property that is security for the loan. A borrower might have a right of first refusal to buy the debt if the lender decides to sell.

RIGHT OF SURVIVORSHIP The right of a joint tenant to acquire the interest of a deceased joint tenant automatically upon death.

RIGHT OF WAY See EASEMENT.

RIPARIAN OWNER Owner of real estate bordering a body of water.

RIPARIAN RIGHTS Rights of a riparian owner to the reasonable use of water flowing past his land.

RISK FACTORS Those elements of a given investment that serve to create a risk of loss of the invested capital. Such elements, depending on the characteristic of the investment, might include but are not limited to
  (1) competition;
  (2) excess leverage;
  (3) lack of demand;
  (4) inexperience of the operator;
  (5) short-term or weak credit leases;
  (6) acts of God (see FORCE MAJEURE);
  (7) labor strikes;
  (8) changes in market conditions;
  (9) change in environment;
  (10) changes in technology;
  (11) acts of war, riot or terrorism and;
  (12) toxic or hazardous substance.

ROYALTY Money paid to landowner in return for taking natural resources from his property. Combined payment for rent and depletion.

RULE AGAINST PERPETUITIES Any contingent interest to be valid must vest within 21 years of a life in being.

RULE OF 72 A widely applied arithmetical formula that permits the investor and his investment advisor to determine how much financial assets must grow to realize a given investment objective within prescribed periods. The number 72, when divided by a quarterly compounded annual rate of interest, indicates the number of years required to double an investment. Conversely, to determine the approximate quarterly compounded rate of interest required to double an investment in a given number of years, divided by 72 by the number of years available. The rules does not take into account the affect of taxes on the rate of return.

RULE OF 78 A widely applied arithmetical formula for assessing a penalty for prepayment of an add-on or discounted contract. The effect of the rule is such that if a loan is paid off before maturity the lender will receive a greater rate of interest than if the loan had been paid according to the original terms.

S

SAFE HARBOR RULE Referring to a ruling of the Internal Revenue Service indicating under what circumstances the service will issue a favorable ruling regarding flow-through accounting treatment for a partnership and agree that it is not an association taxable as a corporation.

SALE AND LEASEBACK Financial transaction wherein owner sells his land to an investor and simultaneously leases it back, thereby freeing his capital and being able under some circumstances to claim lease payments as a tax deduction.

SALE OR REFINANCING (Tax Purposes) Transaction not in the ordinary course of business for example a sale of non-inventory property. Proceeds of such transaction are the amount gained less the costs of the transaction.

SALE OR SELL Includes every contract of sale, contract to sell, or disposition for value.

SALES ASSESSMENT RATIO Ratio calculated by dividing selling price by assessed value.

SALES COMMISSION Fee paid to agent or broker for negotiating sale of property. Generally paid by seller.

SALES CONTRACT Contractual agreement between buyer and seller as to terms of the sale.

SALES COSTS Costs arising from sale as opposed to operations.

SALES DEPOSIT RECEIPT Written acknowledgment of payment of deposit that may also constitute binding contract if executed by both parties and contains sufficient terms.

SALES INCENTIVES   Additional inducements offered to buyers or agents.

SALES PRICE LIST Listing of units available in project with most recent selling prices.

SALES TAX Tax on the sale of certain personal property. What is taxable varies from state to state.

SANDWICH LEASE The remaining interest of an original subleasee after he sublets all or any part of his interest.

SATISFACTION OF MORTGAGE Instrument used to show that a mortgage debt has been paid (receipt).

SBA Small Business Administration of the federal government.

SBB&M San Bernardino Base and Meridian lines.

SBIC Small Business Investment Company under the jurisdiction of the Small Business Administration.

SEC Refers to the Federal Securities and Exchange Commission, which has jurisdiction over the interstate offering of securities.

SECONDARY FINANCING Loan secured by second mortgage or trust deed to the property, subordinated to the first mortgage or trust deed.

SECONDARY ISSUE A sale of stock or interests owned by investors rather than by the issuer.

SECONDARY LENDER See LENDER.

SECONDARY OR RESALE MARKET The market place and the selling of loans to someone other than the original investor.

SECTION (OF LAND) 1/36th of a township. A section contains one square mile (640 acres).

SECTION 1245 PROPERTY – I.R.S Code Definition Any gain made in disposing of this type property may be subject to recapture of depreciation. Consult IRS code for definition.

SECTION 1250 PROPERTY – I.R S. Code Definition Real property not classified as Section 1245 property upon which depreciation is allowed. Part of any gain made upon disposition of such property may be subject to recapture.

SECURITY DEPOSIT   Deposit to assure performance.

SECURITY DEVICE/AGREEMENT An instrument used to make payment of a debt more certain. Mortgages, trust deeds, conditional sales contracts, security agreements, and pledges are all security devices.

SECURITY INTEREST The creditor's interest in a debtor's property.

SEED MONEY Front-end money to organize a project. Term often used in assisted housing projects.

SEIZIN Possession of real estate by one entitled thereto.

SELLER'S CLOSING COSTS Seller's escrow costs.

SELLING EXPENSES Costs of selling particular property.

SELLING GROUP Securities sales organizations that are part of the initial sale. Members of the selling group are not necessarily UNDERWRITERS . Underwriters are those who make a commitment to purchase a portion of the issue being sold. Other members of the selling group are those who merely agree to sell under certain terms and conditions and who are allotted a concession on the sale price. Members

of the UNDERWRITING GROUP, as opposed to those of the selling group, make commitments to purchase a portion of the issue.

SENIOR ENCUMBRANCE In reference to another encumbrance, one that is prior to the other encumbrance.

SEPARATE PROPERTY Property owned by a husband or wife that is not community property.

SEQUENCE SHEET Listing houses or lots within a subdivision in order of their progress.

SERVIENT TENEMENT Land burdened by an easement. See DOMINANT TENEMENT.

SERVITUDE A right in another's property in the nature of an easement.

SETBACK The distance from curb or other established line, within which no buildings may be erected.

SETTLEMENT See ESCROW.

SETTLEMENT COSTS See ESCROW COSTS

SEVERAL See JOINT AND SEVERAL.

SEVERALTY OWNERSHIP Ownership by one person only. Sole ownership.

SHELL CORPORATION A corporation which has a registration or qualification and is available for acquisition by another entity for the purposes of a "back-door" registration or qualification. Generally, a shell has no current ongoing business and its value consists largely in the fact that its shares of stock or partnership interests have been registered or qualified. VANILLA SHELL is standard building specifications offered by a landlord.

SHELTERED INCOME See TAX FREE INCOME.

SHERIFF'S DEED Deed given when property is sold by court order for payment of a debt.

SHORT RATE Unequal portion of an insurance premium or other prepaid or contracted for item or service is to be returned when the purchase cancels before maturity of the period contracted for.

SIMPLE INTEREST Interest paid on money lent at a certain rate agreed upon by the parties or fixed by law calculated on an annual basis.

SINKING FUND METHOD OF DEPRECIATION Setting aside from the income of property an amount, which, with accrued interest, will pay for the replacement of improvements when needed.

SITE PLANNER See LAND PLANNER.

SITUS Location.

SLANDER OF TITLE False statements regarding another's title to land.

SOCIAL OR ECONOMIC OBSOLESCENCE Reduction in value of property due to factors outside the property.

SOFT COSTS Legal fees, architecture and design, studies etc., as opposed to direct cost of land, buildings, and improvements.

SOFT DOLLARS That portion of the funds advanced by the investor for the investment, such as prepaid interest, real property taxes, current excess depreciation, management fees, etc., which are deductible on his personal income tax return and result in a reduction in taxable income of like amount in the year of investment. This is as opposed to HARD DOLLARS, which would be the net funds advanced by the investor in a given year after giving effect to the current tax savings and/or deferments.

SOLDIER'S AND SAILOR'S CIVIL RELIEF ACT Federal Statute assisting those in military service with obligations incurred before entering the military. 50 USC App. Sections 531-532.

SOLICITATION Every attempt or offer to dispose of, or an offer to buy.

SPECIAL ASSESSMENT (TAX) Charge against real estate by a public authority to pay cost of public improvements for the property such as sewers, street lights, etc. In a condominium or homeowners' association, charges over and above the regular periodic assessment to pay for unanticipated expenses.

SPECIAL WARRANTY DEED A deed wherein the seller covenants to protect the buyer against dispossession because of adverse claims to the land by the seller or any other third party.

SPECIFIC PERFORMANCE A remedy in a court of equity compelling the defendant to carry out the terms of the agreement or contract which was executed. SPONSOR Entity acting as manager, of the sale of a syndicate program. The initiator of the project.

SPREADING EQUITY The increase in equity to a wraparound lender on an all-inclusive loan resulting from the fact that payments may be such that the amount of equity held by the lender is increasing every month. This is due to the underlying loan being at a lower rate of interest and the payment on the all inclusive is more than the amount required to keep the underlying principal level or results in positive amortization on the underlying.

S.R.A. Society of Real Estate Appraisers.

STANDARD OF SUITABILITY A description of the investor's background that the respective agency feels is required for an offering to be fair, just, and equitable. For example, certain investors cannot benefit by tax-motivated investments which should only be offered to classes of investors whose circumstances would place them in a position to benefit from a tax-motivated investment (usually either a high annual income or a substantial net worth). Standard of Suitability can be expressed in terms of educational background, business experience and sophistication, profession, geographic location of residence, annual income, net worth, or a combination of these factors.

STANDARDS OF PRACTICE Code of ethics adopted by a state or national trade association governing business practices of members of that association.

STANDBY COMMITMENT An agreement by a lender to make a loan under certain circumstances, wherein it is the intent of both the borrower and the lender that the borrower secure more favorable financing prior to the date that the STAND BY is to be "taken down." The borrower takes the STANDBY COMMITMENT to an interim lender who provides funds for the project during the period that the STANDBY LENDER has his commitment outstanding.

STANDING MORTGAGE Indicates a mortgage where the payments are interest only and there is no reduction of principal during the term of the loan.

STARTS Units begun under construction, determined by number of building permits filed.

START UP COSTS See FRONT MONEY.

START-UP PERIOD See RENT UP PERIOD.

STATE HOUSING ACT California Building Statute setting minimum construction standards. Health and S.C. Sections 15000-17902.

STATUTE OF FRAUDS Law that require certain contracts to be in writing.

STATUTE OF LIMITATIONS See OUTLAWED CLAIM.

STATUTORY DEDICATION Dedication (giving) a right to use (easement) to the public as provided for by the Subdivision Map Act.

STOCK COOPERATIVE PROJECT Corporation formed primarily to hold title to rental property either in fee simple or for a term of years. Shareholders receive right of exclusive occupancy of part of the real property, the corporation holding title. See CO-OPERATIVE APARTMENT HOUSES.

STOP NOTICE California's Mechanic's Lien Law enabling unspent construction funds to be reached before general contractor is paid. C.C.S. 3103.

STRAIGHT DEBT Debt without conversion feature.

STRAIGHT LINE DEPRECIATION Calculating an equal sum of money each year for replacement of improvements when needed.

STRAIGHT NOTE Principal to be repaid in one sum.

STREET IMPROVEMENT ACT (California Str. & H.C. Sections 5000-6794) Statutory method for payment for cost of local improvements.

STRONG HANDS Owner of property with independent resources enabling him to carry the property through poor operating periods. See WEAK HANDS.

SUBCONTRACTOR One who performs contractual work for developer or general contractor, as opposed to owner.

SUBDIVISIONS (Defined by State Subdivision Law). Land divided into parcels with the intent to sell or lease or "finance" now or any time in the future.

SUBDIVISION MAP ACT (B & P C. Sections 11500-11641). California statute regulating subdivision administration by local authorities.

SUBJECT TO (a mortgage or trust deed) When a grantee takes title to real estate "subject to" a mortgage (or trust deed), he will lose the property through foreclosure proceedings if the debt is not paid. However, the grantee is not personally liable and no deficiency judgment may be obtained against him if the property does not bring enough at auction to pay off the loan. SEE ASSUMPTION.

SUBLEASE A lease given by a lessee. See also, LEASE.

SUBLETTING A leasing by a tenant to another, who holds under the tenant.

SUBORDINATION CLAUSE A clause in a mortgage or trust deed by which the lender "relinquishes his priority" to a subsequent mortgage or trust deed.

SUBORDINATED INTEREST One which is junior to the right of other investors to receive a certain return prior to the subordinated interest participating in a distribution of cash or assets. In a SYNDICATE, promotional interests of the syndicator are often subordinated to that of the investors. These may be various classes of investors whose interests are in turn subordinated one to another. Subordination can be either of a right to receive income or right to receive proceeds from sale, exchange or hypothecation of the property, or a combination of both.

SUBROGATE Substitution of one to the rights of another.

SUBSCRIPTION The signing of a binding contract to purchase an interest in a syndicate security. Such subscription may or may not be accompanied by all or a portion of the purchase price. SUBSCRIPTION AGREEMENT is the contract or other agreement binding the subscriber to purchase an interest in what is being offered.

SUBSTITUTED INTEREST or SUBSTITUTED PARTNER A substituted interest refers to a situation wherein the purchaser thereof is becoming an initial subscriber in place and instead of another initial subscriber who has withdrawn. A substituted partner is one who has become the transferee of an initial partner. A substituted interest is listed as an original partner. A substituted partner, however, is not an original partner, but one who purchased after the close of the original syndication.

SUBSTITUTION OF LIABILITY Like a novation. New borrower on a mortgage or trust deed note assumes liability for it and mortgagee or beneficiary releases transferring borrower.

SUBSTITUTION (IN APPRAISALS) The principle of substitution affirms that maximum value of a property tends to be set by the cost of acquisition of an equally desirable substitute property, assuming no costly delay is encountered in making the substitution.

SUFFERANCE See ESTATE AT SUFFERANCE.

SURETY One who guarantees performance by another.

SURPLUS PRODUCTIVITY The net income that remains after the proper costs of labor, organization and capital have been paid, which surplus is imputable to the land and tends to fix the value thereof.

SURVEY The process by which a parcel of land is measured and its area ascertained.

SYNDICATE Any general or limited partnership limited liability company, tendency in common, joint venture, unincorporated association, or similar entity, formed for the sole purpose of or engaged solely as an investment or gain from an interest in real property, including but not limited to a sale, exchange, trade or development.

SYNDICATE AGREEMENT The partnership or other agreements governing the rights, duties, and liabilities of the beneficial owners of the syndicate.

SYNDICATION The action taken as a whole, involved in the formation of a syndicate.

SYNDICATOR'S COMPENSATION The total amount of compensation of all kinds to syndicators of real estate syndications, including commissions, management fees, and promotional interest.

SYNERGISM The additional value that relates to a thing, or process, or activity, by adding it together with another so that the value of the whole is greater than the sum of its parts.

SYNDICATOR An individual or entity involved in the formation of a syndicate. Syndicator includes all persons directly or indirectly instrumental in the organization of a syndicate as well as the persons who will thereafter manage the syndicate, such as general partner. Independent management companies, attorneys, appraisers and accountants, who have no other interest in the syndicate other than performing their usual and normal professional duties, and are not in any way directly or indirectly controlled by people instrumental in organizing the syndicate, are not considered syndicators. See SPONSOR.

T

TAKE OUT LOAN Permanent loan.

TANDEM PLAN Purchase by GNMA of certain mortgages at par for subsequent resale at market price to F.N.M.A.

TAX AVOIDANCE The use of legitimate tax planning taking advantage of the provisions of existing laws and regulations to reduce applicable tax of an entity or individual. The use of schemes and procedures, which would be in violation of the law, is TAX EVASION as opposed to TAX AVOIDANCE.

TAX BENEFITS/TAX ADVANTAGES Total tax benefits from both TAX SHELTER and TAX DEFERRAL.

TAX BRACKET Maximum rate at which a person's taxable income would be taxed.
TAX DEED Deed given when property is sold due to tax delinquency.

TAX DEFERRED INCOME (TAX DEFERRED RETURN) Net spendable income which is received in a given year, but for which there is no current tax due because of tax shelter (usually excess depreciation) It is assumed that at the time the property is disposed of, a tax bill will then be incurred on the difference between the then-basis of the property and the sale price, and that tax-deferred income will then be taxed either by ordinary income rates or by capital gain rates, depending upon the individual circumstances (referred to as "recapture").

TAX EVENT Transfer of property creating an IRS-recognized tax consequence.vv

TAX-FREE EXCHANGE An exchange of real property, exempt from taxation under I.R. Code Section 1031, except for boot received in the exchange.

TAX-FREE INCOME Income that is received, which because of provisions of federal income tax laws, is free from income taxation. An example of such income would be income from tax-exempt municipal bonds. Net spendable income that is tax sheltered because of excess losses is not tax free, but merely tax deferred. It would be correct to label such income tax-sheltered income, but incorrect to label such income tax-free income.

TAX-FREE TRANSFER A transfer under a method other than tax-free exchange that would not result in a tax event.

TAX INCENTIVE INVESTMENT An investment with flow-through tax benefits such as capital gains, high deductions, deferred income, depletion, accelerated depreciation, and excess depreciation.

TAX INCENTIVE PROGRAM Tax incentive investment where flow through tax benefits is the primary motive.

TAX-SHELTERED CASH FLOW See NON-CASH CHARGES.

TAX LOSS A loss which the individual may show in his then current tax return by reason of taxable PROFIT AND LOSS tax (deductions exceeding taxable income) as opposed to a cash loss (negative cash flow from the property due to cash expenses exceeding cash income).

TAX PREFERENCES A minimum federal income tax is imposed on certain tax benefits that have been labeled "tax preferences." This tax is a minimum tax on each person's total of tax preference items in excess of a certain amount plus the regular tax imposed.

TAX RATE The actual highest tax rate that an individual has to pay on his income. Tax rate should always be specified as to whether it is marginal or effective. The marginal rate is the tax rate as applied to the highest level of income being taxed, whereas the effective rate would be the rate as applied to all income being taxed.

TAX (REAL ESTATE) A tax on real estate levied by local governmental bodies such as county, city, school district, etc.

TAX SALE Sale of property by tax collector for non-payment of taxes.

TAX SHELTER An investment that may generate losses for tax purposes greater than the profit for tax purposes. This creates excess losses, which may offset, and thereby shelter, other income of the investor. Only investments which have a large ratio of depreciable assets generally may qualify as tax-sheltered. Non-depreciable property purchased with prepaid interest may not be a tax shelter, although it may create TAX DEFERRAL, in that taxable income of the investor reduced by the payment of prepaid interest may be deductible from his current return. If there are arrangements for resale of the property later in an amount sufficient to return basis plus expenses, the prepaid interest income deduction may be taken back at time of sale as ordinary income or capital gain. The prepayment of certain expenses, if they result in immediate deductions, may be a TAX DEFERRAL, but not a tax-shelter technique. The prepaying of certain expenses in connection with farming or other operations, where these qualify under the Internal Revenue laws as a deduction in the year of payment, may result in shifting taxable income from a high-tax year to a lower-tax year. Again this is TAX DEFERRAL rather than tax shelter.

TAX SHELTER INCOME   Income of the investor that he receives from the investment, which is sheltered by excess depreciation.

TAXABLE INCOME   Net reportable income for income tax purposes, after consideration of all deductible items and exemptions.

TAXPAYER   When referring to income taxes and an individual or entity, the person on whom the tax is imposed. When referring to real property taxes and real estate, a property which generates only enough income to pay operating expenses and real property taxes.

TENANCY OCCUPANCY by a tenant.

TENANCY AT WILL A license to use or occupy lands and tenements at the will of the owner.

TENANCY BY THE ENTIRETY A joint tenancy between husband and wife. Right of survivorship. Neither spouse can convey their interest to break the joint tenancy. Not recognized in California.

TENANCY IN COMMON Ownership by two or more persons who hold undivided interests without right of survivorship.

TENANCY IN PARTNERSHIP Ownership by business partners.

TESTAMENT A will.

TENANT A person who holds real estate under a lease (lessee).

TENANT AT SUFFERANCE One who comes into possession of land by lawful title and keeps it afterwards without any title at all.

TENAMENT All rights in land, passing with a conveyance of the land.

TENEMENT HOUSE Obsolete apartment house.

TENTATIVE MAP Preliminary map submitted by sub divider for approval and approved before final maps pursuant to California Subdivision Map Act. B & PC Sections 11503, 11531, 11550-11555.

TENURE Manner in which title to land is held.

TESTATE Leaving a will upon death.

TESTATOR Man who makes a will

TESTATRIX Woman who makes a will.

TERM a) period of a lease; b) provisions of a loan; and, c) provision of a contract.

THREE-PARTY EXCHANGE Property exchanged between two parcels of land and three parties.

THIRD-PARTY FINANCING Financing from someone other than the seller.

TIER Term used for land descriptions. East and West townships running parallel to north or south of a designated base line.

TIERED FINANCING   Indicates several levels of debt are being used. These might include, but are not limited to, a long-term ground lease, a first mortgage on the improvements, a second mortgage on the improvements, and a secured lien on personal property.

TIME IS OF THE ESSENCE Contract clause requiring performance to be complete and punctual within the stated time.

TITLE Title can be held among others as
   (1) tenancy in common;
   (2) joint tenancy;
   (3) trust;
   (4) real estate trust investment;
   (5) joint venture;
   (6) co-partnership;
   (7) limited partnership;
   (8) Limited Liability Company;
   (9) corporation; or
   (10) community property.
These are some of the methods of holding title. Usually refers to the owner of record, also called RECORD TITLE HOLDER.

TITLE DEFECT A legal right held by another who claims property or makes demand on owner.

TITLE INSURANCE A policy of insurance, which indemnifies the holder for loss sustained by reason of certain specified defects in the title.
TITLE SEARCH Search of public records to disclose current state of title.

TOMBSTONE AD A simple notice announcing the fact that an issue or loan has been sold. It states the name of the UNDERWRITER, name of issue, and date sold. It may also indicate whether it is an original issue or secondary issue.

TORRENS SYSTEM Government title registration system.

TOPOGRAPHY Nature of the surface of land, its contour and elevation as shown by lines on a map.

TOWNSHIP A unit of land containing 36 square miles and 6 miles long on each side.

TRADE FIXTURES Personal property attached to real property, necessary to carry on a trade, removable by their owner, e.g., removable by tenant at expiration of lease.

TRADE NAME Name by which person, firm does business.

TRANSFER FUND See EXCHANGE FUND.

TRANSFER TAX Tax payable on conveyance of real property.
TREND An arrangement of statistical data in accordance with its time of occurrence.

TRESPASS Wrongful, intentional entry onto the land of another.

TRIPLE A TENANT Indicates that the tenant has a triple-A credit rate under a recognized credit rating bureau such as Dunn & Bradstreet or some similar organization of equal structure. It may also be referred to as a PRIME TENANT.

TRUST Fiduciary relationship whereby there is a division of ownership between the legal and equitable ownership. The trustee holding the legal title for the benefit of the beneficiary who holds the equitable title.

TRUST ACCOUNT An account in which funds are held "in trust."

TRUST DEED A conveyance of real estate to a third person to be held for the benefit of a beneficiary.

TRUSTEE One who holds legal title to property for a special purpose without being the actual (beneficial) owner. A trustee is one of the parties to every trust deed.

TRUSTEE'S DEED Deed given by the trustee when property is sold under the power of sale in a trust deed.

TRUSTEE'S SALE Foreclosure sale by trustee under deed of trust when a default has occurred.

TRUSTOR Borrower in a trust deed.

TURNKEY LEASING
(1) privately built housing leased to housing authority for low- income housing;
(2) in commercial leasing, property built for a specific purpose, with all improvements necessary for the purpose provided by the property owner.

TURNKEY PROJECT A project where payment is made by buyer, at completion of project with no further obligation on the seller to do any further work and the project is complete for its intended use.

TWO-PARTY EXCHANGE Property exchanged between two parties

U

U.C.C. Uniform Commercial Code. Uniform and comprehensive scheme regulating security transactions in personal property.

UNDERLYING LOAN Loan covered by an A.I.T.D. or sales contract.

UNDERWRITING The activities of a broker or broker/dealer or syndicator whereby such person undertakes the sale of syndicate or loan interests on one of the following bases:
(1) FIRM – The underwriter agrees to purchase all of the interests and re-offers them to investors.
(2) GUARANTEED – The underwriter guarantees that if he is unsuccessful in selling the interests, or a portion of them, within a given period of time, at the expiration of that time the underwriter will purchase all of the unsold interests.
(3) ALL OR NOTHING – If all the interests offered to be sold are not sold by the underwriter within a given period of time, the issuer has no obligation to offer any interests for sale, and the underwriter will not be entitled to any commission.
(4) BEST EFFORTS BASIS – The underwriter undertakes to sell the interests and is entitled to a commission on the interests sold and issued despite the fact that he might not sell the entire issue and that others, including the issuer, may sell the balance. In all cases, the IMPOUND CONDITION, if applicable, must be satisfied before any party would be entitled to any commission paid from the proceeds of sale.

UNIMPROVED REAL PROPERTY Raw land.

UNDIVIDED INTEREST Nature of each owner's interest when two or more persons own the same property as in tenancy in common, joint tenancy, community property and tenancy in partnership. Not the owner of a "distinguishable part."

UNDUE INFLUENCE Taking advantage of another person's distress or weakness of mind in inducing him to enter into a contract.

UNEARNED INCREMENT Value added to land by and demand for which the owner is in no way responsible. Population increase is an example.

UNIMPROVED LAND Raw land.

UNILATERAL CONTRACT Contract in which a promise is given for an act.

UNIT Each class of investor interest is divided into a number of equal units, each unit representing a prorata share of representation in that class. Mini-mum purchase required is usually expressed in some multiple of the basic unit, such as a minimum purchase of two units (this minimum relating to the standard of suitability for the investment). Normally fractional units are not sold, the smallest incremental pur-chase being in terms of one unit. When referring to property usually means the number of apartments in a building.

UNITIES The four unities necessary to create a joint tenancy; possession, interest, time and title.

UNLAWFUL DETAINER ACTION Lawsuit to evict a tenant who unlawfully remains in possession.

UNSPECIFIED FUND See NON-SPECIFIED FUND.

URBAN PROPERTY City property; property in a developed, relatively densely populated area.

USEFUL LIFE Estimated life of asset allowable in certain circumstances for tax depreciation purposes.

USE PROJECT Indicates a program where the value of the unit to be offered is based on the use that the purchaser will make of the property, as opposed to an investment project where the value and motivation for purchase is to some extent based on investment characteristics. In a use project, investment characteristics are generally negated by a statement that "the property should be purchased only by those intending to make actual use and that there may be little, if any, increase in value."

USURY Indicates the charge or collection of a rate of interest in excess of the lawful rate. Penalties for usury vary from state to state. A distinction should be made between legal rate and lawful rate. The legal rate is the amount of interest which is charged on a court judgment, or which the laws of a particular state provide under certain circumstances where no rate has been stated between the parties. The lawful rate is the maximum rate allowable.

V

VACANCY FACTOR The relationship between the vacant premises and the total premises available for rental. Should indicate whether actual or estimated.

VA Veterans Administration. A "VA Loan" is one guaranteed by this agency.

VALUATION The actual process of estimating value.

VALUE, BOOK (Un-recovered Cost) Accounting balance sheet item that is capitalized; historical cost less depreciation reserve.

VALUE, FORCED LIQUIDATION Amount that might be realized by a seller (with an unduly compelling reason to sell) from lump sum disposition of assets in the market over a relatively short period of time, perhaps through a complete sale to a dealer or speculator.

VALUE, INSURABLE The term is used conventionally to designate the amount of insurance that may be carried on destructible portions of a property to indemnify the owner in the event of loss.

VALUE, MARKET (also FAIR MARKET VALUE) (1) As defined by the courts, is the highest price estimated in terms of money which a property will bring if exposed for sale in the open market, allowing a reasonable time to find a purchaser who buys with knowledge of all uses to which it is adapted and for which it is capable of being used. (2) Frequently it is referred to as the price at which a willing seller would sell and a willing buyer would buy, neither being under abnormal pressure to act. (3) It is the price expectable if a reasonable time is allowed to find a purchaser and if both seller and prospective buyer are fully informed.

VALUE, PLOTTAGE An increase in value arising because of the combining of two or more sites to develop one site having a greater utility on the aggregate of each when considered separately.

VALUE, RENTAL The monetary amount reasonably expected for the right to the agreed use of real estate. Usually it is established by competitive conditions. It may be expressed as an amount per month or other periods of time; or per room, per front foot, or other units of property.

VALUE, SALVAGE The price expectable for the whole (that is, a house) or a part of the whole (that is, a plumbing fixture) for removal from the premises, usually for use elsewhere.

VARA Measurement used in Mexican land grants that is approximately 33 inches.

VARIABLE RATE See FLOATING RATE.

VARIANCE Change of use allowed as a variance from zoning of a single lot.

VEHICLE Refers to the form of entity of the issuer such as partnership corporation, tenancy in common, limited partnership, etc.

VENDEE Receiver of thing being vended, i.e. buyer.

VENDOR Owner of thing being vended, i.e. seller.

VENTURE CAPITAL Indicates investment of funds for a venture as opposed to the lending of funds. Venture capital is usually supplied by an equity investor as opposed to a lender.

VENUE The county in which a lawsuit is brought or tried; or the place in which an acknowledgment is taken.

VERIFICATION Sworn before a duly qualified person that the matters set forth in a pleading or other document are true.

VERTICAL SUBDIVISION Perpendicular condominium.

VEST An immediate, fixed property right with either present or future right of enjoyment. Manner in which title is held.

VESTED INTEREST Property interest that is fixed or determined.

VETERANS TAX EXEMPTION An exemption on assessed value of a veteran's property as provided by law.

VOID Having no legal effect.

VOIDABLE Capable of being made void by a proper declaration.

VOLUNTARY LIEN Lien placed on property voluntarily by owner (debtor).

VOUCHER SYSTEM Relates to construction loan. Subcontractor receives voucher instead of cash, which is redeemed with one who made the construction loan.

W

WALK-AWAY RISK See EXIT PENALTY.

WAREHOUSING Holding mortgage or trust deed notes in inventory for sale. Business of mortgage banker. Short-term loans, which are repaid out of proceeds from sale of those notes, are used to make, or finance the purchase of those notes.

WARRANTS Right to purchase a security on specified terms and conditions for a specified period.

WARRANTY DEED A deed that contains expressly written warranties (guarantees) of title.

WASTE Beyond normal wear and tear, or failure to exercise reasonable maintenance.

WATERED STOCK A method of compensating an underwriter by sale to him, prior to the public issue shares of stock or interest in the property, at a lower price than that to be charged the public. When a substantial amount of interest has been offered at prices considerably below the public offering price, this stock is said to be watered or watered stock. The phrase "watered stock" would refer to all stock or interest outstanding.

WATER RIGHT Landowner's right to use water bordering on or underneath his land. Also may refer to the right of another (other than the owner) to draw water from a parcel.

WATER TABLE Level of water in the ground.

WEAK HANDS An owner of property does not have staying ability to meet negative cash flow. If reversals in operations occur, he will have to sell the property. See STRONG HANDS.

WILLS (TESTAMENT) Witnessed - in writing and witnessed. Holographic – written, dated, and signed in handwriting of testator. Nuncupative – dying declaration, or in contemplation of death.

WRAP-AROUND MORTGAGE OR TRUST DEED A refinancing scheme using an all-inclusive trust deed or mortgage to preserve the terms of the underlying loan.

WRITE OFF Indicating excess deductions from an investment which may be used to reduce income taxes on income from other sources. See TAX SHELTER.

WRIT OF EXECUTION Court order that property of a debtor be sold to pay a debt.

Y

YIELD (1) Unless otherwise specified the term will mean the annual cash flow return on the total investment. Yield can also be expressed in terms of AFTER TAX at a given assumed tax rate, tax sheltered or tax free where appropriate, discounted and current or to maturity. (2) In an agriculture the quality (per acre or per parcel) of the crop.

Z

ZERO LOT LINE Describes positioning of building on a lot with one side resting directly on the lot's boundary line.

ZONING Local government control of the use of land.

OIL AND GAS TERMS

A

ABANDON   Voluntary or involuntary termination of interest in well, equipment or lease or portion thereof.

ABANDONED EQUIPMENT CHARGES   Equipment costs (excluding Special Project Costs) not recouped by salvage: (1) attributable to any well which is abandoned without completion. (2) Attributable to a non-commercially productive well.

AFFILIATE   Any person controlling, controlled by, or under common control of, another person. OF ANOTHER PERSON means: (1) Any person directly or indirectly owning, controlling or holding with the power to vote 10% or more of the outstanding voting securities of such other person. (2) Any person 10% or more of whose outstanding voting securities are directly or indirectly owned, controlled or held with power to vote, by such other person. (3) Any person directly or indirectly controlling, controlled by or under common control with such other person. (4) Any officer, director, or partner of such other person. (5) If such other person is an officer, director or partner, any company for which such person acts in any such capacity. C **AFFILIATED JOINT VENTURE**   Joint venture arrangement for oil and gas exploration.

C

COMMERCIALLY PRODUCTIVE WELL   A completed well considered capable of producing oil, gas, or other hydrocarbons in commercial amounts.

COMPLETED WELL   Producing wells that have been tested and equipped to the extent required to permit commencement of production.

D

DELAY RENTALS   Expenditure incurred to gain additional time to explore or develop leases or to retain leasehold interests.

DEPLETION   Deductions, allowed for federal income tax purposes against income received for oil or gas produced each year.

DEVELOPMENT WELL   A well drilled to a known producing geological zone in a previously discovered field.

DIRECT EXPENSES   Costs, expenses and liabilities charged by third parties, such as independent audit and legal services, insurance.

DRILLING BLOCK   Geographically described area with one or more leases.

DRILLING PROSPECT   Lease and land which according to geological data is reasonably anticipated to contain at least one reservoir.

E

EXPLORATION COSTS   Costs incurred in relation to a Drilling Prospect deductible in the year of expenditure, for Federal Income Tax purposes. Includes the following: (1) Payments to drilling contractors; Payments for service and items incidental to and necessary for drilling and completing wells, or plugging and abandoning, or preparing wells for production, which of themselves have no salvage value. (2) Amounts paid for delay rentals and shut-in or minimum royalties. Excludes the following: (A) Operator Exploration Costs. (B) Special Project Costs (C) Operator's Overhead Expenses.

F

FARMOUT   Agreement between lessee and sub-lessee assigning all or part of lessee's interest in the land, but retaining some interest in it such as a royalty, dependent upon performance by the lessee of a condition such as drilling a well. The right to drill under a farmout agreement is referred to as a Farm-Out Drilling right. Occurs where lease owner does not wish to drill.

L

LANDOWNERS ROYALTY INTEREST   Interest generally retained by the landowner under an oil and gas lease. Royalty owner is entitled to a share of production, free of the production cost and without any operating rights.

LEASES   Instrument by which a leasehold or working interest is created in minerals. Partial or full interests in oil, gas and mineral leases, oil, gas and mineral rights, fee rights, reservations, permits and other rights authorizing the leasee to drill for and take possession of oil, gas and minerals.

LEASE ACQUISITION COSTS   Costs incurred in acquiring leases for oil gas or other hydrocarbon substances.

LEASE OPERATING COSTS   All costs incurred in the production and sale of oil, gas and other minerals including direct supervision charges and monthly charges consistent with industry charges in a particular area and cost excluding equipment and cost of equipment installation incurred maintaining established production from Commercially Productive Wells.

N

NON-CAPITAL COSTS   Costs in connection with the drilling and development of a well which are subject to the election of charging to capital or to expenses as provided in Section 263(c) of the Internal Revenue Code and the Treasury Regulations promulgated there under such as Intangible Drilling and Development Costs, cost of non-salvageable tangible equipment installed in dry holes and the depreciated cost of such equipment installed in abandoned wells, leasehold acquisition costs incurred in requiring oil and gas properties that are not subsequently determined to be productive and are abandoned, delay rentals, operating costs, plugged and abandoned cost, delay rentals and advances, minimum and shut-in royalties, fees and expenses paid for management and administrative services.

O

OPERATING COSTS—OPERATING AND LIFTING COSTS   Costs made and incurred in producing and marketing oil and/or gas from completed wells, such as labor, fuel, repairs, handling, material supplies, utility charges and other costs incidental to and necessary for the maintenance or operation of wells or marketing the oil and gas produced, ad valorum and revenue taxes, insurance and casualty loss, etc.

OPERATOR   Person or corporation engaged in the business of, or exercising direct supervision over, the drilling or production from a well or lease.

OPERATOR—EXPLORATION COSTS   Costs incurred in relation to a Drilling Project which for Federal Income Tax Purposes are required to be capitalized. Including: (1) Costs of purchasing Leases. (2) Fees paid for recording, geological and geophysical reports, legal and brokers fees, etc., with regard to the lease. (3) Equipment costs to drill, test, and complete the well (unless they become Abandoned Equipment charges). (4) Acquisition costs and oil or gas property, royalties, or overriding royalty purchased.

OPERATOR'S OVERHEAD EXPENSE   Expenses which are subject to annual audit such as oil and gas property analysis, lease acquisitions, salaries of officers, directors and employees. Office equipment and rental expense and related general administrative costs.

PAYOUT   Where an entity has been formed for the production of oil or gas, payout occurs when:

(1) the Investors have received distributions from the partnership equal to the minimum required cash capital contribution, plus any amounts which may have

been paid as a result of assessments upon their units, and all letters of credit furnished by Investors have been cancelled and returned to the Investor.

(2) The Investors have received distributions from the entity equal to their total capital contributions, plus any amounts which may have been paid as result of assessments upon their units.

R

RELATED ACTIVITIES   Activities related to operations previously commenced, such as further drilling, deepening, plugging back, reworking, repairing, etc.

S

SEMI-PROVEN LEASES   Leases in an area in which producing wells have been completed usually at scattered points—but in which the confines of the reservoir have not been determined.

SPACING UNIT   Area of land included in the production spacing unit or similar unit assigned to a well, by a regulatory authority, or if not so assigned, the area attributed for such purposes to wells drilled under the normal spacing pattern in the area, or if there is no such spacing pattern, under the spacing pattern designated by the operator in keeping with generally accepted industry practices.

ENTERTAINMENT TERMS

A

ABOVE THE LINE Terms used in relation to certain production costs of motion picture such as – producer's expenditures for story and other rights, writing, producer and staff, director and staff, artists, talent, supplemental labor. May be used with reference to those who carry out "above the line services".

ACCELERATE An employer's negotiated/contractual right to move up the commencement of a contract year to a date during the preceding contract year. START DATES may also be accelerated.

AFMA Trade organization for film distributors. Used to be abbreviation for American Film Marketing Association, but this organization now just calls itself AFMA.

ALL RIGHTS Includes motion picture and allied rights, publication, dramatic stage, radio, sound recording, live television and all other such rights in a literary work.

AMPTP – ASSOCIATION OF MOTION PICTURE AND TELEVISION PRODUCERS Includes major studios and independent producers. It researches methods of improving motion picture production.

ANIMATED Using drawings, puppets, or other substitutes for actual people or places.

ANSWER PRINT Completed, edited movie judged adequate for public viewing.

ART THEATER Shows specialized art films, generally in exclusive engagements, rather than mass-market studio films.

ATTORNEY'S LOG Synonym—Contract Status Report.

AUTEUR A French term; the auteur theory holds that the director is the true creator, or author, of a film, bringing together script, actors, cinematographer, editor and molding everything into a work of cinematic art with a cohesive vision. Another view is filmmaking is a collaborative endeavor and the director is only one of the contributors.

AUTHOR Creator, originator. Under U.S. copyright law, the author may be the employer of the person who actually creates the work. See "work for hire."

AUTHOR One who writes a book, music lyrics, etc.

B

BACK END Profit participation in a film after distribution and/or production costs have been recouped.

BALANCE STRIPE   A magnetic stripe on the film, which is on the opposite edge from the magnetic sound track.

BEGINNER   Definition per SAG Codified Basic Agreement of 1967, Theatrical Motion Pictures—which also applies to television employment (1) A person over 30 with no professional acting experience prior to twelve months before the commencement of his term of employment; or, (B) A person 30 or over with no professional acting experience prior to the commencement of his term of employment. One employed as a beginner under a term of contract is a beginner for 12 months from the commencement of the term.

BELOW THE LINE   Relates to certain motion picture costs, computed together with ABOVE THE LINE expenses and producer's indirect costs to find total budget of a motion picture. Includes such items as producer's expenditures for production staff, camera, set construction, set operations, electrical, set dressing, action props, special photography, wardrobe, makeup, hairdressing, sound-production, locations, transportation studio, film-production, tests (except for costs), editing and projection, music, post production sound, film and post production stock shots, titles, opticals, and inserts, insurance, supplemental laborer, unit publicist and stillman, general expenses. People who perform these services are referred to as "below the line" personnel.

BELOW-THE-LINE COSTS   The technical expenses and labor including set construction, crew, camera equipment, film stock, developing and printing.

BILLING   See Synonym CREDIT.

BLIND BIDDING   Requiring theater owners to bid on a movie without seeing it. Several states and localities require open trade screenings for each new release. Guarantees and advances may be banned

BLOW-UP   Optical process of enlarging a film, usually from 16mm to 35mm.

BOX OFFICE RECEIPTS   What the theater owner takes in from ticket sales to customers at the box office. A portion of this revenue is remitted to the studio/distributor in the form of rental payments.

BREAK   To open a film in several theaters simultaneously, either in and around a single city or in a group of cities, or on a national basis.

BREAKEVEN   Time at which distributor's gross receipts cover all distribu-tion fees, distribution expenses, third party gross participation, negative costs which includes interest and overhead, and contingent deferments.

BREAKOUT To expand bookings after an initial period of exclusive or limited engagement

BUSINESS DAY Any day except Sunday or a holiday under the SAG Agreement, or a legal holiday in the State. In other industries M-F excluding holidays.

BUY-BACK PERIOD Time during which seller may buy back his property, repaying purchaser's expenses or another specified amount. Usually found in sale of literary work. See REVERSION OF RIGHTS.

C

CEL A transparent sheet of cellulose acetate used as an overlay for drawing or lettering. Used in animation and title work.

COLOR CORRECTION Changing tonal values of colored objects or images by the use of light filters, either with a camera or a printer.

COLOR TEMPERATURE The color in degrees Kelvin (K) of a light source. The higher the color temperature; the bluer the light, the lower the temperature, the redder the light.

COMMERCIAL RECORDS Records included primarily for sale for business use, and/or jukeboxes.

COMMERCIAL TIE-UP Agreement wherein a photoplay is advertised together with another product or service, excluding advertising relating to the producer or distributor or its products, and licenses for the exhibition of the photoplay on sponsored television programs.

COMPLETION BOND A form of insurance, which guarantees financing to complete a film in the event that the producer exceeds the budget. Completion bonds are sometimes required by banks and investors to secure loans and investments in a production. Should a bond be invoked, the completion guarantor may assume control over the production and be in a recoupment position superior to all investor.

COMPOSERS AND LYRICISTS GUILD AGREEMENT Relates to theatrical and television motion picture employment. Collective bargaining agree-ment between the Guild and certain motion picture production companies.

CONSIDERATION The reason or inducement for a party to contract with another. Usually money, but can be anything of value. The right, interest or benefit to one party, or the loss or forbearance of another. A necessary element for a contract to be binding.

CONTRAST   The density range of a negative or print. The brightness range of lighting in a scene

CONTRACT DIGEST   Detailed outline of important contract provisions.

CONTRACT STATUS REPORT   Progress report on negotiations and drafting of contracts.

CONTRACT YEAR   Period commencing on the first day of any year within the TERM and ending 12 months thereafter. Synonyms: EMPLOYMENT PERIOD, ORIGINAL TERM, TERM OF EMPLOYMENT.

CO-PRODUCTION AGREEMENT   Agreement between two or more motion picture producers who share in the ownership of the production. Synonyms: JOINT VENTURE, PRODUCTION DISTRIBUTION AGREEMENT.

COST OF PRODUCTION   Total direct expenditures related to production of motion or television picture, including overhead and indirect charges.
CREDIT   Contractual provisions specifying size of type, position, etc., of individuals name in main and/or end titles on the positive print of a motion or television picture Contract; may include paid advertising of motion or television picture.

CROSS COLLATERALIZATION   Practice by which distributors off-set financial losses in one medium or market against revenue derived from others. For example, the rentals obtained from France are combined with those from Italy, and after the expenses for both are deducted, the remainder, if any, is net revenue. Filmmakers don't like to have revenues and expenses pooled because it may reduce the amount of money they receive.

CROSSOVER FILM   Film that is initially targeted to a narrow specialty market but achieves acceptance in a wider market.

D

DAILIES (RUSHES)   Usually an untimed one-light print, made without regard to color balance, from which the action is checked and the best takes selected.

DAY AND DATE   The simultaneous opening of a film in two or more movie theaters in one or more cities.

DAY PLAYER   An actor who works on a daily basis. Usually used for actors with small parts

DEAL MEMO   Outline of deal points—the important provisions of an agreement, given by the deal maker—the one who made the agreement—to a lawyer, used as the basis to draft the formal contract. When signed by all parties concerned it is called a DMX—executed deal memo.

DEFAULT   A failure, refusal, or neglect of the actor/artist pursuant to an Agreement to perform, (except where such failure results from an incapacity)or to carry-out their obligations under the Agreement of an intention not to perform.

DEFERMENT   (1) Fixed sum payable from gross proceeds or net profits from the distribution of a motion picture generally paid just before net profits are reached or from first 100% net profits. (2) Accrued compensation payable at a later date.

DEFERRED PAYMENT   When writers, directors, cast, crew or others accept some or all of their compensation later in order to reduce production costs. A deferred fee is generally paid from revenues generated from a completed motion picture, and if a movie is not finished, or it does not generate significant revenue, then the deferred payment holder may not be paid the deferred portion for his contribution.

DERIVATIVES   See PHONOGRAPH RECORDS.

DEVELOPMENT   The process by which an initial idea is turned into a finished screenplay. Includes optioning the rights to an underlying literary property, and commissioning writer(s) to create a treatment, first draft, second draft, rewrite, and polish

DISTRIBUTION AGREEMENT   Agreement to distribute motion picture, giving the producer a cash advance against a future percentage or a flat lump sum payment. May be for the whole world or limited territorially. For a television film or series it is generally for a share of gross receipts over a period of years.

DISTRIBUTION EXPENSE   Distributor's charges to the producer for distributing a motion picture, such as cost of prints, advertising, promotion, shipping and all other distribution costs. Synonym EXPLOITATION.

DISTRIBUTOR   A company that distributes a motion picture, placing it in theaters and any media, and advertising and promoting it. The major studios nowadays are mostly in the business of financing and distributing films, leaving production to smaller independent companies.

DISTRIBUTOR'S GROSS RECEIPTS   Gross receipts annually received and earned by the distributor from exploitation of a motion picture, less certain miscellaneous costs.

DGA AGREEMENT   Collective bargaining agreement between Directors Guild of America, Inc., and certain motion picture production companies. Applies to theatrical and television motion picture employment.

DMX   Executed deal memo.

DOMESTIC RIGHTS   Usually defined as U.S. and English-speaking Canada.

DOUBLE DISTRIBUTION FEES   Occurs when a distributor uses a sub-distributor to sell a film. If multiple distributors are allowed to deduct their full fees, the filmmaker is less likely to see any money.

DOUBLE-SYSTEM SOUND   The recording of sound on tape and picture on film so that they can be synchronized during editing.

DUBBING   (A) Sound recording to be synchronized with previously shot motion picture footage. (B) Re-recording several separate sound tracks onto a single track which becomes the final sound track for a motion picture. (C) Recording dialogue of a completed film in a foreign language. (D) For radio and recording – adding material to a sound track that was separately recorded. Synonym: LOOPING.

E

EMPLOYMENT PERIOD   Occurs with a SERIES OR MULTIPLE contract. The term which each employee is assigned to actually work on a picture.

END TITLE   Credits run at the end of a theatrical or television film.

ENTERTAINMENT COSTS   Monies spent to promote an attraction such as main attraction, supporting acts, money paid to performers, money paid to booking agents, money paid to performer's agents, money paid to supporting musicians, room, board and transportation.

EXCLUSIVE OPENING   A type of release whereby a film is opened in a single theater in a region, giving the distributor the option to hold the film for a long exclusive run or move it into additional theaters based on the film's performance.

EXECUTED CONTRACT   (1) A fully performed contract. (2) A contract signed by all the parties.

EXHIBITION AGREEMENT
(1) Agreement between distributor of a motion picture and exhibitor such as a theatre.
(2) Agreement between producer or distributor of a television series and a television network or other exhibitor for the first new telecast. Subsequent telecasts as termed Distribution agreements.
See SYNDICATION AGREEMENT.

EXHIBITOR   Operator of a motion picture theater.

EXPLOITATION   Distribution Expenses.

EXPOLITATION FILM   Directed to an ethnic audience.

EXTENSION   Contract provision enabling the employer to extend the employment period, contract year term and option dates of a contract, to enable the employee to complete services under the contract.

F

FACILITIES AGREEMENT   Agreement between a motion picture company and an outside company, whereby the motion picture company contracts to allow the outside company to use its facilities and personnel.

FEATURE FILM   Full length, fictional films (not documentaries or shorts), generally for theatrical release.

FILM NOIR   Dark, violent, urban, downbeat films, many of which were made in the 40's and 50's.

FILM RENTAL   What the theater owner pays the distributor for the right to show the movie. As a rough rule of thumb, this usually amounts to about half of the box office gross but can be as much as 90% or as little as 25% depending on film.

FINAL CUT   The last stage in the editing process. The right to final cut is the right to determine the final version of the picture. Usually the studio or the financier of a picture retains final cut.

FIRST-DOLLAR GROSS   The most favorable form of gross participation for the participant. Only a few deductions, such as checking fees, taxes and trade association dues are deductible.

FIRST MONIES   From the producer's point-of-view, the first revenue received from the distribution of a movie. Not to be confused with profits, first monies are generally allocated to investors until recoupment, but may be allocated in part or in whole to deferred salaries owed to talent or deferred fees owed a film laboratory.

FIRST RUN   The first engagement (public showings) of a new film.

FLAT SALE   Sale of the license to use a theatrical exhibition for a stated period of time for a price which is not tied to a percentage of the receipts from the theatrical exhibition.

FLOORS   In distributor/exhibitor agreements, the minimum percentage of box office receipts the distributor is entitled to regardless of the theater's operating expenses. Generally floors decline week by week over the course of an engagement. Generally range from 70 to 25 percent.

FORCE MAJEURE   Any event beyond the control of the Producer which causes an interruption or materially hampers or interferes with the production of a photoplay, play, etc. Same meaning in other industries.

FOREIGN SALES   Licensing a film in various territories and media outside the U.S. and Canada. Although Canada is a foreign country, American distributors typically acquire English-speaking Canadian rights when they license U.S. rights.

FOUR-WALLING   Renting a theater and its staff for a flat fee, buying your own advertising, and receiving all the revenue. The exhibitor is paid a flat fee regardless of performance and receives no split of box office receipts

FREELANCE CONTRACT   Agreement giving the licensee the right to pro-duce, exploit and distribute a single theatrical or television motion picture based on licensor's property. Synonym: SINGLE PICTURE LICENSE.

G

GROSS PROCEEDS   Total income from exhibition and for distribution of the-atrical or television motion picture.

GROSS AFTER BREAK-EVEN   The participant shares in the gross after the break-even point has been reached. The break-even point can be a set amount or determined by a formula.

GROSS PARTICIPATION   A piece of gross receipts without any deductions for distribution fees or expenses or production costs. However, deductions for check-ing and collection costs, residuals and taxes are usually deductible. A "piece of the gross" is the most advantageous type of participation from the participant's point of view. In an audit, it is the most easily verified form of participation.

GROSS RECEIPTS Proceeds received by distributor from theatres and others for the right to exhibit or otherwise exploit a picture, less deductions for trade association fees, industry assessments, applicable taxes, costs of collection and checking exhibitors.

GUARANTEE Contractual agreement setting out the payment that will be made.

GUILD WAIVER Document by which a Guild waives a part of its collective bargaining agreements.

H

HIATUS Break between production periods for television series episodes.

HOLD OVER Where employee is under a term or multiple series contract, the employer has the right to extend the employment term in order to complete the project.

HOT Anyone whose last picture was a big hit, won an Academy Award or is being lionized by the media. A transitional state.

HOUSE NUT Weekly operating expenses of a movie theater.

HYPHENATES Persons who fulfill two or more major roles such as producer-director, writer-director or actor-director.

I

INCAPACITY An inability to perform which is considered excusable at law.

J

JOINT VENTURE Synonym: CO-PRODUCTION AGREEMENT.

L

LAW Rule or principle of common law or equity, a present or future, municipal, county, state or federal ordinance or statute, on executive, administrative or judicial regulation, order, judgment or decree.

LAY-OFF Period during which the employee does not work. Varies depending on type of contract: Term contract employee may be laid off for all or any of the difference between the guarantee period and the contract year or employment term. Series contract time when actor is told his services are not required. Multiple contract no lay-off periods as actor completes project he is engaged for.

LEGITIMATE THEATRE A place where live performances are given.

LICENSE   To permit to use of photoplay, phonograph records, etc for specific purposes.

LICENSEE   Person who is given a license or permission to do something.

LICENSOR   The person who gives or grants a license

LITERARY RIGHTS   See ALL-RIGHTS, MOTION PICTURE and ALLIED RIGHTS.

LIVE PERFORMANCE   A play put on by actors as opposed to record a film.

LOAN OUT   When an employer, with an employee under contract, has a contractual right to lend the employee to other companies and receive the payment for such services.

LOOPING   Method of obtaining improved soundtracks.

LP   A 12 inch, 33 1/3 rpm double-sided phonograph record embodying thereon the equivalent of not less than 9 sides and not more than 12 sides.

M

MAIN TITLE   Complete list of credits, usually run at or near the beginning of the television or theatrical motion picture.

MASTER   Equivalent of a 7 inch, 45 rpm, single sided recording embodying the recorded performances of an Artist and intended for use in the manufac-ture and sale of phonograph records.

MASTER RECORDING   The original object in which sounds are fixed.

MOTION PICTURE AND ALLIED RIGHTS   Rights obtained from the author or owner of a literary material for use as a motion picture.

MPAA— MOTION PICTURE ASSOCIATION OF AMERICA   Responsible for ratings given to motion picture, maintaining Title Registration Bureau, and maintaining an arbitration committee to resolve disputes.

MPRF— MOTION PICTURE RELIEF FUND   Organization to assist retired and/or other motion picture employees who have problems, maintained by volun-tary contributions.

MULTIPLE CONTRACT   Contract engaging employee for a specific number of assignments to begin within a specified time.

MUSICAL ATTRACTIONS   Includes concerts, stage shows, variety shows, sym-phonies, recitals, chamber music, and similar performances where music is performed.

N

NAME AND LIKENESS   Includes name, professional name, sobriquet, photograph, caricature, biography, actual or simulated likeness, signature, voice.

NEGATIVE COST   Actual cost of producing a film including the manufacture of a completed negative (does not include costs of prints or advertising). It may be defined to include overhead expenses, interest and other expenses, which may inflate the amount way beyond what was actually spent to make the film.

NEGATIVE PICKUP   A distributor guarantees to pay a specified amount for distribution rights upon delivery of a completed film negative by a specific date. If the picture is not delivered on time and in accordance with the terms of the agreement, the distributor has no obligation to license the film. A negative pickup guarantee can be used as collateral for a bank loan to obtain production funds.

NOVELIZATION   A book adapted from a motion picture.

NTSC   National Television System Committee. The standard for North America, Japan and several other countries, which is 525 lines, 60 fields/30 frames per second. Compare to PAL.

NET PROFITS   Net Producer's Shares of Gross Receipts remaining after deduction of total amount of Picture final production costs with interest thereon.

O

OBLIGATION   A duty imposed by law, courtesy or contract.

OFF-HOLLYWOOD   American independent films made outside the studio system

OFF THE TOP   The first monies paid before anyone else receives payment.

ON SPEC   Working for nothing on the hope and speculation that something will come of it.

OPTION   The ability to choose whether or not to take action on or before a specified date.

ORIGINAL   A work that has not been adapted from another work.

ORIGINAL MATERIAL   Not derived or adapted from another work

ORIGINAL TERM   First employment term of a Multiple Series or Term Contract.

P

PARI PASSU   At an equal rate.

PAY OR PLAY   Employer is under no obligation to use employee's services – only to pay him.

PERCENTAGE PARTICIPATION   Contractual provisions giving person right to receive a specified percentage of the profits. Synonym: PROFIT PARTICIPATION.

P.G.A. AGREEMENT   Collective bargaining agreement between Producers Guild of America and certain motion picture production companies.

PHONOGRAPH RECORDS   All forms of recording and reproduction now known or which may become known in the future, manufactured or sold primarily for home use and/or jukebox use, and/or use on or in a means of transportation, such as magnetic recording tape, film, electronic video re-cordings, and any other medium or device for the reproduction of artist performances manufactured or sold primarily for home and/or jukebox and/or use on or in a means of transportation, whether embodying sound alone, or sound synchronized with visual images such as sight and sound devices.

PHOTOPLAY   Any recording for future visual reproduction (with or without sound) using any device now or hereafter known or conceived.

PICK UP AGREEMENT   Agreement by a Studio to distribute or buy an existing motion picture.

PILOT   Sample episode of a proposed television series enabling the network to decide if it will buy the series for first run exhibition.

PLATFORMING   A method of release whereby a film is opened in a single theater or small group of theaters in region and later expands to a greater number of theaters

PLAYOFF   Distribution of a film after key openings.

POST PRODUCTION SERVICES   Artist's services regarding a photoplay required by the Producer such as photography, recording, editing, etc. Publicity is generally limited to interviews, voice transcriptions, and stills.

PRE-EMPT   Right to prevent a non-exclusive employee accepting other employment by giving him work which would conflict with the proposed outside work.

PRE-PRODUCTION SERVICES   Services regarding a photoplay, required by the Producers, such as tests, readings, rehearsals, location searches, etc.

PRINCIPAL PHOTOGRAPHY   Daily photography of the main story line of a motion picture.

PRODUCER'S SHARE OF NET PROFITS   That portion of net profits left after payment of third party net profit participation.

PRODUCTION DISTRIBUTION AGREEMENT   Agreement for production and distribution of a theatrical motion picture generally between a studio which provides facilities, financing and distribution and an outside company which generally provides the producer, director, star and literary material or some of these. The outside company does not own any part of the picture.

PROFIT PARTICIPATION   Contractual right to receive specified percentage of the profits from distribution of theatrical or television series.

PUBLIC DOMAIN MUSIC   Musical composition not protected by copyright.

R

RAW STOCK   Motion picture film that has not been exposed or processed.

RECORDS— RECORDINGS   See PHONOGRAPH RECORDS.

RECORDING COSTS   Costs incurred for the production of sides embodying Artist's performances. Include such items as union scale, instrument costs, musicians, vocalists, conductors, arrangers, orchestrations, copyists, payments to a trustee or fund based on wages, to the extent required by an agreement between the Recording Company and any labor organization or trustee, all studio costs, tape, editing, mixing, mastering, engineering, travel and per diems for individuals involved in production of the Sides, rehearsal halls, costs of non-studio facilities and equipment, dubbing transportation of instruments, producer's fees, and other items customarily recognized in the phonograph record (including tapes cd's and dvd's) industry.

REGIONAL RELEASE   As opposed to a simultaneous national release, a pattern of distribution whereby a film is opened in one or more regions at a time.

RELEASE PRINT   A composite print made for general distribution and exhibition after the final answer print has been approved.

REMAKE   Motion picture using the same characters and story line as a previously produced motion picture.

RESALE SUSPENSION   Only applies to television where an actor under a TERM or SERIES contract, playing a continuing role in a television series on the last day for the exercise of an option for an actor's next employment term when the employer does not have a firm order for additional series episodes. The employer may insert an additional option term

RESALE TERM   Between the preceding employment term and the next employment term. SAG rules govern the length of this term and the rate of pay.

RESERVED RIGHTS   Rights reserved by author or owner of a literary work apart from those granted to a rights purchaser.

RESIDUALS   Specific payments made per guild agreements, to actors, writers, directors for the use of results and proceeds of their services in television reruns, theatrical exhibition, and foreign telecasting of television films.

RETAIL LIST PRICE   Selling price fixed by Recording Company exclusive of taxes, discounts, duties and packaging.

REVERSION OF RIGHTS   Clause in Purchase Agreement for literary rights giving a reversion of the literary rights to the original owner without cost, if the rights purchaser fails to fulfill his conditions within a specified time. See: BUY-BACK PERIOD.

ROLL-OUT   Distribution of film around the country subsequent to either key city openings or an opening in one city.

ROUGH CUT   A preliminary assemblage of footage.

RUN   Length of time feature plays in theaters or territory

S

SAG   Screen Actors Guild, Inc.

SAG AGREEMENT   Collective bargaining agreement between SAG and AMPTP.

SCALE   The minimum salary permitted by the guilds.

SEATING CAPACITY   Total number of seats permanently affixed in any theatre, plus any temporary seats added within the theatre for a particular performance. If the seating of a theatre has been altered for a particular performance seating capacity shall be the total number of seats available for that performance. If there are no permanent seats at a site, seating capacity shall mean the number of persons attending a particular performance.

SEPARATION OF RIGHTS   Occurs where a writer is employed by a production company to write format, story or story line and teleplay not based on previously exploited material for a pilot or for a television film, and is not part of an established series with continuing characters. Separation of rights means that the production company may only exploit television sequel rights.

SEQUEL   Motion picture with the same characters but a different story line than a previously produced motion picture and/or also as the basic literary property, if any. Distinguished from REMAKE.

SEQUEL ROYALTIES   Payments to writers whose work is the basis of a television series or theatrical or television picture with the same characters but a different story.

SERIES CONTRACT   Employment agreement whereby an employee is hired to perform for a particular television series in a stated role and paid on a per film basis.

SIDE   Equivalent of a 7 inch, 45 rpm single sided recording embodying recorded performance of an Artist and intended for use in the manufacture and sale of phonograph records.

SINGLE   Equivalent of a 7 inch, 45 rpm double sided phonograph record embodying thereon two sides.

SINGLE PICTURE CONTRACT   Employment agreement whereby an employee is hired for a single television or theatrical film.

SINGLE PICTURE LICENSE   Agreement granting licensee the right to produce, exploit and distribute a single theatrical or television motion picture based on licensor's literary work or other property.

SLEEPER   An unexpected hit. A film that audiences fall in love with and make a success.

SLICKS   Standardized ad mechanicals, printed on glossy paper, which include various sizes of display ads for a given film, designed for the insertion of local theater information as needed

SPECIALIZED DISTRIBUTION   As opposed to commercial distribution, distribution to a limited target audience, in a smaller number of theaters, with a limited advertising budget and reliance upon publicity, reviews and word-of-mouth to build an audience for the picture

SPIN-OFF   Television series based on characters or story originally in another series. It may be: PLANTED- originating with material in pre-existing series expressly to be used as a pilot for the spin-off. NATURAL- originating with an integral part of the pre-existing series which is taken and used as the basis of a new series.

STADIUM SEATING   Similar to an athletic stadium with steeper elevation than a "flat floor" (slooping at a lesser elevation). Older theaters will have a flat floor and newer theaters are usually stadium seats.

SSH   Saturdays, Sundays and holidays.

START DATE/NOTICE   Starting date of an employment period under a SINGLE PICTURE, SERIES Or MULTIPLE CONTRACT. Legal written notice must be sent to an employee a specified number of days before the start date. On or about period gives the employer leeway to start the employee around the start date for example "24 hours excluding SSH".

STORY ANALYST OR READER   A person employed by a studio or producer to read submitted scripts and properties, synopsize and evaluate them. Often held by young literature or film school graduates.

STORY CONFERENCE   A meeting at which the writer receives suggestions about how to improve his/her script.

STRIKING ANSWER PRINT   Printing of the ANSWER PRINT. Used as a date to calculate the option period for further work for an employee engaged on the photoplay.

SUB-DISTRIBUTOR   In theatrical releases, distributors who handle a specific geographic territory. They are contracted by the main distributor, who coordinates the distribution campaign and marketing

SUSPENSION   Standard contractual provision enabling employer for cause, to temporarily stop the running of the contract term and stop paying the employee. When lifted the employer can elect to extend the employment Term or reduce the guarantee.

SYNDICATION   Distribution of motion pictures or tv series to independent commercial television stations on a regional basis.

SYNDICATION AGREEMENT   Agreement for market to market exhibition of television series in the U.S. See: EXHIBITION AGREEMENT

T

TALENT   The word used to describe those involved in the artistic aspects of film-making (i.e., writers, actors, directors) as opposed to the business people.

TARGET MARKET   The defined audience segment a distributor seeks to reach with its advertising and promotion campaign, such as teens, women over 30, yuppies, etc.

TAXES   Any governmental fee placed on all or part of a photoplay, entertainment, phonograph record, etc. or on the gross receipts, license, distribution, exhibition or use of same, or collection, conversion or remittance of monies connected with.

TBA   To be announced.

TELEVISION DISTRIBUTION FEE   Typically 10-25% for U. S. Network broadcast sales, 30-40% for domestic syndication and 45-50% for foreign distribution.

TELEVISION SPIN-OFF   A television series or mini-series based on characters or other elements in a film.

TERM CONTRACT   Employment agreement whereby employee is paid periodically over the time of employment as opposed to payment by the photoplay.

TERMINATION FOR CAUSE   Termination of Artist's employment because of incapacity, default force majeure, or other specified cause.

TERM OF EMPLOYMENT   Total time of employment under a contract.

TEST MARKETING   Pre-releasing a film in one or more small, representative markets before committing to an advertising campaign. The effectiveness of the marketing plan can thereby be assessed and modified as needed before the general release.

TERRITORY   A given geographic area.

THEATRES   Includes concert halls, theatres, auditoriums, amphitheatres, stadiums and similar places of performances whether enclosed or not.

THEATRICAL   Includes exhibitions in theatres, transportation facilities such as airlines, armed forces, V.A. and other institutions, television—pay cable and subscription, audio visual cassettes, and similar devices, which transmit audio and/or visual images.

THEATRICAL DISTRIBUTION FEES   Generally between 30% and 40% of gross film rentals.

THEATRICAL PRODUCTION   A live performance

TITLE REGISTRATION AGREEMENT   Maintained by MPAA

TOP OF THE SHOW   Highest per assignment fee being paid at the time to employees for a television series.

TRADES   The daily and weekly periodicals of the industry, such as "Variety" and "The Hollywood Reporter."

TREATMENT   A prose account of the story line of a film. Usually between 20 and 50 pages. Comes after an outline and before first draft screenplay.

TURN AROUND PERIOD   (1) See: REVERSION OF RIGHTS (2) Period of postponement of option date of employee assigned to a regular television series when the series is cancelled.

U

UNION SCALE   Relevant minimum payments required to be paid to an Artist under applicable collective bargaining agreement in force and controlling at the time, or last in effect.

UPSET PRICE   Price set only by WAG AGREEMENT as minimum which a producer must initially pay for the services of a television writer entitled to separate rights.

W

WAG AGREEMENT   Collective bargaining agreement between Writers Guild of America, West and AMPTP.

WEEK TO WEEK   Employment on a weekly basis, which can be terminated by either party subject to guild requirements.

WIDE RELEASE   The release of a film in numerous theaters usually 800 – 3,000.

WINDOW   Period of time in which a film is available in a given medium. Some windows may be open-end, such as theatrical and home video, or limited, such as pay television or syndication.

WORK-FOR-HIRE (or work-made-for-hire   Under the Copyright Act this is either 1) a work prepared by an employee within the scope of employment; or 2) a specially ordered or commissioned work of a certain

.

Order More Books

The useful facts found within the pages of this book can be ordered directly from the publisher. Please call, email, or mail us your inquiries with shipping quantity amounts for your schools, libraries, or corporate gifts.

All questions that you may have regarding the contents of this book will be answered. Please contact the publisher.

If you would like to be contacted for seminars, reviews, or events, please send us your contact information; and we will inform you of occasions or opportunities to network with others interested in syndication in your area.

Call DEPARTMENT B
1-800-LA-KNOW (1-800-521-5669) or 1-310-854-0705
fax: 1-310-854-1840, email: contact@bevhillspub.com

Major Credit Cards Accepted
Mail your order now

Enclosed is my check
for _____ copies @ $69.95 each
plus CA sales tax
(8.25% CA residents only)
and $5 shipping. Total = $80.72

Beverly Hills Publishing Dept. B
Suite 107/108
291 South La Cienega Blvd.
Beverly Hills, CA 90211-3325

Name: _____

Address: _____

_____

Phone: _____ Fax: _____

email: _____